DECADENT ECOLOGY IN BRITISH LITERATURE AND ART, 1860–1910

Casting fresh light on late nineteenth- and early twentieth-century British art, literature, ecological science, and paganism, *Decadent Ecology* reveals the pervasive influence of decadence and paganism on modern understandings of nature and the environment, queer and feminist politics, national identities, and changing social hierarchies. Combining scholarship in the environmental humanities with aesthetic and literary theory, this interdisciplinary study digs into works by Simeon Solomon, Algernon Swinburne, Walter Pater, Robert Louis Stevenson, Vernon Lee, Michael Field, Arthur Machen, and others to address transtemporal, trans-species intimacy; the vagabondage of place; the erotics of decomposition; occult ecology; feminist decadence; and neo-paganism. *Decadent Ecology* reveals the mutually influential relationship of art and science during the formulation of modern ecological, environmental, evolutionary, and transnational discourses, while also highlighting the dissident dynamism of new and recuperative pagan spiritualities – primarily Celtic, Nordic-Germanic, Greco-Roman, and Egyptian – in the framing of personal, social, and national identities.

DENNIS DENISOFF is McFarlin Professor of English in the College of Arts and Sciences at The University of Tulsa. His awards and recognitions include the President's Award from both the Nineteenth-Century Studies Association and the North American Victorian Studies Association. A past Sarwan Sahota Distinguished Scholar at Ryerson University, in 2022, he is Visiting Distinguished Researcher at Queen Mary University of London.

CAMBRIDGE STUDIES IN NINETEENTH-CENTURY
LITERATURE AND CULTURE

Founding Editors
Gillian Beer, *University of Cambridge*
Catherine Gallagher, *University of California, Berkeley*

General Editors
Kate Flint, *University of Southern California*
Clare Pettitt, *King's College London*

Editorial Board
Isobel Armstrong, *Birkbeck, University of London*
Ali Behdad, *University of California, Los Angeles*
Alison Chapman, *University of Victoria*
Hilary Fraser, *Birkbeck, University of London*
Josephine McDonagh, *University of Chicago*
Elizabeth Miller, *University of California, Davis*
Hillis Miller, *University of California, Irvine*
Cannon Schmitt, *University of Toronto*
Sujit Sivasundaram, *University of Cambridge*
Herbert Tucker, *University of Virginia*
Mark Turner, *King's College London*

Nineteenth-century literature and culture have proved a rich field for interdisciplinary studies. Since 1994, books in this series have tracked the intersections and tensions between Victorian literature and the visual arts, politics, gender and sexuality, race, social organization, economic life, technical innovations, scientific thought – in short, culture in its broadest sense. Many of our books are now classics in a field that since the series' inception has seen powerful engagements with Marxism, feminism, visual studies, postcolonialism, critical race studies, new historicism, new formalism, transnationalism, queer studies, human rights and liberalism, disability studies, and global studies. Theoretical challenges and historiographical shifts continue to unsettle scholarship on the nineteenth century in productive ways. New work on the body and the senses, the environment and climate, race and the decolonization of literary studies, biopolitics and materiality, the animal and the human, the local and the global, politics and form, queerness and gender identities, and intersectional theory is reanimating the field. This series aims to accommodate and promote the most interesting work being undertaken on the frontiers of nineteenth-century literary studies, connecting the field with the urgent critical questions that are being asked today. We seek to publish work from a diverse range of authors, and stand for anti-racism, anti-colonialism, and against discrimination in all forms.

A complete list of titles published will be found at the end of the book.

DECADENT ECOLOGY IN BRITISH LITERATURE AND ART, 1860–1910

Decay, Desire, and the Pagan Revival

DENNIS DENISOFF
The University of Tulsa

Shaftesbury Road, Cambridge CB2 8EA, United Kingdom

One Liberty Plaza, 20th Floor, New York, NY 10006, USA

477 Williamstown Road, Port Melbourne, VIC 3207, Australia

314–321, 3rd Floor, Plot 3, Splendor Forum, Jasola District Centre, New Delhi – 110025, India

103 Penang Road, #05–06/07, Visioncrest Commercial, Singapore 238467

Cambridge University Press is part of Cambridge University Press & Assessment, a department of the University of Cambridge.

We share the University's mission to contribute to society through the pursuit of education, learning and research at the highest international levels of excellence.

www.cambridge.org
Information on this title: www.cambridge.org/9781108994279

DOI: 10.1017/9781108991599

© Cambridge University Press & Assessment 2022

This publication is in copyright. Subject to statutory exception and to the provisions of relevant collective licensing agreements, no reproduction of any part may take place without the written permission of Cambridge University Press & Assessment.

First published 2022
First paperback edition 2024

A catalogue record for this publication is available from the British Library

Library of Congress Cataloging-in-Publication data
NAMES: Denisoff, Dennis, 1961– author.
TITLE: Decadent ecology in British literature and art, 1860–1910 : decay, desire, and the pagan revival / Dennis Denisoff.
DESCRIPTION: Cambridge ; New York : Cambridge University Press, 2021. | Series: Cambridge studies in nineteenth-century literature and culture | Includes bibliographical references and index.
IDENTIFIERS: LCCN 2021030246 (print) | LCCN 2021030247 (ebook) | ISBN 9781108845977 (hardback) | ISBN 9781108991599 (ebook)
SUBJECTS: LCSH: British literature – 19th century – History and criticism. | Decadence (Literary movement) – Great Britain. | Decadence in art – 19th century. | Paganism in literature – 19th century. | Paganism in art – 19th century. | Ecology in literature – 19th century. | Ecology in art – 19th century.
CLASSIFICATION: LCC PR468.D43 D46 2021 (print) | LCC PR468.D43 (ebook) | DDC 820.9/008–dc23/eng/20211012
LC record available at https://lccn.loc.gov/2021030246
LC ebook record available at https://lccn.loc.gov/2021030247

ISBN   978-1-108-84597-7   Hardback
ISBN   978-1-108-99427-9   Paperback

Cambridge University Press & Assessment has no responsibility for the persistence or accuracy of URLs for external or third-party internet websites referred to in this publication and does not guarantee that any content on such websites is, or will remain, accurate or appropriate.

Contents

List of Figures		*page vi*
Acknowledgments		*viii*
	Introduction: Thoughts at Imbolc 2021	1
1	Decadent Ecology and the Pagan Revival	7
2	"Up & down & horribly *natural*": Walter Pater and the Decadent Anthropocene	34
3	The Lick of Love: Trans-Species Intimacy in Simeon Solomon and Michael Field	61
4	The *Genius Loci* as Spirited Vagabond in Robert Louis Stevenson and Vernon Lee	96
5	Occult Ecology and the Decadent Feminism of Moina Mathers and Florence Farr	140
6	Sinking Feeling: Intimate Decomposition in William Sharp, Arthur Machen, and George Egerton	174
Epilogue		*219*
Notes		*225*
Index		*256*

Figures

1.1 Frederick Sandys, *Medea* (1868), Birmingham Museum. Oil on canvas, 102 by 122 cm, 40 by 48 in, Artepics/Alamy Stock Photo *page* 29

3.1 Simeon Solomon, *Babylon Hath Been a Golden Cup* (1859), Birmingham Museum. Pen and pencil on paper, 25.5 by 28.3 cm, 10.5 by 11.125 in, Artepics/Alamy Stock Photo 77

3.2 Simeon Solomon, *Habet! In the Coliseum A.D. XC* (1865). Private Collection. Oil on canvas, 101.5 by 122 cm, 39.875 by 48 in, Artepics/Alamy Stock Photo 79

3.3 Simeon Solomon, detail from *Habet! In the Coliseum A.D. XC* (1865). Private Owner. Artepics/Alamy Stock Photo 83

3.4 Simeon Solomon, detail from *Babylon Hath Been a Golden Cup* (1859). Private Owner. Artepics/Alamy Stock Photo 84

3.5 Correggio, *Jupiter and Antiope* (c. 1528). Louvre Museum, Paris. Oil on canvas, 190 by 124 cm, 74.8 by 48.8 in, vkstudio/Alamy Stock Photo 87

3.6 Piero di Cosimo, *A Satyr Mourning Over a Nymph* (c. 1495). The National Gallery, London. Oil on poplar, 65.4 by 184.2 cm, 25.7 by 72.5 in, Peter Horee/Alamy Stock Photo 90

4.1 Walter Crane, frontispiece to Robert Louis Stevenson, *An Inland Voyage* (London: Kegan Paul, 1878). McFarlin Library, The University of Tulsa 119

4.2 Walter Crane, frontispiece to Robert Louis Stevenson, *Travels with a Donkey in the Cévennes* (London: Kegan Paul, 1879). McFarlin Library, The University of Tulsa 120

4.3	Walter Crane, cover illustration for *Pan Pipes: A Book of Old Songs, Newly Arranged* (London: George Routledge and Sons, 1883). Dennis Denisoff	121
4.4	Joseph Mallord William Turner, *The Golden Bough*, 1834. Tate Museum, London. Engraving of Painting by T.A. Prior. 36.3 by 23.8 cm, 14.3 by 9.4 in, JAK Historical Imates/Alamy Stock Photo	129
5.1	Photograph of Moina Mathers, c. 1900, printed in André Gaucher, "Isis à Montmartre," *L'Écho du merveilleux*, 94 and 95 (December 1900), 446–53, 470–73, at 471. The Picture Art Collection/Alamy Stock Photo	156
5.2	Photograph of Florence Farr. Abbey Theatre archives, 1903. The Picture Art Collection/Alamy Stock Photo	163
6.1	William Sharp, "The Norland Wind," Headpiece by John Duncan, *The Evergreen: A Northern Seasonal*, 1 (1895), 109. Dennis Denisoff	193

Acknowledgments

My research was funded by The University of Tulsa, the Social Sciences and Humanities Research Council of Canada, and the Research Society of Victorian Periodicals. I would like to thank these bodies for their support, as well as scholars from the following institutions for the funding and opportunities to share my scholarship and conduct additional research: the British Institute – Florence, Michigan State University, the University of Exeter, the University of Glasgow, the University of Houston, the University of Kent, Queen's University – Belfast, Ryerson University, the University of Stirling, the University of Stockholm, the University of Sussex, Birkbeck – University of London, Queen Mary – University of London, the University of Oxford, and the William Andrews Clark Memorial Library – UCLA.

I am grateful to more friends and colleagues than I can recall for supporting, engaging with, and commenting on my work in progress over the past eight years; these include Rachel Ablow, Joseph Bristow, Alicia Carroll, Bénédicte Coste, Gowan Dawson, Lovette Denisoff, Jane Desmarais, Joy Dixon, Jill Ehnenn, Stefano Evangelista, Christine Ferguson, Kate Flint, Dustin Friedman, Randall Fuller, Regenia Gagnier, Daniel Hack, Susan Hamilton, Nathan Hensley, Kate Hext, Leslie Higgins, Morgan Holmes, Neil Hultgren, Mark Knight, Deanna Kreisel, Cassandra Laity, Austin Lawrence, Deborah Lutz, James Machin, Teresa Mangum, Kristen Mahoney, Diana Maltz, Catherine Maxwell, Michèle Mendelsohn, Richard Menke, Alex Murray, Jesse Oak Taylor, Lene Østermark-Johansen, Ana Parejo Vadillo, Federica Parretti, Matthew Potolsky, Patricia Pulham, Charlotte Ribeyrol, Talia Schaffer, Michael Shaw, Jonah Seigel, Rachel Teukolsky, Chip Tucker, Lynn Voskuil, Corinna Wagner, David Weir, Giles Whitely, Carolyn Williams, Paul Young, the members of the British Association of Decadence Studies and the Decadence and Aestheticism caucus and Vcologies caucus of the North American Victorian Studies Association, and my colleagues at The

Acknowledgments ix

University of Tulsa. My graduate students at Middlebury College, Ryerson University, and The University of Tulsa have been crucial to my ideas as this project developed, especially Jacob Crystal, Beth Csomay, Caleb Freeman, Dennis Hogan, Steven Maulden, Colleen McDonnell, Leila Meshgini, Chelsea Miya, Amy Ratelle, and Sydney Rubin. I extend my love and gratitude to Morgan Holmes for his patience, encouragement, guidance, and contributions to the ideas and spirit that have given body to this and so many other projects. And I thank him for building a bagpipe studio at the bottom of the yard, giving me and the cats a bit more quiet time for our occasional labors and serious naps.

An earlier version of my discussion of Moina Mathers appeared in "Performing the Spirit: Theatre, the Occult, and the Ceremony of Isis" in *Cahiers victoriens et édouardiens*, 80 (2015); an earlier version of part of Chapter 2 appeared in "Decadent Animal Sympathies in Simeon Solomon, Ouida, and Saki," *Studies in Walter Pater and Aestheticism*, 1.1 (2016); and an earlier version of part of Chapter 5 appeared in "The Queer Ecology of George Egerton's Neo-Paganism," *Victorian Sustainability in Literature and Culture* (2018). Some ideas found in this monograph were first explored in "The Posthuman Spirit of the Neo-Pagan Movement," *21st-Century Approaches to Literature: Late Victorian into Modern, 1880–1920*, ed. Laura Marcus, et al. (Oxford University Press, 2017) and "Women's Nature and the Neo-Pagan Movement," *History of British Women's Writing: 1880–1920*, ed. Holly Laird (Palgrave Macmillan, 2016). I am grateful to the editors of these journals and collections for their feedback on these works in progress and for permission to incorporate these materials here.

Introduction
Thoughts at Imbolc 2021

On a cool autumn evening about eight years back, I found myself scanning the sky in search of the forecasted Blood Moon. A couple of friends – decadence scholars like myself – had invited me to dinner and, having never experienced a Blood Moon before, I was imagining offering an animated description of the gleaming copper disc that I would have seen on my walk over to their place. "It hung like a giant, glittering prop from Farr's English production of Wilde's *Salome*," I would wax. "It seemed to swing lightly in the evening breeze, as ragged, chiffon clouds rushed past." I surrendered myself to my musings and the night air, the occasional rattle of leaves in the trees making it seem colder than it was. A tattered plastic bag skittered across St. Cross Road and into Holywell Cemetery. I followed.

I had visited the old graveyard just a few days earlier to see whether Walter Pater's and Kenneth Grahame's tombstones held any pagan elements. It was the graveyard's various denizens, I now realize as I finish up this monograph, that made me first sense the idea of a decadent ecology in Britain that encompassed both Pater's and Grahame's lives and careers. The sky over Oxford turned out to be too overcast for me to see the moon, but Holywell Cemetery at night, with its deep purple shadows and musty smell of fermentation and flowering, exuded its own mysterious aura. The burial ground's roots go further back than recorded history, the site deriving its name from the Anglo-Saxon toponym *haeligewielle*, a term that's been used to refer to various springs and water sources that pagans, Christians, and often both identified as spiritual.[1] The earliest known reference to Holywell's location in Oxford is in the 1086 Domesday Book, where it is described as a meadow. In 1847, Merton College donated the land for a burial site. In the later twentieth century, it became, in many ways, a meadow again, a wildlife refuge for which the Friends of Holywell Cemetery adapted an ecologically sensitive approach that minimizes human impact on the homes and lives of the

1

Introduction: Thoughts at Imbolc 2021

resident and visiting birds, reptiles, insects, foxes, and other creatures. The cemetery's trees, grasses, and flowers flourish basically untended except for, at least when I last visited, the occasional mowing of a few paths and the lopping of some limbs. The moss is thick and pungent, many of the tombstones almost inaccessible among the overgrown tendrils of ivy.

Holywell's fusion of nature, spirituality, ancient history, and overlapping functions as meadow and cemetery seems especially appropriate in light of the layers of ecological and pagan interests of so many of those whose bodies are decaying there. With over 1,000 graves,[2] corporeal contributors to the cemetery's ecosystem include natural scientists, such as George Claridge Druce, a botanist and Royal Society fellow who helped found the Ashmolean Natural History Society of Oxfordshire; and George Rolleston, a zoologist friend of Thomas Henry Huxley, and the author of *Forms of Animal Life: A Manual of Comparative Anatomy* (1870). The decomposed bodies of scholars of pagan culture are also here, including those of John Rhys, the first professor of Celtic studies at Oxford, and famed Egyptologist Francis Llewellyn Griffith, who endowed Egyptology studies at Oxford and served as a professor of the subject. Griffith's extensive knowledge of Egyptian paganism can be found in his *Stories of the High Priests of Memphis* (1900) and the three-volume *The Demotic Magical Papyrus of London and Leiden* (1904–1921), among others. We also find a marker for Max Müller, the influential specialist in comparative philology and mythology who focused much of his work on arguing that Sanskrit documents could demonstrate the influence of Vedic nature worship on European paganisms. While Gifford Lecturer at the University of Glasgow, Müller gave a series of talks on the development of spirituality from nature worship,[3] leading some to accuse him of being anti-Christian, while Theosophist Helena Blavatsky and others saw him as someone sympathetic to their own interests in paganism, occultism, and the traces of universal spirit within diverse regional beliefs and practices.

The verbal arts are also well represented at Holywell. There is Kenneth Grahame, whose love and veneration of nature can be found in many works, including *Pagan Papers* (1893) and *The Wind in the Willows* (1908). The American James Blish is also part of this sepulchral community. His writings include *A Case of Conscience* (1958) – a reworking of his 1953 novella *If* – in which a Jesuit priest has his faith shaken when he and his team visit the planet Lithia and encounter alien reptiles who have, without the aid of the Judeo-Christian God, attained a perfect moral

Introduction: Thoughts at Imbolc 2021 3

state. Of all the individuals who have enhanced the soil of Holywell Cemetery, the most relevant to an understanding of what I call British decadent ecology is Walter Pater. He and Algernon Charles Swinburne were key catalysts of the flourishing of decadent culture and the pagan revival in Britain. Pater's own ideas were influenced by the work of Müller, and the two were well acquainted as Oxford dons living across the street from each other.[4] Pater died in 1894 and Müller six years later. Even in Holywell, Pater's rather conventional grave marker stands just across from the Celtic cross on Müller's burial plot.

When I speak of Holywell's denizens, I am thinking of the specialists in diverse fields who contributed to these changing ecological visions, as well as the creatures, plants, and other forces that contributed to their enquiries, engaged their imaginations, and flourished on their graves. Their physical intermingling is a helpful model for envisioning the decadents' own mix of ideas about ecology, decadence, and pagan spiritualities. A number of scholars have conducted research on ways in which British decadent authors and artists turned to paganism for exotic and erotic metaphors and motifs. Others have addressed how the decadents used paganism's spiritual, aesthetic, and philosophical discourses as cultural coding through which to engage nonnormative desires or to foster community. My study builds on this valuable work, although paganism's symbolic and mediatory functions are not my main focus. Rather, in this study I address paganism as a force in itself – one that made a vital contribution to the decadent ecological models articulated by authors, artists, and scientists in the nineteenth and early twentieth centuries. In *Decadent Ecology*, I address literary and visual works of decadence as they engaged with discourses that also operated through modern science, politics, and spirituality. The decadents, I argue, found sustenance from and gave nourishment to their ecology, with paganism a particularly vital component of their thinking, writing, performances, and art.

Despite its image in the press, British decadence, even from the 1860s to the 1910s when it was most popular, was not a monolithic movement. Rather, it engaged with and changed in response to diverse developments in science, philosophy, aesthetics, politics, and ethics. Within this familiar time period, there remain today under-acknowledged works that propound temporal, spatial, and conceptual expansions of what the British understood as decadence. In the chapters that follow, I explore less recognized aspects of decadence, such as animal empathy, the intimacy of the peripatetic, and the feminist potency of occult ritual. While not assuming lines of influence, *Decadent Ecology* also notes

4 Introduction: Thoughts at Imbolc 2021

conceptual overlaps with recent inquiries into issues such as queer ecology, pagan civic responsibility, and ecosophical articulations of animal–vegetal communication. In *Through Vegetal Being* (2018), Luce Irigaray ponders, "How can we speak of the vegetal world? Is not one of its teachings to show without saying, or to say without words? I imagine that we will try to display and signify on this side or beyond any discourse."[5] How to think less like a human? How to allow others to perceive and process on one's behalf? How to break open the logic of familiar discourses? Such queries underlie British decadence as a creative force of cultural disturbance and the eco-paganism through which so many of these radical interests and methodologies were experienced.

There are two main reasons why the eco-morphological aspect of British decadence has, to date, not garnered greater scholarly attention. First, from the start of the cultural phenomenon, decadence has been associated with the urban, the cultured, the artificial, and, not infrequently, the insincere. Second, the popular press canonized decadence largely by parodying or condemning the persona of the dandy-aesthete, the penchant for bons mots, the celebration of gender and sexual liberties, and certain Pre-Raphaelite aesthetics in fashion and home décor that became markers of middle-class pretension. Swinburne, Dante Gabriel Rossetti, Pater, Ouida, Wilde, James McNeill Whistler, Aubrey Beardsley – these prominent authors and artists were refashioned into the comic embodiments of the decadent type at the expense of other contributors to the movement who did not fit so readily into the popular vision and were, therefore, arguably also less influential. To help avoid losing those subject threads of British decadence that, to date, have been underappreciated, I conceive of decadence as multidisciplinary, interweaving strands of interests whose interactions fostered a conceptual elasticity and suppleness. Each of my chapters is designed around one of these strands. Some strands are temporally longer and others are not as tightly interwoven with the rest, so I have organized the chapters as chronologically as possible in order to signpost more easily notable influences, redirections, and integrations.

Following the Strands

Because Swinburne and Pater were the main catalysts for a British culture of eco-pagan decadence, they are my starting points in Chapters 1 and 2. My first chapter defines, historically positions, and captures the intersections among decadence, ecology, and the pagan revival in literature and art. I establish the ecological aspects of decadence as articulated

Following the Strands 5

by such influential writers as Charles Baudelaire, Paul Bourget, and Max Nordau, while, in the process, offering close analyses of works by Swinburne and the Pre-Raphaelite artist Frederick Sandys that help demonstrate the complex interplay across these concepts. In Chapter 2, I explore Pater's turn to Classical paganism to formulate his vision of the individual subject as dissipated through a range of spatiotemporal landscapes. Situating Pater's *Studies in the History of the Renaissance* (1873) and *Marius the Epicurean* (1885) within the context of scientific claims by Charles Darwin, Ernst Haeckel, and Antonio Stoppani, I demonstrate the way in which Pater's paganism melds the Classical with recent scientific developments to present an ecological fusion of humans, other animals, plants, cultures, and even architecture. Of equal importance, I note that people such as Stoppani turned to metaphors rooted in Classical mythology in order to formulate, in his case, a pseudo-scientific, Christian conception of the rise of the Anthropocene.

My discussion of the term "new paganism" in Chapter 1 notes the homophobic intimations present in some critics' responses to Swinburne's and Pater's decadent works. However, as Swinburne's poem "The Leper" (1866) and Pater's *Marius the Epicurean* make apparent, the intimacies that construct ecological communities are often far more amorphous or unprecedented than homophobic innuendos suggest. My third chapter addresses decadent desires as complicated modes of perspectival code-switching accomplished through trans-species intimacies. Focusing on the strategic paganism in works by painter Simeon Solomon and poets Katherine Bradley and Edith Cooper, known together as Michael Field, I offer two queer models of what Henry Salt theorized, in *Animals' Rights Considered in Relation to Social Progress* (1892), as imaginative sympathy.

Decadence turned to paganism to grasp not only animal intimacies but also engagements with the environment more generally. Building on the queer trans-species intimacies articulated by Swinburne, Pater, Solomon, and Field, in Chapter 4 I address Robert Louis Stevenson's and Vernon Lee's renderings of the environment as *genius loci*. As I argue, for Stevenson and Lee the *genii locorum* are not fixed locations in nature but ecological entanglements among animal and vegetal species, geographic formations, and climate. Stevenson and Lee extend Pater's ecological correspondences by presenting the immersive experience of the peripatetic as sensual and psychological engagements with nature that result in a more vital identification outside the self. And in situating their analysis within the growing cultural practice of the nature walk, their writings redefine the *genius loci* as a dynamic engagement suggestive of early environmentalism.

In her writings, Lee at times formulates the spirit of place as a transhistorical, gynocentric paganism, but a number of her contemporaries took on a more explicit consideration of the pagan as a site of feminist self-realization. Chapter 5 turns from literature about the spirit of moving through place to works addressing another form of spiritual movement: actual pagan ritual. Enmeshed within both the London decadent community and New Woman politics, Moina Mathers and Florence Farr were among the most influential occultists of the pagan revival. These two leaders of the Hermetic Order of the Golden Dawn developed ecological models in which human-centered measures of space and time are replaced by an understanding of the self as an evanescent engagement within an occult ecology. Taking a lesson from Sandys, this chapter is not about searching for occult symbols in decadent art or literature. Rather, it addresses the decadent spirit within occult works aimed, in part, at destabilizing modern gender inequality.

While my discussion of occult feminism in Chapter 5 shifts the foundations of my study to a reality beyond the veil, in Chapter 6 I return to the turf on which I began with my ruminations on Holywell Cemetery. The last chapter examines works by George Egerton, Arthur Machen, and William Sharp, each of whom introduces a different form of paganism to their earthy decadent ecologies. The authors find in paganism scalar distortions and other forms of eco-excess that problematize distinctions between the spiritual, secular, and scientific. At the same time, while all are, today, recognized as part of the cosmopolitan, fin-de-siècle culture of Wilde and Beardsley, each, in fact, turns to the local and the rural as the site of their decadent intimacies. We hear in their often conflicted renderings of the pagan landscape voices for sexual, eco-spiritual, and regionalist politics.

As I sit at my desk now, discouraged by a global plague from travel and socializing, I look out at the new raised garden beds in our backyard on this bright Oklahoma February day. Morgan, the cats, and I keep hypothetically safe in our bubble, while the virus and international politics rage on. And I am left in awe, inspired at least, by the idea that the ecological remains so inescapable and that the regional and the earth-centered have become so much a defining element of my life.

Dennis Denisoff
Tulsa, Imbolc, 2021

CHAPTER I

Decadent Ecology and the Pagan Revival

Ernst Haeckel coined the term "ecology" (German: oikologie, from the Latin *oikos* for home or place of being) in his *Generelle Morphologie der Organismen* (1866). Citing Charles Darwin's scholarship as his main influence, Haeckel defines ecology as "the whole science of the relationship of the organism to the environment including, in the broad sense, all the 'conditions of existence.' These are partly organic, partly inorganic in nature."[1] It was also in 1866 that Algernon Charles Swinburne let his paganism-riddled and shockingly sexual collection *Poems and Ballads* loose upon an unwary populace, marking the beginning of British decadence as a cultural phenomenon encouraging a view of individuals' relation to their environments as rapturous, rupturing, and unstable. The collection confronted the many ecological models of the time that, in accord with natural theology, favored human-centered, closed systems or coordinated, self-moderating biospheres. A decadent ecology such as that envisioned by Swinburne differs in being characterized by disruption, defilement, and excess operating beyond human comprehension, modeling, or management. Such an open ecology is decadent not only in its historical and cultural references but also in its destabilizing forms. Devin Griffiths and Deanna K. Kreisel observe that much of nineteenth-century eco-theory "did not assume that these interactions were coherent, harmonious, or tightly integrated"; instead, they offered a "more mutable notion of ecology."[2] To the proposition of a less determinate model of ecology, Darwin and his contemporaries "responded creatively, developing notions of ecology that were extremely wide-ranging and flexible." Decadent ecology constitutes part of this response, but it is unique in the cultural resources it accessed, the conscious imbrication of the aesthetic and the textual within the model, the hackle-raising character of its popular identity, and its diverse adaptations of eco-spirituality.

Decadent Ecology and the Pagan Revival

The Eco-morphology of Modern Decadence

The term "decadence" entered common English usage in the eighteenth century as what now, in retrospect, can be understood as an ecological phenomenon. The word was applied predominantly to the immorality and deterioration of a society or civilization, an application that was extended – especially in the nineteenth century – to signify the immorality or deviancy of specific individuals or subsets of a society. Montesquieu's naturalist political study *Considérations sur les causes de la grandeur des Romains et de leur décadence* (1734) and Edward Gibbon's *History of the Decline and Fall of the Roman Empire* (1776–1788) familiarized the literate public with a biological model of a decaying society. For Gibbon, the downfall of the Romans was principally precipitated by the rise of Christianity, which shifted people's commitment away from the political vitality of the empire to the afterlife, thereby weakening their patriotism and civic virtue.[3] Gibbon articulates the period's discord between individual rights, on the one hand, and the need to sustain a cohesive, collective program, on the other. The issue arose, in part, from Voltaire, who, in his *Essai sur l'histoire générale et sur les mœurs et l'esprit des nations* (1756), advocates for freedoms of the individual, questioning recent claims that Christianity marked the pinnacle of civilization. Building on this thesis, Gibbon offers examples of what he saw to be other highly civilized cultures and belief systems, such as those of China and some Muslim nations. Admiring "naked and unpresuming simplicity" in literature, he critiques Byzantine works characterized by "gigantic and obsolete words, a stiff and intricate phraseology, the discord of images, the childish play of false or unseasonable ornament, and the painful attempt [by authors] to elevate themselves, to astonish the reader, and to involve a trivial meaning in the smoke of obscurity and exaggeration."[4] One notes in this quotation some of the rhetoric that would be turned against decadents as preening, urbane individualists.

Charles Baudelaire, perhaps the main foreign catalyst of British decadence, privileged the urban and self-centered over the natural. In 1853, after receiving Fernand Desnoyers's request for a contribution to a collection of nature poetry, he wrote a response (revised and published as an open letter in 1855) in which he challenged popular convention by portraying nature as spiritless, yet, curiously, also quite upsetting:

> [Y]ou well know that I am incapable of being moved by plants, and that my soul rebels against this singular new religion, which will always have, it seems to me, for any *spiritual* being something *shocking* about it. I will

The Eco-morphology of Modern Decadence 9

> never believe that *the soul of God inhabits plants*, and even if it did live there, I would care little, and would consider my own soul worth far more than the soul of sanctified vegetables. I have always thought that there was in *Nature*, flourishing and rejuvenating, something impudent and distressing.[5]

Despite the declarative tone, we find here not a confident separation of the natural and spiritual, but a sense of uncertainty ("even if it did live there"). While the letter is a repudiation of late-Romanticist pap, it is not an utter devaluation of the natural; instead, it depicts nature as showing disrespect for, or even cruelty toward, Baudelaire's soul (with the poet adding the word "cruel" in the version of the letter that he later published). Baudelaire's distinction between nature and spirit has been read as one between the real and the artificial, with the latter seen as purer, because closer to the spiritual. Thus, poems in *Les Fleurs du mal* (1857) such as "Je t'adore à l'égal de la voûte nocturne" ("I Adore You as Much as the Nocturnal Vault"), "Une charogne" ("A Carcass"), "Remords posthume" ("Posthumous Remorse"), and "L'Irréparable" ("The Irreparable") see the sanctity of death infiltrated by the voracious vitality of maggots, flies, or other species, suggesting he had found the decadent fecundity and persistence of nature a spiritual and philosophical threat.

Théophile Gautier's 1868 notice to *Les Fleurs du mal*, however, problematizes such a juxtaposition by understanding ecological excess as itself nurturing the hyper-refined modern aesthetic. Baudelaire's work, Gautier proposes, is the refuse of modern society as it, like past civilizations, falls from a "natural" to an "artificial life." The poet's language is "already marbled with the greenness of decomposition, savouring of the Lower Roman Empire and the complicated refinements of the Byzantine School, the last form of Greek art fallen into dissipation."[6] Gautier here addresses Baudelaire's literary style and themes but, by echoing political and scientific language of decay, mingles the poetics with these other disciplinary discourses. Influenced by Gautier, Paul Bourget's *Essais de psychologie contemporaine* (1883) includes a subsection entitled "Theory of the Decadence" that offers his well-known discussion of decomposition as a negative yet natural process, which he then extrapolates into other contexts. Bourget establishes Baudelaire and his writing as dangerously absorbing: "He was a man of decadence, and he made himself a theorist of decadence. This is perhaps the most troubling feature of this troubled figure. It is perhaps that which exercises the most disturbing seduction on a contemporary soul."[7] Bourget writes, "Wherever there shimmers what Baudelaire calls, with a necessary strangeness, 'the phosphorescence of decay,' he feels himself drawn by an irresistible allure."[8] Quoting Gautier's notice to *Les Fleurs du mal*, Bourget proposes that Baudelaire and other decadents are the psychologically disturbed products of their environments, their writing articulating "a troubled life whose language is 'already marbled with the greenness of decay.'"[9] The references to seduction remind one of the sensually alluring imagery of so much of Baudelaire's poetry. But the putridity that draws the attention of Gautier and then Bourget, the view of decay as glimmering invitingly with a cold light, elicits not simply a yearning for the repulsive or to repulse, but a lingering sense that those elements that a society marks as abject are not only inherent but actually contribute to that society's self-identity and form. With this conception of decay, Bourget creates a technology of excess involving mutually reinforcing models rooted in biology, psychology, desire, economics, sociology, civilization, and aesthetics. According to him, societies operate like organisms that sustain an overall healthy, living force only if they maintain a coordinated effort for growth and life:

> If the energy of the cells becomes independent, the organisms composing the total organism likewise cease to subordinate their energy to the total energy, and the anarchy which takes place constitutes the decadence of the whole. The social organism does not escape this law. It becomes decadent as soon as the individual life becomes exaggerated under the influence of acquired well-being and heredity.[10]

Similarly, in Bourget's terms, when artists and authors begin taking things to extremes (as Gibbon criticizes the Byzantine authors for having done), they have a disproportionately high impact on the perceptions and understandings of the whole; the rise of such creative individuals is the result of the excess encouraged by contemporary society in general. And just as a healthy society relies on the teamwork of self-sacrificing individuals, decadent literature sacrifices the healthy relational cohesion of a text to the malignant independence of the paragraph, and that of the paragraph to that of the sentence. Bourget is arguing for a model in which both organic and inorganic elements are understood as occasions of interaction, with a decadent ecology pulsating through textual relations as much as through biological ones.

In *Degeneration* (1892; English trans. 1895), we find Max Nordau repurposing Bourget, citing him as proof that the contributors to modern decadence were not righteous cultural scientists exposing modernity's greed and gluttony, but elitists whose drive to distress the middle classes was actually what first fostered contemporary society's egomania and corrosion.

The Eco-morphology of Modern Decadence

Nordau builds on anthropologist Cesare Lombroso's theories of innate criminality to argue that the decadent movement and other affiliated developments in the arts were marked by the works of deranged individuals exacerbating the degeneracy (that is, criminality) of society. Nordau's position reflects a broader struggle to quarantine decadence after it had already infected various, at times conflicted, political and cultural perspectives and positions. In response, Alfred Egmont Hake anonymously published *Regeneration* (1895), depicting Nordau as little more than "an irascible toy-terrier barking at the moon."[11] Hake's writing career engaged with a range of subjects, including free trade and, in *Suffering London* (1892), the hygienic, moral, and political relations between voluntary hospitals and society. He is best known for editing the journals written by General Charles George Gordon regarding his involvement in the Taiping Rebellion and the Siege of Khartoum. For Hake, if we follow Nordau's logic, "we pay the penalty of our individuality in being found to be 'morbid deviations from an original type,' and are therefore degenerate."[12] "Who but a 'degenerate,'" however, Hake counters, "would treat all these alike?" As he points out, Nordau "goes out of his way in order to protest against the misconception which represents him as having insinuated that the whole of humanity exhibited signs of decay, and he declares that his remarks apply exclusively to the educated classes"; and yet, "he speaks of the masses as partly affected by degeneration, and of the danger of the contamination spreading from the educated classes to the masses."[13] Hake follows this inversion – declaring Nordau to be the actual degenerate – by linking Nordau's views to issues of imperial decline.

Hake's reading encourages us to recognize the illogical effort to take what is biologized as a healthy society and separate it from what are seen as its illnesses, infections, and expulsions. What if, one might ask, we entered the inquiry with a regard for the seemingly useless and excessive? What if we appreciated more those ambiguous attractions, transmissions, and dissipations that preceded the nominal and classificatory practices that privilege an artificial image of a stable society against which decadence is then described as a secondary reaction? Decadents, in engaging mutation, excess, and inconstancy, envisioned comingling forces moving through species, as well as through the organic and inorganic, and the generative and degenerative. Decadent ecology does not turn to some ideal of nature and its processes in order to understand society, but encourages an appreciation of the indeterminacies that are part of all of its manifestations. Like biological decay, decadent culture is not a threat, but an inherent aspect of an open ecology. One sees cultural decadence,

12 Decadent Ecology and the Pagan Revival

then, not simply as applications of ecological theory, but as vital ecological engagement itself. This helps explain why, while decadence has often been associated with illness, deviancy, and immorality, authors and artists also *accepted* accusations of decadence; it was not just rebelliousness on their part, but a sign of their awareness of the inevitable cross-influences that gave shape to themselves, their ideas, and their works.

Disparaging the accusations of decadence, meanwhile, inadvertently also drew attention to anxieties regarding Britain's naturalization of imperialist activities and human exceptionalism in order to justify its exploitation and abuse of other elements of its ecology. The concerns noted by Gibbon regarding national and regional differences remained, with xenophobic and racist metaphors continuing to resonate. The system of co-option and abuse is far from simple. Decadence has been a global phenomenon not only because Europeans (and Westerners more generally) objectified and sexualized people from other countries and cultures as exotic markers of their own refined tastes. It has also been so because many non-Europeans, non-Americans, Black people, Indigenous people, and others participated and continue to take part in shaping decadent culture and politics, often by appropriating and adapting the same tropes and perspectives by which they themselves had been objectified or erased. Monographs by Regenia Gagnier, Kristin Mahoney, and Robert Stilling, and essay collections edited by Liz Constable, Matt Potolsky, and myself and by Kate Hext and Alex Murray, among other works, demonstrate that one can find strong decadent strains and elaborations on through to the present day in cultures around the globe.[14] At the same time, influential engagements fostered conflict on local or provincial levels. Moreover, Mary Ellis Gibson observes that the provincial "usually operates in an implicit – and sometimes explicit – binary with the metropolitan," and "as an ideological construction of the metropole rather than a place or space or set of social practices in itself."[15] The nationalist agendas of Scottish and Irish independence that I discuss in later chapters, for example, were played out simultaneously on the local and international stages, and within both the nature-centered and city-centered decadence of the period and on various spatial, temporal, and political fronts.

Ecological Swinburne

The main catalyst for literature having a voice in the formulation of British decadence, Algernon Swinburne's *Poems and Ballads* (1866) took shape in relation to other disciplinary discourses of the time. Writing in

Ecological Swinburne

1904, William Barry declares that those who desire "the simplest version ... of what the movement intended when it began, will find it ... in Mr. Swinburne's 'Poems and Ballads.'"[16] In his oft-cited review "The Fleshly School of Poetry" (1871), Robert Buchanan (Thomas Maitland) turns to an ecological framework to declare "unnatural" the works of primarily Swinburne and Dante Gabriel Rossetti, whom he describes as "public offenders ... diligently spreading the seeds of disease broadcast wherever they are read and understood. Their complaint too is catching, and carries off many young persons."[17] Buchanan's turn to a language of illness, infection, and procreative excess is not simply figurative. Gowan Dawson has demonstrated that "sexual debauchery, aesthetic approaches to literature, unbelief and naturalistic forms of science were all, in Buchanan's critical writing during the mid-1870s, elided in a single pejorative term: materialism."[18] Other writers for the popular press, Dawson observes, particularly encouraged conflations of Swinburne's work with Darwin's. When Buchanan jokes that Swinburne's passionate poetry makes him wish that "things had remained for ever in the asexual state described in Mr. Darwin's great chapter on Palingenesis," we find the term "unnatural" being used to critique not artifice but, in fact, a hyper-sensuality that is all too sexual and rejuvenating – the untameable nature that Baudelaire had likewise criticized.[19] Buchanan notes that this poetry in fact impacts the minds of readers, seeding a perspective that undermines the moral standards necessary for maintaining a healthy, social organism. Fleshly poetry, Buchanan suggests, is a form of ecoterrorism.

With the release of *Poems and Ballads*, the flaming-haired, erratically energized Swinburne was quickly sensationalized as the "libidinous laureate of a pack of satyrs," positioning him as Britain's voice of aesthetic sensuality, cultural morbidity, and what was called (often disparagingly) the new paganism.[20] This neo-paganism has been understood as part of his campaign against institutional Christianity's blind faith. In a discussion of Robert Browning's poetry, Swinburne juxtaposes "the viler forms and more hideous outcomes of Christianity, its more brutal aspects and deadlier consequences" with the imaginative talents Browning derived from "the mythological side of the creed," from the tradition in which "the sacred sirens have sung to this seafarer."[21] The distinction is engaged in various of Swinburne's poems, from the Germanic pagan "Hertha" to the Classical pagan "The Garden of Proserpine," and the nonpagan "The Leper."

Published in his collection *Songs before Sunrise* (1871), "Hertha" is, as Swinburne described a draft of the poem, "another mystic atheistic democratic anthropologic poem."[22] Noting the essential, if ambiguous, pagan element in his own work, he wrote to Dante Gabriel Rossetti, "I have tried not to get the mystic elemental side of the poem swamped by the promulgation of the double doctrine, democratic and atheistic, equality of men and abolition of gods."[23] In "Hertha," Swinburne uses the Germanic goddess of earth, nature, and fertility to propose a female-centered myth of Creation, although, as Margot K. Louis details, his formulation is inspired particularly by Eastern spiritualities, and Hinduism in particular.[24] Jerome McGann has noted that while Hertha is for modern society a "dead god long delivered into the regions of comparative mythology," it is indeed death that "gives Hertha's voice its prophetic authority."[25] She speaks from outside of history and the models of evolution or rewarding afterlife, self-identifying as the source of all existence: "Out of me man and woman, and wild-beast and bird; | Before God was, I am." With the sudden shift from past tense to present (with its parodic echo of Exodus 3:14), Swinburne establishes Hertha as both the original force (preceding God) and also timeless, ongoing, and yet not tied to a narrative of progression or improvement.

"The Garden of Proserpine," from *Poems and Ballads*, depicts the ancient Roman goddess and her eternal garden of the underworld. There, she maintains her "bloomless buds" and "fruitless fields of corn,"[26] what Sara Lyons has described as "a kind of Eden under erasure."[27] Swinburne does not present this landscape as either a subversion of nature or Christianity, nor as a respect for artifice; rather, the emphasis is placed on sustained uncertainty, on "doubtful dreams of dreams."[28] One finds a concerted challenge to institutionalized convictions regarding what exists beyond mortality and those earthly acts of virtue inspired by a hope of improving one's chances in the afterlife:

> I am tired of tears and laughter,
> And men that laugh and weep
> Of what may come hereafter
> For men that sow to reap.[29]

The poetry's decadent weariness, soothing aural sway, and pagan imaginary serve as implicit arguments against rigid, moral edict and action driven by an expectation of posthumous reward.

Swinburne takes a distinctly different approach to modern morality in "The Leper," which was published in *Poems and Ballads*. The poem is decadent not only in its nonnormative affections, sensual detail, and cultural morbidity, but also in its use of infection and rot to formulate an ecology of interpenetrations and mutual consumptions operating beyond human comprehension. In the poem, a poor scribe tells of his unfaltering but unrequited love for an aristocratic woman who becomes leprous and, shunned by all others, dies and decays. At the time of the poem's publication, the boom in Britain's popular periodical industry brought forward analogies for decadent ecology not only in the sciences but also in fields such as the architectural, nationalist, and military. For example, in 1860, William Makepeace Thackeray, as editor of *The Cornhill Magazine*, published an uncredited essay by geologist and Royal Society member David Thomas Ansted demonizing those "natural enemies" that cause the "defacement," "decay," and "decomposition" of wood, stone, and metal constructions.[30] Ansted's "Our Natural Enemies" discusses ways of combatting the damage of "the progress of decay" set on by fungus, worms, boring insects, and water, while at the same time equating the affected structures with national identity: "constantly on the watch to attack us," these forces are "more insidious, more treacherous, and more unscrupulous than any foes in human shape; they are everywhere around us."[31] Buckingham Palace, Westminster Abbey, St. Paul's Cathedral, the Houses of Parliament, the colleges of Oxford – all these bastions of Englishness are described as under threat. With "the glories of the Victorian period of England's wealth and prosperity ... already defaced" by these attackers, the author declares, it is no less than "a point of honour that we have to fight for, and, if defeated, we are irretrievably disgraced."[32] The hyperbole reveals the ready formulation, even by an acclaimed scientist such as Ansted, of natural decomposition not as a process of wear or multispecies interaction, but as a calculated attack by an invisible foreign agent. In this article intended to stimulate readers of *The Cornhill* to support the cause of protecting architecture from erosion, he portrays decay as a form of biological, national, and moral aggression, evoking the same anxieties Buchanan voices in his reading of Swinburne and Rossetti as biological threats to the core of national identity.

This was also a period of extensive research and popular publication on fungal infections, including leprosy, today more commonly referred to as Hansen's disease, after the Norwegian physician Gerhard Armauer Hansen who discovered the disease-causing fungal bacterium in 1873. A kingdom of species of multicellular microorganisms, including mildew, mushrooms, and mould, fungi do not produce their own food but generally exist in symbiotic relations with bacteria and plants, contributing to the diffusion of nutrients through their ecosystem. The transmission of

16   Decadent Ecology and the Pagan Revival

fungi across species and ecologies is understood, from a human perspective, as decay or rot, although it is just as accurate to see it as the thriving of a microorganism within an ecology that includes the human. But, just as this perspective is difficult for most humans to adopt, others – over the many centuries of discussion and research on the phenomenon – have become familiarized. The term "leprosy" has been used to refer not only to the physical disease but also to the general illness and uncleanliness of humans, buildings, locations, and ideas. The implications of this expansive application can be seen in Swinburne's "The Leper" and its formulation of the decadent as part of an uncontainable infection that was simultaneously ecological, sociopolitical, and philosophical. The poet's rendering of Hansen's disease, preceding as it does modern progress in treatment (a reliable cure was not established until the mid-twentieth century), retains the historical associations of the disease with putrefaction, issues of sensory reception, and the dangers of the unsanitary, the foreign, and the immoral.

Poems and Ballads received heavy criticism but, according to Clyde K. Hyder, it was "The Leper" that took the brunt of the attacks.[33] *The Spectator* of September 22 described it in passing as "foul stuff, worst of all, … which we think no critics can speak worse of than [it] deserve."[34] Writing anonymously for *Fraser's Magazine*, John Skelton liked the collection but recommended the suppression of "The Leper" and a few other poems.[35] And *The Athenæum*'s critic described the poem as a "horribly impure" and "utterly loathsome" story of an "unclean priest and his leprous mistress," commenting that there is nothing "much more revolting than when the graves of poor mortality are torn open to exhibit the tenants influenced by feelings which have the fierce passions of earth about them."[36] Curiously, *The Athenæum*'s reviewer refers to the scribe and the woman who shuns him as a priest and a mistress, which implies she is a willing lover.[37] The reviewer insinuates, moreover, that the key immorality of the poem is not the obsession of the lover but the fact that his beloved is leprous and that somebody would have such feelings for a leper. On a more general register, the language of impurity and uncleanliness extends the critique implicitly to a sense of poverty as itself a moral weakness.

Not long before Swinburne published "The Leper," an acquaintance,[38] the minor poet Frederick Locker, had published a poem entitled "A Human Skull." The piece appeared in *The Cornhill Magazine* in 1860, upon the encouragement of Thackeray, the magazine's editor.[39] Not a decadent work, Locker's poem nevertheless foreshadows Swinburne's in

Ecological Swinburne   17

presenting a narrator who contrasts a fleshless skull with the beloved's
original dewy beauty (which, in Locker's poem, is only imagined):

> Time was some may have prized its blooming skin:
>   Here lips were woo'd perhaps in transport tender:
> Some may have chucked what was a dimpled chin,
>   And never had my doubt about its gender!

In a recent essay on putrefaction and natural theology in the Victorian
period, Christopher Hamlin notes that Locker intended the poem's closing
image of the rotted body converted to a patch of meadow flowers as a sign
of God's grace and assurance of an overarching social cohesion. "[W]hat is
praiseworthy," Hamlin sees Locker proposing, "is the transformation of
matter from one beautiful and useful occupation to the next, or, in more
technical (and more evocative) terms, the putrefaction, decomposition, or
decay of organic matter and its subsequent reconstitution in a new
form."[40] Locker envisions a natural theology, a holistic ecological system in
which the productivist ethos of modern Western society was an innate,
ethical element. One suspects that Thackeray, as the *Cornhill* editor, realized what he was doing when he chose to position Locker's poem on decay
directly after Ansted's essay "Our Natural Enemies," which I addressed
earlier. While Locker situates corporeal rot within a religious framework
intended to reaffirm his faith, the geologist envisions micro-organismic
consumption as a threat to a national and spiritual cohesion that must be
addressed through science. As "The Leper" makes clear, this is also the
unstable terrain of decadent ecology.

"The Leper" captures a young man's impassioned lament for the death
of his beloved. In a manuscript of the poem in Swinburne's handwriting
held at Georgetown University, three lines are revised to make two fundamental changes to the work. First, the new lines now identify the servant
as a writer – a "poor scribe," as if Swinburne wished to suggest an affinity
between the poem's narrator and himself.[41] Second, it describes the
beloved as having "curled-up lips and amorous hair," the author thereby
re-affirming his affinity with the Pre-Raphaelites by evoking the
Brotherhood's voluptuous ideal of female beauty as found in paintings
completed near the time, such as Dante Gabriel Rossetti's *Helen of Troy*
(1863) and *Bocca Baciata* (1859) and Frederick Sandys's *Love's Shadow*
(1867) and *Proud Maisie* (1868). The latter alludes to Sir Walter Scott's
ballad "Proud Maisie" (1818), in which a cheery robin informs a vain
young woman that her marriage will occur at death, and her marriage
bed made by the grave digger. Swinburne described Sandys's

then-untitled *Proud Maisie* on exhibition at the Royal Academy as "one of his most solid and splendid designs; a woman of rich, ripe, angry beauty, she draws one lock of curling hair through her full and moulded lips, biting it with hard bright teeth, which add something of a tiger's charm to the sleepy and crouching passion of her fair face."[42] While it is unknown whether Swinburne knew that Sandys had Scott's dead heroine in mind, his language echoes his own depiction of the proud, dying noblewoman in "The Leper."

Swinburne's poem contributes to the familiar Pre-Raphaelite trope of the *femme fatale*, but the image is frankly problematized by the beloved's leprosy. His rendering of the woman's decaying body remains highly sensual:

> Love bites and stings me through, to see
> Her keen face made of sunken bones.
> Her worn-off eyelids madden me,
> That were shot through with purple once.[43]

This macabre devotion situates the poem comfortably within the necrophiliac tradition to which Pre-Raphaelitism, aestheticism, and decadence contributed, as found in Alfred Tennyson's "The Lady of Shalott" (1833), Robert Browning's "Porphyria's Lover" (1836), Edgar Allan Poe's "Annabel Lee" (1849), Charles Baudelaire's "I Worship You" (1857), and John Everett Millais's *Ophelia* (1865–1866). "I served her ... " "I served her ... " begin the first two lines of the second stanza of "The Leper,"[44] emphasizing the scribe's sense of himself as a dependent functionary. This is an identity that the tenacity of his devotion overturns, with him gaining authority in the relationship as she relies increasingly on him for sustenance. In the process, Swinburne gradually shifts the source of social discord from the heartless, selfish female to the groveling male whose insatiable love for the deteriorating body proves an increasingly repulsive, counterproductive obsession. In this sense, Swinburne is himself the lowly scribe rejected by the dominant order for his voracious devotion to sensual themes and aesthetics.

Through a broader lens, Swinburne portrays decadent aesthetics itself as a hyper-emotional excess disturbing the mainstream vision of a harmonious ecology in which all components operate toward ensuring the vitality of the British middle class. "The Leper" correlates the actual desensitizing numbness often caused by the disease with the beloved's cold response to the narrator's sensual advances. This juxtaposition of repulsion and attraction also operates in the poem on a larger scale, contrasting the common impulse to shun the other – whether deemed abject, sickly, foreign, or unnatural – with the decadent drive for appreciative incorporation (what Baudelaire captures in "The Carcass" in his vision of the beloved as a maggot-ridden corpse). Appropriately, in contrast to Locker's piece, Swinburne's decadent poem concludes with far greater skepticism. He offers the distinctly ambivalent query "Will not God do right?," as if the deity can or can choose to act against the ethics that he himself embodies.[45] By doubting God's morality, "The Leper" questions the very existential logic behind Locker's notion of a benevolent, organizing force. Swinburne's poem shifts in its conclusion not simply to spiritual doubt, but to a skepticism or even a determinism that jeopardizes the basis of free will and ethical responsibility. The lines could be read as a simple reflection of the crisis of faith some Victorians were feeling at the time in light of new scientific discoveries and arguments. I am arguing, however, that the poem offers the alternative of an expansive conceptualization of ecological reality. A reader's human perspective and control is destabilized by the agency of leprosy long enough to note currents of engagement not simply operating outside of human consideration, but permeating the philosophical, spiritual, and aesthetic of human understanding.

In the mid-nineteenth century, scientific, medical, and religious institutions seemed particularly concerned with organic changes that humans were unable to explain or harness; a biologized economic model that accommodated the possibility of production beyond purpose did not simply undermine the overarching claims of the closed ecology, but proposed that there were engagements operating independently at the potential expense of the bourgeois order. Simply declaring that these engagements produced only excess and waste failed to account for the other forces' apparent compulsion to act and produce. And so, we see the support of the natural theology described by Hamlin, in which waste is evil unless converted into a resource. The contrast between "The Leper" and "The Human Skull" suggests that decadents such as Swinburne used literature and art to challenge what they saw as an uninspired, conformist culture, but also out of skepticism regarding the anthropocentric privileging of humans within their ecology. Their works consider rot, filth, and the seemingly lesser creatures that thrive on them as an inspiration to engage philosophically and ethically the notion of an indeterminate, open set of relationships from which humans are unable to extricate themselves. It is through pagan formulations that decadent writers have most often rendered the ethics of these values.

Decadent Paganism in the Popular Imagination

Paganism is not a single, homogenous belief system or cultural tradition, but a broad range of past and present earth-, biosphere-, and cosmos-reverent spiritualities. Various twenty-first-century activities, such as green burials, animal liberation, Indigenous activism, and what the Federal Bureau of Investigation refers to as ecoterrorism (not too long ago defined as the greatest domestic terror threat in the United States),[46] reflect a spiritually inflected re-assessment of the relation that humans have to nonhuman sentient beings and the planet. In the United Kingdom, the Pagan Federation has articulated official codes of belief somewhat grudgingly and only to the minimum degree required for the association to attain legal rights and recognition. This caution regarding established institutions reflects not only a historically justified skepticism regarding the aims and methods of those in power, but also the polytheism and polyvocality of paganism characterized by actions and engagements rather than by individuals' identifications.[47] Most current politicized pagans who are drawn to the loss of self through practice, ritual, or what British Druid Emma Restall Orr refers to as "genuine experience" find themselves in seeming contradiction, needing to take advantage of their species' privilege in order to argue that other species (or elements of the cosmos) deserve the right to assert their own genuine experience. Orr concludes that "it is never sound simply to follow, for to do so is to abdicate our personal and sacred responsibility as an individual and also as a part of society. Sharing the existentialist's suspicion of the individual's submersion into the collective, the Pagan emphasizes retaining personal moral responsibility."[48]

Neofascist appropriations of pagan traditions have exacerbated the importance of articulating individuals' responsibilities within their beliefs and practices.[49] Recently, more pagans have become explicit in their fusion of worship with the argument for responsible citizenship linked to environmentalist action. In the January 6, 2021, violent insurrection at the Capitol building in Washington DC, one of the terrorists – the QAnon-supporting part-time actor Jacob Chansley – stood out for wearing a fur cap and horns and showing various tattoos related to Norse and Viking imagery, such as the *mjolner* (Thor's Hammer), the *Yggdrasil* (Tree of Life), and a *valknut* (knot of the slain). The group The Troth – which represent the polytheistic religions of Northern European Heathenry – quickly released a statement condemning "the events today by all who committed acts of violence and terror in the strongest manner possible."[50]

Decadent Paganism in the Popular Imagination

The Troth's mission statement also makes a clear declaration of its support for gender and sexual diversity: "The Troth welcomes all people, whatever their religious, cultural, or ancestral background, gender or sexual orientation, and would like to know more about Asatru or other forms of Heathenry."[51] Politics, in short, is explicitly engrained within The Troth's identity in part because contemporary issues make it necessary to be clear in this regard.

Writing in 2005, feminist pagan Starhawk declared that "at this moment in history, we are called to act as if we truly believe that the earth is a living, conscious being that we're part of, that human beings are interconnected and precious, and that liberty and justice for all is a desirable thing."[52] Taken from the US Pledge of Allegiance, the phrase "liberty and justice for all" is loaded with a nationalist intensity and yet, at the same time, is couched in a humbling deflation of its own authoritarian rhetoric: "*as if* we truly believe" (italics added). The word "all" meanwhile gains a novel political potency here by referring to more than humans. "A community is necessarily *a community of individuals*," notes scholar Thom van Dooren:

> As such, individuality is not dissolved by this view; it is simply placed within a different context, in which what it means to be an individual is not as "individual" as we may have initially thought. To lose sight of the individual in favour of more "holistic" understandings of the world is to fail to recognize and honour all of the ways in which we are different from one another, both those of our species and others.[53]

In addressing the politics of individualism, civic responsibility, and spirituality, recent pagan scholarship is engaging in issues that have arisen throughout pagan history.

Such politics is even suggested by the likely derivation of the word "pagan" from the Latin *paganus*, meaning a person living in a rural area or village. It probably gained currency as part of Roman military language that was later adopted by Christians who cast nonbelievers as rustic and simple, regardless of whether their spirituality arose in the countryside or not. There is no solid proof of any continuous line of pagan practices in Britain that extended from the pre-Christian period to the nineteenth century. Most archaeologists and historians currently agree that, in Britain, paganisms as sizable religious institutions more than likely ended in the early Middle Ages, at a time when Christianity was cohering as the dominant belief system, albeit maintaining elements of the pagan. Advocates of what is often called "alternative archaeology" (or the less affirming "pseudo-archaeology") are more than skeptical of such conclusions, but Ronald Hutton points out in *The Stations of the Sun* (1999) that, even if claims to lineage are tenuous or not provable, contemporary paganism and witchcraft still offer genuine new practices echoing those indeterminate ones of the past and can be worthy of the respect given to any spiritual belief system.[54]

Much as today, during the nineteenth and early twentieth centuries paganism was understood both as pre-Christian polytheistic spiritualities and cultures and as contemporary manifestations with new interpretations and creative renderings. An 1839 article in *Chambers's Edinburgh Journal* that was part of the ongoing column "Sketches of Superstitions" makes apparent early in the Victorian period the hotchpotch of concerns that found a place in the public's growing interest in paganism:

> Neither the Greeks nor Romans, two of the most refined nations of antiquity, had any just idea of the operations or works of nature, as arising from a train of immutable laws established and supported by an all-wise Providence for the government of the universe. In this respect they stood exactly on a parallel with those uneducated persons of the present day who believe that the winds can be raised by incantation, and that bodily illnesses are an effect of the evil eye. … Thus, the fisherman in our own day, who will not put to sea because he has met a woman with a pair of particularly broad thumbs, is not more justly a subject of ridicule than the grave legislators of Athens eighteen hundred years ago.[55]

Just as notable as the comingling of Classical myth and modern folk beliefs is simply the fact that *Chambers's Edinburgh Journal* chose even to have a running column offering its readers a rich history of paganism, magic, and the occult – addressing not only folk and Classical, but also Egyptian, Persian, Syrian, and other belief systems most readers would have found unfamiliar.

At this time, influences on knowledge of past paganisms included developments in anthropology, archaeology, and ecology, the rise of folklore studies, and the German folk movement.[56] There was also growing general interest in Northern European cultures, such as the Celtic and Scandinavian. These operated in tandem with nationalist initiatives, such as the Scots Renascence (as Patrick Geddes referred to it) – spurred on by people such as Geddes, William Sharp, and members of the Glasgow School[57] – and the Irish Celtic Revival – whose participants included Maude Gonne, Augusta Gregory, and W. B. Yeats. Another influence came through the back-to-the-land interests sparked by John Ruskin,

Decadent Paganism in the Popular Imagination

William Morris, and others, encouraged by Edward Carpenter, questioned by E. F. Benson, and mocked by Saki. The rise of popular occulture was inspired by Egyptomania, Theosophy, the Golden Dawn, and Eastern studies, and reinforced by the problematic penchant for collecting and exoticizing those spiritualities and cultures of societies that the British found less common. Occultists and decadents were both also invested in symbolism and new psychological articulations of synaesthesia as accessing other realms of being, as were authors of pagan- and occult-inflected supernatural fiction, such as Sheridan Le Fanu, Arthur Machen, and Edith Nesbit.

In order to address the obstinance of pagan practitioners of the Classical period, Christianity had found it necessary to incorporate many of its beliefs into its own practices. With regard to the nineteenth-century rural poor, David Hempton emphasizes that a conceptual distinction between Christianity and paganism is problematic, because the two terms "themselves inadequately describe the complex patterns of religious inheritance, ecclesiastical penetration, community solidarity, primitive security and rural entertainment which all contributed something to rural religious life."[58] James Obelkevich similarly argues that it is even an issue to envision paganism as separate from Christianity in nineteenth-century rural England. Using the term "paganism" to refer to "the non-Christian elements in popular religion is convenient but misleading, since like popular religion as a whole, it was not a distinct movement or organisation but a loose agglomeration of religious phenomena. It was not a counter-religion to Christianity; rather, the two coexisted and complemented each other."[59] Obelkevich later observes that, rather than the view often propounded of Christianity's usurpation of paganism, "[i]t is hard to avoid the conclusion that paganism was dominant and Christianity recessive in popular religion. Paganism was rarely christianized, but Christianity was often paganized."[60] And in fact, Yeats found himself having to defend Irish theatre from newspaper accusations of pagan infiltration; in his discussion of Lady Augusta Gregory's play *The Travelling Man* (1910), he argues that an allusion to a pre-Christian Irish culture was not addressing earth-veneration as superior to Christianity, but rather pointing out that "in Ireland every great landmark has its meaning in sacred or heroic legend."[61]

By the 1890s, the pagan revival had become a full-fledged cultural movement consisting of a variety of morphing sub-interests. Terms such as "neo-pagan" and "the new paganism" were adopted not only by some of those sincerely invested in pagan myth and practice, but possibly more

24   Decadent Ecology and the Pagan Revival

so by people anxious about paganism's influence. Critics were keen to see this "new" fad (like that of the New Woman, new hedonism, new journalism, and so on) fizzle out, especially after the deaths of decadent authors who made major contributions to its momentum, such as John Addington Symonds, Pater, Wilde, and Swinburne (in 1893, 1894, 1900, and 1909, respectively). Because critics frequently deployed "neo-pagan" as a term of disparagement, in this study I avoid it and simply use "pagan" to address this historical revival of interest.

Pagan practices and beliefs are often seen as part of folk tradition, but it was the urban middle class, with its enhanced educations, access to scholarly resources, and increased artistic and spiritual adventurousness, that engaged most forcefully in pagan-inflected decadent culture. Influenced by Romanticism's mingling of the Classical with nature worship, and with Classical language and culture being standard teaching within institutions of higher learning throughout the nineteenth century, Greco-Roman paganism became a familiar medium that members of intellectual communities such as the decadent used to explore their unconventional interests.[62] When, in the early twentieth century, Joyce Kilmer writes that Ernest Dowson "could not write poems that really were pagan. He was not a true decadent," he assumes his readers make a direct link between the two.[63] About the same time, Edmund Gosse similarly envisioned Swinburne as "a young Bacchus ... now preparing to burst, in the company of a troop of Maenads," into the "beautifully guarded park" that was mid-Victorian poetry,[64] just as T. E. Welby saw the poet as "some pagan creature, at once impish and divine, leaping on to the sleek lawn, to stamp its goat-foot in challenge."[65] Linda Dowling cites an undergraduate student's denunciation in 1877 of "Pater-paganism and Symonds-sophistry for encouraging the worst passions and most carnal inclinations of humanity."[66] Writing in 1918, Mrs. Humphry Ward followed her reminiscences of Swinburne with memories of Pater and the "cry of 'Neo-paganism' – and various attempts at persecution" of Pater that arose with the publication in 1873 of his *Studies in the History of the Renaissance*.[67] As Ward's recollection suggests, Classical paganism was more than a historical curiosity; it was seen by many (including Ward herself) as a contemporary threat to established institutions of social order and spiritual belief.

In "How Long Halt Ye" (1905), Goldsworthy Lowes Dickinson offers a rich articulation of some of the sources of these anxieties. In this short article, he considers as modern the values he had championed more extensively in *The Greek View of Literature* (1896), asking, "Are we, in our

Decadent Paganism in the Popular Imagination 25

inmost and ultimate convictions, Christians, or Pagans, or perhaps both?"[68] Rather than strain for an unattainable Christian ideal, he argues, modern society must incorporate the view of Classical paganism, where the spiritual and the material were not seen as distinct:

> They had grasped from the first the truth which Christianity did its best to obliterate: that the life of the spirit grows out of the life of the flesh, as the flower grows out of the soil. Hence their cult of the body; which was, be it observed, a cult, not only of health and strength and skill, but also of beauty. The Greeks, I suppose, are the only people who have conceived athletics spiritually.[69]

Critiquing Christianity for being falsely idealist while inadequately addressing how one should aspire to live spiritually in the present, Dickinson writes, "Speak to men of leisure, of hope, of poetry, of beauty, of love; and you will stir something far deeper than what can be evoked by the vision of three acres and a cow, or the formula of the expropriation of the capitalist and the landlord."[70] The primary Christian contribution to this set of otherwise pagan values is the conviction that the leisure to follow personal interests should not be the exclusive purview of a privileged class.[71]

Dickinson brings together physicality, paganism, and elements of socialism to give form to a spirituality for modern times. Friends with Edward Carpenter, Kenneth Grahame, E. M. Forster (who published a biography of Dickinson in 1934), and members of the Bloomsbury Group, he worked not only as a Greek Classics scholar at Cambridge, but also on a farming cooperative and as a lecturer for the University Extension program. His *The Greek Way of Life*, through its veneration of the healthy, active body captured in the all-male athletic culture of the palaestra, elevates same-sex attraction as a pure experience of wholesome spirituality. Using the body as a marker of pagan understanding (as opposed to the Christian emphasis on the soul), Dickinson – himself homosexual – celebrates the vigorous male athlete as the core of not only Greek religion but also his vision of a modern political reality in which all can aspire to a life of leisure activity. Hutton has proposed that, following the notoriety of Wilde's trials in the 1890s, decadent paganism saw "not so much a decline as a more subdued and thoughtful continuation," one that was "less provocative and flamboyant," offering Dickinson's work as an example.[72] However, for G. K. Chesterton, Dickinson's mix of interests positioned him squarely within the dangerous decadent tradition. Chesterton's 1905 commentary on the latter's *The Greek Way of Life* opens with a declaration that the latest surge in paganism has been defeated:

> Of the New Paganism (or neo-Paganism), as it was preached flamboyantly by Mr. Swinburne or delicately by Walter Pater, there is no necessity to take any very grave account, except as a thing which left behind it incomparable exercises in the English language. The New Paganism is no longer new, and it never at any time bore the smallest resemblance to Paganism.[73]

For the Roman Catholic apologist Chesterton, British decadence was not true to Classical culture and spirituality, which he asserts was primarily characterized not by leisure, as Dickinson proposes, but by responsibility, dignity, and civic obedience. The vast majority of contributors to the pagan revival, however, were not attempting to re-assert, let alone replicate, the values and practices of Classical paganism. Bénédicte Coste insightfully argues that, although in Chesterton's view the latest paganism "was used to undermine the authority of Christianity," it was actually part of a larger cultural shift that had been propelled through developments that included "the Higher German Criticism as well as through scientific discoveries including Darwin's evolution."[74]

Writing during the period when British decadence had hit its peak of notoriety, the Roman Catholic priest William Francis Barry offered one of the most extensive critiques of its paganism in his articles "Neo-Paganism" and "Latter-Day Pagans," which appeared in *The Quarterly Review* in 1891 and 1895, respectively, and then in slightly revised versions in his *Heralds of Revolt: Studies in Modern Literature and Dogma* (1904). In the first, Barry describes the "new paganism" as having been developing for 140 years, initiated by the works of the eighteenth-century Germans Johann Wolfgang von Goethe, Gotthold Lessing, and Johann Winckelmann. For him, its rise followed from Goethe's sense of the seductiveness of Classical beliefs being gradually replaced with intense doubt: "The intoxication and the awakening, the defiance which modulates into despair, and the despair which would fain lose itself in a never-ending whirl of passion, – these are notes of a significant and widespread movement in our time, which has been called the New Paganism."[75] This movement, he declares,

> when it lived at all, had these gruesome and forbidding associations. It was the dark but defeated rival of the creed which openly triumphed in churches and saintly shrines. It lingers still, but like a half-forgotten dream, or whines and murmurs in odd and apparently trivial superstitions, for which those who practise them can render no reason. The great Pan is dead.[76]

Decadent Paganism in the Popular Imagination

However, undermining his declarations of paganism's feeble, indeed departed, state, he spends considerable time demonstrating the inadequacies of "the school known as Decadent," whose "disciples," "though by no means classic in a noble sense, are unquestionably Pagan."[77] Here, he focuses on the influences of Swinburne, Pater, and Symonds, which, he concludes wishfully, ultimately had minimal long-term impact:

> The essays and histories of Mr. Symonds, the thoughtful and languorous prose of Mr. Pater, may have drawn students to expend a vacant hour upon them. But in England all this, like any other literary movement, is for the few to whom politics, business, philanthropy, and sectarian interests, hold out less attraction. The nearest approach an English lad makes to Paganism is when he gives himself to athletics; and in doing so he is delightfully ignorant of the tradition of the palæstra. If there is one thing which he hates and does not understand, it is effeminacy. He would call Marius the Epicurean disparaging names, were he compelled to read about him; it is certain that he would never get to the end of the second volume.[78]

Barry's attempt to discredit Symonds's and Pater's aesthetic philosophies illuminates the vibrant multidimensionality of modern paganism and decadence within contemporary culture. Not only does his essay show how each was used to condemn the other by association, but he also demonstrates the way in which the pagan and decadent movements had been woven into the nationalist, imperialist, gender, and sexual politics of the time. Notable among his concerns is his sense of modern paganism as a disruptive force that comes from abroad – specifically, from Germany. The context here is the increasing British anxiety around growing German militarization and imperial expansion. Through the emphasis on the English male, Barry's technology of marginalization incorporates xenophobia into its machinery along with noninstitutionalized spirituality and nonheteronormative desires. The act of encouraging English male youths to hate that which they do not understand sets a template for future cultural misogyny, homophobia, transphobia, and xenophobia, while presenting anti-intellectualism as a sign of manliness. Thus, despite taking a dig at rural superstition, embedded in Barry's rhetoric is a curious shift from the very early Christian critique of rural, less educated people as backward pagans toward, now, a middle-class critique of the urbane and well educated as pagan faddists.

Barry does not simply note the element of paganism within decadence, but repeatedly presents paganism as its key characteristic, both in this essay and his 1895 "Latter-Day Pagans." At the same time, however, he inadvertently undermines any hope of articulating a coherent juxtaposition between Christianity and pagan decadence by recognizing the diversity of cultural artefacts and conceptual characteristics the latter embodies. In his second essay, Barry speaks principally to Pater's novel *Marius the Epicurean* (1885) and Horatio Brown's *John Addington Symonds: A Biography, Compiled from his Papers and Correspondence* (1895); however, he formulates his general subject as "that movement wherein Medievalism, the Renaissance, Mr. Ruskin, Japanese ware, old blue china, and the French symbolists were to play their several parts" – "that esthetic movement which has been with us these thirty years, the principles of which run up into Paganism, Cyrenaic or Stoic, but avowedly pre-Christian."[79] Barry here characterizes canonical decadent authors as part of a broader cultural wave that encompasses aestheticism, symbolism, Orientalism, Pre-Raphaelitism, the house beautiful, and the Arts and Crafts movement. He distinguishes between, on the one hand, the "lower Paganism" of "all who choose to be 'exquisite humanists' rather than humane, who prefer sensations to principles and intoxication to duty" and, on the other, the "better Paganism," characterized by "solitude, in the hope of communion with what was divine."[80] For Barry, Pater's and Symonds's decadence embodies the former, while what he earlier describes as "classic in the noble sense" is not apparent in this new paganism at all.[81] It has replaced "sovereign self-direction according to the moral law, or life everlasting" with an acceptance of a life of indeterminacy, of "moral relaxation, effeminacy, sickly self-consciousness, morbid tastes, *tædium vitæ.*"[82] The fashionable ennui of the fin de siècle is thereby conflated with an ecology simultaneously too organic and too artificial, and a paganism devoid of sincere spirituality.

The Palpability of Frederick Sandys's *Medea*

As Dickinson, Chesterton, and Barry make apparent, paganism became a central aspect of decadent ecology because of its popularity and the malleability of its anthropomorphic renderings of humans' relationships to the natural. But it also did so because paganism engaged with human ecology as a philosophical, political, and spiritual problematization of the image of society characterized by organicist cohesion. There was, in fact, an astounding diversity of pagan interests that incorporated and were incorporated into nineteenth-century culture, making any mainstream efforts at containment difficult. Even a work early in the rise of British decadence, such as Frederick Sandys's 1868 painting *Medea* (Fig. 1.1),

The Palpability of Frederick Sandys's Medea

Figure 1.1 Frederick Sandys, *Medea* (1868), Birmingham Museum. Oil on canvas, 102 by 122 cm, 40 by 48 in., Artepics/Alamy Stock Photo.

which Swinburne declared a masterpiece, found inspiration from this immeasurable excess.[83] In Pre-Raphaelite artworks such as *Medea*, the extensive detail, rich coloring, tendency (especially in early works) toward elaborate backgrounds, forceful vibrancy of the female figures, and hyper-emotional expressions readily signaled a sensual intensity that was also celebrated in decadent writing.

The subject of the painting, the priestess Medea in a state of distress, captures her conflicted emotions of love and need for revenge famously rendered in Euripides's tragedy *Medea* (first produced in 431 BC). In Greek mythology, Medea used her skills as a pagan priestess to help Jason attain the Golden Fleece from her own father, king of the region of Colchis, and bring it back to his hometown of Iolcus. In some versions of the myth, Medea's roots are presented as barbaric, in comparison to those of Jason, with her seemingly less civilized culture possibly the reason why he eventually left her for Glauce. In revenge, Medea infused a cloak with poison and sent it to the other woman as a gift, killing both Glauce and her father. Medea then went on to punish Jason further by also murdering two (or more) of her and Jason's own children. The sitter for the painting, Keomi Gray (who took Sandys as a lover), was of Romany descent and Elizabeth Prettejohn has noted that, in using her, Sandys was perhaps "alluding to Medea's barbarian origin, something … which is important in ancient sources; Ovid's Hypsipyle, for example, calls her 'barbara venefica' and 'barbara paelex,' barbarian poisoner and barbarian prostitute; and in the *Metamorphoses* Medea muses on how she will exchange her barbarian origin for the civilized world of Jason."[84] In a more general sense, it is also likely Sandys realized that Gray's complexion, physiognomy, and rich, thick hair would suggest the pagan subject's outsider status to most of his viewers (even those unaware of Medea's story).

Sandys's painting was accepted for the Royal Academy Summer Exhibition of 1868, but then withheld from display. It remains unknown whether the reason was internal politics, that the committee felt the subject matter was in poor taste, or that space simply was not found for it. Critics quickly raised concerns of censorship through a debate in *The Times* and both Swinburne and William Michael Rossetti, in their co-published reviews of the 1868 exhibition, regretted the absence of the work.[85] Perhaps as a consequence of the critical response, the painting was shown the following year. While what exactly might have been particularly offensive is uncertain, *Medea*'s combination of beauty and pained expression, enhanced by the rich, fluid color combination of gold, brown, and cream, offers a particularly intense sensual experience. The two frogs copulating in the foreground would surely have given viewers pause, while also imbuing stronger sensationalist connotations into other elements in the scene, such as the seashell filled with what appears to be blood or wine, the detailed blue veins against the pale skin of Medea's hands, even the suggestive position of two of the fingers on her left hand straddling a cup from which an unknown liquid flows, which one then notes is echoed on the right hand clawing at the strings of ox-blood coral beads around her throat (repeated in the red thread circling the chafing dish in which she prepares a potion). In short, the diverse elements in the foreground – most with one or more pagan or occult connotations – draw a viewer into a sensual reading that risks spiraling into a sensational over-reading bubbling with desire, death, and paganism.

The Palpability of Frederick Sandys's Medea   31

It is not certain what scene from Medea's mythology Sandys intended to evoke, although the amorous amphibians have encouraged most often a reading of the painting as capturing the sorceress preparing the poison with which she will take revenge against her cheating husband. But then, so many elements in the painting do not easily affirm any single interpretation. The cranes, owl, reptile, beetles, cobras, dragon, Egyptian statuette (evoking Bastet, the cat-human goddess of the home and of women's secret lives), dried stingray twisted into a human figure (sometimes called a Jenny Hanniver), oak trees, herbs of henbane, aconite, and nightshade (according to Swinburne's review), and various other items assure no single meaning is coherently represented. One's attempt to formulate a cohesive reading of all these intercultural appropriations extending across the spatial, temporal, spiritual, scientific, and aesthetic would go against the dominant force of the painting – Medea's intense expression of anguish.

The highly artificial background makes the emotion only more pronounced. Although a depiction of nature and the outdoors, it is suggestive of an opulent interior. Sandys's stylized imagery reflects the decadents and aestheticists' admiration for and adaptation of Japanese and Chinese aesthetics. While the intensity of the gold coloring brings to mind the golden fleece central to Medea's story, which is itself displayed like an artwork stretched among the branches of the oaks, the flat backdrop evokes, as Prettejohn notes, the gold leaf used in religious paintings of the very early Renaissance. This reading suggests a sort of iconography, with Sandys's painting not only representing a pagan ecology, but also functioning as itself a pagan artefact, an object of spiritual engagement. The artist implies his own sense of the painting as affectively engaged within the transhistorical, trans-spatial reality of paganism. In 1867, a year before Sandys's *Medea* was displayed, Swinburne published a review of William Morris's poem *The Life and Death of Jason* (1867) in which he observes of Medea, "At her first entrance the poem takes new life and rises out of the atmosphere of mere adventure and incident."[86] Sandys's painting is not a close rendering of Morris's piece but, considering Swinburne's reading, one recognizes the visceral emotions of Sandys's Medea come to life against the flat context of her myth. The background evokes Classical mythology as an artistic artefact akin to the golden fleece, while Medea acknowledges the presence of paganism within the contemporary viewer's investment in the heroine's emotions. It is not that the Argonauts and the multicultural symbology are in the past but that Medea's alchemical influence and emotional investment have brought their spirit into the present.

32   Decadent Ecology and the Pagan Revival

Alfred Bate Richards was so taken by the painting's expressive vitality, that he was inspired to write a sixty-page poem based on the work, published in 1869, a year after *Medea* had its public showing:

> How far the story of Medea is a fable is immaterial to my treatment of Medea as a human being. ... I have dealt with a great artist's conception of a flesh-and-blood Medea, although I am conscious of treating even this occasionally as the suggestion of a wider theme. I admit that my Poem is not strictly classical, simply because I am not an ancient Pagan author.[87]

Like the critics discussed in the previous section, Richards distinguishes between Classical and contemporary paganism, boldly declaring that his poetry is the work of a modern spirit, a paganism of flesh and blood. The narrator of the piece, evoking a variety of pagan options, calls on the painting itself to tell him both the future and the dark mysteries of the past, fading into myth: "A being with a history untold; A picture framed in glory of pale gold."[88] The art of British decadence becomes a major site of contemporary paganism. More precisely, Richards's formulation decomposes the separation of ancient myth and contemporary emotion. In his adaptation, the artwork is both a rendering of a pagan phenomenon and a palpable engagement with the modern viewer.[89]

Flourishing with Indeterminacy

Sandys's Medea seems almost to spill outside the confines of the picture plane and the marble divider that keeps her separate from the viewer, just as his *Medea* offers a proliferation of significations that refuses a viewer's containment of the artwork within one coherent aesthetic reading. *Decadent Ecology* proposes that the concept of decadence is itself part of an open ecology that encourages disruptive interfusions among the natural, cultural, spiritual, and imaginative, as well as the individual and the collective. A number of decadents evoked a pragmatic empathy for the ecology of which a person was a part, exploring the extensibility of affective experience not simply among humans, regions, and species, but through organic and inorganic components, including art itself. These individuals took discourses of alliance, colonization, and refinement that were used to naturalize the rise and fall of civilizations and applied them to issues of speciesism, human exceptionalism, and false idealism, although this was not a consistent strategy or one that was consistently altruistic. As Sandys's painting suggests and as the following chapters attest, decadents did not always encourage inclusivity or an egalitarian

Flourishing with Indeterminacy

order. In fact, the subordination of human agency to the forces of an indeterminate ecology was as likely to have encouraged the existential ennui or *taedium vitae* that characterized much of fin-de-siècle decadence. We find decadent works marked not only by a sense of liberty or an aura of eco-veneration, but also by fatalism, fear of the ecological unknown, and a disregard for human life.

CHAPTER 2

"Up & down & horribly natural*"*
Walter Pater and the Decadent Anthropocene

> The incidents of a fully developed human personality are superinduced on the mystical and abstract essence of that fiery spirit in the flowing veins of the earth – the aroma of the green world is retained in the fair human body, set forth in all sorts of finer ethical lights and shades.
>
> – Walter Pater, *Greek Studies*[1]

Contributors to pagan decadence had diverse agendas and did not operate as a single coherent force in their views on either nature or human perceptions of it. However, they did collectively encourage a spiritually inflected respect for the environment of which they saw themselves to be a part. Walter Pater, a major catalyst for the pagan revival, portrays pagan myth as a changeable living medium for spiritualities that preceded Christianity and continue to exist today. He presents paganisms (he explicitly notes their plurality) not as the veneration of particular idealizations but as interweaving philosophical and aesthetic perspectives that are sensitive to an ecological medley that includes not only humans, other animals, and other aspects of nature, but also cultural elements ranging from human-crafted landscapes and architecture to labor, pleasure, and reading. Thus, we see the titular hero of Pater's novel *Marius the Epicurean* (1885) "surrender[ing] himself, a willing subject, as he walked, to the impressions of the road,"[2] with the meandering journey that was his life taking him often seamlessly across both rural and urban landscapes, among villagers and Romans, and through real and textual worlds. Moreover, Pater has Marius's persona as a pagan of the Classical age mediated through the nineteenth-century narrator's perspective, and the scientific, aesthetic, and philosophical ideas that, while often still inchoate during Pater's lifetime, were already entangled among modern formulations of paganism.[3] Pointing to the novel's dual temporality, the narrator observes that "[t]hat age and our own have much in common, many difficulties and hopes," and asks readers for their pardon "if here and there I seem to be passing from Marius to his modern representatives – from Rome, to Paris or London" (149). Pater himself never explicitly enters the plot, and the narrator remains unspecific about the precise age in which they exist. The phrase "modern representatives," however, makes it clear that the more current speaker is conceptually in tune with Marius's mental machinations, reflecting Pater's view of the spiritual philosophies central to the novel as pagan-centered and transhistorical.[4]

Pater himself encourages such an awareness of the constructed components of perceived reality through *Marius the Epicurean*'s self-referentiality. At one point in the novel, the narrator describes a scene in which the hero and his friend Flavian are "lounging together over a book, half-buried in a heap of dry corn, in an old granary," while "the western sun smote through the board chinks of the shutters. How like a picture!" (33). It is unclear from Pater's wording whether it is the young men or their "golden book" that is half-buried in the sun-saturated grains – an ambiguity that proves to be appropriate. As the narrator observes, the scene in which the two youths are buried turns out to be "precisely the scene described in what they were reading," the "poetic touch in the book" enlivened with "the ray of sunlight transforming the rough grain among the cool brown shadows into heaps of gold." It is through such meta-textual gestures that Pater keeps his readers sensitive to the place of the imagination and interpretation in their understanding of the world.

In the previous chapter, I explain the concept of decadent ecology and the diverse disciplines that together supported its cultural manifestations across a number of decades. I also note various, often conflicted trajectories within this ecology that encouraged politicized self-identification but also self-dissipation, a call to action but also a sense of ennui or even fatalism. As one of the main influences on the ideas and values of British decadence, Pater's writings both absorbed various decadent models of the time and crystallized them into a singular aesthetic vision in which the eco-pagan was a major element. To illuminate the interweaving of science, aesthetics, and spirituality that created the network of ideas that supported the energies of Paterian paganism, I wish first to point out some of the ways in which aesthetic and spiritual elements permeated wider Victorian ecological discourse. Situating Pater's views within this contemporary context, I then use *Marius the Epicurean* to demonstrate his vision of eco-spirituality as a living, transhistorical force that is often indeterminate in its structure and direction. This vision of a contemporary, socially engaged paganism helpfully modifies the more reclusive, idealizing formulations

36 "Up & down & horribly *natural*"

that have dominated discussions of the author's paganism to date, while also capturing a sense of the actual energy and politics of the pagan revival.

The Pagan Strain in Victorian Ecology

Many manifestations of paganism today, as with those of Pater's time, have an ethos invested in a Romantic view of the natural realm as unmarred by negative human influence and thus offering the most intense spiritual experiences. At the same time, for a number of decades, environmental theorists such as Raymond Williams, William Cronon, Graham Huggan, and Helen Tiffin have pointed out that this vision of nature has functioned, intentionally or otherwise, not only to reassure humans of their self-centered worldview and their position as conquerors or designated stewards of the ecological domain, but also to sanction (particularly Western) nations' colonization of other groups of humans. Timothy Morton, meanwhile, emphasizes some of the practical difficulties with the Romanticist veneration of nature when it comes to modern environmental ethics. For Morton, ensuring the welfare of all forms of sentient beings requires the rejection of the common Romanticization of nature because it assumes a humanist perspective that aestheticizes the ecological and thereby offers a view of reality that leaves humans pining for some untainted utopia rather than actually taking on the work of addressing the real ecological damage we continue to cause.[5] In an argument that brings to mind Swinburne's attitude to Christian creed, which I discuss in Chapter 1, Morton proposes instead a model of action that is void of the idea of nature precisely because it has become a "transcendental principle" tethered to a politics of truth and purity that is not inherent to our organic and inorganic reality.[6] For Morton, the dysfunctional obfuscations that culture has cast over our understandings of nature need to be avoided in our current sense of ecology. As many Victorians appear to have realized, however, scientific articulations of ecology themselves often rely on forms of idealization.

The issue Morton raises can be traced back to Ernst Haeckel's *Generelle Morphologie der Organismen* (1866), which appeared during the same period as Pater's works on pagan decadence. Haeckel describes ecology as the science of "the relationship of the organism to the surrounding exterior world," for which the conditions of existence are "partly of organic, partly of inorganic nature; both, as we have shown, are of the greatest significance for the form of organisms, for they force them to become adapted."[7] According to Haeckel, physiology has, in the most one-sided fashion, almost exclusively investigated the conserving functions of organisms (preservation of the individual and the species, nutrition, and reproduction), and among the functions of relationship [it has investigated] merely those which are produced by the relations of single parts of the organism to each other and to the whole. On the other hand, physiology has largely neglected the relations of the organism to the environment, the place each organism takes in the household of nature, in the economy of all nature.[8]

Emphasizing the intricate relationship of part to whole, Haeckel notes that there is never a fixed environment because the inorganic (by which he means the context) is itself shaped and reshaped due to its own relationships. Paul Bourget's formulation of decadence, summarized in the previous chapter, echoes not only some of Haeckel's language but also the spirit of the ecologist's concern regarding the *oikos*, suggesting a richer sense of what the inorganic constitutes by extending evolutionary theory to our understanding of not only social relations, but also textual ones.

In his later *History of Creation* (1880), Haeckel argues for a superindividual conception of ecology marked by "the mutual dependence of all living creatures on one another, and in general the universal connection between cause and effect – that is, the monistic causal connection between all members and parts of the universe."[9] He saw degeneration not as a counter-evolutionary process generating a negative excess, but as a necessary and important part of a biospheric means of adaptation, where certain parts of an organism (or, on a larger scale, of a branch of a species or even of an entire species) are increasingly ineffective and thus become less useful and are gradually lost.[10] The ongoing accommodations of mutually influential components of an ecology means that the standard state is not constancy or balance but sustained reactions and adaptations among morphing components, with some elements of the ecology always dying off while new ones develop – resulting in new species, civilizations, and so on.

From his earliest works, Haeckel established that no pure nature can really exist *out there* for humans or any other organisms because a human is always a constituent element of an ecological web. His view of ecology aligns with Morton's model in explicitly acknowledging the presence of the inorganic within any organism's environment. Notably, however, the earlier scientist's own views were influenced by German Romanticism and Goethe's emphasis on the spirit as a crucial organizing force of reality. Haeckel combined these beliefs with the Hegelian premise of progress toward a universal ideal and elements of Darwin's *On the Origin of Species* (1859) to formulate an evolutionary model of ecology. He promoted Darwin's work heavily in Germany and the two men developed an extensive correspondence, although the German's understanding of evolution was distinct from Darwin's in key ways. Specifically, Haeckel's ideas became increasingly invested in a fusion of species selection with the racial distinction of polygenism (the theory that human races are separately created species), eventually leading him to argue in favor of the killing of certain types of criminals, as well as newborns seen to have abnormalities.[11]

That said, Haeckel does appear to have understood the impermanence of *any* biological element of either an organism or some larger formation; the dominance of a particular trait at one point in time does not ensure its future vitality or even survival. Moreover, while Haeckel's model relies conceptually on an ideation of progress toward perfection, it also acknowledges that the perfection of any particular species can neither be accurately envisaged nor actualized. There is, for example, the very real and very decadent possibility that a particularly successful organism or species, such as the human, in its myopic drive for self-enhancement will eventually eradicate a resource on which it relies, ultimately itself degenerating and becoming the resource of some other organic process and the flourishing of some other organism or species. Similarly, Morton's issue is not with the term "nature" per se, but with the false ideal with which it has come to be associated, and one can assume he would offer a similar critique of Haeckel's evolutionary perfectionism. Scholars, Morton argues, must reject the view that humans and their environment ever existed as distinguishable phenomena, and particularly since the start of the Anthropocene, the geological period in which, he explains in a more recent work, "humans have a direct effect on the substrata of their earthly reality."[12]

The concept of the Anthropocene is actually central to Pater's decadent ecology, especially as embodied in *Marius the Epicurean*. Regardless of when the Anthropocene actually began, it was around the 1860s and 1870s that the scientific *idea* of such an age took shape, at the same time that Pater formulated his decadent ecology and Haeckel developed his evolutionary one. As Paul J. Crutzen notes, it was the Italian geologist and paleontologist Antonio Stoppani who coined the term "anthropozoic" (which would become a synonym for the later "Anthropocenic") in his 1871 study *Corso di Geologia*, articulating a model of the concept similar to the way in which it is often understood today, albeit unique in certain aspects.[13] A Roman Catholic priest, Stoppani turned to the study

The Pagan Strain in Victorian Ecology

of the earth and eventually became a professor of geology at the Milan Polytechnic, a founder of the Museum of Geology, and the acting president of the Geological Society in Italy. He had read *Origin of Species*, but did not fully adopt evolutionary theory in his own work because he could not support what he saw as Darwin's suggestion that humans are not divinely superior members of the planet. For Stoppani, the Anthropocene began with the birth of Christ. Despite his faith, he describes this new geologic era as a time when humans are not only observers of deep-time alterations in nature, but engrained participants in the creation of ecological change, operating as a force whose impact has become increasingly apparent in the earth's own records. "Everywhere, the bosom of the ancient Mother discloses, and the shadows, broken by vagrant splendors, resign to man treasures that were hidden by centuries,"[14] he declares with celebratory vigor:

> In vain you would look for a single atom of native iron in the earth: already its surface is enclosed, one could say, within a web of iron, while iron cities are born from man's yards and float on the sea. How much of the earth's surface by now disappears under the masses that man built as his abode, his pleasure and his defense, on plains, on hills, on the seashores and lakeshores, as on the highest peaks! ... Let us not forget, then, that man has been, since his incipit, cosmopolitan. Unlike speechless animals that preceded him on the surface of the planet, he knows no geographical confine, he makes no distinction of zone or of climate; rivers, seas, valleys and mountain crests are no obstacle to him.

Evoking the pagan earth as "ancient mother," Stoppani briskly celebrates her disembowelment, her inner wealth dug up by humans to bury the planet beneath itself, an utterly global reconstitution. This record of human influence, he makes sure to point out, is the product of European humans, inspired as they were by Christianity. As cosmopolitans – literally citizens of the entire world (from the Greek, kosmos + politēs) – Christian Europeans own the planet because their global impact is on anthropozoic record. Other animal species lack such a record of influence, despite having existed before humans (as per Genesis I: 24–27); this absence of material evidence is the basis of Stoppani's claim for human's species superiority.

The term "Anthropocene" was coined in the 1980s by Eugene F. Stoermer, and has been used to signify a variety of ideas regarding the measurable impact of humans on the planet. As with Stoppani's Anthropozoic record, Stoermer's term refers to the period during which our species has either been the dominant influence on the earth's ecosystem, or at least has had an influence so significant as to be geologically recorded. In their brief but highly influential article "The 'Anthropocene'," published in *The Global Change Newsletter* in 2000, Stoermer and the chemist Paul J. Crutzen propose that the epoch that Charles Lyell dubbed "the Holocene" in 1833 does not capture the fact that the "expansion of mankind, both in numbers and per capita exploitation of Earth's resources has been astounding." They therefore propose that "Anthropocene" be adopted "to emphasize the central role of mankind in geology and ecology."[15] From the various examples they summarize to make their proposal, their measure of human centrality is defined by degrees of influence. What exactly constitutes the amount of influence sufficient for the realization of the Anthropocene remains undetermined, and scientists have yet to agree on when this latest geological age began. Acknowledging that "to assign a more specific date to the onset of the 'Anthropocene' seems somewhat arbitrary," Crutzen and Stoermer suggest it began in the later eighteenth century with the invention of the steam engine,[16] while others have gone further back in time, to the rise of agriculture, for example, or even fourteen to fifteen millennia back. For Stoppani, it began with the birth of Christ and Pater likewise marks a global ecological shift occurring at the time of Christianity's expanse at the expense of paganisms.

Neither Pater nor Stoppani had any noted impact on the other, but they did have similar influences – including E. B. Tylor's cultural anthropology and, especially, Darwin's *On the Origin of Species*, which both men had read.[17] Tylor's *Primitive Culture: Researches into the Development of Mythology, Philosophy, Religion, Art, and Custom* (1871) popularized the argument that animism, the view that all objects have some essence or soul, was the pagan spark of the earliest forms of human spirituality. Influenced by Lyell's uniformitarianism – a deep-time model of planetary development – and coming soon after Darwin's *On the Origin of Species*, Tylor offered an evolutionary model of spirituality, where certain "primitive" beliefs and customs somehow anachronistically survived to the present day. Tylor's ethnocentric views, although now generally rejected, nevertheless beg the question of whether or not a person's intense relations with others in their ecological context could not inspire some new form of paganism. Pater proposes such a vision of a morphing paganism in *Studies in the History of The Renaissance* (1873; renamed *The Renaissance: Studies in Art and Poetry* in later editions). "Religions, as they grow by natural laws out of man's life, are modified by whatever modifies his life," he declares.

The Pagan Strain in Victorian Ecology

41

They brighten under a bright sky, they become liberal as the social range widens, they grow intense and shrill in the clefts of human life, where the spirit is narrow and confined, and the stars are visible at noonday; and a fine analysis of these differences is one of the gravest functions of religious criticism. Still, the broad characteristic of all religions, as they exist for the greatest number, is a universal pagan sentiment, a paganism which existed before the Greek religion, and has lingered far onward into the Christian world, ineradicable, like some persistent vegetable growth.[18]

In Chapter 1, I discuss work by recent pagan scholars Emma Restall Orr, Thom van Dooren, and Starhawk that articulates an individualism inherent to the reverence of an ecological collective. Pater similarly puts forward the idea of a universal impetus combined with inevitable variations arising from different people's contexts and relations. Unlike Tylor in his distinction of the primitive as inferior to the modern, Pater does not present ancient paganism as less developed than the contemporary variation he felt through his decadent sensibility. While the decadents often alluded to paganism as a means of exoticizing their specialist tastes, their veneration usually (but not always) avoided implying that contemporary pagan engagements were superior to earlier experiences.

Darwin was, of course, an influence on Pater's thoughts during the writing of the essays in *Studies in the History of the Renaissance*. Michael Levey has observed the intense debates that characterized Pater's Oxford regarding issues of Christian faith and evolutionary theory.[19] Gowan Dawson has noted a complex allusion to Darwin in *Marius the Epicurean*, as the hero considers all the "various and competing hypotheses, which, in that open field for hypothesis – one's own actual ignorance of the origin and tendency of our being – present themselves so importunately, some with so emphatic a reiteration" (*Marius*, 177).[20] Kate Hext further argues that, in various works, Pater merged Darwinian evolutionary theory with Heraclitean flux, resolving the problem of the individual in the context of Darwinian deep time by turning to aesthetics and art.[21] These readings of Darwin's influence on Pater portray the latter as an individual who was inspired and driven by fresh explorations and new inquiries – what he in the conclusion to *Studies in the History of the Renaissance* describes excitedly as "the inward world of thought and feeling" – "the race of the midstream, a drift of momentary acts of sight and passion and thought" (118). Pater's and Stoppani's fusions of geology and Classical mythology to envision a modern Anthropocenic world help mark out the nineteenth-century shift in European conceptions of the relationship of humans to the rest of the planet. This shift was characterized by an awareness of mutual contingency among sentient beings and an awed acknowledgment of humans' limited knowledge of the way these contingencies operate, elements that invite the potential of a paganism inspired as much, if not more, by scientific imagination than by religious tradition.[22]

This new vibrancy is apparent, for example, in Stoppani's investment in both spirituality and geological objectivity, offering an example of the pagan imaginary infecting (or, perhaps, more accurately, assisting) modern scientific discourse. The result is a creative fusion of myth and science in which the telluric becomes no less than a personified creature. "It is not enough to consider earth under the impetus of telluric forces anymore: a new force reigns here," he dramatically declares, "ancient nature distorts itself, almost flees under the heel of this new nature."[23] The human is not positioned as distinct from the natural but explicitly as part of a new ecological paradigm, one that Stoppani describes as more of the future than the past, albeit for him rooted in a Judeo-Christian mythos: "We are only at the beginning of the new era; still, how deep is man's footprint on earth already! ... How many events already bear the trace of this absolute dominion that man received from God."[24] Describing the same historical period that Pater would focus on in *Marius the Epicurean*, Stoppani proposes that the Anthropozoic age began when,

> in the bosom of the aged fabric of ancient pagan societies, the Christian ferment was introduced, the new element *par excellence*, that substituted ancient slavery with freedom, darkness with light, fall and degeneration with rebirth and true progress of humanity. ... But the new being installed on the old planet, the new being that not only, like the ancient inhabitants of the globe, unites the inorganic and the organic world, but with a new and quite mysterious marriage unites physical nature to intellectual principle; this creature, absolutely new in itself, is, to the physical world, a new element, a new telluric force that for its strength and universality does not pale in the face of the greatest forces of the globe.[25]

In this passage, the geologist adopts the familiar language of decadence – "fall and degeneration" – to capture a period when Christian and rationalist ferment are reborn from a paganism that already combined, as does Haeckel's theory of ecology, the organic and inorganic, the natural and cultural, but did not (in fact, could not) alienate the human from the experience of geological change through intellectual distancing. Stoppani primarily presents the newer religion as a replacement, a "creature, absolutely new in itself," but he also sees it as a development born from the

The first known English use of Stoppani's term "anthropozoic" was by the American conservationist George Perkins Marsh, in the 1874 edition of his highly influential *Man and Nature: Physical Geography as Modified by Human Action* (1864). An expert in ancient Mediterranean cultures, Marsh adopts a distinctly environmentalist position when he proposes that the decline of Classical Greco-Roman civilizations was due to a failure to recognize humans as a component of the environment.[26] Marsh's biographer, David Lowenthal, notes that his conservationist vision was inspired, in part, by Nordic myth and "contained a congery of themes: an idealized pagan past, racial determinism, militant anti-Catholicism, nativist exclusion of aliens, praise of rural virtues, fear of city vices."[27] The result, Lowenthal summarizes, was a dualistic and often contradictory set of values that did, however, become modified over time as Marsh softened some of his positions. In the 1874 revised version of *Man and Nature*, Marsh proposes that "the influence of human action on the surface of the globe" has been "superior in degree" than that of other animals, but notes that "the eminent Italian geologist" Stoppani makes an even greater claim by arguing for an understanding of "the action of man as a new physical element altogether *sui generis*."[28] The key distinction for Marsh is that the Italian envisions the difference across the influence of species not only as one of scale but also one of kind; it has an impact that is not only vaster, but also of a different sort entirely. Stoppani, according to Marsh, proposes that the "creation of man" "was the introduction of a new element into nature, of a force wholly unknown to earlier periods" and that "in power and universality may be compared to the greater forces of the earth." Stoppani understood himself as able to make this claim because he is referring to the birth of Christianity, which he viewed as divine truth and, indeed, *sui generis*. Marsh's position is more pragmatic: the human impact on deep time has persisted beyond human realization, but this does not, for Marsh, position it beyond our ethical responsibility or nonspiritual agency.

Read throughout Europe, Stoppani became particularly well known in his homeland as an influential advocate of the earth sciences. By the end of the century, Darwin, Haeckel, and Stoppani were being addressed collectively for their contributions to these sciences. In 1891, Mario Cermenati described Haeckel as the "German Darwin," comparing him to Stoppani for the popularization in their home countries of evolu-

44   "Up & down & horribly *natural*"

tionary and geological sciences, respectively.[29] Stoppani's inspirational, even celebratory, perspective of Italy's natural environment is apparent in passages such as the following, which in Italian is an equally charming piece of rambling prose:

> From the humble brook, that springs from cliff to cliff, to the river that widens its mouth as it debouches into the sea, all flowing waters, oblivious of ancient laws, beat the path that man has traced for them. The old alluvial expanses, already beaten by them with whirling winding, and drowned by their overflowing floods, subtracted by force to their capricious domain, are converted into greening meadows and fertile fields, periodically mowed by their new owner.[30]

Rather than trying to avoid Romantic cultural mediation in the articulation of his ecological vision, as Morton argues is necessary for environmentalist purposes, Stoppani incorporates the beautiful, and arguably the beatific, both formally and thematically into his language.

Stoppani's narrative of the water gradually transforming from a small, erratic brook in the mountains into a grand, flooding delta reinforces his own argument regarding the rise of the anthropozoic, and of the wilds gradually tamed by human hand. The depicted water, moreover, is never sublime in Stoppani's description, personified as "humble" even in its highest climbs, and then "oblivious of ancient laws," passively accepting the revised tracks that our species has carved out for it. Explicitly marking the place of not only the human but also the spiritual in the landscape, the geologist's ecological formulations remain invested in a rhetoric that superimposes human authority over all stages of geologic development, and not only that of the new age introduced with Christ's birth. Thus, in the passage just quoted, the landscape is modified by people, but this is not presented as an intrusion so much as a contribution to a protean design. Humans mark new waterways just as the water alters the shape of the river's delta. It is for this reason that Stoppani refers doubtfully to "so called virgin lands (if there are still any that deserve that name)," his anthropozoic skepticism foreshadowing Morton's argument that contemporary models of nature are too often idealistic fantasies. The religious politics of the discourse is apparent again when he declares that "[b]otanists can only look into the furthest depths, into mountains' fissures, on the highest peaks, for the untamed daughters of virgin nature, that carry unaltered the features of their mother."[31] Bringing to mind the "humble brook, that springs from cliff to cliff," any element of the planet that humans have not yet reached is nevertheless mastered by the geologist's very conceptualization of the anthropozoic age. This human-centered vision is part of the Christian premise that he retains in his scientific writing and, as such, a reflection of the common patriarchal logic to which the religion adheres. In the process of subjugating untouched nature by gendering it female, however, he also attempts to vanquish the pagan mythology on which, ironically, he relies for his own articulations. The flights of the imagination arising from Stoppani's efforts to articulate the anthropozoic age suggest a real difficulty that both Christianity and the earth sciences had in extricating the pagan imaginary from modern ecological thought.

Universal Sentiment and Pater's "aroma of the green world"

Stoppani's, Darwin's, and Haeckel's works reflect a growing Western interest in geology, archaeology, landscape aesthetics, and the changing place of the human and other beings within the physical world. As part of this development, the new environmental interests and ecological paradigms that arose in the nineteenth century in large part due to industrialization and urbanization fostered fresh understandings and adaptations of paganism itself. Pater's decadent ecological model arose as part of the burgeoning network of modern ideas engaging ecology, evolution, and a geological age demarcated by the record of human influence. His works offer a sympathetic conception of paganism as a transhistorical force relevant to the values and ethics of the modern age. In *Marius the Epicurean*, Pater extends these considerations to envision a decadent ecology that addresses the fundamental issues of selfhood, collective intimacy, and mutual responsibility.

In the essay "Pico della Mirandola" (1871), which appeared again two years later as a chapter in *Studies in the History of the Renaissance*, Pater encourages "effecting a scientific reconciliation of Christian sentiment with the imagery, the legends, the theories about the world, of pagan poetry and philosophy. For that age the only possible reconciliation was an imaginative one, and resulted from the efforts of artists trained in Christian school to handle pagan subjects" (*Studies*, 27). Certain humanist individuals, such as the philosopher Pico (1463–1494), he argues, bore "generous instincts" that allowed for such a reconciliation, replacing the pre-Renaissance view of Greek gods as "so many malignant spirits, the defeated but still living centres of the religion of darkness, struggling, not always in vain, against the kingdom of light" (18). For Pater, pagan myths are to be viewed not purely as creative, cultural works, but also as vital repositories of pre-Christian spirituality that continues to exist through them to the present day. The fifteenth century in Italy, he proposes, "was too familiar with such language to regard mythology as a mere story; and it was too serious to play with a religion" (18). Pater's attention to the interaction between Classical and Christian belief systems brings to mind Stoppani's own incorporation of pagan myth into his articulation of a Christian Anthropocene. Stoppani's position is contingent on his Christian faith, however, and it is his sense of the fundamental conceptual shift in human perspective arising from the birth of Christianity that leads him to define the period in terms so forceful that they would result in a ground-breaking vision of geological time among modern scientists.[32] While Stoppani's new age marks the rise of Christianity as the one true religion, Pater, in "Pico della Mirandola" and elsewhere, brings forward a sense of an inherent place for paganism within a robust ecological vision.

Like Stoppani's turn to hidden mountain-stream maenads, in "Pico della Mirandola" Pater reminds us of Heinrich Heine's depiction in the essay "Gods in Exile" (1854) of the Classical pagan deities having "had then to take flight ignominiously, and hide themselves among us here on earth under all sorts of disguises" (19). For Pater, this shift can only be temporary, as every spiritual belief system is the result of the imagination. "A modern scholar occupied by this problem might observe," he proposes,

> that all religions may be regarded as natural products, that, at least in their origin, their growth, and decay, they have common laws, and are not to be isolated from the other movements of the human mind in the periods in which they respectively prevailed; that they arise spontaneously out of the human mind, as expressions of the varying phases of its sentiment concerning the unseen world; that every intellectual product must be judged from the point of view of the age and the people in which it was produced. (19–20)

For Pater, spiritualities develop from each other, creating the "religious sense" of whatever the current age may be (20). Moreover, using a model of decay, rebirth, and growth, he emphasizes that spirituality is extensively organic, rather than utterly cultural or otherworldly.[33] In the natural qualities of their origins, fluctuations, and eventual transformations, not only those religions commonly recognized as pagan but all religions are eco-spiritual.

The same organic model of spiritual regenesis can be found in his essay "Winckelmann" (1867), also to become part of *Studies in the History of the Renaissance*. Here Pater cites Hegel in describing the ancient Greeks as "free, and hav[ing] grown up on the soil of their own individuality,

Universal Sentiment and Pater's "aroma of the green world" 47

creating themselves out of themselves, and moulding themselves to what they were and willed to be," but being able to do so because they are part of what he calls the "Greek spirit," which is also comprised of the environment itself (110). Pater's reference to "soil" alludes to the very materials of the sculptures that he is describing in this passage to explain that the "artistic point of view" is central not just to artists but to all of Greek society, including its orators, philosophers, and statesmen (110). The language, however, also parallels an earlier reference to soil in "Winckelmann," in a section cited above, in which he discusses a transspiritual paganism that preceded Greek culture and persists to the modern day, "ineradicable, like some persistent vegetable growth, because its seed is an element of the very soil out of which it springs" (99). Paganism here is presented as literally of the earth – arising from the soil – but also part of "human nature" (100), with cultural variations making contributions to the unique formulation of ecological contexts and their concomitant spiritual belief systems. While some Christian institutions historically denigrated nature- or planet-centered spiritualities by categorizing them as pagan, Pater sees all religions as some form of paganism tempered by their practitioners' contexts. Like the artistic perspective that he portrays in the later passage of "Winckelmann" describing the soil of sculptural aesthetics, the author envisions paganism as an overarching influence on ecologically varied religious permutations, as well as an organic element of each individual's own makeup.

Ten years after "Winckelmann," in his 1876 "A Study of Dionysus," Pater addressed the place of the rationalist model of intelligence within this polyvalence of pagan ecology. The initial kernel of spiritualism itself, he proposes, is a panpsychic belief in the sentience of nature (*Greek Studies*, 8). Citing this essay, Stefano Evangelista explains that "the origin of myth is for Pater in the act of recognition of a 'kindred spirit' in nature, followed by the development of physical sympathy with the outer world. This is the mental attitude that enabled the early Greeks to see the 'spirit of life in the green sap'"[34] and, from this, gradually to develop a mythology. This changed, Pater tells us in "Dionysus," into "the spirit of a severe and wholly self-conscious intelligence" that eventually became "the entirely humanised religion of Apollo" (29). Apollonian self-conscious intelligence and the rational mental thought it supports is juxtaposed here with an instinctual sense of being that is not characterized by a humanist idea of the self or even, necessarily, of the human species. Because what Pater calls the Greek spirit "belongs to all ages," Apollonian religion may be "entirely humanised," but living beings are

48 "Up & down & horribly *natural*"

never entirely Apollonian (*Greek Studies*, 9). As Lene Østermark-Johansen notes, in Pater's depiction of Denys l'Auxerrois's death in the imaginary portrait by that name, his "interweaving of pagan and Christian mythology slurs such issues," suggesting, "perhaps, that paganism is not all that easy to pin down."[35] Østermark-Johansen's interpretation reinforces Pater's claim that the pagan spirit is a universal animist sympathy and an innate element of the human.

Pater's language in "Dionysus" is notably invested in using contemporary experience as evidence of a transhistorical pagan spirituality. "Who has not at moments felt the scruple," he asks his readers, "which is with us always regarding animal life, following the signs of animation further still, till one almost hesitates to pluck out the little soul of flower or leaf?" (11). The subtle hesitance one feels over hurting a plant, he proposes, reflects a sense of a shared vitality coursing through the veins of every living thing. Pater's argument here is not exceptional, affirming the panpsychism that was common within nineteenth-century European philosophies of the mind, including those of Schopenhauer and Haeckel.[36] Panpsychism is the view that there exists a primordial consciousness shared by all things. As Pater goes on to argue, this collective bond, which he often presents as a pagan animism, is then modified by the influence of each individual's ecological situatedness. "Writers on mythology speak habitually of the *religion* of the Greeks," he notes, but this language (which Pater himself uses) is inaccurate not only because paganism extends beyond the Greeks, but also because the language homogenizes the diversity of the cultural formulations of this innate sense of trans-species empathy. These writers, he argues,

> are really using a misleading expression, and should speak rather of *religions*; each race and class of Greeks – the Dorians, the people of the coast, the fishers – have had a religion of its own, conceived of the objects that came nearest to it and were most in its thoughts, and the resulting usages and ideas never having come to have a precisely harmonised system. (9)

For Pater, paganism is not so much a fundamental spirituality, but an implicit result of the way in which humans perceive their ecological engagements at any given moment. Those laboring among the grapevines become followers of Dionysus, those working in farms and cornfields are drawn to Demeter. Ovid's *Metamorphoses*, he argues, captures only "a fossilised form of one morsel here and there from a whole world of transformation" that the Ancient Greeks' imagination explored.

Universal Sentiment and Pater's "aroma of the green world" 49

In his conclusion to *Studies in the History of the Renaissance*, Pater addresses the tension between the overarching, animist spirit of paganism and the Apollonian or humanist vision of the individual that had come to dominate modernity. Although he offers up an image of "the individual in his isolation, each mind keeping as a solitary prisoner its own dream of a world" (119), he begins the piece by portraying the individual as neither temporally nor spatially isolated. Referring to the transformations that occur on an inseparable, ongoing basis, he proposes:

> Our physical life is a perpetual motion of them – the passage of the blood, the wasting and repairing of the lenses of the eye, the modification of the tissues of the brain by every ray of light and sound – processes which science reduces to simpler and more elementary forces. Like the elements of which we are composed, the action of these forces extends beyond us; it rusts iron and ripens corn. Far out on every side of us these elements are broadcast, driven by many forces; and birth and gesture and death and the springing of violets from the grave are but a few out of ten thousand resulting combinations. (118)

For Pater, a person's perspective of reality arises from a state of "isolation," and for this reason they can never adopt or enter fully into the perspective of another. The experience is one of separation from other human beings specifically. But when he describes the individual as part of a collective, he imagines a person not only as a cluster of interactive organs and other bodily materials, but also as contributing to an ecology so vast it can never be accurately conceived. His imaginative rendering of the relations leak into and outside the human in a way that dissolves the fleshly exterior of the body. The sentience of the individual is realized as a trans-species, collective experience. Moreover, Pater situates this interactive web in a graveyard bustling with transformations of death, decay, and, through the image of the Shakespearean "springing of violets from the grave" (118), animistic rebirth, thereby changing the idea of "our physical life" from that of any single human existence – whether Ophelia or, ultimately, Pater himself – to that of an ecological, panpsychic history.

According to Pater, while science tends to simplify these processes by trying to compartmentalize them in an effort to understand them, he prefers to adopt an impressionist prose style that foregrounds the actual porousness of physical reality, wherein human fluids become the means of agricultural growth and mineral deterioration. The often flowing styles of both Pater's and Stoppani's prose buttress parallels in their spiritual models. Unlike Stoppani, however, Pater emphasizes relationality rather than the entities having the relations, as systems of connectivity seep into and out of the individual, such that objects become "dissipated," as he puts it (118). Declaring that scientists have oversimplified human experience, in the "Conclusion" Pater encourages his readers to develop a sense of themselves as each an indistinguishable element of an ecological network of immeasurable interactions – a vision that expands ethical responsibility beyond one's community or species by defining the collective itself as an organic, sentient, and ultimately indeterminate macroorganism. Approaching the subject through Greek mythology, Pater's "The Bacchanals of Euripides," which he wrote five years after publishing *Studies in the History of the Renaissance*, turns to Dionysus and the maenads to portray paganism not as a fixed catalogue of spiritual values but as a perpetual process of dissolution and transmutation.

The ritual of the maenads is made comprehensible only if one understands it as requiring, paradoxically, both the individual agency central to humanism and the nonindividualist collectivist animism of pre-Renaissance paganism. Pater describes, for example, the worship of Dionysus, where "the *Thiasus*, or wild, nocturnal procession of Bacchic women, retired to the woods and hills for that purpose, with its accompaniments of music, lights, and dancing" (*Greek Studies*, 52). Meanwhile, he notes, the "[r]ational and moderate Athenians ... despised all that." Here, Pater offers an explicit distinction between "rational" urban and pagan rural minds. Of greater complexity is his suggestion that the celebrants, although their actual aim is a loss of individual agency, are acting purposefully – organizing music and lights for their procession. To make his readers sensitive to the way in which he sees the seeming contradiction reconciled, Pater evokes their own experiences to suggest the innate stimulus for the arrangement – "that giddy, intoxicating sense of spring – that tingling in the veins, sympathetic with the yearning life of the earth" (52–53). Pater has the feeling of sympathy entwine the veins of the human with those of vegetation, as both engage in the act of yearning. In this sense, the maenads' ritual veneration of Dionysus is always in part beyond their control, being rooted in the veins of organic sympathy and vegetal ontology. This innate impulse gradually results in raving frenzies that, at times, lead to inhumane activities, such as the bare-handed killing of animals, the dismembering of humans (*sparagmos*), and cannibalism.[37] Within Classical culture, it was proposed that, during these states, participants were also able to get wine or milk to flow from the earth, acts of transmutation that notably occur outside what is depicted as the maenads' own physicality, albeit not uniquely miraculous in Pater's own porous model of ecology.

Universal Sentiment and Pater's "aroma of the green world" 51

Quoting Samuel Taylor Coleridge, Pater goes on to describe the maenads as being like "the swarming of bees together," with their worship itself becoming a singular act of transmutation:

> The sympathies of mere numbers, as such, the random catching on fire of one here and another there, when people are collected together, generates as if by mere contact, some new and rapturous spirit, not traceable in the individual units of a multitude. Such *swarming* was the essence of that strange dance of the Bacchic women: literally like winged things, they follow, with motives, we may suppose, never quite made clear even to themselves, their new, strange, romantic[,] … woman-like god. (*Greek Studies*, 53)

Pater is highly attentive to the slippage between being and performance. He describes the maenads as being "literally like" another species – both the embodiment of ("literally") and the more distanced signification of ("like") insects. As a swarm, they operate as a collective force rather than individuals with distinct motives; yet, the minds of these insects are not utterly void of comprehension, for they only "never quite" understand the full knowledge of their pagan inspiration. Pater gradually reimagines the maenads' shift from personal isolation – "one here and another there" – to a single hyper-sensual movement embodied in the god Dionysus himself as pagan sympathy. The sublimation of the subjects into the "strange, new, romantic" collective experience demands an unconventional notion of the phenomenon called Dionysus, it being more appropriate from Pater's description to conceive of the god as a poly-agential transmutation rather than as an individual entity who inspires others to dissident action. For this reason, he portrays the demi-god in "Dionysus" not as a being but as "a single imaginable form, an outward body of flesh presented to the senses, and comprehending, as its animating soul, a whole world of thoughts, surmises, greater and less experiences" (2–3).

The extension of the action through multiple entities in ambiguous states of self-awareness brings to mind the ecologically leaky language of "The Conclusion" to *Studies in the History of the Renaissance*. In "Dionysus," Pater describes the god "becoming, in his chase, almost akin to the wild beasts – to the wolf" (*Greek Studies*, 42). In this context of pagan ambiguity, human sacrifice cannot be taken literally; or rather, what is represented here is the sacrifice not of the individual, but of liberal humanism itself, with "the beautiful soft creature become an enemy of human kind" like the "were-wolf" (42–43). The metaphors of the moth swarm and the pack of beasts allow Pater to sustain both the individual and collective perspectives that "The Bachannals" blends

52   "Up & down & horribly *natural*"

together in depicting the submergence of individual identity within a universalizing passion, one where "the aroma of the green world is retained in the fair human body, set forth in all sorts of finer ethical lights and shades" (58). The earthy sensuality in Pater's work that critics attacked as decadent is here described as innately ethical. As I wish to demonstrate in the final section of this chapter, it is in the character of the eponymous hero of *Marius the Epicurean* that the author offers his most sustained consideration of the place of ethics within pagan sensuality and the parallel issue of the place of the individual within a world that can never be fully understood. At the same time, adopting a semi-omniscient, contemporary perspective outside of the novel's hero himself, Pater also offers a vision of the way in which broad shifts in cultural perspective reverberate on a macro-ecological scale.

Deep-Time Paganism in *Marius the Epicurean*

The Victorian poet and scholar John Addington Symonds spent much of his adult life in Davos, Switzerland, which he found to be the best environment for the health issues he had experienced since childhood. Becoming an active and engaged citizen of the town, it was also here that Symonds wrote many of his works, including his most famous publication, the seven-volume study *The Renaissance in Italy* (1875–1886). On March 30, 1885, nearing completion of this major work, he wrote to his friend Mary Robinson that he would, "of course," eventually read *Marius the Epicurean*, which had been published the previous month, although he hoped it would be "in a gondola."[38] Pater had taken his first trip to Italy in 1865, two years after the appearance of Symonds's *The Renaissance: An Essay* (1863), the published version of a talk he had delivered at Oxford in which he had emphasized the multiple origins of the early-modern concept of humanism.[39] Pater's 1865 trip (not repeated until a quarter century later, in 1889 and 1891) was an experience that, Michael Levey observes, proved to be a key inspiration for his own *Studies in the History of the Renaissance*, a collection of essays noted for its loose conception of the individuals and time periods that were part of the Renaissance.[40]

Despite their somewhat frosty relationship, Symonds and Pater's overlapping interests led the former to have high respect for his contemporary's ideas and writing. Nevertheless, Symonds's association – in his letter to Robinson – of the other man's prose with Venetian waterways stands as a suggestive distinction that he wished to make between his

Deep-Time Paganism in Marius the Epicurean   53

own ideas regarding historical Italy and Pater's. As Symonds explained to Robinson regarding his hesitance to engage with *Marius the Epicurean* until he had arrived in Venice,

> my brain is so badly made that I cannot easily bear the sustained monotonous refinement in his style. To that exquisite instrument of expression I dare say that I shall do justice in the languor & the largeness of the lagoons – better than I can in this eager air of mountains, where everything is jagged & up & down & horribly *natural*.[41]

The previous year, the prolific Symonds had just republished his own *Sketches and Studies in Italy* and *Italian Byways* as a single work entitled *New Italian Sketches* (1884), while his friend Horatio Brown had published *Life on the Lagoons* (1884), describing the natural topography, architecture, gondoliers, and fisherman that he and Symonds experienced during their Venetian boat rides. His performance of disinterest in reading *Marius the Epicurean* was clearly not due to a waning interest in Italian history. For Richmond Crinkley, Symonds's comments reflect a sense of reading the novel as "a dubious duty and certainly not a pleasure."[42] His familiarity with Italian history and Pater's writings led him to expect that the novel would prove ill-suited to his tastes. As Crinkley proposes, the work would not offer Symonds either "a clearly worded historical novel with easily perceived allegiances" or "a well-researched reconstruction of an earlier culture, like some of his own volumes."

And sure enough, as it seems Symonds feared, Pater's *Marius the Epicurean* stands as a challenge to the timelines, narrative structures, and pacing common to most Victorian histories and novels, the author using style as a form of argument. According to Edmund Gosse, in explaining why he chose not to read Rudyard Kipling or Robert Louis Stevenson, Pater apparently declared: "I feel, from what I hear about them, that they are strong: they might lead me out of my path. I want to go on writing in my own way."[43] This susceptibility to being led astray was not only a concern about originality, but about the ideas and meanings being enacted through the style itself. The lulling alliteration in Symonds's letter to Robinson is an off-the-cuff parody of Paterian prose that implies that he expected the novel to be as heavily invested in formal elements as were Pater's earlier publications. A few years later, Symonds would complain that, in trying to read Pater's *Appreciations, with an Essay on Style* (1889), "I found myself wandering about among the precious sentences, just as though I had lost myself in a sugar-cane plantation."[44]

Symonds's view on Pater's form also effectively foreshadows both the listless hero of the novel Symonds himself appeared in no rush to read and the landscapes through which Marius allows himself to be carried much like the epicurean passenger of a Venetian gondola.

Pater's decadent style contributes to his efforts, as Angela Leighton puts it, to let the "intrinsic and extrinsic leak into each other" (17). Meanwhile, the novel presents a more expansive, leaky manoeuvre through which Pater offers an eco-pagan consideration of the permeability among the self, the sentient, and the landscape – an enactment sympathetic to a pagan vision that allows the imagined historical and the embodied present to be recognized as elements of each other. That is, *Marius the Epicurean* offers a turn to Classical paganism not only as a mythopoeic strategy for exploring other issues of interest or concern to Victorians, but also as a formulation of an ecological model that was contemporary but maintained a vision of deep time, and that was characterized by the inter-permeations among environment, vegetation, and animals, including humans. In recalling his own languorous journeys through the lagoons, Symonds speculates, accurately as it turns out, that Pater's novel captures a sustained spiritual engagement with the landscape, one that embodies his decadent ecology.

The novel in its meanderings – whether into philosophical musings, elaborate descriptions, or retellings of myths – plays havoc with common understandings of time and history. The opening sentence seems to prepare, or at least forewarn, the reader for this: "As, in the triumph of Christianity, the old religion lingered latest in the country, and died out at last as but paganism – the religion of the villagers, before the advance of the Christian Church; so, in an earlier century, it was in places remote from town-life that the older and purer forms of paganism itself had survived the longest" (3). The disruptive punctuation and heavy alliteration immediately encourage temporal confusion. The novel opens with a two-letter word followed by a comma, while mellifluous phrases such as "the old religion lingered latest" may have inspired Symonds to close his copy of the novel and write a letter to Robinson about the "languor & the largeness of the lagoons." The first sentence also warns us of the confusingly loose formulation of time that Pater engages in much of the work. Does the sentence say that pre-Christian spirituality did die out as paganism or that it died out in all *but* paganism? The narrator states that older and purer forms specifically lasted longest in the countryside, but what of the newer and less pure? And what exactly is the date the narrator is proposing here for Christianity's triumph and pure paganism's

Deep-Time Paganism in Marius the Epicurean

dissipation? From this sentence, the reader can only discern that, according to the narrator, "the triumph of Christianity" did occur, but that this story was going to start at some point before whenever that happened.

In defining paganism as no more than the religion of villagers, the novel's narrator is not echoing the view that Pater articulates in *Studies in the History of the Renaissance*. It is Marius himself who reflects the inquisitiveness and multi-perspectival approach to life that Pater encourages in the earlier collection of essays. This outlook on the world results in a hero who cannot help but appear as rather inert for somebody who is supposed to be on a journey. He delays for three days before even beginning his travels and then comes across as far less the adventurer on a path to self-discovery than a piece of driftwood caught in the back currents of a lagoon. "Surrender[ing] himself, a willing subject, as he walked, to the impressions of the road," Marius does not actively choose to venture forth to Luca (today commonly spelt "Lucca"), but instead finds that his journey "brought him" there (91–92).[45] And Luca itself is full of lethargic locals who, having lingered a moment on the threshold of their homes, "went to rest early" (92). In the "Conclusion" to *Studies in the History of the Renaissance*, Pater famously reproves people who go "to sleep before evening" (120), while in the novel the listlessness of Marius and the other humans is countered by the broader environment itself, which sustains a distinctive inner energy. Notably, Pater had removed the "Conclusion" from the essay collection's second edition but restored it to the third (published in 1888), declaring that he now deals "more fully in *Marius the Epicurean* with the thoughts suggested by it."[46] While it has been generally understood that, by removing the section, Pater had been responding to the outcry over the essay collection's sensuality and support for nonnormative desires, it may also be that the issue of lethargy and temporal attenuation briefly engaged in the "Conclusion" (with a suggestion of living a life of pleasure) and much expanded in the novel was also a point of conceptual elaboration. In the novel, even after the villagers have gone to bed, "there was still a glow along the road through the shorn cornfields, and the birds were still awake about the crumbling grey heights of an old temple: and yet so quiet and air-swept was the place, you could hardly tell where the country left off in it, and the field-paths became its streets" (92). In this passage, Pater emphasizes the inseparability of the rural and urban, creating the image of a single ecology fused by the interrelations among plants, animals, topography, and architecture. The environment itself appears as a sort of character in the novel, going about its activities and engaging the changes influenced by humans, and not as a mere passive backdrop or resource for them.

As this passage suggests, Pater's famous recommendation in the "Conclusion" that one always seek new sensations is not only depicted in the novel but also encouraged through its style and narrative form. If Pater had simply defined the ecology of *Marius the Epicurean* as pagan, he would have risked his readers – like the novel's Victorian narrator – assuming the common dichotomy of Christianity and paganism, a model that does not reflect the complexity of what in "Winckelmann" he calls a "universal pagan sentiment, a paganism that existed before the Greek religion" (*Studies*, 99). Instead, he draws the novel's readers into a sense of an all-encompassing, panpsychic spirituality with a deep-time understanding of history. Thus, in Luca, "the rough-tiled roofs seemed to huddle together side by side, like one continuous shelter over the whole town" (*Marius*, 160). Apparent throughout the novel is this same vision of the individual not as a singular agent moving through the landscape but as an element more effectively realized as an interlacing of changing relationships, as Marius explores various philosophies in his efforts to establish how to live his life. The overarching trajectory of the hero is one of an inner journey, almost exclusively a Bildungsroman of the mind that Marius himself describes upon reflection, in the novel's final chapter, as "the unbroken placidity of the contemplation in which [his life to date] had been passed" (258). "How little I myself really need," observes the hero a short time earlier, "when people leave me alone, with the intellectual powers at work serenely." Drops of water, wildflowers, dying leaves – he gives a few examples of the humble stimuli he finds sufficient, but Marius's main example of inspiration is a child's delicacy, an image that he makes more fleeting by immediately placing it within an ahistorical frame. Describing an imagined girl's father, "the rudest of brick-makers as he comes from work," Marius explains that "through her, he reaches out to, he makes his own, something from that strange region, so distant from him yet so real, of the world's refinement, ... a touch of the *secular* gold, of a perpetual age of gold." Marius's inspiration here proves to be the same as that of the crude laborer, or of any human. The two men ultimately move through the inspiration together, toward a timeless, golden age that defines their point of unity, of singularity. The turn to "perpetual" gold brings to mind Frederick Sandys's use, as discussed in Chapter 1, of a flat gold background and the image of the Golden Fleece in his painting *Medea* (1868) to address the transmission of pagan vitality across history, geography, and culture. Pater attended the Royal Academy

Deep-Time Paganism in Marius the Epicurean   57

exhibition both in 1868 (when the absence of Sandys's painting led to rich speculation on the reason) and in 1869, when it was finally displayed.[47]

As the character's example suggests, he venerates most those journeys that are rooted in internal stimulation. Any actual movement in his life's narrative, he proposes, has been driven by his temper "inward; movement of observation only, or even of pure meditation" (258). Appropriately, Pater goes out of his way to mark as coincidental Marius's pivotal assumption of his friend Cornelius's Christian identity – an action that eventually leads to the hero's death. At this point in the narrative, the two friends come in touch with each other utterly by chance, Cornelius having shown up out of the blue "as it happened, on a journey and travelling near the place, finding traces" of Marius. Nor are the two friends any more driven on their joint excursion than when they had been traveling alone, proceeding together to move "hither and thither, leisurely, among the country-places thereabout, … till they came one evening to a little town," one that Marius realizes only then that he had been to before. This lack of awareness of physical surroundings reaches its most extreme manifestation when the hero – despite his intellectual depth and moral sensitivity – seems to have almost fully lost any sense of his own physicality, becoming like a worshipping maenad apparent in the world only as brief flashes of light here and there.

On the spur of the moment, Marius decides to protect his Christian friend by claiming his identity, a loving gesture of which Cornelius himself is unaware. It may seem ironic that Marius, who has most sincerely quested all his life for an ideal way of being in the world, dies from the plague in part because he has chosen an act of subterfuge, assuming a false identity for the sake of his friend. On another level, however, it is not a death; as with the overarching conception of spirituality in *Studies in the History of the Renaissance*, the novel's closing chapter encourages one to read the new religion of Christianity as an outgrowth of paganism, just as Marius sees Cornelius as not just a brother, but "like a son also" (258). Much as Stoppani describes a modern geological age arising as a "new nature" replacing the "old nature" or "old planet," Pater's narrator describes Cornelius as embodying "a new hope [that] had sprung up" upon "the aged world" (259).

The trope of a new age was not unique to Pater and Stoppani, having been made popular in the latter half of the nineteenth century through decadence, but especially through scientific discourses of evolution and degeneracy. *Marius the Epicurean*'s ecological metaphor, however, does

"Up & down & horribly *natural*"

not resolve itself with a shift from one perspective to another. Rather, Pater depicts his hero's transformation between Classical paganism and Christianity as incomplete. Moreover, Pater has the key moment of Marius's mental turn occur as part of a paradigm shift on the grandest scale. At the same time that Marius inhales the plague that will kill him, there is a sudden surge in pre-Christian spirituality. "[T]he old gods were wroth," concludes the narrator, "at the presence of this new enemy among them!" (259). It is a shift of cosmic proportions as, "[u]nder this sunless heaven the earth itself seemed to fret and fume with a heat of its own." Marius is uncertain whether it is just an illusion brought on by his illness or whether the environment has actually begun to tremble, as if the very world

> had sunken in the night, far below its proper level, into some close, thick abysm of its own atmosphere. ... [O]n a sudden the hills seemed to roll, like a sea in motion, around the whole compass of the horizon. For a moment Marius supposed himself attacked with some sudden sickness of brain, till the fall of a great mass of building convinced him that not himself but the earth under his feet was giddy. A few moments later the little marketplace was alive with the rush of the distracted inhabitants from their tottering houses; and as they waited anxiously for the second shock of earthquake, a long-smouldering suspicion leapt precipitately into well-defined purpose, and the whole body of people was carried forward towards the band of worshippers below. (259–60)

It is difficult at this moment in our twenty-first-century history not to feel compelled to transpose metaphors of environmental catastrophe and devastating contagion onto Pater's novel. But then, social models of decadence that preceded *Marius the Epicurean* themselves formulated social discord as ecological crises. Interestingly, however, the novel's narrator conceptualizes the spiritual shift as taking place within an atemporal ecology that Pater elsewhere calls a "universal pagan sentiment," literally an earth-shattering phenomenon. The reader's own interpretation of the depicted experience vacillates among an actual catastrophe, mental delusion brought on by the plague, and a metaphor for Marius's spiritual transformation. In this moment, the "rush of inhabitants" exists not only as a merged collective, a swarm, but also as a fluid extension of the hills, which are now themselves a "sea in motion." Pater explicitly muddies the readers' understanding of the scene as a means of representing the polyvalence of his decadent ecology. As he notes, the flow of the townsfolk is the result of not only a geologic effect but also a pagan one, the "whole body of people," we are told, being "carried forward" by a spiritual momentum to challenge the Christian worshippers as the source of this seismic catastrophe. In this way, Pater's model envisions the human impact on geological change not principally as a physical influence but as a spiritually inflected shift in human understanding of the world, its structure, and its malleability. If Marius comes across as the most languorous, meandering hero in history, it is because he is an embodiment of paganism's movement through a time so deep as to exist beyond the methods of comprehension and categorization that influenced not only the Victorian novel genre, but much of the earth sciences.

The Persistence of Aftershocks

Marius the Epicurean describes a historical decadent ecology in which eco-spirituality is portrayed as a persistent but adaptable influence.[48] It is for this reason that the narrator observes that, rather than having destroyed and replaced pagan practice, early Christianity "had adopted many of the graces of pagan feeling and pagan custom; as being indeed a living creature taking up, transforming, accommodating still more closely to the human heart, what of right belonged to it" (211). And in the previous chapter of the novel we are told, "So much of what Marius had valued most in the old world seemed to be under renewal and further promotion" (207). This shift of established belief systems into newer but still linked ones is enlivened by the hero's actions for the sake of Cornelius, whom he describes as both brother and son – Christianity as both the sibling and the descendant of a belief system that came before it. From an ecological perspective marked by a universal, transhistorical paganism, the two friends are a personification of a religion being reinvigorated or reborn through its own disruptive offshoot. In this sense, à la Stoppani's anthropozoic, the plague-infested, eco-catastrophic climax of the novel marks the shift into a new geologic era in which human influence became recorded in deep time – a radical spiritual alteration inseparable from geologic change. One cannot help but feel a touch sorry for Symonds. He entered into *Marius the Epicurean* expecting to replace a world "where everything is jagged & up & down & horribly *natural*" with "the languor & the largeness of the lagoons." Instead, he found himself and his modern conception of Italian history swept up in an earth-shattering wave that was disrupting Victorian society's very understanding of its place in the world and in the depths of time.

Pater participated in a broad nineteenth-century sense of paganism not only as a part of late-Romanticism or as a general interest in Classical

60 "Up & down & horribly *natural*"

mythology, but also as an influential, contemporary panpsychism that was culturally modified and that persisted precisely because of its adaptability. As a key instigator of the decadent pagan imaginary, he also had a considerable influence on other contributors to this cultural development, such as Simeon Solomon and Michael Field, whose representations of trans-species engagements are the focus of my next chapter. Pater's writing in *Studies in the History of the Renaissance, Marius the Epicurean,* and elsewhere discourages a view of Victorian paganism as entirely circumscribed by the popular understanding of decadence, or as primarily an artistic interest in Classical mythology as a source of creative and sexual inspiration. Instead, Marius's own signs of self-awareness dissuade readers from searching for primary origins, while encouraging recognition of Pater's ecological vision as part of an expansive exploration, within the scientific, philosophical, and cultural thought of the time, of the earth not principally as an object that humans influence but as a disruptive, indeterminate force. Moreover, the author envisions these vibrant interests in the biosphere, the trans-historic, and cross-species relations as themselves signaling a mutable and at times destructive paganism too vast for him and his contemporaries ever to appreciate fully.

CHAPTER 3

The Lick of Love
Trans-Species Intimacy in Simeon Solomon and Michael Field

Decadent animals, we know a few: there is the swine on a lead in Félicien Rops's painting *Pornocrates* (1878), des Esseintes's bejeweled tortoise in Joris-Karl Huysmans's novel *À rebours* (1884), the goddess-like subject of Rachilde's "The Panther," and the domesticated lobster that Gerard de Nerval took for a walk on a blue silk leash, which, if the story is true (highly unlikely), says less about the crustacean's peripatetic inclinations than the owner's need for bourgeois notice. In Britain, we have the beloved serpent of Vernon Lee's "Prince Alberic and the Snake Lady" (1896); Arthur Machen's disturbingly protracted depiction in *The Hill of Dreams* (1907) of the strangulation of a little girl's puppy; and the ferret in Saki's "Sredni Vashtar" (1911) who becomes the deity of a child's personal paganism. Popular novelist Ouida (Marie Louise Ramé) lived with up to thirty dogs and, in her novel *Puck* (1870), bestowed the role of a narrator upon a Maltese terrier. And Michael Field celebrated through poetry their intimate affections for their dog Whym Chow (although my analysis of Field in this chapter focuses on their 1892 collection of poems, *Sight and Song*). This far from rounds out the list, but its diversity of types and scenarios suffices to suggest that animals among the decadents were more than decorative or metaphors for human-centered concerns. While decadents such as Ouida engaged with pet politics, in this chapter I wish to propose that, in a number of instances, their consideration of the intimacies between humans and other animals extends to the vegetal, as well as beyond affection to a consideration of other bonds that undermined contemporary conventions of species distinction.

Consider Ouida, who was noted for the "ultra-Swinburnean fleshiness" of her style,[1] being described in an article entitled "Ouida's Decadence" as "very eccentric," misogynistic, and having propagated "dreadful wickedness."[2] A contemporary reviewer of her novel *Ariadne: The Story of a Dream* (1877) commented that her narrator appears over-influenced by Walter Pater. The reviewer spends much energy criticizing the florid

The Lick of Love

excess of Ouida's sentimental descriptions, and ends by lifting one of Pater's most memorable lines: "Perhaps the small but lively school of Neo-pagans may turn from the error of their literary ways when they find that Ouida can burn, with a hard gem-like flame, with the best of them."[3] Despite the reviewer's assessment of her work, Ouida ultimately did more during her career to popularize rather than stymy British pagan decadence. This is, in part, because her literary intentions were driven by what the 1877 critic, in describing a quality Ouida *lacked*, refers to as "an acute and almost universal sympathy, which does indeed often degenerate into a false and illogical sentiment, yet serves to redeem an age of egotism."[4] Decadents who were mocked for their pagan interests were also often recognized for their strong sympathetic drive, interpreted by some as an act of submission marked by deindividuating languor. In some instances, this attribute is portrayed as overemotionalism, in others as a deviant male effeminacy. As I argue in this chapter, however, their efforts to integrate themselves imaginatively into the emotions of other species and sentient beings from across time can also be understood as reflecting a politically inflected engagement with trans-species intimacy.

Ouida wrote criticism of vivisection, fur clothing, and hunting, as well as essays on animal rights in general, for journals such *The Fortnightly Review* and *Gentleman's Magazine*. Upon her death, the town where she was born, Bury St. Edmunds, installed a drinking fountain for dogs and horses with the inscription: "Here may god's creatures whom she loved assuage her tender soul as they drink." In an article in *The Fortnightly*, Ouida quotes Pierre Loti's description in *The Book of Pity and of Death* (1891; English trans. 1892) of the thoughts his cat expresses through its eyes:

> In this sad autumn day, since we are both alone in this floating prison, rocked and lost in the midst of I know not what endless perils, why should we not give to one another a little of that sweet exchange of feeling which soothes so many sorrows, which has a semblance of some immaterial eternal thing not subjected to death, which calls itself affection, and finds its expression in a touch, a look?[5]

Ouida's discussion of Loti appeared in the same 1892 volume of the periodical as a piece by decadent Pierre Bourget, a second in which Elizabeth Pennell refers to the "mystic creed" of "artistic decadence,"[6] and a review by Arthur Symons of Joris-Karl Huysmans's works in which Symons describes the author as not only "the type and symbol" of that "decadent civilisation" characterized by an "exquisitely perverse charm," but also as physically and mentally akin to a cat.[7] Even though it does not mention

The Lick of Love 63

decadence or paganism, Ouida's piece on Loti is, I propose, a more insightful contribution to pagan decadence than these others because – rather than regurgitating the common trope of a decaying society, a mystical, symbolist aesthetic, or the persona characterized by cultured perversity – Ouida offers an attempt to evoke a sense in her readers of a feline existentialism she believes they will find comforting, just as she has. In so doing, the author calls to mind the broad Victorian cast of cultural entanglements among decadence, sympathy, and trans-species intimacy, interlocutions that contributed to a view of nonhuman animals as kin and community, rather than property or resource.

The threads joining eco-paganism to intimacies among sentient creatures are not the sort that can be disentangled, and to try to do so risks de-eroticizing or de-emotionalizing the possibility of one's own trans-species affections. This chapter offers depictions of humans and other animals in erotic engagement or emotional co-reliance, but I am especially interested in the ways in which decadents used the defamiliarizing perspective of the species other (sometimes animal, sometimes plant) as a form of sympathy or shared soul communicated through an acknowledged experience of pleasure. Benjamin Morgan has argued that the "nineteenth-century interface of science and aesthetics powerfully reframed and displaced the aesthetic, extending its boundaries beyond the domain of art or beauty to consider broader questions about how meaning and emotion are meditated through human bodies."[8] I wish to extend this insight a touch further to consider intimacies between humans and other sentient beings that break down assumed, even subconsciously imposed, limits to affective engagements, as well as to consider whether the site of identity formation exists not in Loti's "floating prison" of the self, but in what he calls the "sweet exchange" across sentient beings that affirms, in passing, the existence of each.[9]

In the previous chapter, I summarized Pater's paganism from an ecological perspective, situating it in the context of other related approaches of the time, before reading *Marius the Epicurean* as rendering a decadent ecology operating on both emotionally intimate and Anthropocenic scales. Turning to Simeon Solomon's artwork at the start of the pagan revival and Michael Field's poetry collection *Sight and Song* (1892) in the decade of probably its greatest popularity, this chapter addresses the pagan visuality of decadent ecology that, I argue, allowed Solomon and Field to render affections operating beyond normative models of desire. Both Solomon and Field engaged in same-sex intimacies that support the use of a queer framework of analysis. In their engagement with Classical paganism, these British decadents were not only building a space for their desires, but also developing an ecological politics based on intimacy. These individuals offer unique formulations of what Pater presents as a transtemporal and trans-spatial form of community in order to acknowledge more richly the importance of affect within the experience of sympathy.

As my placement of imaginative sympathy within British decadence suggests, I use the term "queer" not to refer to a sexuality built from individual identity categories or sharply delineated types of desire, but to emphasize attractions and intimacies that seem so malleable and so fluid as to operate outside the possibility of accurate cultural categorization at all. I agree with the more common definition of "queer" that engages with the political empowerment of individuals who are abused because of desires and self-identities deemed nonnormative. For this chapter, by focusing on particularly evanescent attractions I hope to attain a stronger sense of the freedom and power that pagans have repeatedly found in remaining uncategorized and unregulated. In this context, my use of queer theory accords with the sense articulated by David Halperin, where the queer acknowledges its connection to sexuality and/or gender, while extending into more general states and strategies that disrupt the normative (even if unintentionally): "Queer is by definition whatever is at odds with the normal, the legitimate, the dominant. *There is nothing in particular to which it necessarily refers*" (italics in the original).[10] This lack of referent is crucial for the consecration of desires because it foregrounds and maintains queerness's articulation not through a particular institutional system of categorization; it is not simply reactive and thus does not inadvertently reassert the primacy of the normative in its own act of self-declaration.

Sympathy and Victorian Animal Rights

The decadents did not discover species intimacies on their own. Solomon's and Field's works arose within a vibrant animal rights activist movement that was rhetorically framed through a philosophical and ethical discourse of sympathy. Victorians developed models of affection for the domestic animals whom they allowed to share their space, doing much to build the momentum for animal rights, anti-vivisection, and vegetarian movements. Following extensive eighteenth-century philosophical and practical discussions of sympathy for nonhuman animals, the next century saw some of the most conceptually radical and culturally disruptive developments in

Sympathy and Victorian Animal Rights 65

animal rights and subjectivity. A key shift during this time was from the common understanding of domestic and wild creatures as property or resource to an acknowledgment that other animal species have emotions and feelings that demand they also be given rights as members of modern society. In his *Introduction to the Principles of Morals and Legislation* (1781), Jeremy Bentham, comparing the mental and discursive competencies of equines, canines, and day-old babies, argues that no individual's interests are of greater value than those of any other. It is only "on account of their interests having been neglected by the insensibility of the ancient jurists," Bentham states, that nonhuman species "stand degraded into the class of things":

> The French have already discovered that the blackness of the skin is no reason why a human being should be abandoned without redress to the caprice of a tormentor. It may one day come to be recognized that the number of the legs, the villosity of the skin, or the termination of the *os sacrum* are reasons equally insufficient for abandoning a sensitive being to the same fate. … The question is not, Can they reason? Nor Can they talk? But, Can they suffer?[11]

Employing a strategy that would become familiar among nineteenth-century animal rights advocates, Bentham parallels speciesism to a practice of human subordination, specifically slavery, as a rhetorical means of bringing home his key contention. In his *Theory of Legislation* (French 1802; English trans. 1864), Bentham offers another analogy in the hopes of evoking sympathy:

> A multitude of innocent animals suffer a continual persecution, because they have the misfortune to be thought ugly. Everything unusual has the power of exciting in us a sentiment of disgust and hatred. What is called a *monster* is only a being which differs a little from others of its kind. Hermaphrodites, whose sex is undetermined, are regarded with a sort of horror, only because they are rare.[12]

As Bentham observes, both animal abuse and sex-based denigration arise not from the individual but from attitudes rooted in cultural norms. However, he foregrounds the individual in pain by focusing on the italicized, singular "*monster*" – measured as a deviation when the very cause of alienation is actually humans' unwillingness to acknowledge the ontological and affective connections across conceived difference.

The first anti-cruelty legislation of any country was the United Kingdom's 1822 Act to Prevent the Cruel and Improper Treatment of Cattle. Also known as Martin's Act, it was brought forward by the politician

The Lick of Love

Richard Martin, who also fought for prison reform, anti-slavery, and the rights of Roman Catholics in his home country of Ireland, suggesting the complex ethical imbrications being recognized among diverse forms of rights politics during the period. Ivan Kreilkamp observes that "Martin had achieved something monumental, a national legislation testifying (if not to a point and provisionally) the legal personhood of certain nonhuman creatures, their standing as legal subjects possessing rights and protections beyond those due to them as possessions."[13] The year 1824 saw the formation of the Society for the Prevention of Cruelty to Animals (SPCA), to which Queen Victoria gave Royal status in 1840. Further acts addressing cruelty to animals passed in 1835, 1849, and 1876, challenging certain blood sports and scientific vivisection, extending protections to dogs, bulls, bears, and roosters, and to any animals that were being made to suffer for the sake of science. In the latter case, abuse was not made illegal; physiologists could commit acts of violence as long as they were deemed necessary for their science and were seen as the least painful option. The 1900 Wild Animals in Captivity Protection Act extended rights further and all were repealed when consolidated under the 1911 Protection of Animals Act.[14]

While expanding the types of nonhumans protected by the law, legislation consistently reflected an awareness only of those animals with which humans chose to engage, generally for work, sport, or pleasure. Meanwhile, philosophical debates around species empathy and rights were being framed predominantly through a liberal consideration of social stability as weighed against the individual's rights to personal growth, freedom, and happiness. A major conceptual shift arose as emphasis moved from species-based rights to an understanding of animals as sentient individuals. In *Utilitarianism* (1863), John Stuart Mill turns to nonhuman animals in order to distinguish the basis for human rights, arguing that the "beast's pleasures" do not define the "better and nobler object of pursuit."[15] Choosing swine as his example, he argues:

> If the sources of pleasure were precisely the same to human beings and to swine, the rule of life which is good enough for the one would be good enough for the other. The comparison of the Epicurean life to that of beasts is felt as degrading, precisely because a beast's pleasures do not satisfy a human being's conceptions of happiness.[16]

Mill's homogenized rendering of all nonhuman animals as swine assumes that human perspective is not limited, that all humans have the same sense of pleasure, and that he has a clear awareness of all of nonhuman animals' pleasures. He also assumes that all people would prefer individual

Sympathy and Victorian Animal Rights

agency to de-individuated pleasure and would prefer "elevated" pleasures to the sensual pleasures he interprets as the only ones accessible to other animals, all issues that Solomon, Field, and other decadents challenge in their works.

Despite certain anthropocentric assumptions, Mill does affirm that nonhuman animals should have the right to happiness. Later, in his *Principles of Political Economy* (1885), he declares that the reasons established for legal intervention on behalf of children apply equally to "those unfortunate slaves and victims of the most brutal part of mankind, the lower animals."[17] Notably, the first trial in Britain for child cruelty was instigated by the Royal Society for the Prevention of Cruelty to Animals, whose legal argument was based on the claim that, technically speaking, a child was not a parent's property but fell into the category of a "small animal." The case was successful, eventually leading to the formation of the National Society for the Prevention of Cruelty to Children.[18] A Society for the Prevention of Cruelty to Children was founded in New York in 1875 and in Liverpool in 1883, with many others following.

At roughly the same time, Henry Salt adapted Mill's position to argue that every animal has the right to a life that "permits of the individual development – subject to the limitations imposed by the permanent needs and interests of the community."[19] Salt counted among his friends and acquaintances Swinburne, Ouida, William Morris, Edith Nesbit, George Bernard Shaw, Annie Besant, Edward Carpenter, Mohandas Gandhi, and Havelock Ellis, bringing together a broad set of interests that included decadence, paganism, occultism, environmentalism, vegetarianism, pacifism, and sexual rights. Like Salt, most of these people believed strongly in rights and protections for nonhuman animals based on their subjectivity and right to sympathy. In 1891, Salt founded the animal rights group the Humanitarian League, serving as editor of both of its journals, *Humanity* and *The Humanitarian*, making him arguably the most committed advocate of the cause during the fin de siècle. In his most influential work, *Animals' Rights* (1892), he reiterates the interpretations of previous scholars that humans' abuse of the nonhuman animal sanctions their abuse of other humans as well, not just logistically but psychologically, creating a philosophy of life in which such violence is normalized. Bentham made a similar argument roughly a century earlier in *Theory of Legislation*: "Cruelty towards animals is an incentive to cruelty towards men, & c."[20] According to Salt, it is impossible to attain multi-species justice if humans "continue to regard [nonhumans] as

68 The Lick of Love

beings of a wholly different order, and to ignore the significance of their numberless points of kinship with mankind" (9). In language sympathetic to the claims of authors such as Pater, Ouida, and Field, Salt argues that this persistent refusal to accept others as ethically worthy of respect is founded on "a lack of imaginative sympathy" and "sense of affinity" or "kinship" (21).

Various anthropologists understood sympathy, within a Darwinian framework, as a sign of moral evolution that distinguished humans from other species. In "The Origin of Human Races and the Antiquity of Man deduced from the Theory of 'Natural Selection'" (1864), Alfred Russel Wallace argues that, as civilization accommodates individuals' strengths and weaknesses in collective progress toward a stronger holistic order, we will each understand that our greatest happiness relies on that of the greatest happiness of the collective: "[T]he well balanced moral faculties will never permit any one to transgress on the equal freedom of others; restrictive laws will not be wanted, for each man will be guided by the best of laws; a thorough appreciation of the rights, and a perfect sympathy with the feelings, of all about him."[21] Vernon Lee similarly addressed vivisection through a Darwinian logic. "[O]ur physical nature has been evolved by the selection and survival of those physical forms which are in harmony with the greatest number of physical circumstances," she argues in "Vivisection: An Evolutionist to Evolutionists":

> [S]o also has our moral nature been evolved by the more and more conscious choice of the motives including consideration for the greatest number of results from our actions, of the motives which, instead of merely enlarging the shapeless and functionless moral polyp-jelly of ego[,] work out, diversify and unify, lick into shape, the complicated moral organism of society.[22]

In accord with Lee, Salt wished to erase species distinctions that he saw as unfounded impediments to humane justice (21). For Keith Tester, Salt's greatest contribution to the modern discussion of trans-species respect and sympathy is his declaration that nonhuman animals deserve not just our protection and support, but their own rights as individuals.[23] Salt's main conceptual shift in *Animals' Rights* occurs through his advocacy not simply for trying to adopt something like the perspective of someone from another species, but for exposing the biased systems of understanding that shape the human perspective through which species relations are mediated.

Sympathy and Victorian Animal Rights

Salt's formulations have found like-minded articulations in later scholarship. Approaching the issue from a philosophical perspective, Peter Singer, in his paradigm-changing *Animal Liberation* (1975), argues that, ethically speaking, nonhuman animals must be brought within the human "sphere of moral concern and [we must] cease to treat their lives as expendable for whatever trivial purposes we may have."[24] Brian Massumi proposes that "sympathy" and "creativity" are necessary in any consideration of the rights of nonhuman animals, even if this approach makes some degree of anthropomorphism inevitable. We need to develop, he contends, a nonhuman revision to "our image of ourselves as humanly standing apart from other animals; our inveterate vanity regarding our assumed species identity, based on the specious grounds of our sole proprietorship of language, thought, and creativity. We will see what the birds and the beasts have instinctively to say about this."[25] While Salt advocates for the acknowledgment of kinship, Massumi moves to a conceptualization of alternative perspectives and voices, a way of perceiving that moves away from species entirely.[26] Massumi proposes a fundamental recalibration that could make humans' current controlling status irretrievable. Salt himself does not conjecture on what such a dissolution of the human might entail, but decadents such as Solomon and Field simulated the crossing perspectives of different types of animals, the artist and authors speaking to the act of attraction as an ethics of care, longing, and belonging. Replacing a singular viewpoint with a plurality does not in itself ensure or even propose a more empathic way of being in the world. The transience of engagements and the impermanence of outlooks, however, do entice a sustained awareness of the politics of perspective.

The apocalyptic climax of Pater's *Marius the Epicurean*, discussed in the previous chapter, makes it apparent that, in understanding a decadent ecological model, one must remain aware of the way in which humans – including scholars such as myself – are compelled to consume and regurgitate what decadent writers themselves propose as the unknown and unknowable. The very compulsion to understand carries humanist assumptions (regarding scales of size, space, and time, for example). A key conundrum in this situation is that ecologies are defined as much by the *acts* of engagement, as the subjects; however, humans train each other to distinguish first different animal types, and only then the possible modes of interaction. Decadents such as Solomon and Field, however, through their attention to allure and enticement, suggest the possibility of foregrounding imaginative sympathy. In the spirit of Massumi's call to hear what others have to say, they proffer ways of opening oneself up not to other species, but to compulsions and desires, the intimate licks, strokes, and glances that extend through others and the self.

Queer ecology studies has enhanced recent conceptions of such ideas regarding trans-species attractions. It engages with the practices, cultures, and politics of desire, procreation, and proliferation among various components of an ecological network. As Catriona Sandilands (elsewhere Mortimer-Sandilands) notes, the field has generated "a proliferating array of queer ecological possibilities, including provocative considerations of cross-species and eco-sexualities as part of an ethico-political opening of love to include more-than-human corporealities."[27] A common premise among queer ecology scholars is that nonhuman sexual and gender diversity undermines human exceptionalism, demanding the reconsideration of standard methods of establishing identities (such as species categorization) and of any such thing as authentic nature.[28] Queer ecology proposes that what humans have included within the rubric of "nature" has so often been *not* exclusively natural that we must look beyond the human for ecologies defined by mutual investments. "Although Foucault rightly notes the tenuous early connections between the two discourses [of nature and sexuality]," Sandilands observes, "the establishment of sex as a matter of biopolitical *truth* could not help but be connected to ideas of nature, and especially to racialized, sexualized, and other anxieties over hygiene and degeneracy."[29]

As my previous chapter on Pater suggests, paganism could and has espoused both the dissolution of the self and the impossibility of experiential immersion while sustaining a political mandate. Notably, the claim reinforces key positions within queer ecology studies. Catriona Mortimer-Sandilands and Bruce Erickson point out that, although there have been queer ecological articulations in earlier scholarly work, contemporary Western ideas of nature have been extensively explained through a paradigm that they see as indebted particularly to nineteenth-century evolutionary and sexological discourses.[30] Such scholarship, they suggest, helped essentialize a heteronormative scientific eye. At the same time, in relying on an implicitly moral aim of improving the species, but not engaging the possibility of humans' own amoral degeneration as an eventually useless by-product of some other ecological development, such models of nature insinuate a type of anthropocentrism that decadents such as Solomon and Field challenge.

Simeon Solomon's Animal Appetites

William Blake Richmond described his friend Simeon Solomon as "spasmodically intense, sensitive to extreme touchiness," and also with "something of the mystic about him which was Pagan."[31] As Richmond implies, Solomon was often understood as a peripheral figure – a visual artist somewhere on the margins of the Pre-Raphaelite Brotherhood. But he can just as accurately be portrayed as an innovative artist well integrated within a broad community of artists, writers, and scholars that included the Pre-Raphaelites. One need only envision (as per Gerard Manley Hopkins's journal) Hopkins and Pater enjoying lunch before popping by Solomon's studio and the three of them going off to visit the 1868 Royal Academy exhibition. This was the exhibition that I mentioned in Chapter 1, for which Frederick Sandys's *Medea* was accepted but, for some reason, ultimately excluded. The three men would have seen, among the works on display, a number of Pre-Raphaelite pieces, including a variation on Sandys's *Proud Maisie* (also discussed in Chapter 1); in his journal, Hopkins summarizes Sandys's piece as "a study of a head, long hair fully detailed; she bites one lock."[32] In his "A Study of Dionysus," first published in the *Fortnightly Review* in 1876, Pater mentions also seeing at the same exhibition a work by Solomon himself, depicting Bacchus.[33]

Like Pater, Solomon was one of the Victorians who most imbued the Classical paganism of British decadence with what we now can conceive of as a proto-queer sexual politics. In a consideration of Solomon's investment in what Victorians saw as decadent aspects of ancient Greco-Roman culture, Elizabeth Prettejohn concludes that his "Classicism constantly asks us to question the customary divisions of the Western tradition, between Greek ideal beauty and Roman decadence, religious contemplation and erotic fervour, Hebraism and Hellenism."[34] Most scholars of Solomon's work, meanwhile, have recognized his investment in nonnormative desire as particularly fundamental to his turn to Classicism in the first place. Classical paganism offered a context for rendering alternative erotics, as a number of Victorian reviewers themselves had suggested in their critique of his mystical ambiguities; limp, odd-shaped, young men; and tones of melancholy and loneliness. Classical paganism, though, would have encouraged Solomon to consider the channels of respect and affection outside of exclusively human networks as possible sources for visualizing his own queer nature. In the "Conclusion" to *Studies in the History of the Renaissance*, Pater describes any human as being an "individual in his isolation" because of each person's subjective perspective on the world.[35] But Pater begins this closing section with a very different image of the individual as a "perpetual motion" of intermingling processes, such as the flow of blood, the deterioration and repair of the eyes, and changes to the brain, as well as external but connected processes such as metal rusting and corn ripening.[36] Isolation is, for Pater, a formulated model through which we attain a sense of self, but it does not negate or even subordinate our own relationality within an ecological network of experiences. The individual is no more a circumscribed set of mutually supporting organs than part of a larger, never wholly comprehensible, macro-organism. For example, appreciating decay as itself part of the process of rebirth, Pater encourages an understanding of decadence not as a cycle but as simultaneous interchanges, not the rise and fall of empires but simultaneous shifts of energy and attentions engaging a greater diversity of linkages and impacts than human history can record.

A study of Solomon's representation of human–nonhuman animal relations requires an appreciation of the role of paganism in his sense of sexuality and desire. Pater turned to a Classical model of animism wherein all objects have some form of soul. In "A Study of Dionysus," Pater evokes the comparative science of religion to describe the worship of Dionysus as "one of many modes of that primitive tree-worship which, growing out of some universal instinctive belief that trees and flowers are indeed habitations of living spirits, is found almost everywhere in the earlier stages of civilization."[37] Just as Pater addresses what he, in his essay "Winckelmann," refers to as the "pagan manner" of Classical aesthetic sensuality, he also explores the philosophic implications of paganism's animism and veneration of nature, the "universal pagan sentiment" that preceded and persists within the Christian world.[38] Solomon similarly, early in his career, began conceptualizing other sentient beings, including animals and plants, as engaging through the politics and desires circulating within Victorian human society. His renderings of other species spoke to the emotions and spiritual faiths of humans; however, with Solomon, it did so in subtler, less declarative ways that allowed him to engage his own personal desires, sense of cultural isolation, and spiritual uncertainties.

In 1856, Augustus Egg proposed Solomon to the Royal Academy Schools and he was accepted. Soon after, around 1858, Dante Gabriel Rossetti, who became a major influence on Solomon's work, helped him become part of the Pre-Raphaelite movement. Meanwhile, his sensual

Simeon Solomon's Animal Appetites 73

style and the mystical expression of his subjects contributed to the inauguration of modern decadence in Britain. Around this time, Solomon also met Swinburne, who himself had recently become part of Rossetti's chosen circle of artists and authors. Solomon's attention gradually shifted from Shakespearian and biblical subjects to Classical themes, enhanced by similar interests among other Pre-Raphaelites such as Frederic Leighton and Edward Poynter, not to mention Solomon's travels to Italy. As Roberto C. Ferrari points out, however, whether painting Classical, biblical, or other subjects, Solomon's wish to capture his same-sex desires continue to come through in his depictions of "effete or languorous youths," beautiful, religious men (*Two Acolytes Censing,* 1863), and nonheteronormative passions (*The Bride, the Bridegroom, and Sad Love,* 1865; *Sappho and Erinna in a Garden at Mytilene,* 1864).[39]

Solomon's works sustain a vaguely lonely, almost trembling energy in both facial expressions and physical postures, but also in the muted coloring and blurriness of texture in a painting as a whole. The artist's persistent rendering of this tenuousness of affection ultimately instils within both the art and, indirectly, the artist an aura of admirable tenacity that brings to mind the strategic persistence of contemporary camp politics. Describing the artist's representations of Sappho and Bacchus, Swinburne notes in 1871 that the "wasted and weary beauty of the one, the faultless and fruitful beauty of the other, bear alike the stamp of sorrow; of perplexities unsolved and desires unsatisfied."[40] For Swinburne, as Catherine Maxwell observes, Solomon's paintings presented the "metaphysical expression of the ambivalent joy and sorrow of Life itself."[41] In 1906, the year after Solomon's death, a writer for *The Studio* described his work as "in places nothing more than languidly sentimental" but as also embodying "a proud and remote mysticism which only meets its equal in Blake," this disparity being the result of "the unhappiness for which the artist's temperament seemed fated in its curious incompatibility with life's daily traffic."[42] Regardless of whether they were written before or after Solomon was arrested in 1873 for indecent exposure and "attempting to commit sodomy,"[43] for which he did not serve jail time, a number of descriptions of his work adopt this theme of the suffering Solomon as a means of alluding to indecent desires while avoiding being explicit.

Even in recent decades, while the artist's Jewish, Christian, and pagan investments continue to be analyzed, the most common issue for discussion has remained his sexual interests and the negative impact his persecution for those interests had on his career and life. Susan Moore has

74 The Lick of Love

recently declared it "a cruel trick of fate that the scandal that ruined his life has continued to overshadow a complex creative vision more in tune with continental Symbolism than the Victorian tradition."[44] I agree with Moore's observation, but would also note that Solomon's symbolism is actually in accord with his decadence, paganism, and sexuality, and that the issue of desire was for Solomon not only a personal concern but also a central element of his aesthetic. Moreover, recent new conceptualizations of desire within gender/sexuality studies in general more than justify continuing the queer work that has already been done on Solomon's art. Indeed, Solomon's investment in pagan decadence incorporates a consideration of animal sympathies that itself expands our understanding of desire, attraction, and fulfillment. His pagan works shift the possibility of these affective channels outside of human constructions of the normative and the deviant, rendering a queer emotionalism into which viewers find themselves drawn.

To imagine queerness in the Victorian period requires sensitivity to such euphemistic terms as the "lonely" and "suffering" artist, which point to the fuzzy boundaries through which nonnormative desires were often envisioned and potentially engaged. Dustin Friedman has argued for an "erotic negativity" in queer Victorian aesthetes, where the mainstream condemnation of homoerotic desire in fact gives it a type of value: "By transforming the painful recognition of one's queer desire into a profoundly consciousness-transforming experience, erotic negativity allows one to tarry at the very limits of what is thinkable in one's culture."[45] Colin Cruise demonstrates a keen thoughtfulness regarding this liminality when he describes Solomon as "the first to attempt a pictorial representation [of] same-sex desire."[46] Gayle Seymour similarly notes the ambiguities of queer subjectivity when she argues that Solomon used Old Testament themes not only to address contemporary Jewish culture and identity, but also "to explore and acknowledge his own emerging homosexual identity."[47] As with the artist's creative mingling of Jewish and homosexual alienation, his work also reveals a sustained sense that sexual discrimination and species discrimination were not readily separable. Indeed, the need to articulate one's desire at a slant would have made Solomon sensitive to a broad range of signifiers and techniques for extending affective invitations across diverse sentient beings, tapping into the Victorians' growing attention to animal rights and sympathies.

Even before his 1873 arrest, Solomon's artwork was being characterized as decadently deviant. In 1869, the reviewers for *The Art Journal* and *Blackwood's* both described Solomon's "The Toilette of a Roman Lady" as decedent in style.[48] Soon after, another reviewer surmised in seeming befuddlement that "Mr. Simeon Solomon also must find that nature puts him out." Referring to *The Evening Hymn (An Offering)* (1870), the reviewer goes on to observe that the work is "non-natural: such a figure could not sustain life for four and twenty hours, and so this sadly-stricken creature sighs out his soul, and looks suicidal."[49] The critic describes as unnatural, here, that which they feel is unrealistic. The scene itself is quite saturated by nature, having as its subject a moment of Classical pagan worship in a forest where a young man stands almost naked in seeming spiritual communion with the *genius loci*. The critic's choice of language, however, is not intended to condemn paganism itself as unnatural; rather, their claim parallels other reviewers' rhetoric in interpreting Solomon's representation of androgynous beauty as a technical weakness in painting realistically.

One of the more insightful attempts to come to terms with Solomon's unique entanglement of pagan and queer natures appears in a piece written somewhat earlier, in 1868, for *The Art Journal*. "Solomon is a genius of eccentricity," writes this critic,

> he can do nothing like other people, and in being exclusively like himself, he becomes unlike to nature. As for choice of subject, most religions of the world have struck by turns the painter's fantastic and splendor-loving fancy. On the present occasion "Bacchus," "A Patriarch of the Eastern Church," and "Heliogabalus, High Priest of the Sun," obtain from the painter about equal favour, whether as to ritual, robes, or anatomies. The latter, however, would not be recognized by the College of Surgeons. "Bacchus" is a sentimentalist of rather weak constitution; he drinks mead, possibly sugar and water, certainly not wine.[50]

Conflating Solomon with his art, the critic follows the standard negative approach to decadence by interpreting the artist's "eccentric" individuality and "genius" as a threat to organic social progress. He becomes the very prototype of the pagan decadent who is seen as both weak and yet a threat to modern British society. In the watercolor *Bacchus* (1867), Solomon portrays the lithe youth as curiously elongated and slack in posture, the leopard skin hanging limp rather than vibrant over his shoulder, while he gazes downward with a distant, tired, even suffering expression on his face. Immersed in, but seemingly not open to, the natural surroundings, Bacchus can be read as a symbolic embodiment of Solomon's isolated sense of himself, but can just as readily be understood as the embodiment of the decadent worldview that the reviewer finds threatening.

As this reviewer observes, Solomon's spiritual interests included Christian ritualism, paganism, and Hebraism, but he seems to approach each with the same intent. In Cruise's words, it is "hard to ignore the religious subject-matter of many of Simeon Solomon's paintings," but it is "also hard to define either the nature of the religious experience they outline or the precise denominational position they indicate."[51] Pater, in his essay "A Study of Dionysus," while not mentioning Solomon by name, compliments Solomon's *Bacchus* (1868) for capturing not only the god's "incorporation" into nature, but also the "darker side" of "a melancholy and sorrowing Dionysus."[52] This pagan spirituality evokes, for Pater, an animal kinship embodied not in the demi-god's energized summer persona but in his melancholy winter one, when Bacchus "become an enemy of humankind," like one of the "wild beasts."[53] *Bacchus* evokes an ambiguous androgyny and eroticism that is also found in a number of Solomon's other spiritual works, such as *The Mystery of Faith* (1870) and *Sacramentum Amoris* (1868). Like Pater, Swinburne understood these spiritual, androgynous characters as signifying desires beyond those recognized through contemporary models of realism and sexuality: "Many of these, as the figure bearing the eucharist of love, have a supersexual beauty, in which the lineaments of woman and of man seem blended as the lines of sky and landscape melt in burning mist of heat and light."[54] In Swinburne's interpretation, spiritual devotion mingles with an ethereal eroticism that he describes, using language suggestive of Pater's "Conclusion," as dissipating into the natural landscape. In complimenting Solomon's ability to capture a sensual spirituality, both Pater and Swinburne emphasize its presence within an interchange of ecological forces, where species distinctions are subordinated to the emotional drive.

Solomon offers a rendering of such an experience of trans-species sympathy in his 1859 pen and ink drawing, *Babylon Hath Been a Golden Cup* (Fig. 3.1). The piece was initially intended as a contribution to the Dalziel brothers' "Bible Gallery" of 100 or more wood engravings, but it proved "much too risqué for that purpose," being exhibited as an independent piece in 1859 at the *Seventh Annual Winter Exhibition of Cabinet Pictures, Sketches and Watercolour Drawings* at the French Gallery in London.[55] Beneath the image in the show's catalogue is the following passage from Jeremiah 51:7: "Babylon hath been a golden cup in the hand of god, which hath made all the earth drunken: the nations have drunken of her wine, therefore the nations are mad."[56] The passage refers to the fulfillment of Jeremiah's prophecy that the Jews' captivity in Babylon

Figure 3.1 Simeon Solomon, *Babylon Hath Been a Golden Cup* (1859), Birmingham Museum. Pen and pencil on paper, 25.5 by 28.3 cm, 10.5 by 11.125 in., Artepics/Alamy Stock Photo.

would lead to them choosing, among other things, to burn incense to the god Baal and follow foreign gods, resulting in the ruin of their kingdom. According to E. H. Plumptre, in *An Old Testament Commentary for English Readers* (1884), the passage describes the Babylonian civilization as materially attractive but immoral at its soul, drawing people to "wild ambitions, and dark idolatries."[57] The same commentary also directs us to the scene as it appears again in Revelations, where the cup is held by a harlot personifying Babylon (17:4–5). The subject thus offers a textbook example of Victorians' own conceptions of a decadent society as one fallen into anarchy through key individuals investing too much into their personal pleasures, at the expense of the health of the larger order.

While Seymour reads the piece as addressing mid-Victorian Jews' concerns regarding secularization, the connection to idolatries,

78 The Lick of Love

bacchanalian revelry, and trans-species sympathies all suggest that Solomon's artwork should also be seen as engaging with paganism associated with the demi-god Pan and the Bacchic maenads, where individualism is sacrificed to an uncategorizable, spiritualist sensuality. Pater had noted such an element of animalistic revelry even in Solomon's painting of the distinctly mellower *Bacchus* (1868). In the foreground of *Babylon Hath Been a Golden Cup*, the artist offers the image of a male in ecstasy while an androgynous figure strokes a harp situated suggestively in the man's lap. The naked figure is Semiramis, the queen of Babylon,[58] although in Solomon's rendering the character's sex is indeterminate. Moreover, the piece is so intensely detailed and the eroticism so lush that, as with many decadent works that followed, it discourages a singular reading; desire spills beyond the fingering of the central figure's instrument to all of the sentient members of the revelry. With the various transient signifiers of the senses – the incense to Baal, the spilt wine and various grapevine motifs, diverse musical instruments, the texture of the leopard's fur, and the sensuality in general – a viewer's habitual compulsion for structured coherence ultimately remains unfulfilled. Interestingly, the use of only pencil and black and brown ink does offer an overall stylistic glazing to the piece, but this compels the viewer to blur the elements together; rather than focusing on the singularity of each participant, one, instead, is engaged by the aesthetic continuities that join the elements with each other.

The very intricacy and excess of *Babylon Hath Been a Golden Cup* fosters unification through its detailed entanglement. Solomon reflects the human viewer's perspective in the vacant eyes of Semiramis but even more seductively in the pseudo-human eyes of the leopard lounging in the foreground with its gaze at the viewer read as easily as a challenge, an invitation, or indifference. The feline's seeming immersion in the sensual moment suggests a mutually rewarding experience, as if the cat and the harpist (and the invited viewer) are familiars. The leopard's legs are bent at the same angle as both of the other figures', a detail that further unites them visually. And both the musician and the leopard appear connected to their physical reality but, as their eyes suggest, they also share a mystical engagement with some alternative plane of being. Seymour notes that the image of the drunken leopard is often associated with Greek Orphic rites,[59] creating a concise linkage between Solomon's recognition of the animal's sensual engagement and pagan spirituality in general. And the allusions to other animals – the dove drinking or cooing on the central figure's lap, the serpentine bracelets of the harpist, the

Simeon Solomon's Animal Appetites 79

Figure 3.2 Simeon Solomon, *Habet! In the Coliseum A.D. XC* (1865). Private Collection. Oil on canvas, 101.5 by 122 cm, 39.875 by 48 in., Artepics/Alamy Stock Photo.

peacock feathers tucked into the harp itself – reinforce this motif of species interrelations.

There is a distinctly different positioning of human–nonhuman animal relations in *Habet! In the Coliseum A.D. XC* (1865), Solomon's most ambitious painting and, for many, his most successful (Fig. 3.2). The oil portrays a group of wealthy women and a meek male servant enjoying gladiatorial death sports from their coliseum balcony. The central figure, probably an empress, looks on with seeming indifference, while one of the other women signals, thumb down, her judgment on whether the victorious combatant should kill his opponent. In ancient Rome, the two options for gestures were a thumb turned up (kill the losing combatant) or a thumb pressed against a fist (spare them). As Merrill Fabry notes, Jean-Léon Gérôme's famous painting *Pollice Verso* (1872) may have got it historically wrong, as the title – translated as "with a turned thumb" – does not definitively clarify whether it is turned up or down, and the audience members' facial expressions are unclear on their position.[60]

80   The Lick of Love

Solomon's *Habet!*, exhibited seven years earlier, is also ambiguous, although the rapt glare and exposed teeth of the woman passing judgment implies a lusty engagement with the blood sport that encourages a reading of her thumb-down gesture (albeit historically inaccurate) as intended to signal the slave not be spared.

While Gérôme's *Pollice Verso* explicitly displays the various gladiators in combat, Solomon's work gives us no combat and only a small section of the audience, leaving the spectacle to the imagination of the artwork's viewer. It is quite possible that the figures are witnessing a battle between gladiators and animals, called a *venatio* or wild-beast hunt. Over 9,000 nonhuman animals (wild and domestic) were killed in the opening ceremonies for Rome's Coliseum alone, and such torture and murder were a standard spectacle, often taken to gruesome extremes involving the mass slaughter of various beings.[61] In *Marius the Epicurean*, Pater's narrator describes the spectacles of the amphitheater, including the slaughter of human and nonhuman animals, as religious occasions: "to its grim acts of bloodshedding a kind of sacrificial character still belonged," marking "man's amity, and also his enmity, towards the wild creatures, when they were still in a certain sense his brothers."[62] As the narrator notes, however, in the spectacles of mass killing, "the humanities of that relationship were all forgotten to-day in the excitement of a show, in which mere cruelty to animals, their useless suffering and death, formed the main point of interest" (136). Pater goes into gruesome detail: baby animals pouring from the spilt guts of their pregnant mothers, a criminal performing the role of Icarus as he plunges into a sea of hungry bears. Marius averts his eyes, judging the practice as unjustified and cruel. The narrator does likewise, even acknowledging having possibly over-extended the descriptions. The scene is both a critique of the inhumanity of certain forms of decadent excess and a decadent rendering of that inhumanity. After forcing upon the reader a distended experience of the brutality and grotesque bloodlust, the narrator then asks the reader whether they perhaps should question their own ongoing tolerance of "the slave-trade, for instance, or of great religious persecution," "each age in turn, perhaps, having its own peculiar point of blindness, with its consequent peculiar sin" (138). Pater shifts the animal rights issues of the Roman empire (as well as, for that matter, pagan acts of co-engagement that were not in any way sanctioned by the other creatures themselves) into the context of the contemporary, at the very time when anti-vivisection politics was in full swing.

Simeon Solomon's Animal Appetites

Later in *Marius the Epicurean*, Pater adds greater affective nuance to the issue by offering a scene in which the novel's hero describes seeing a beautiful but lame horse, wounded probably in the Coliseum, being taken to slaughter, and well aware of it:

> [H]e cast such looks, as if of mad appeal, to those who passed him, as he went among the strangers to whom his former owner had committed him, to die, in his beauty and pride, for just that one mischance or fault; although the morning air was still so animating, and pleasant to snuff. I could have fancied a soul in the creature, swelling against its luck. And I had come across the incident just when it would figure to me as the very symbol of our poor humanity, in its capacities for pain, its wretched accidents, and those imperfect sympathies which can never quite identify us with one another. (239)

The decision to murder the horse is that of the same humans engaged in injuring the creature in the first place. The phrase "although the morning air was still so animating" subtly extends the vitality of the abused victim into a larger spirit (Latin *anima*: soul), with the engagement of the air being directly linked in the next sentence to the "soul" of the creature. Pater, here, foreshadows Salt's theory of "imaginative sympathy" by noting the lack of sympathy that keeps most humans from recognizing our shared spirit.

In Solomon's *Habet!*, despite their absence from the scene, the spirit of nonhuman animals still comes through. Victorians were culturally trained to read visually for narrative, with the woman's cruel gesture the prominent narrative element of the piece. The viewer's attention is drawn to the woman's hand at the bottom center of the painting, and the intricate, serpentine bracelet on her wrist. The gold coiled snake is conjoined to the woman's own identity through the golden robe and the blonde coils of her hair, both of which are unique to her in the scene. The most vibrant and detailed element of the painting, her robe has the oily sheen of satin, thin layers of folds leading upward to yet another golden snake coiled around the woman's neck. If this were not enough to signal the reptilian spirit of the character, her own hand coils around the necklace as if she is half-imagining crushing the life out of the vanquished in the arena. The intensity of her gaze brings to mind Medusa, serpent-haired and able to turn people to stone with her stare. Solomon engages pagan myth to bring forward the woman's animality and thereby signal her inhumaneness. Meanwhile, the fact that the woman has chosen this reptilian jewelry in advance, the indifferent gaze of the empress, and the coiled snake bracelet of a woman in the upper left can be read as

82   The Lick of Love

extending the moral judgment to decadent Rome in general. Pater makes
a similar equation in *Marius the Epicurean*, where Marius, despite his
"sympathy for all creatures, for the almost human troubles and sicknesses
of the flocks, for instance" (13–14), reveals an innate revulsion to snakes
that the narrator characterizes as a "vague fear of evil, constitutional in
him" (14). One of two scenes of snakes mentioned in the novel is of them
breeding on the roadside, while the other has a serpent writhing on an
"African showman" (14), Pater thereby offering an efficient conflation of
the animal, the sexual, and the foreign – the trifecta of the decadent
imaginary. Solomon, however, signals a less clear-cut formulation that is
more in accord with Pater's sympathetic discussions of the victims of
Roman blood sport.

There is at least one additional coil to Solomon's snake–human correlations that warrants consideration. The woman on whom I have focused
my analysis also wears an earring, again in the golden snake motif. From
this small detail to her own coiling, golden figure, she is the embodiment
of an animalistic excess. But the serpent also signifies, through its biblical
allusion, both forbidden knowledge and sexuality, and the motif was
interpreted in such a way by various members of British decadence. In
1865, the same year as Solomon's painting, Dante Gabriel Rossetti had
made initial drawings for *Aspecta Medusa*, a commissioned work
depicting Andromeda looking at the reflection of Medusa's head in a
pond (thereby avoiding direct eye contact and certain death). The piece
was never finished, but Rossetti did do other red-chalk drawings of an
auburn-haired Andromeda as late as 1867. He also wrote a brief poem on
the subject, intended to accompany the picture, which reads in part:

> Let not thine eyes know
> Any forbidden thing itself, although
> It once should save as well as kill: but be
> Its shadow upon life enough for thee.

The poem suggests that, just as Andromeda saves herself by looking only
at the reflection of Medusa's head, one might avoid the risks of engaging
in deviant pleasure by experiencing a diluted version through art. We are
perhaps similarly encouraged by Solomon's *Habet!* to engage the cruel,
decadent spectacle at a remove, through his painting of the golden
woman's relish and not through an image of the actual cruelty.
Swinburne's poem "Faustine" appeared a bit earlier, in 1862, with the poet
taking the heroine's sadistic pleasures at watching gladiatorial blood sport
and twisting it around not only "Sapphic song" and "sterile growths of

sexless root | Or epicene," but also the nest of "coiled obscene | Small serpents with soft stretching throats" that caress her.⁶³ His essay "Notes on Designs of the Old Masters of Florence" (1868), which also mentions the Medusa motif, appeared later in the decade, written about the same time as Pater's own "Notes on Leonardo da Vinci" (1869). Pater's essay addresses the *Medusa* at the Uffizi Gallery (attributed at the time to Leonardo da Vinci), focusing like Solomon's painting on "the fascination of corruption [that] penetrates in every touch its exquisitely-finished beauty."⁶⁴

In an analysis of Solomon's turn to Sappho as a way for the artist to engage his own homosexuality, Stefano Evangelista notes his frequent depiction of his initials SS as a snake twining around a rod, the ancient Greek *asklepian*, named after Asclepius, the demi-god associated with medicine and healing. As Evangelista points out, this allusion introduces "echoes of spiritual sickness into Solomon's canvases."⁶⁵ This rendering of the snake as simultaneously seductive and disagreeable brings to mind Pater's later depiction in *Marius the Epicurean* of the hero's negative reaction to breeding snakes. The serpentine image is also possibly an allusion to the Greek myth of the blind Tiresias who, separating a pair of breeding snakes, is transformed by Hera into a woman, who then goes on to marry and have children. Due to his own less common desires, Solomon recognized such conflicted compulsions as also part of himself. Therefore, Solomon directs our attention in *Habet!* not to the repulsive

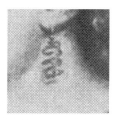

Figure 3.3   Simeon Solomon, detail from *Habet! In the Coliseum A.D. XC* (1865). Private Owner. Artepics/Alamy Stock Photo.

Figure 3.4   Simeon Solomon, detail from *Babylon Hath Been a Golden Cup* (1859). Private Owner. Artepics/Alamy Stock Photo.

object on view in the stadium, but to the acts of affective engagement, to the golden woman eagerly leaning forward with an expression of blood-lust on her face that, while comparatively contained, brings to mind the maenads (themselves often wearing snake-crowns) in their bloody Dionysian rites. In *Habet!*, the artist's sense of his own affinity with this primal drive is most subtly captured when one notes that the figure's serpentine earrings are the very design Solomon would adopt as the signature for many of his works, including *Babylon Hath Been a Golden Cup* (Figs. 3.3 and 3.4). Through the graphic echo, Solomon connects his queer desires with a violent energy; the link is made all the more apparent when one recalls that Britain had only relatively recently begun to make certain blood sports illegal.

Michael Field and Species Compassions

Poets and lovers Katherine Bradley and Edith Cooper (aka Michael Field) did not develop as strong a set of relationships as Solomon had with the dominant members of the British decadent community, but their inter-ests did richly overlap with Solomon's and others'. They began their literary career at a time when middle-class society was particularly invested in issues both of women's suffrage and animal sympathies. "It was an era when Higher Education and Women's Rights and Anti-Vivisection were being indignantly championed," as Mary Sturgeon notes in her biography of the authors, "and when 'æsthetic dress' was being very consciously worn – all by the same kind of people. Katharine [sic] and Edith were of that kind."[66] The two attended Classics and Philosophy lectures at University College Bristol and engaged in the debating society.[67] Katherine even served for a number of years as secre-tary of the Anti-Vivisection Society in the Bristol suburb of Clifton.[68] These interests also touched on Field's investment, like Solomon's, in paganism as a context for exploring same-sex attraction. Field's writings, however, repeatedly turn away from coherent formulations of desire as fixed, let alone sutured to identity. Jill Ehnenn and Yopie Prins have both brought attention to this ambiguity as a queer formulation.[69] With regard to their poetry collection *Whym Chow: Flame of Love* (1914) – privately printed upon the death of their beloved dog, "Our Bacchic Cub"[70] – David Banash has also argued that the dog in a sense gave a means for the poets to "enact their passion through the mediating body" of the pet as "a space of possibilities to transform themselves."[71] At various times in their lives, both women felt intense affections not only for each other and for Whym Chow, but also for various men, literary luminaries, art works, and, I would argue, spiritual forces. As their work suggests that they recognized, any single formulation of polysexuality could not capture the fluctuations of type and intensity among these attractions across time and it is this skewed affect, more so than their same-sex desires, that drives their decadent ecological vision. Decadent paganism, for them, served not simply as a source of a coy symbolism or a spirituality sympathetic to their nonnormative interests, but as a free-floating, pseudo-naturalized space of possibilities that did not demand their articulation as such. This is the spirit in which I described the concept of queer desires earlier, in line with Halperin's broader vision of the queer as referring to that which is "at odds with the normal, the legitimate, the dominant."[72]

The queer ecological linkages embodied in the ekphrastic poetry collection *Sight and Song* affirm Field's understanding of their desires as not coherently trans-species, but as mutating engagements beyond ready comprehension. In these poems, Field work to give themselves up to sympathetic correspondences that existed centuries earlier. As Marion Thain proposes, Field's aims with this collection reflect Pater's argument that the sensuous elements of each art form foster aesthetic experiences and imaginative engagements that cannot be translated into another art form. One is not encouraged to read the collection for the literal meaning of the poetry, nor the meaning of the paintings represented, nor even the sensual beauty of the figures, but for affective responses to qualities beyond human embodiment. This "synaesthetic metamorphosis," Thain argues, "is not dependent on abstracting content from form in order to represent it within another mode, but a more complete apprehension of something designed for one sense through another sensory channel."[73] The process brings to mind Vernon Lee and Kit Anstruther-Thomson's experiments at the time with psychological aesthetics, as well as Lee's nature writing discussed in the next chapter, where emphasis is placed on the body's affective relation to another object.

In proposing that the poems in *Sight and Song* express "not so much what these pictures are to the poet, but rather what poetry they objectively incarnate,"[74] Field ask for an impressionistic erasure of any sense of agency, including that of the visual artists and the poets themselves. They aim at something from which human "theory, fancies, [and] mere subjective enjoyment" are removed, "suppressing the habitual centralisation of the visible in ourselves" (v, vi). The call for a decentering of the human encourages readers to try to engage with form from its own standpoint,

86 The Lick of Love

and yet it is a request Field believe will result in "an impression, clearer, less passive, more intimate" (vi). The absence of the anthropocentric individual, the poets propose, results in a more vital experience, one that extends beyond the ego to a collective intimacy (bringing to mind Solomon's *Babylon Hath Been a Golden Cup*). Affections, for Field, are not simply a set of linkages between the individual and the art object, but a current, vital paganism manifest as imaginative eco-engagements. While *Sight and Song* sustains a human agenda that can usefully be read as a queer aesthetics, intimacy arises through the surrender of identity – as poet, as human, as self.

As with Solomon's ecological aesthetics, nature in *Sight and Song* is not the context for experience but part of the sentient engagements, just as the poets themselves can be understood as immersions into the channels of transhistorical pagan collectivism. In "Correggio's *Antiope*," for example, a response to Correggio's painting *Jupiter and Antiope* (*c.* 1528), Field sandwich the glowing nude Amazon between a sleeping cupid and a satyr (one winged, the other goat-legged – both already trans-species), offering a polytheistic rendering of Antiope's sensual spirituality (Fig. 3.5).

Following the traditional myth, the poem notes that the satyr is actually Zeus in disguise, who, enamored by the hunter, is about to rape her. The god's deviousness imbues paganism with a note of cruel deception, but Field offer a unique contribution to the myth that undermines a correlation of paganism purely with characters who, like Zeus here, enact heteronormative power paradigms. The poem focuses almost entirely on the figure of the sleeping Antiope, with Zeus appearing only toward the end and doing little more than allowing the reader a new perspective through which to continue getting pleasure from the heroine's beauty. The ocular indulgence is formulated, meanwhile, as part of a set of tendrils of engagement that work to characterize the Amazon as the focus of various attractions and disseminations of desire. As Antiope "cuddles on the lap of earth," next to her lies "her woodland armory," a reference to the "doe-skin" quiver of arrows in Correggio's painting, but also more subtly to the trees in which she is bowered. She lay

> curled beyond the rim
> of oaks that slide
> Their lowest branches, long and slim,
> Close to her side;
> Their foliage touches her with lobes
> half-gay, half-shadowed, green and brown.

Figure 3.5   Correggio, *Jupiter and Antiope* (*c.* 1528). Louvre Museum, Paris. Oil on canvas, 190 by 124 cm, 74.8 by 48.8 in., vkstudio/Alamy Stock Photo.

"The supineness of her sleep," we are told, is "Leaf-fringed and deep," with not animality but ecology more broadly becoming an element of the erotic, sliding its limbs along her body, caressing her with its leaves (16–18). Antiope is sensually enwrapped by the protective folds of the environment with which, even in sleep, she shares connections.

88   The Lick of Love

A similar ecological dynamism can be seen represented in the poem
"Botticelli's *Birth of Venus*." The 1486 painting *The Birth of Venus* on
which Field's piece is based has been interpreted as rendering the
Neoplatonic notion that the admiration of physical beauty functions as
an avenue to comprehending that of the spiritual. Field, however, disturb
the focus on the beautiful central figure of the goddess by engaging first
with elements in the ecological periphery – the waves, a shell, roses.
Gradually, there is intermingled among these natural items mention of
Venus's garment, her hair in the wind. The depiction eventually coheres
at the end of the first stanza, in the acknowledgment of "a girl" (13). Just
as the elements surrounding Venus are given primacy, the goddess herself
is diminished as no more than a "chill, wan body" needing protection
from the very crispness of the air. Botticelli's painting captures this
moment of Venus's realization as an opportunity for sexualized consumption sanctioned in later readings as a spiritual experience. Field, however,
desexualize the figure but enhance its function as a site of linkage among
diverse ecological elements. At the moment of the female body being
realized in the poem, it is already being enfolded again within the
ecosystem, as Flora's flower-bedecked "rose" cloak enwraps her exposed
flesh. Rather than confirming a Neoplatonic ideal, the poem dallies on
the earthly elements in the artwork, eventually revealing the goddess in a
fragile moment of a state of selfhood that, even in the painting, seems
formulated by others, and then only to submerge her again, in the
remaining three stanzas, among the natural elements and the pagan
deities Flora, Zephyrus, and Boreas. These are respectively, the goddess of
flowers and spring, the god of the west wind (the wind of spring), and
the god of the north wind. In Field's rendering, then, Venus is a sentient
point of convergence among elements that conflate the sensual and the
mythological, a formulation that actually is not in conflict with the
Neoplatonic reading.

Similarly, in "Correggio's *Saint Sebastian*," the Christian martyr and
"pagan saint"[75] tied to a tree and shot with arrows is himself likened to
aspen leaves that, despite being held to their stems, rejoice. At the time
the poets were writing, the saint was already being used as a symbol for
same-sex male desire[76] and, in their poem, Field associate his painful
martyrdom and his relationship with Christ to their own same-sex love
and, one might assume, the network of desires signaled in *Sight and Song*
in general. As the poem's narrator says to St. Sebastian, in admiration of
his sustained faith despite the arrows piercing his flesh, "Oh might my
eyes, so without measure, | Feed on their treasure, | the world with thong

and dart might do its pleasure!" (33). In the face of modern persecution, Field call for a forbearance sustained by their own "treasure" – perhaps spiritual devotion, perhaps love. In these examples, where pagan gods and Christian martyrs are depicted as extensively wrought constructions that remain invested in a multispecies ecology, Field bring attention to the artifice of both representation and perception, while countering the separation between human and other natural elements. In contrast to the visual artists' objectification of their subjects as the central focus of the artworks, in each of these poems, the anthropocentrism of Field's own society's value systems is disturbed through the veneration of a perspective that leaves the key figures not only decentered, but conceptually sustained through relationships within an eco-spiritual network. Rather than an escape from contemporary society's hypocrisy, the collection's paganism (often suggested through images of nature-based intimacy) offers a confrontation with it. And the more their vision appears an overwrought, idealized fantasy, the more fully is the poetry demanding that the realism in both the arts and social convention acknowledge the fabrications of their own character.

Field's poem "Piero di Cosimo's *The Death of Procris*" is the most poignant rendering in their collection of this type of trans-species affection, in part because of its emphasis on an intimacy among animals. Cosimo's own life appears to have prepared him to capture the complex emotional exchanges among diverse sentient beings. A contemporary of Botticelli, another Florentine artist, Cosimo vacillated between Christian and pagan subjects. He apprenticed under Cosimo Rosselli, contributing to Rosselli's frescoes for the Sistine Chapel, but he was also influenced by Hugo van der Goes and his naturalist attention to landscape. Cosimo's mythological works are particularly notable for their often playful rendering of human–nonhuman animal hybrids. According to Giorgio Vasari, in his foundational *Lives of the Most Excellent Italian Painters, Sculptors and Architects* (1550), Cosimo was during much of his life not only a loner and eccentric, but also emotionally intense, showing fear or impatience with everything from thunder and shadows to crying children, coughing men, and flies. For Vasari, Cosimo's relationship to nature was especially notable:

> He would never have his rooms swept, he would only eat when hunger came to him, and he would not let his garden be worked or his fruit-trees pruned; nay, he allowed his vines to grow, and the shoots to trail over the ground, nor were his fig-trees ever trimmed, or any other trees, for it pleased him to see everything wild, like his own nature; and he declared

that Nature's own things should be left to her to look after, without lifting a hand to them. He set himself often to observe such animals, plants, or other things as Nature at times creates out of caprice, or by chance; in which he found a pleasure and satisfaction that drove him quite out of his mind with delight.[77]

Vasari's vibrant rendering creates an individual who was eccentric and misanthropic in relation to his society but was more viscerally and emotionally in sympathy with nonhuman animals and the wilderness, his own untamed character echoing the untrammeled nature he admired. As Vasari observes, because "his life was that of a beast," Cosimo's art captures "a certain subtlety in the investigation of some of the deepest and most subtle secrets of Nature."[78]

Field's poem suggests they recognized this intensely natural sympathy in Cosimo's work. The untitled painting that Field reference is now best known as *A Satyr Mourning over a Nymph* (c. 1495) (Fig. 3.6), evoking parallels with Pan and the Death of Syrinx. During the nineteenth century, however, it was commonly known as *The Death of Procris*, and read as a depiction of a scene from Ovid's tale in which Procris, distrustful, spies on her husband Cephalus while he is hunting. Mistaking his wife for a wild animal, Cephalus kills her with one of his arrows. Notably, unlike virtually all other visual renderings of the myth, Cosimo's dying female is consoled by a satyr rather than by her husband. In addition, Cosimo's version is unique in having her wounded in more than one place, intended perhaps to evoke St. Sebastian's martyrdom.

Joseph Bristow has argued that "[d]eath, especially its link with regenerative powers, always summoned Michael Field's greatest pagan energies."[79] Initially, however, the image Field offer of Procris dying is

Figure 3.6   Piero di Cosimo, *A Satyr Mourning over a Nymph* (c. 1495). The National Gallery, London. Oil on poplar, 65.4 by 184.2 cm, 25.7 by 72.5 in., Peter Horee/Alamy Stock Photo.

Michael Field and Species Compassions 91

seemingly less about regeneration than isolation and solitude: "Far from the town she might not gain | Beside a river-mouth | She dragged herself to die" (48). The isolation is specifically from society, just as Cosimo, Vasari tells us, himself refused attention from others in his dying days. Field follow Cosimo's artwork in ensuring that, despite the absence of humans, a plethora of other species is insinuated in Procris's passing, rendered as "foolish Procris! – short and brown" (47) melding into the very earth itself:

> And thus she lies half-veiled, half-bare,
> Deep in the midst of nature that abides
> Inapprehensive she is lying there,
>   So wan;
> The flowers, the silver estuary afar— ...
> unto themselves they are:
>   The dogs sport on the sand,
> The herons curve above the reeds ... (49)

The sense of the female figure buried within the natural environment is reinforced by the grammatical structure, which leaves it ambiguous as to whether it is Procris or nature that is "inapprehensive," with Cosimo's own image actually suggesting both. The sentence "So wan; | The flowers, the silver estuary afar ... | unto themselves they are" similarly leaves the reader uncertain whether it is the dying figure or nature that is described as wan. This conflation of the heroine with the natural environment echoes Cephalus's mistaking her for a wild animal in the myth, as well as Cosimo's positioning of the two key subjects that witness her death. The painting shows her consoled by a faun, while the hunting dog she had given her husband as a gift stands devotedly at her feet. The image echoes the species sympathies of other poems from *Sight and Song*, such as "Botticelli's *Birth of Venus*" and "Correggio's *Antiope*." In the former, the earth goddess is flanked by the pagan deities Flora, Zephyrus, and Boreas. In the latter, Antiope lays on the ground sandwiched between two trans-species entities – an angel and a satyr. However, Field's attention to the details of the satyr's expression and gestures in "Piero di Cosimo's *Death of Procris*" is unique.

What stands out in Field's poem on Procris is that it offers a less humane rendering of the two consoling figures than does the visual artist himself, but one more akin to what humans perceive as the harsh realities of nature, as well as the limited comprehensibility of trans-species affections. The satyr in the painting is shown gently cupping Procris's shoulder and brushing her hair from her brow while gazing down with

92   The Lick of Love

sympathy. In Field's poem, however, the "creature of wild fashion" with "boorish bristles" "grips | Her shoulder [while] the right [hand] | along her forehead moves." The gestures come across as cold, even gruff, and are echoed by the satyr's "indecisive" eyes and the "coarse pity" on his lips (50). Field go on to conflate the satyr's and dog's conception of the death, as they display "like expression of amaze | and deep, | Respectful yearning." What the poem captures here is not human love and loss, but an engagement among diverse, sentient contributors to a queer ecology. In a remarkably astute articulation of this nonhumanist experience, the poets write:

> These two watchers pass
> Out of themselves, though only to attain
> Incomprehensible, half-wakened pain.
> They cannot think nor weep
> Above this perished jealousy and woe,
> This prostrate, human mass. (50–51)

The roughness of the satyr is a personification of the landscape, the "tide and bloom and bird" that surround the trio and carry on "unstirred" (51). At the same time, however, it is remarkable that Field allow the satyr and the dog not only to conceptualize the existence of lives and realities outside themselves, but also to communicate their emotions.

As with Solomon, Field turned to Classical mythology in *Sight and Song* not only to carve out a cultural space for recognizing unconventional love and desire between two humans. The poets did so also in order to engage with an eco-spirituality committed to decentering the human and the individual. Unbeknown to Field, they would later in life develop a shared affection with a dog that would be so intense as to redefine as interspecies both their own collective relationship and arguably their individual senses of self. In *Whym Chow: Flame of Love*, the women celebrate what they tell God is their own "trinity":

> I did not love him for myself alone:
> I loved him that he loved my dearest love. … .
> It is to feel we loved in trinity, …
> So I possess this creature of Love's flame, …
> O symbol of our perfect union, strange
> Unconscious Bearer of Love's interchange.[80]

As with the technique of conflation that they use in "Piero di Cosimo's *Death of Procris*," both the perfect union and the dog are described as strange simultaneously, because they are indeed both part of the same

Queer Engagements or Faunus-Haunted Ways 93

strange affection. One notices the concerted effort to complicate any sense of individuality, with affection marked by a tangled set of exchanges: "I loved him that he loved my dearest love" and "we loved in trinity," respectfully queering the orthodox concept of the Christian holy trinity. Both symbol and partner, the dog allows Field a pagan "interchange" of respect and desire as pure and intense as those so often attributed exclusively to human–human intimacy, a trinity they first experienced twenty years earlier, through Cosimo's tender image of a dog, a satyr, and a nymph.

Queer Engagements or Faunus-Haunted Ways

Ouida's novel *Ariadne: The Story of a Dream* (1877) opens with a sleep-deprived narrator appreciating a marble sculpture in the Caesars' Gallery of the Villa Borghese:

> Outside the sun was broad and bright upon the old moss-grown terraces and steps, and not a bough was stirring in the soft gloom of drooping cedar and of spreading pine. There was one of the lattice casements open. I could see the long lush grass full of flowers, the heavy ilex shadows crossing one another, and the white shapes of the cattle asleep in that fragrant darkness of green leaves. The birds had ceased to sing, and even the lizards were quiet in these deep mossy Faunus-haunted ways of beautiful Borghese, where Raffaelle used to wander at sunrise, coming out from his little bedchamber that he had painted so prettily with his playing gleeful Loves, and flower-hidden gods, and nymphs with their vases of roses, and the medallions of his Fornarina.[81]

Of the statue he is admiring, the narrator observes, "It is not called an Ariadne here in Villa Borghese: it is called a young Bacchus; but that is absurd."[82] And as his semiconscious ruminations continue, he laments, "if only the old myths could but have been kept pure they had never been bettered since Pan's pipe was broken."[83]

This opening scene depicts the narrator as an aesthetically sensitive, educated man whose admiration of a sculpture becomes confused not only with the languid heat of the afternoon and the sights, sounds, and aromas of the landscape, but also with the long sentences of tangled descriptors rambling down the page. Even the artworks and architecture, as he goes on to explain, become part of the melding experience as they seem to come to life, with the sculpture of the androgynous Ariadne and then other deities even speaking to him. It is understandable that the emphasis on Classical paganism and the extended, sensuous descriptions would lead the critic for *The Saturday Review* to define the novel as an exemplar of decadent aesthetics and the animal-rights activist herself as one who is able to "burn, with a hard gem-like flame, with the best of them."[84] The uncertain gender of the "young Bacchus" does lead one to wonder if Ouida is alluding to one of the drawings or paintings of a youthful, languid Bacchus that Simeon Solomon had on show over the previous decade. In the context of this chapter, I am taken by Ouida's dissolution of time and space and the novel's immediate melding of the human, the ecological, and the aesthetic, with the very pillars of the institution, we are told, bending like flowers while the marble statuary is given voice. The novel's dominant conceit is that Classical paganism does persist through the dream, but also through the emotional investment and imaginative engagement of the narrator. With the added gender ambiguity of Ariadne/Bacchus, Ouida offers a pagan decadence that is wholly enmeshed within a discourse of trans-species sympathy mediated, in part, through aesthetic pleasure.

In this chapter, I have turned to Solomon's artwork and Field's ekphrastic poetry to consider what decadence contributes to the modern model of imaginative inter-species sympathy formulated by Henry Salt. For him, modern humanist individualism relies on a conceptual separation of the human from the other species and elements of one's environment, often resulting in callousness, if not cruelty. Sympathy, as he conceives of it, is not simply kindness but the sincere effort (however faulty) to maintain a sustained integration throughout one's sentient ecology. Solomon and Field both found their nonheteronormative desires drawing them to a pagan aesthetic that produced art not only representing but stimulating intimacies in its viewers or readers. Such a decadent ecology is queer, in part, by acknowledging underrepresented desires, but particularly by celebrating transhistorical affective engagements among humans, animals, plants, and ecologies in general. While Solomon's works produced in the mid-nineteenth century brought forward the possibilities of melancholy and sorrow that are part of such engagements and that accord with the experiences at that time of many men with same-sex attractions, Field's poetry, which arose in the context of a vibrant animal rights and suffrage context, more openly celebrates the erotics of species relations. Both envisioned an eco-spirituality that disturbed the technology of anthropocentric, heterosexual privilege, while also contributing to a sympathetic collective, what Edward Carpenter described in 1889 as an "intimately knit" network that extends to the core of all living entities.[85] This is not to be generalized as a

Queer Engagements or Faunus-Haunted Ways

community of individuals extending every-present kindness across species; rather, it is a network dominated by the affections themselves. What we find in decadent engagements among species is not principally arguments for other animals' rights, but a sense of sympathy maneuvering along channels whether with or without human (or other species) recognition.

It is with such a network that Field attempt to interact in *Sight and Song* when they search for "intimate" aesthetic engagements by "see[ing] things from their own centre, by suppressing the habitual centralisation of the visible within ourselves" (vi). As was the case for Solomon, the poets' explorations of destabilizing systems of engagement operated on a different scale than the gender debates of the age, as in fact at times did their approach to living in the world. In addition, Field's respect for the immersion of being within a sympathetic ecological network is to be recognized as a feminist gesture in itself, given that it works in support of respect for diversities of desire and community. The works by Solomon and Field addressed in this chapter offer not just examples of nonnormative attractions, but queer visions of affective engagements extending into distant space and time, even across different notions of space and time. In this sense, their works make a distinct contribution to our understanding of queer decadent ecology, marking affects, compulsions, and yearnings that thrive beyond normative human formulations of purpose and value.

CHAPTER 4

The Genius Loci *as Spirited Vagabond in Robert Louis Stevenson and Vernon Lee*

[A] walking tour ... should be gone upon alone, because freedom is of the essence; because you should be able to stop and go on, and follow this way or that, as the freak takes you; and because you must have your own pace[.] ... And then you must be open to all impressions and let your thoughts take colour from what you see. You should be as a pipe for any wind to play upon.

– Robert Louis Stevenson, "Walking Tours"[1]

In *Marius the Epicurean*, Walter Pater conceptualizes paganism as a variety of philosophical and aesthetic perspectives, each engaged with the eco-spiritual politics of its moment. As I mentioned in my second chapter, the character Marius himself comes across less as an adventuresome hero or a soul on a trip of self-discovery in the tradition of the standard Bildungsroman than as a meandering introvert often seemingly surprised by the surroundings through which "the freak" takes him. This image of the cerebral traveler is complicated by Pater's representation of humans as principally intermingling contributions to networks of engagements with their ecological traces marked on a global geography and through the furthest reaches of time. One can get a sense of human effect on this grand scale only if one adopts a nonhumanist lens, such that speciesism has a less distorting control over the perspective of the landscape of existence. In this de-individuating model, Pater's hero appears not as a character but as the decadent embodiment of the Anthropocene itself – more an earthly immortal than a person. Through this lens, the novel can be understood to be making it easier to conceptualize and comprehend an extended period of geologic transition. The reader is now able to perceive the extremely slow process of the human species' contributions to ecological change because Pater has taken geological history and sped it up, like a film on fast-forward, so that an entire transhistorical process is concentrated into one human lifetime, what Pater condenses even further in the "Conclusion" to *Studies in the History of the Renaissance* into a "short day of frost and sun."[2] In light of the author's view of paganism as an atemporal life force, Marius comes across as wandering so glacially across the Italian countryside because he in fact *is* the landscape itself as it morphs through deep time.[3]

Most earnest contributors to the pagan revival were aware that their veneration of nature or the environment vacillated between a Marius-like state of passive absorption into the experience, on the one hand, and a more disconnected consideration and assessment of such engagements, on the other. As the previous chapter's look at Simeon Solomon and Michael Field suggests, those who were spiritually invested in some form of paganism often saw the environment as a fundamental element of their sense of self – the living embodiment of their belief system, for example, or an essential element of their sexuality or ethnicity. And yet, conversely, many also perceived themselves and their surroundings as an inseparable tangle of mediations, a perspective that humbled the ego, coupling any sense of individuality with one of trans-elemental mutability operating beyond both personal agency and analytical distance. In this chapter, I extend my discussion of the sensual eco-immersions found in works by Solomon and Field by addressing the ways in which both Robert Louis Stevenson and Vernon Lee turned to the *genius loci* to render these two aspects (the immersive and the analytical) of their identification with nature. Each of these authors offer a useful expansion of the decadent canon because they arrived at the issue along different currents of thought and conceived of both "nature" and "the self" in different ways that reflect their cultural origins, political concerns, and life opportunities. Both, however, frame their inquiries within the changing landscapes of industrialization, commerce, and nationalism. Moreover, both use models of desire and decay, as well as the persona of the wandering adventurer, akin to Marius, to signify the individual as a shifting, often undirected force within a decadent ecology interfusing the spiritual, material, and psychological.

It is not just place but the movement through it, or its movement through you, that proves crucial to both authors' conceptions of the *genius loci* in their travel writing. Andrea Kaston Tange has noted the immense generic range that nineteenth-century travel writing covered, creating a field of study for those scholars "interested in questions of empire, identity, diaspora, geography, botany, colonial settlement, environmental studies, art history, and tourism, among other topics."[4] As Tange points

98   The *Genius Loci* as Spirited Vagabond

out, a particular emphasis in scholarship for the past thirty years has been on such writing that engages with "the intersection of identity and empire."[5] Stevenson traveled and, indeed, lived all across the globe, while Lee spent her life moving around and living in Western Europe. Although both spent considerable parts of their lives residing in cities, this chapter addresses their writings on traveling primarily in nature. Such nonfiction was a well-established subgenre by the time Stevenson and Lee turned to it, having gained traction with the Romantic writers and their formulations of fresh modes and degrees of pleasure in engaging in the experience. Nature-centered travel writing in Britain was reinforced by different forms of imperialist expansion and exploration, the rise of tourism, and developments in transportation, communication, and travel accommodation. The writings by Stevenson and Lee on which I focus do not represent even the diversity of their own works within the subgenre. Rather, the pieces I address are those that use aspects of decadent aesthetics and philosophy to explain a sense of the self as a momentary coalescence of ecological forces.[6] As I argue, the very pacing of modern experiences within the environment influenced Stevenson's and Lee's formulations of their sentiments regarding nature. Their pagan-invested works encourage sensitivity to the passing of time itself as part of people's ecological engagements – their experience of, and as, the *genius loci*.

This chapter looks at Stevenson and Lee as figures of British decadence who, in their efforts to formulate a sense of the dissipated, modern self, developed pagan ideas of a wandering *genius loci*. Lee has been recognized as a major contributor to decadence who, despite her disagreements with key aspects of it, was deeply appreciative of the writing of her "kind personal friend" Pater.[7] Stevenson, meanwhile, is not part of the established canon of decadent authors, his work not offering provoking challenges to sexual convention or sustained engagements with more familiar aspects such as the urban *flâneur*, a hyper-refined style, or evocations of languor and ennui. And yet Pater himself may have sensed overlapping interests, for he chose not to read Stevenson for fear that the latter was such a strong writer that he "might lead me out of my path."[8] As I explain in my introduction, a major aim of my study overall is to acknowledge such paths or currents that, while often underappreciated, contributed to the larger flow of British decadence – a phenomenon best appreciated as not clearly circumscribed, nor monolithic or internally consistent. Stevenson is a prime example of such a contributor, early in his career not only echoing some of Pater's major arguments but exploring similar aspects of Classical paganism and historical figures such as Marcus Aurelius. His work also engages in fresh ways with cosmopolitanism, international aesthetics, the exoticization of foreign cultures, and the politicization of national or regional paganisms. Both Stevenson and Lee appreciated the interweaving of natural, rural, regional, and urban models of understanding that nurtured the rise of pagan interest in their time. Indeed, as Stevenson and Lee suggest, it is precisely because paganism sustained interest in both modern modes of progress and the sensual, affective realities of the natural that the *genius loci* came to mark so boldly the mutual imbrications of the two.

Genius Loci and the Pagan Panpsychic

Contributors to a Victorian understanding of the *genius loci* were drawn by a desire to conceptualize the ways in which history, collective memory, and mythic tradition shaped locative spirituality and helped make it culturally significant.[9] Stevenson and Lee developed different formulations of the *genius loci*, but their investments were spurred on by much the same modern sense of individuals' special relationships to nature. The concept of the *genius loci* arose with the Roman view that each person had his or her own accompanying spirit, which gradually led to the belief that families, buildings, and locations had their protective spirits as well. With veneration not being a purely religious act, such a spirit could be attributed to an extremely broad range of objects. As the Christian poet Aurelius Prudentius Clemens (348–c413) observed to his fellow Romans, "[w]hy talk to me of the genius of Rome, when your wont is to ascribe a genius of their own to doors, houses, baths, and stables; and in every quarter of the town, and all places, you feign thousands of genii as existing, so that no corner is without its own ghost?"[10] Among Romans, the term "genius" could also mark respect for an emperor, an empire, or the denizens of a region. In fact, the earliest articulations of *genii locorum* arose with a view of them not as secret bowers to which one might escape from the bustle of modern human society, but as locations marking a spiritual investment in the politics of the age.

There are various reasons why Victorians were drawn to the Roman understanding of the *genius loci* as a protective force associated with a particular location. It could be seen to align with the popular Romantic rendering of nature as imbued with a divine vitality that marked a special relationship between the viewer and the world, while it also fit effectively with the strong Classical influence on nineteenth-century paganism, which more explicitly addressed the possibility of the human as an engrained element of a larger ecology. Moreover, the veneration of the spirit of places and objects is not exclusive to Classical models of paganism. Celtic, Germanic, occult, and what in the twentieth century came to be called Wiccan practitioners can welcome a spirit to virtually any location through the use of affective objects in ritual. Members of the occult Hermetic Order of the Golden Dawn, for example, used particular objects, clothing, arrangements of items, and so on to convert private homes, meeting halls, and theaters into sites appropriate for magic ceremonies, with the removal of the sacred items then dispelling the spiritual force that had been invoked. Attention was further heightened during the nineteenth century with increased popular interest in British sites of Roman altars to *genii locorum*, including even one in Scotland to the spirit of all of Britain.[11] Meanwhile, Celtic sites developed strong nationalist connotations in England, Ireland, Scotland, and Wales. As in the Roman era, the locations were understood to manifest an eco-spiritual energy, but their significance often arose in response to particular historical or political events. The rise of interest in both archaeology and folklore studies in Britain during this time further developed the idea of specifically natural locations being imbued with their own unique energy or soul. More people became familiar with the traditional awareness that trees, groves, springs, and rocks carried their own animist qualities or that they were populated by spirits such as fairies, elves, or goddesses.

Science, of course, played a key role in understandings of the *genius loci*. Based on the concept of the *anima mundi*, or "world soul," the term "animism" was coined in 1720 by the German physicist George Ernst Stahl to describe the view that sentient beings are produced through an immaterial soul. Meanwhile, Stahl maintained the Cartesian view of humans as superior to other animals, the latter functioning not through an immortal soul but more as mechanical entities. By the time E. B. Tylor introduced the term "animism" into common English usage with his influential *Primitive Culture* (1871), a century and a half later, animal rights activism had brought forward the ethical contradictions in Stahl's speciesism and his privileging of humans over other animals and life forms.[12] Partly rooted in Darwinian evolutionary theory, Tylor's idea that there is a universal purpose behind the cultural development of religions encouraged Victorians to understand animism as supporting the position that all natural things (trees, water, crystal formations, and so on) have forms of vitality akin to souls or minds that warrant respect.

The issue of the nonhuman soul was also being engaged at this time through the philosophical concept of panpsychism (discussed in Chapter

2), the view that all matter had a form of mind or consciousness, and thus also an element of agency, force, or pull.[13] As Adela Pinch notes, by the end of the nineteenth century "the dominant position in British philosophy was absolute idealism: a belief in reality as a single unified consciousness or conscious experience."[14] A key issue in this field is the distinction between animism and panpsychism, the former referring to the presence of a soul and the latter to a presence of some form of consciousness. George Henry Lewes, who coined the term "panpsychism" in English in 1879 as part of his magnum opus *Problems of Life and Mind* (1874–1879), acknowledged the attributes of vitality and sensibility in plants as in animals, albeit operating in distinctly different ways. He did not accept the claim, however, that the presence of sensibility established the presence of a soul.[15] Efforts to articulate the sensibility of plants or crystals as soul-driven, he argues, are flawed "anthropomorphism," while also concluding that the concept of panpsychism relied on a law of continuities that erases crucial differences.[16] "Does not oxygen *yearn* for hydrogen?," he mockingly queries at one point.[17] He writes:

> To some minds eager for unity, and above all charmed by certain poetic vistas of a Cosmos no longer alienated from man, the hypothesis has attractions. But while its acceptance would introduce great confusion into our conceptions, and necessitate a completely new nomenclature to correspond with the established conceptions, it would lead either to a vague mysticism enveloping all things in formless haze, or to a change of terms with no alteration in the conceptions. By speaking of the souls of the molecules we may come to talk of the molecules as men "writ small."[18]

As with the concept of the *genius loci*, that of panpsychism goes back at least to the ancients; however, during the nineteenth century it was marked with a popularity far greater than anything that has been seen since. The contingencies between discussions of panpsychism and pagan worldviews have also surfaced in recent theoretical works. Gregory Nixon opens his review of David Skribna's essay collection *Mind that Abides: Panpsychism in the New Millennium* (2009) with the rhetorical query: "Is the great god Pan reborn? For a while there, it seemed every intellectual movement began with the prefix 'post,' implying non-totality, but now there are indications that 'pan' (all) is returning to provide another answer to one of the most basic of ontological questions: What is the relationship of mind to matter?"[19] Nixon's mythological reference is intended as a bit of light homonymic humor, but his turn to the demi-god nevertheless affirms the cultural memory that still connects panpsychism to Pan, who not only leaves his mark throughout the modern history of decadence, but who rose during the Victorian and Edwardian periods to become the most popular pagan deity of the age.

Within recent eco-paganism, one of the most discussed conceptual variations on panpsychism is the idea that the earth or universe operates like a single organism or an intersubjective mass of indistinguishable organisms sharing one consciousness. In 1979, the British chemist James Lovelock put forward what is now the most popular of these models, known as the Gaia Hypothesis. "The evolution of organisms," Lovelock proposes, is "so closely coupled with the evolution of their physical and chemical environment that together they constitute a single evolutionary process, which is self-regulating."[20] In models such as Lovelock's, humans are seen as influential but not necessarily essential components of the biosphere in which they exist. In response to critiques of his argument as not taking into consideration evolutionary theory, Lovelock declares, "[i]n no way is this a contradiction of Darwin's great vision. It is an extension of it to include the largest living organism in the Solar System, the Earth itself."[21] Lovelock situates his hypothesis effectively within scientific discourse, and has vehemently argued against the adaptation of his argument by pagans who, since the book's publication, have been drawn to his work for its framing through Classical mythology. He takes the term Gaia from the myth in which Chaos gave birth to the siblings Gaia and Eros, respectively, mother earth and the god of sex, lust, and love. The myth personifies the Earth as a living goddess, a formulation that harmonizes with pagan animism, which does not only see natural objects as imbued with a soul but also sees these instances of sentience as enmeshed, co-reliant forces. Of equal importance, the myth also offers an early fusion of the earth-centered spirituality and nonnormative sexuality – the pagan and the queer – that characterizes not only decadent ecology but also current pagan politics and that, not surprisingly, has consistently contributed to forms of spirituality characterized by human's affective relations with nonhuman beings, including not only animals and plants, but also all things with animist or panpsychic force. In addition to its mythological conceptual frame, Gaia theory is in line with paganism in its effort to shift away from a human-centered perspective. "I see the world as a living organism of which we are a part"; Lovelock states, "not the owner, nor the tenant, not even a passenger on that obsolete metaphor 'spaceship Earth.' To exploit a living world on the scale that we do is as foolish as it would be to consider our brains supreme and the cells of other organs expendable. ... The philosophy of Gaia is not humanist."[22]

While the term Gaia has attained common usage among current pagans, they are not only interested in offering hypotheses on the way in which our planet or biosphere is formulated but are also drawn, in stark contrast to Lovelock, to engaging with and celebrating a spiritual dissipation of the self within a natural collective. Today's various paganisms are united in their nature-based polytheism and their respect for the diversity of peoples' views and values. As with the feminist, queer, trans, Black, Latinx, and other rights movements whose histories parallel in insightful ways that of the modern pagan movement, pagans' rejection of any one discourse as capturing their diverse worldviews and value systems has come with an intense caution regarding organized authorities and fixed laws and systems of categorization and differentiation. As I note in my first chapter, Thom van Dooren warns pagans that the desire for a dissipation of selfhood within some protean collective risks disempowering the diversity politics by which earth-veneration today often defines itself. Modern paganism's equal-but-diverse holism risks formulating the sort of homogenizing panpsychism about which Lewes warned. As Stevenson's early writings make apparent, the conundrum also echoes the bind of nineteenth-century liberalism, where the values of independence and personal growth were weighed against the rights of society at large and the importance of collective stability. In *On Liberty* (1859), John Stuart Mill attempted to formulate a collective utilitarian ethic that would support, yet minimally impinge upon, the freedom of the individual. As van Dooren and others note, however, paganism asserts that nonhuman species and entities are also members of this collective. The conception of multi-sentient subjectivity suggests that much of Victorian liberal philosophy framed the debate in such a way that presupposed a humanist elitism that itself, in spirit, undermines the values espoused by philosophers such as Mill, even accounting for the ambivalences within their work. In his writing, Stevenson explicitly acknowledges an early investment in Classical myth as a guide for his philosophy of life. But it is in the engagements that he portrays himself having with the nonhuman that he most succinctly captures his simultaneous efforts to be transfused by the *genius loci* and render the experience in words.

Stevenson's Pagan Vagabondage

Many of Stevenson's contemporary readers envisioned him as a pagan, but of a type that held a wholesome and surprisingly broad set of connotations in Victorian culture. He was not called a pagan because he was

104   The *Genius Loci* as Spirited Vagabond

seen to be a devout worshipper of Classical or other non-Christian goddesses and gods. Nor, generally speaking, was he referred to as such as a euphemism through which to point out his affiliations with other contributors to modern decadent culture. Stevenson does not come to mind when one thinks of British decadence, but it does not take much processing to recognize the influence of Pater on his early works and their pagan rebelliousness. There are also links between Stevenson's rallying for individualism and similar concerns in decadent authors such as Algernon Charles Swinburne and Oscar Wilde. As a popular and much admired author, Stevenson produced works that brought decadent interests in such ideas as an open ecology and dissipated ego into the mainstream. His paganism was seen as showing itself primarily in his anti-bourgeois investment in living a full and adventurous life as free as possible from the constrictions of consumerism and conservative tradition, an attitude that his admirers found articulated throughout his writings, but especially in his earlier work. In a review of *An Inland Voyage*, Stevenson's first published book, which appeared in *London* in May 1878, a reviewer (possibly W. E. Henley)[23] emphasized the author's individualism and free will in relation to other humans. Stevenson's piece of travel writing, we are told, presents the author as "almost a pagan in his fine indifference for dogma and tradition, no less than his freshness of spirit, his vigorous elasticity of temper, his pleasant open-heartedness."[24] Fresh, vigorous, and open-hearted – one can sense an easy extension of this combination of values to a Victorian model of masculinity that stood in contrast to the delicacy and detail found in other works of the period that were being read as pagan, such as Swinburne's poetry or Simeon Solomon's paintings.

Other readers, however, saw Stevenson's investment in living life to the fullest as a sign of irresponsibility and sensual excess. Such a view can be found in the first expansive assessment of the author's writing – William Archer's 1885 piece "Robert Louis Stevenson: His Style and His Thought," which appeared a year before *Strange Case of Dr Jekyll and Mr Hyde* (1886). In Archer's view, Stevenson was a "lover of literature for its own sake," far more concerned with style and surface than with substance and the difficult realities of life.[25] His writing is marked by a disarming "happy-go-lucky-ism," Archer declares, that never fully engages with deeper, moral issues.[26] While, for the 1878 reviewer, this attitude was a part of Stevenson's paganism, for Archer it reflected an ethical lassitude suggestive of the urban dandy-aesthetes who had begun gaining so much attention. Stevenson was displeased by his fellow-Scotsman's reading and, in a letter to Henry James dated October 28, 1885, he criticizes the persona Archer created of him as "the rosy-gilled 'athletico-aesthete'."[27] While Archer actually never refers to Stevenson as pagan, James in an 1887 piece critiques Archer for portraying the author as "a happy but heartless pagan, living only in his senses" and for failing to appreciate the "appeal to sympathy and even to tenderness ... beneath the dancing-tune to which he moves."[28] These three pieces – Archer's essay, Stevenson's letter to James, and James's own later essay – effectively portray the Stevensonian pagan as embodying a range of connotations that include the superficial aesthete, the wholesome nature lover, and the ethically mature and sensitive writer.

As with James's essay, Richard Le Gallienne's 1895 collection *Robert Louis Stevenson and Other Poems* admires the moral politics within the author's work, with Le Gallienne giving more attention to Stevenson's panpsychism. The nature worship that, by the 1890s, had become a common complement to a growing skepticism regarding organized religion is apparent in many of the works in Le Gallienne's collection, including "Tree-Worship." This poem describes various animals and pagan spirits who partake of the bounty and protection of a huge, old tree – a "grim fortress" and "old monster."[29] Dryads, fairies, and witches scooch along the branches of this natural temple to make room for doves, larks, nightingales, owls, moths, bats, all accompanied by cattle, a ghost, and a "ghastly Æolian harp" that like a "human corpse swings, mournful, rattling bones and chains."[30] Despite being chosen to be the first poem in the inaugural volume of *The Yellow Book* (to which James contributed the first story), the piece was not well received. Jason Boyd notes that, despite its declaration of nature worship, the poem ends with a contradictory "reference to 'all-loving' God and a description of the tree not as a god, but as 'God's best Angel of the Spring'."[31] Philip Gilbert Hamerton criticizes "the fallacious theology of the last stanza as being neither scientific nor poetical."[32] A similar but often more ambiguous folding of paganism and Christianity into each other also concludes other pieces in Le Gallienne's poetry collection, such as "Natural Religion," "Faith Reborn," and "The Animalcule on Man."

As Boyd suggests regarding "Tree Worship," Le Gallienne's effort to bring together his diverse images and allusions under a Christian God in the last of eighteen quatrains comes across as rushed and unconvincing. The previous three stanzas, however, maintain a pagan perspective that proves more sincere in its evocation of lost hope, even desperation. "All other gods have failed me always in my need," laments the narrator,

"Unto thy strength I cry – Old monster, be my creed!"[33] The language offers the combination of awe and terror that had already proven especially evocative among literary depictions of otherworldly experiences in works such as Arthur Machen's *Great God Pan* (1890, 1894). The pre-penultimate and penultimate quatrains capture the panpsychic sympathies of paganism in general. Here the narrator, "with loving cheek pressed close against thy horny breast," asks the tree to "fill full with sap and buds this shrunken life of mine."[34] The intense intimacy of the engagement speaks to the more sexual or violent pagan depictions in works such as Machen's *The Hill of Dreams* (1907), Michael Field's "Pan Asleep" (1908), and Aleister Crowley's "Hymn to Pan" (1919). Unlike Machen and Crowley's works, however, Le Gallienne's emphasizes the spiritual desire for a permanent fusion of the self with the tree and, by extension, the other sentient beings, spirits, and natural elements with which it is enmeshed and mutually reliant.

One finds strong metaphoric parallels between "Tree Worship" and the opening poem in Le Gallienne's collection, "Robert Louis Stevenson: An Elegy." The poet's efforts to capture his predecessor's genius as a writer result in a panpsychic model of the biosphere, indeed the cosmos:

> The shell that hums the music of the seas,
> The little word big with Eternity,
> The cosmic rhythm in microcosmic things—
> One song the lark and one the planet sings,
> One kind heart beating warm in bird and tree—
> To hear it beat, who knew so well as he?[35]

While lacking the desperation found in "Tree Worship," the elegy harmonizes with that poem in its sublime metaphors. This particular passage stands out for capturing Stevenson's pagan spirit through an evocation of transience, enhanced by an emphasis on the aural. Le Gallienne incorporates into this cosmic schema the art of writing, the "little word" effectively containing some sign of the universe of things. Le Gallienne works to suggest that Stevenson's paganism, like his own, was not in conflict with Christian beliefs, so much as complementary or cooperative. Stevenson's writings sustain, the later poet proposes, an eco-spiritual appreciation of the world that melds not only the individual but also his immortal writing into the organic, universal consciousness to which paganism draws us.

Writing at the start of the twentieth century and clearly hoping that his pagan contemporaries had hosted the last of their ritual gatherings,

Stevenson's Pagan Vagabondage

G. K. Chesterton assures us that "Of the New Paganism (or neoPaganism), as it was preached flamboyantly by Mr. Swinburne or delicately by Water Pater there is no necessity to take any very grave account, except as a thing which left behind it incomparable exercises in the English language." After conflating paganism with the British fathers of decadent style, he goes on to note its ready connection to modern immorality: "The ideas about the ancient civilization which it has let loose in the public mind are certainly extraordinary enough. ... The pagans, according to this notion, were continually crowning themselves with flowers and dancing about in an irresponsible state[.] ... Pagans are depicted as above all things inebriate and lawless."[36] However, while Chesterton attacks Pater's and Swinburne's takes on paganism for the sensuality of their writing, in another essay he celebrates Stevenson as "a highly honourable, responsible and chivalrous Pagan, in a world of Pagans who were most of them considerably less conspicuous for chivalry and honour."[37] Later in this work, Chesterton conflates paganism with the literary qualities of the admirable artist. Stevenson, he says, "believed in craftsmanship; that is, in creation. He had not the smallest natural sympathy with all those hazy pagan and pantheistic notions often covered by the name of inspiration." Rather than accept a "doctrine of mystical helplessness," Stevenson believed in human will and, in particular, in "the act of creative choice essential to art."[38] What Chesterton criticizes from those elements culturally gathered under the modern umbrella of paganism is the set of styles that had come to characterize modern British decadence, as well as what he sees as a lazy approach to artistic creation where one maximizes one's sensual experience of life while waiting for inspiration to hit, or not. But while Stevenson has no affinity with this attitude, Chesterton proposes, he is nevertheless pagan in his desire to experience life and engage his writing fully, energetically, and with a commendable moral core. What makes him a pagan is his drive to appreciate the natural world not by aestheticizing it but by allowing himself to be immersed in it, and returning to it repeatedly without the strictures of social habits and customs. While this interpretation is distinct from Le Gallienne's formulation of Stevensonian paganism as spiritual, it does not contradict it; rather, each writer is foregrounding that aspect of Stevenson's interests that he sees as supporting his own.

Stevenson was a tourist of life in many ways but, as Chesterton emphasizes, not in the sense of being a passive viewer of the changing landscape or others' experiences. Rather, he took on adventures marked by novelty

108   The *Genius Loci* as Spirited Vagabond

and risk, and adopted a pagan eye that allowed himself to be more intensely engaged with the sentient energies he encountered. Stevenson perhaps most vividly captures this persona in Mr. Hyde. A chimeric character, he is most often interpreted, within the reality of the narrative, as an actual person, a psychological vision, or a mental state. But Hyde can also be seen as the cityscape itself – as a primal life force whose affective energies feed into each member of the populace as much as draw from them. Hyde is, in this reading, the spirit of the place, while the struggles that Dr. Jekyll experiences are those of the rational individual who refuses to accept that the wild and the rational feed off of and into each other, are indeed part of the same visceral network. For Stevenson, a major manifestation of such cultural denial was the increasing control that middle-class mores and consumerist economics were having on the freedom to imagine and develop one's sensual extensions through space. In this context, Stevenson's paganism stands as a critique of liberal humanist subjectivity, a position that he maintained throughout his career. The question becomes whether his work ever really escapes the constrictions that contemporary culture imposed upon his idea of self, whether he at best simply replaces a bourgeois self-identity with a popu-list Romantic one, or whether he ever sincerely accepts the possibility of a shift of authority away from both society and the humanist ego to a vaster organic force of life, death, and decay.

Well before his problematization of speciesism and sentience in *Jekyll and Hyde*, his consideration of the innate virtues of the savage in *Treasure Island*'s character of Ben Gunn, or his exploration of the nature-based belief systems of people from the South Seas, Stevenson had turned to Classical mythology to address humans' relations to their environments. Both *An Inland Voyage* (1878) and *Travels with A Donkey in the Cévennes* (1879) foreground the narrator's sensorium: his sensations, perceptions, and culturally inflected understanding of them. In this process, the jour-neys become not simply the movement of Stevenson-as-narrator through space and time, but the exploration of his being as a part of the sensory environment of *other* life travelers (such as animals, plants, and the river on which he takes his inland voyage). The representations of place in both of these travelogues capture perhaps more boldly than anything he produced afterward the sensitivity that James, Le Gallienne, and others throughout Stevenson's career recognized in his sense of his own transient role in the *genius loci*. When, in a discussion of Walt Whitman, Stevenson conjectures that "there is a sense in which all true books are books of travel,"[39] he is referring not to physical trips but to immersions in imaginative adventure and exploration through the various arts. Similarly, in "Providence and the Guitar," Stevenson complements musicians and painters as "people with a mission – which they cannot carry out."[40] And in *An Inland Voyage*, he characterizes even the least successful of actors as dignified because "he has gone upon a pilgrimage that will last him his life long, because there is no end to it short of perfection."[41] Stevenson's ideal artist – whether a musician, painter, actor, or writer – is one whose aesthetics are an extension of their sensorial vagabondage.

Even before his first publication, the author was engaging Classical renderings of *genius loci* and mythologizing place as a site of transience and self-dissolution. In an 1872 letter to his friend Charles Baxter, he frames a recent country walk as a form of mythic memory. A close companion of Stevenson's and the son of the prominent Edinburgh lawyer Edmund Baxter, Charles would eventually become Stevenson's legal and financial advisor. After a winter of ill health, Stevenson took some time in March of 1872 seeking relief in the village of Dunblane, Scotland. In a friendly, rambling message curtailed only when he runs out of paper, the author explains to Baxter why he cannot meet him for a stroll the next day:

> I came yesterday afternoon to Bridge of Allan, and have been very happy ever since, as every place is sanctified by the eighth sense, Memory. I walked up here this morning (three miles, *tu-dieu!* A good stretch for me) and passed one of my favourite places in the world, and one that I very much affect in spirit, when the body is tied down and brought immovably to anchor in a sick-bed. It is a meadow and bank at a corner on the river, and is connected in my mind inseparably with Virgil's Eclogues. "*Hic corulis mistos inter consedimus ulmos*," or something like that the passage begins (only I know my short-winded Latinity must have come to grief over even this much of quotation); and here, to a wish, is just such a cavern as Menalcas might shelter himself with from the bright noon, and, with his lips curled backward, pipe himself blue in the face, while *Messieurs les Arcadiens* would roll out these cloying hexameters.[42]

For much of his life, Stevenson's chronic tuberculosis meant that any notable amount of exertion was difficult and yet, a consistency of his character, he found walking crucial to his engagement with nature, just as he found traveling through the landscape a central element of works such as *Travels with a Donkey*, *Silverado Squatters* (1883), and even *Jekyll and Hyde*. As this passage from his letter to Baxter suggests, there is for Stevenson a crucial connection between the way he experiences memory (both personal and cultural) and the way he moves across a location. In a

110   The *Genius Loci* as Spirited Vagabond

highly original set of correlations, he writes not that he stopped at his special location but "passed" it. It is a place, he goes on to explain, that he "affect[s] in spirit" when, due to illness, he is "immovabl[e]." In a form of reciprocal engagement, just as he at times meanders through the *genius loci*, the location likewise permeates through the immobile author via spiritually inflected reminiscence.

Adding a third layer to these interactions between individual and location, Stevenson goes on to describe the spiritually invested spot as linked to Virgil's *Eclogues* not simply by an imaginative correlation, but by a sort of anamnesis. The setting is a configuration of the site of the encounter between the shepherds Menalcas and Mopsus who, in Virgil's text, consider playing the pipes and singing the praises of the shepherd Daphnis under a leafy bower of hazels and elms before deciding instead to retreat to the coolness of a cave. Although Daphnis was mortal, later shepherd-poets deified him, just as Menalcas and Mopsus do in the *Eclogues*. Stevenson, meanwhile, by conflating his memories with mythology, in his letter, effectively constitutes himself within the tradition of Virgil's shepherd-poets for whom life and art, labor and pleasure, are inseparable. The author's engagement with a particular location animates his memory of Virgil's works, as well as his veneration of Daphnis's legacy, a spatiotemporally dynamic, spiritually inspired aesthetic worldview that he then attempts to capture in his epistle to Baxter. Through this Scottish Arcadia, Stevenson realizes himself not as a circumscribed individual but as a component of an immortal shepherd-poet lineage and, more importantly, animist pastoral tradition. In this sense, the contemporary assessments of Stevenson's paganism as, in his own dismissive words, that of an "athletico-aesthete,"[43] actually fits the author's own early articulation in this private missive, where his creative interests are an innate element of his physically taxing experience of the *genius loci*.

In a letter to his friend Sidney Colvin sent in February 1878, however, Stevenson notes his investment in a somewhat different pagan persona, one that Victorians would come to see primarily as Swinburnian. Here he states his hope that Walter Crane's drawing of the demi-god Pan for the frontispiece of his forthcoming *An Inland Voyage* – his record of a canoe trip down the River Oise – appears "'cruel, lewd, and kindly,' all at once."[44] "[T]here is more sense in that Greek myth of Pan," he goes on, "than in any other that I recollect except the luminous Hebrew one of the Fall. ... If people would remember that all religions are no more than representations of life, they would find them, as they are, the best representations." The language echoes that of Pater's "A Study of Dionysus," which appeared in the *Fortnightly Review* only a few months before Stevenson plunged into the Oise. In the essay, Pater represents Pan as "half-way between the animal and human kinds," "a presence; the *spiritual form* of Arcadia, and the ways of human life there." Pan is not just a myth, an entity, or a collection of entities for Pater, but a locative spirit and a process, "the ways of human life."[45] According to Eli Edward Burriss, Pan was the mythological character "nearest in [Stevenson's] heart"[46] and, in the same spirit as Pater's essay, the subject of Stevenson's letter to Colvin shifts from a description of the significance of the frontispiece first to a celebration of the pagan myth of Pan and then to a conception of spirituality as a vital presence. Not only does Stevenson appreciate paganism as a viable spirituality but also, like Pater, he describes it as a living, organic, mediatory force warranting his respect and self-investment.

This conviction is made stronger in Stevenson's 1881 essay "Pan's Pipes," in which he declares that "Pan is not dead, but of all the classic hierarchy alone survives in triumph; goat-footed, with a gleeful and an angry look, the type of the shaggy world."[47] Stevenson opens the piece with ideas and language reminiscent of Pater's "Conclusion" to *Studies in the History of the Renaissance*:

> The world in which we live has been variously said and sung by the most ingenious poets and philosophers: these reducing it to formulæ and chemical ingredients, those striking the lyre in high-sounding measures for the handiwork of God. What experience supplies is of a mingled tissue, and the choosing mind has much to reject before it can get together the materials of a theory. ... There is an uncouth, outlandish strain throughout the web of the world, as from a vexatious planet in the house of life. Things are not congruous and wear strange disguises: the consummate flower is fostered out of dung, and after nourishing itself awhile with heaven's delicate distillations, decays again into indistinguishable soil.[48]

In passages such as this, one senses both the author's skepticism of scientific materialism and his impassioned investment in an earth-based spirituality, as well as his desire to conceptually subordinate his ego to a greater, ecological force. In the 1875 essay "An Autumn Effect," he refers to this site of energy precisely as the "spirit of the place."[49] Jean Perrot argues that Pan represented for Stevenson "a genuine natural energy which was lacking in the hearts of those of his contemporaries who were unnerved by ambient decadence and dominant materialism."[50] As Stevenson writes in "Pan's Pipes," "Highly respectable citizens who flee life's pleasure and responsibilities[,] ... how surprised they would be if they could hear their attitude mythologically expressed and knew themselves as tooth-chattering ones, who flee from nature because they fear the hand of Nature's God!"[51] This combination of life's pleasure with responsibility may be what led Chesterton to describe Stevenson as an "honourable, responsible and chivalrous" pagan. While Chesterton's language emphasizes an anthropocentric moral order, however, Stevenson's sense of responsibility frequently undermines the privileging of humans over other forces of nature. The trans-species spiritual conflation can be seen in "Pan's Pipe's" and its image of a "shaggy world,"[52] where the planet is envisioned as an ecological entity that can be read in the contemporary eco-pagan sense both as a collective of interdependent, living phenomena and as a pagan cosmos, what Stevenson here calls "the web of the world."[53] The piece encourages an approach to life "where the salt and tumbling sea receives clear rivers running from among reeds and lilies; fruitful and austere; a rustic world; sunshiny, lewd and cruel."[54] These last words echo those in his 1878 letter to Colvin – "cruel, lewd, and kindly" – to describe the emotional energy that we find embodied by Pan in *An Inland Voyage*.

In *An Inland Voyage*, Stevenson expands upon the philosophical vision he sketched out in his 1872 letter to Baxter regarding Pan's Arcadia as a turbulent interfusion of identification and location. The publication demonstrates the author's early investment in a pagan conception of the world and especially nature, marking him as a particularly virile, wholesome devotee. The travelogue would become, in William Gray's words, "a cult classic of the neopagan movement," with Stevenson having no less than "anticipated, and indeed helped to create, the neopaganism and ruralism of the aesthetic 1890s,"[55] as represented, for example, by Le Gallienne's 1895 collection of poems. In this work, Stevenson's concept of nature is not sublime but, more akin to works such as William Wordsworth's "Tintern Abbey," engages an agrarian pastoralism as a background of affective cohesion upon which to explore less fixed emotional experiences. In this spirit, the work echoes Classical paganism in which humans are portrayed not as passive connoisseurs/consumers of the landscape but as organically integrated components in biological processes of being. That said, Stevenson's engagement is clearly that of a temporary visitor, a youth who comes across as performing the rougher lifestyle of camping and canoeing before inevitably returning to a more civilized world. This is not, however, to suggest a falsity or weakness in the adventure, so much as to recognize the author's own ready acknowledgment of the pragmatic realities by which humans' paganisms are always to some degree shaped or curtailed.

An Inland Voyage recounts a canoe trip that the twenty-six-year-old and his friend Walter Grindlay Simpson took through France and Belgium in the autumn of 1876. In their sail-rigged boats Arethusa and Cigarette, the two men made their way from the town of Maubeuge to that of Pontoise, stopping at various towns and natural sites to rest or restock. In addition to descriptions of the trip down the river, the work offers passages of self-analysis and philosophical speculation and, as such, can easily be read as the author's voyage into himself. In this sense, the piece follows in the self-exploratory spirit of works by Henry David Thoreau and Whitman, both of whom Stevenson greatly admired and on both of whom he wrote essays published first in the *New Quarterly Magazine* (1878) and *Cornhill* (1880), respectively, and then in his 1882 collection *Familiar Studies of Men and Books.*[56]

The chapter of *An Inland Voyage* in which Stevenson's pagan epiphany is most overtly portrayed is "The Oise in Flood," in which he elaborates on a view of Pan not as a character but as "the beauty and the terror of the world" (104). The climactic realization occurs when Stevenson and his canoe are entangled in a low-slung tree that throws the author into the swollen river's current. In this scene, it is not only the author on the verge of drowning who is depicted as terrified, but the river itself, which he portrays as something akin to what Deleuze and Guattari would call a pack, as "[e]very drop of water ran in a panic, … so numerous [yet] so single-minded" (105). As the chapter moves from a meditation on Pan to a description of the swift, swelling currents, Stevenson also depicts the processes of nature as increasingly one with his own. One recalls Pater's "Conclusion" to *Studies in the History of the Renaissance*, which first appeared as part of an unsigned review of William Morris's poetry. In it, Pater notes "one characteristic of the pagan spirit these new poems have which is on their surface – the continual suggestion, pensive or passionate, of the shortness of life; … the desire of beauty quickened by the sense of death."[57] In the review, Pater also discusses Morris's meditation on a dreamlike otherworldly engagement, a type of "delirium" that "reaches its height with a singular beauty" in the poem "Blue Closet," which centers on a depiction of drowning.[58] In language Paterian in its quick flow and tumultuous clauses, Stevenson describes how his "blood shook off its lethargy, and trotted through all the highways and byways of the veins and arteries, and in and out of the heart, as if circulation were but a holiday journey." "We could no longer contain ourselves and our content," he rejoices, vowing "eternal brotherhood with the universe" (107, 111). In the chapter's final reference to Pan, the author is no longer

114   The *Genius Loci* as Spirited Vagabond

depicted merely as an embodiment of nature's beauty and terror but *as interfused* with it through a loss of self-identity marked by awed humility.

In an 1887 essay, published but two years after Pater's *Marius the Epicurean* in which Marcus Aurelius is a key character, Stevenson declares of Aurelius's *Meditations*: "The dispassionate gravity, the noble forgetfulness of self, the tenderness of others, that are there expressed and were practiced on so great a scale in the life of its writer, make this book a book quite by itself."[59] The qualities Stevenson venerates in Aurelius's works are akin to those that Pater's Marius develops in combining Aurelius's Stoic philosophy with a grace and humanity that leads Marius eventually to sacrifice himself for the sake of his persecuted Christian friend. It is a similar combination of loss of self and affection for humanity that the author attempts to represent in this scene of submersion from *An Inland Voyage*, a single image that distilled Stevenson's sense of the *genius loci* as a self-negating process. Here we note again the quality of nobility – of self-sacrifice for the greater good of society – that Chesterton felt distinguished the author from those decadents who – as Paul Bourget explained – disruptively privileged the individual over the collective. It is, however, the more extensive periods of repetitive, half-conscious paddling through the landscapes that result in Stevenson's ultimate apotheosis. "What philosophers call ME and NOT-ME, EGO and NON-EGO, preoccupied me whether I would or no," he explains of these periods of calm, evoking Ralph Waldo Emerson's *Nature* (1836). Stevenson writes:

> There was less ME and more NOT-ME than I was accustomed to expect. … [M]y own body seemed to have no more intimate relation to me than the canoe, or the river, or the river banks. Nor this alone: something inside my mind, a part of my brain, a province of my proper being, had thrown off allegiance and set up for itself, or perhaps for the somebody else who did the paddling. I had dwindled into quite a little thing in a corner of myself. I was isolated in my own skull. Thoughts presented themselves unbidden; they were not my thoughts, they were plainly some one (*sic*) else's; and I considered them like a part of the landscape. (198–99)

With the self no longer needing or caring to keep its head, Stevenson allows himself to pass through a pagan state, having finally, as he tells us, become "the happiest animal in France" (201). In these passages, as elsewhere in *An Inland Voyage*, the author suggests that any being is more than one sentient phenomenon or, more precisely (as the water drops would suggest), more than one panpsychic force. At the start of the travelogue, Stevenson directs his critique most blatantly at "the bear's hug of custom gradually squeezing the life out of a man's soul," declaring his wish to avoid becoming "a mere crank in the social engine" (25, 26). "To know what you prefer," Stevenson proposes, "instead of humbly saying Amen to what the world tells you you ought to prefer is to have kept your soul alive" (25). By the end of the work, however, he has shifted away from making combative demands for his freedom from bourgeois constraints, now reveling in those passive "incurious" moments (199) when he loses himself in a "low form of consciousness" (198). "What a pleasure it was! What a hearty, tolerant temper did it bring about! There is nothing captious about a man who has attained to this, the one possible apotheosis in life, the Apotheosis of Stupidity; and begins to feel dignified and longævous like a tree." This conclusion suggests a wholly different understanding of Le Gallienne's "Tree-Worship" than that which I offered earlier; it is a piece that can now be interpreted as the veneration of Stevenson as a vegetative ideal or, for Le Gallienne, as a component of the *genius loci* much as the shepherd-poets that Stevenson himself, early in his career, depicted in such a role.

The animistic attitude that Stevenson celebrates in his sub-beastly apotheosis surfaces in different forms elsewhere in his writings, receiving extended consideration in his second travelogue, *Travels with a Donkey*. This work depicts a young Stevenson in France conducting a twelve-day, 120-mile hike with a donkey principally for the recreational adventure, but also to write a populist work. The piece, however, also proves to be a study of what he finds to be the peripatetic requirement for his spiritual engagement with the landscape, and an analysis of this experience as transspecific. Like *An Inland Voyage*, this travelogue introduces early on the narrator's disdain for the drudgery of most people's work-a-day lives: "People were trooping out to the labours of the field by twos and threes, and all turned round to stare upon the stranger. I had seen them coming back last night, I saw them going afield again; and there was the life of Bouchet in a nutshell."[60] In contrast to this daily march of the masses, Stevenson celebrates his own peregrinations as undirected and incomplete, like those of the artists he admires. "For my part," he tells us, "I travel not to go anywhere, but to go. I travel for travel's sake. The great affair is to move; to feel the needs and hitches of our life more nearly; to come down off this feather-bed of civilization" (81). The language echoes that of William Hazlitt's 1822 essay "On Going a Journey," which Stevenson greatly admired.[61] Hazlitt opens his piece with the declaration "Nature is company enough for me. I am then never less alone than when alone."[62] "When I am in the country," he explains in an elaboration of this sense of de-humanized sensualism, "I wish to vegetate like the country." Stevenson describes his own spiritual outlook as likewise capacious, open, and undirected; when, noting in *Travels* his respect and admiration for a group of Trappist monks whom he encounters, he brings to mind Whitman in "Song of Myself," distinguishing himself as "one who feels very similarly to all sects of religion, and who has never been able, even for a moment, to weigh seriously the merit of this or that creed on the eternal side of things" (118–19). Stevenson appears compelled to invite a universal spirituality, but he continually complicates the gesture by his concerted effort not to assume a vision grander than his personal impressions allow. This conflict between a compulsion to capture a sense of holistic spiritual cohesion and an awareness of the subjectivity of his perceptions results in the narrator's ongoing frustration with himself, rendered by his efforts to write as if wholly transfused by the ecological experience.

For Stevenson, the hike itself is ideally a sustained and immersive experience. "To wash in one of God's rivers in the open air seems to me a sort of cheerful solemnity or semi-pagan act of worship. To dabble among dishes in a bedroom may perhaps make clean the body; but the imagination takes no share in such a cleansing" (181). Paganism is portrayed here as a spiritual practice that purifies the spirit and re-aligns one's perspective with that of a more profound reality. On more than one occasion, however, the words ring hollow, as the narrator appears to forget his admiration for drifting. He describes a traveler such as himself as "hurrying by like a person from another planet" (27). Elsewhere, he speaks of "the glee of the traveller who shakes off the dust of one stage before hurrying forth upon another" (127). While Stevenson-as-narrator appears uncharacteristically goal driven in such passages, elements of the environment with which he engages themselves often come across as understanding the aesthetic value of undirected wandering. The author, I suggest, wrote a travelogue in which Stevenson as the pagan narrator operates as a check on Stevenson as the more pragmatic traveler. During one passage, the hiker can see in the distance the mountain peak that marks his destination, but his efforts to reach it are thwarted repeatedly. "Choose as I pleased," the writer bemoans, "the roads always ended by turning away from it, and sneaking back towards the valley, or northward along the margin of the hills" (34). The traveler's frustration becomes apparent when, as dusk begins to set in, he reaches "a wilderness of turf and stones" that he describes as having "the air of being a road which should lead everywhere at the same time" (35). A road of infinite possibilities is, of course, a succinct image for the process of ego-dissolution that he elsewhere suggests should be his philosophical ideal. Here, however, the actual traveler (as opposed to Stevenson as pagan philosopher) marks the occasion with a sense of futility rather than inspiration.

While there is a realism to the narrator's shifts between moments of pleasurable emersion and frustrated misdirection, the author is using this conflict as a means through which to explore his eco-spiritual beliefs more fully. As part of this visioning process, he has the donkey Modestine, the traveling "companion" with whom he literally breaks bread (231), make the most valiant effort to exist in a state of vagabondage; the term is appropriately rooted in the Latin for "to wander," but it also fits the care-free, positive spirit of Stevenson's own poem "Vagabond" in his collection *Songs of Travel* (1896). At the same time, the allusion to bondage brings forward not only Modestine's state of forced labor but also her seeming lack of tactical curiosity or even awareness of possible choice in her position within the landscape. It is this latter crucial component that the narrator, as human, is unable to sustain. The philosophical depth of the travelogue arises in Stevenson's portrayal of his fraught relationship with the wily equine who, carrying his pack, persistently refuses to follow the travel plans of the man with whom she is saddled.

Much of the text is taken up with the seemingly ornery donkey's unwillingness to cooperate. Modestine constantly feels compelled to stop and eat the roses. But, more than this, she seems to take stoic pleasure in belligerence, and, as Morgan Holmes notes, Stevenson's repeated beatings fostered much of the negative response the work received upon publication.[63] Stevenson often depicts Modestine as a rather lazy, indifferent beast of burden. "What that pace was, there is no word mean enough to describe"; he complains, "it was something as much slower than a walk as a walk is slower than a run; it kept me hanging on each foot for an incredible length of time; in five minutes it exhausted the spirit and set up a fever in all the muscles of the leg" (23). Should the author move at all ahead of his colleague or lag at all behind, she immediately stops to nibble on some clump of grass, utterly unconcerned with Stevenson's aims. "In a path," he explains,

> she went doggedly ahead of her own accord, as before a fair wind; but once on the turf or among heather, and the brute became demented. The tendency of lost travellers to go round in a circle was developed in her to the degree of passion, and it took all the steering I had in me to keep even a decently straight course through a single field. (58)

Stevenson balks at the delay in completing his scheduled journey of ten miles a day for twelve days. In this passage, however, he effectively

118   The *Genius Loci* as Spirited Vagabond

demonstrates his own inability to adopt the pacific acceptance he proposes to be the state of the ideal vagabond. Elsewhere, he describes whipping Modestine, while here he limits his language to describing her as unintelligent and a "brute" (a callous term that was receiving rhetorical evaluation at this time through the animal rights movement). What ultimately stands out in the conflict is the way in which Stevenson's narrator is the one who comes across as erratic in spirit, while the seemingly irrational donkey maintains an attitude more akin to that of the undirected travelers whom the author venerates for their sensorial receptivity. In fact, it is not despite but due to Modestine's seeming indifference to the destination that the narrator eventually accepts an incurious view of his adventure distinctly different from the

Figure. 4.1   Walter Crane, frontispiece to Robert Louis Stevenson, *An Inland Voyage* (London: Kegan Paul, 1878). McFarlin Library, University of Tulsa.

goal-oriented one with which he began: "I had a vision ever present to me of the long, long roads, up hill and down dale, and a pair of figures ever infinitesimally moving, foot by foot, a yard to the minute, and, like things enchanted in a nightmare, approaching no nearer to the goal." Much like the roads to nowhere and everywhere, Modestine does no less than draw the narrator to accept a perspective of travel as meandering and endless, the very elements the author defined repeatedly throughout his career as the ideal type of travel. And the text ends with a portrayal of trans-species affection not apparent until after the narrator has sold his "lady friend" (232). Now, Stevenson describes Modestine as his beloved, and goes so far as to associate her with the dead beloved in Wordsworth's "She Dwelt Among the Untrodden

Figure. 4.2   Walter Crane, frontispiece to Robert Louis Stevenson, *Travels with a Donkey in the Cévennes* (London: Kegan Paul, 1879). McFarlin Library, University of Tulsa.

Ways" (*Travels*, 234), in which the poet depicts the eponymous Lucy as being as unnoticed and inconsequential as "a violet by a mossy stone."[64] Stevenson marks the intimacy of the two species by having the narrator comically recall their travels as they "jogged along with our six legs" (*Travels*, 234). He is in mourning for the animal, he says, and the story closes with the narrator weeping publicly as the stagecoach takes him back to civilization.

This final paragraph offers images of species intimacy and transfusion, on the one hand, but also disingenuous portrayals of Modestine as some sort of worthy female used and sold into bondage. The donkey, moreover, is never explicitly understood by the hiker as his ideal pagan traveler. Interestingly, however, Walter Crane's frontispieces for *An Inland Voyage* and *Travels with a Donkey* do acknowledge such complex trans-species politics (Figs. 4.1 and 4.2).[65] These are the only two drawings Crane ever did for Stevenson and they are only a year apart, so he would have been thinking of the first when he made the second, although the connection is more than just a mnemonic echo. The first is set in a Renaissance-style frame characterized by Classical myth, symmetry, and detailing, while the second has no such decoration, and instead offers a medieval visual design depicting the author and the donkey at different stages of their travels. The two pieces exist as counterimages, each with a reclining figure in the foreground, in the reader's full view but embedded among plants and obscured from the rest of the scene. The main figure watches over his shoulder a depiction of Stevenson as a sort of man-of-the-woods; in *An Inland Voyage*, he is the canoeist of the Arethusa paddling down the river Oise, while in *Travels with a Donkey*, he is the intrepid hiker reappearing in various scenes from the book. The name "HMS Arethusa," common among ships in the British Royal navy, is taken from a water nymph in Greek mythology. In a later frontispiece for the aestheticist poet and composer Theo Marzials's *Pan Pipes* (1883), Crane copies the Pan he had drawn for the frontispiece of *An Inland Voyage* but wittily replaces the background figure of the canoe named Arethusa with the nymph herself (Fig. 4.3).

Crane acknowledges Stevenson's self-identification with Classical myth in the frontispiece to *Travels with a Donkey*, presenting the author performing a modern version of Pan, a cross-species conflation of reality and myth that is not apparent without an awareness of the first frontispiece. In both illustrations, the character in the foreground is a relaxed male surveying the natural landscape with a self-assured, pseudo-omniscient gaze. Both figures have shaggy locks, Stevenson recording that, on his journey through the Cévennes, he wore a fur

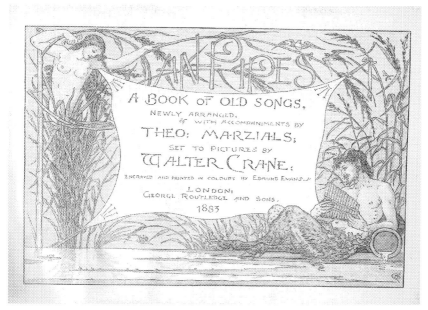

Figure 4.3 Walter Crane. Cover illustration for *Pan Pipes: A Book of Old Songs* (London: George Routledge and Sons, 1883). Dennis Denisoff.

cap over his long hair. More amazingly, both figures have woolly legs; according to Stevenson, for his hiking trip, he had somebody make him a wool-lined sleeping bag (*Travels*, 14), accurately rendered here by Crane. In his conquest of the moon goddess Selene, Pan himself disguised his goat legs by wrapping them in sheepskin. Crane extends the species conflation by foregrounding in the second frontispiece the hind legs of Stevenson's beloved Modestine, evoking even more strongly the hooved goat-legs of the mythic god in the earlier drawing.[66] Crane's renderings suggest he saw in Stevenson's work strategies akin to those I explore in the previous chapter regarding Michael Field's attempts in their poetry to "suppress[] the habitual centralisation of the visible in ourselves" in order to capture "an impression, clearer, less passive, more intimate."[67] Field describe their efforts as using their poems to submerge themselves within a pagan aesthetic. Crane, however, takes into account Stevenson's choice of the genre of nonfiction travel writing, with his illustrations portraying not Stevenson's writing – as is the case with Field and their poems – but the author himself not only as observing nature through a mythic lens, but as less exclusively human and more a vital part of the spirit of the place with which he engages.

In his illustrations, Crane offers an image of Stevenson as a wanderer characterized by movement without ego, caught in a current of one sort or other. The author himself suggests this standpoint not only in his portrayal of Modestine's meanderings but also in the travelogue's conception of a synchronized, emotional universe akin to that suggested a century later by Lovelock. "At what inaudible summons," he asks one early dawn in *Travels with a Donkey*,

> at what gentle touch of Nature, are all these sleepers thus recalled in the same hour to life? Do the stars rain down an influence, or do we share some thrill of mother earth below our resting bodies? ... We have a moment to look upon the stars, and there is a special pleasure for some minds in the reflection that we share the impulse with all outdoor creatures in our neighbourhood, that we have escaped out of the Bastille of civilisation, and are become, for the time being, a mere kindly animal and a sheep of Nature's flock. (113)

Pater similarly writes of Pan that he "has almost no story; he is but a presence."[68] Acknowledging the Classical conception of Pan not as a singular demi-god but as a flowing multiplicity of fauns, Pater sees the figure as akin to Arcadia's "children, agile as the goats they tend, who run, in their picturesque rags, across the solitary wanderer's path, to startle him, in the unfamiliar upper places." Similarly, with *Travels with a Donkey*, Stevenson – himself the wanderer – turns to the nonhuman to realize a pagan conception of subjectivity that questions the assumption that the individual always already exists. The formulation brings to mind the fluid and uncontainable qualities of queer political strategy that I mentioned in the previous chapter. Pan's reputation as sexually indiscriminate is effectively in synch with the shared impulse of "all outdoor creatures in our neighbourhood," as Stevenson puts it. Stevenson's spirit of animality is queer in its combining of sensuality and identificatory fluidity with a challenge to the dominant and legitimate within his society. His efforts undermine what would become the common condemnation of decadent culture as threatening social cohesion by overemphasizing the experience of the individual. He does so by foregrounding a model of being that is rooted in the sensory relations among different entities – "never less alone than when alone," as Hazlitt put it.[69] In this vision, paganism is a form of vagabondage, a protean intersubjectivity that sustains an acknowledgment of both its wandering and its intransience.

Vernon Lee's Peripatetic Engagements

When Stevenson decides it is time to end his travels, he is nothing if not efficient. Having been informed that Modestine needs rest after having been overtaxed by his demands, he simply gets rid of her: "She would need at least two days' repose, according to the ostler; but I was now eager to reach Alais for my letters; and, being in a civilised country of stage-coaches, I determined to sell my lady friend and be off by the diligence that afternoon" (232). And so, he flogs his companion "saddle and all" to the highest bidder and grabs a coach. There is something cold, even callous, in the way he severs all ties with his wandering ways and declares that, in selling Modestine, he bought his "freedom," just as there is something crass and unaesthetic in the efficiency of his celebration of modern transportation. This model of convenience and speed is something Vernon Lee takes on directly in her own exploration of the *genius loci* as a form of movement. Although Lee's travel writings on the sense of place emphasize the passing moment, she does not portray speed or almost any type of movement other than the perambulatory as contributing to the quality of the experience. In particular, her essay collection *The Enchanted Woods* (1905) repeatedly undermines any possible benefit of vehicular travel through the landscape. At one point, Lee discusses her experiences of the *genius loci* and mockingly bewails the "dreary moment, well known and dreaded by all of us who worship that most coy of all divinities" when, whether due to the "stress of time, or footsoreness, or dread of dislocation on a pavement scorning bicycles, or mere lack of moral courage," the lover of landscapes must on occasion take a turn in "the cab of alien lands."[70] But vehicular travel, for Lee, is too brisk and too disengaged to allow for one's submergence into the spirit of a place.

Lee's model of the traveler's experience of the *genius loci* is complicated by what she presents as its corollary in the reader's psychological, aesthetic experience of a piece of writing; words are akin to landscapes that one moves through, that move through one, and that one is moved by. In "The Craft of Words" (1894), she offers a complement to Pater and Stevenson that says as much about herself as her contemporaries. For her, in the essay "The School of Giorgione" (1877) and a section of the novel *Catriona* (1893) respectively, Pater and Stevenson offer "the most perfect fusion of style and subject," in which "it is quite impossible to say where style begins and subject ends. One forgets utterly the existence of either, one is merely impressed, moved, as by the perfectly welded influences of outer nature, as by the fusion of a hundred things which constitute a fine

124 The *Genius Loci* as Spirited Vagabond

day or a stormy night."[71] These samples of Pater's and Stevenson's writings are exemplary, for Lee, because the subject and medium work together to create in the reader a singular psychological movement, much as elements of one's consciousness fuse to create one's sense of a particular moment.

As she readily acknowledged, Pater's writings on the relationships among nature, spirit, writing, and aesthetics had a particular influence on her work. The two had met in 1881 and maintained a long-term friendship through visits, when she was in England, and correspondences, while she lived in Italy. Lee dedicated her essay collection *Euphorion: Being Studies of the Antique and the Mediaeval in the Renaissance* (1884) to him and, ten years later, ended its sequel *Renaissance Fancies and Studies* (1895) with a eulogy to him and a defense of his aesthetic vision. Here, she describes Pater as "the natural exponent of the highest æsthetic doctrine – the search for harmony throughout all orders of existence."[72] "[I]n the words of the prayer of Socrates to the Nymphs and to Pan," she muses on Pater's values, "ask for beauty in the inward soul, and congruity between the inner and the outer man; and reflect in such manner the gifts of great art and of great thought in our soul's depths."[73] Nicholas Dames addresses Lee's "The Craft of Words" as influenced by the psychophysics of E. H. Weber and Gustav Fechner when she describes "literary form as a psychological mediation between two consciousnesses," that of author and reader.[74] Dames is addressing in particular Lee's observation that "the ideas and emotions stored up in the mind of the Reader" as "units of consciousness" constitute "the chaos of living moving things," "living molecules of memory";[75] it is for the writer to use words to configure this vital, plastic pile of units in any potential reader's mind into an intended shape. Adela Pinch has noted that Fechner was also a panpsychist, theorizing "the existence of consciousness going all the way down to plants at least, and up to the earth as a whole, in a kind of nested hierarchy in which each individual consciousness is a unit of a larger one, up to the whole universe."[76] In Lee's theory of writing, Pinch proposes, one finds a similar panpsychism of nesting consciousness among readers and writers, ultimately drawing on "analogies between words, letters, consciousness, and the living particles of the world, a chain of analogies that is one of panpsychism's recurring rhetorical patterns." The other Victorian author Pinch notes for his panpsychic formulations is Swinburne, himself one of the main catalysts for cultural decadence flourishing in Britain.

At the same time as Lee's model suggests the panpsychic, it echoes Paul Bourget's discussion of decadence as the destabilization of influences, in

Vernon Lee's Peripatetic Engagements 125

which he argues that "If the energy of the cells becomes independent, the organisms composing the total organism likewise cease to subordinate their energy to the total energy, and the anarchy which takes place constitutes the decadence of all."[77] As I discuss in my introduction, Bourget's *Essais de psychologie contemporaine* (1883) famously presents decadence as a destabilization of nested units that operate across the biological, the social, and the textual. The following year, in 1884, he would, thanks to Lee's friend John Singer Sargent, visit her in London, followed by another meeting two days later, and then an exchange of letters, articles, and books.[78] In one letter, he distinguishes his focus on the "inner psychological life" and her own "more courageous" contribution to the collective "inquiry into modern sensibility,"[79] but the general sense from his letters to her is that she was not particularly quick to accept his more cerebral, psychological version of decadence. Her own formulation ultimately proves equally ethical but less conclusive in its rendering of the individual's relations to the other elements of their ecology.

Just as readily recognized by her readers for her pagan interests as Stevenson was by his, Lee was more richly engaged in decadent culture and has been canonized by scholars in recent decades as a major contributor to it. Her acquaintances and friendships with others involved in modern decadence such as Amy Levy, Mary Robinson, Bourget, Pater, and Wilde established her as part of the network. Her novel *Miss Brown* (1884), meanwhile, with its sustained critique of the urban figure of the dandy-aesthete, complicated her relations with one cohort of the decadent set, even if, as various scholars have pointed out, the novel itself addresses subjects common to decadence, including paganism, the aestheticization of the female, queer desires, and an overarching narrative of social upheaval marked by both decay and rebirth. In her life, she had intense relationships with various women, and sympathized with Wilde during his trials. Like Wilde, Lee took issue with the logic of capitalism, seeing possible alternatives in socialism. Her decadence is most unique, meanwhile, in its ground-breaking theorization of a psychological aesthetics that was not only more sensually attuned than Victorians could find almost anywhere else, but also among the most queer.

The decadence of Lee's writing is not to be found primarily in a richness of detail and sustained intensity of emotion. Rather, it arises in a spirit of comradery that she theorizes through psychological aesthetics and paganism, and her sustained consideration of how to be most alive in one's environment and most attuned to the affective opportunities it offers. Lee's analysis of the landscape aesthetic from a moving vehicle, in her 1904 essay "Motor Cars and the Genius of Places," can be read as much as an early manifesto of the slow movement as a precursor to Ratty's denunciation of the calamitous driving adventures of Toad in Kenneth Grahame's pagan-invested *Wind in the Willows* (1908). While she acknowledges that her car ride is democratic and individualist in contrast to the forced time schedules and rail routes of trains, the experience itself proves far from liberating:

> In motoring things remain ocular, mere visions, unaccompanied by the sympathizing measuring of our muscles and will. They lack the tangible joy, working deep into our nerves, of the massive real. ... [L]acking the corroborating evidence of my limbs, or of any movement I have learned to time against my limbs' movements, these things remain *seen*, without the ineffable sense of having been there, or of its having been in me. ... There was, moreover, a vague dissatisfaction: this couple of hours in the far-off places *had made too little difference in me*. I missed the sense of strangeness which brings with it so much refreshment and renovation. ...
>
> It seems, in a way, right that such should be the case; and one seems to guess at one of the underlying concordances of things, in the fact that such effortless seeing and knowing should lack the mark of complete possession working deep into the soul, which belongs to desires that struggle for their accomplishment. How poignantly, pathetically almost, we feel the lines and colours of the hills remaining for ever on the horizon! What a nostalgic fondness, as for the unattainable past, we often have for the twist of the valley, the reach of the river – nay, the very tuft of trees or pointing steeple just beyond the limits of our daily walk or ride! (*Enchanted*, 99–101)

Lee's melancholic language of the unattainable evokes Stevenson's philosophic contrast of the mountain in the distance that marks his destination and the meandering paths and travel partner in his immediate moment. The tactile experience, for Lee as for Stevenson, is necessary for a full engagement with a sense of place, for an empathic relationship that extends not only through the body but into the psychological and spiritual, permeating one's desires and soul. Thus, for Lee, the key issue with traveling in motor vehicles is the inability to embody the aesthetic, a problem that she establishes as the difference between sight and touch, the automobile creating a dysfunctional analytical distance between the individual and the landscape. Such drive-by encounters undermine any compulsion or desire one might have to experience oneself as part of the spirit of the landscape.

Vernon Lee's Peripatetic Engagements

There is a broader sociopolitical implication to this situation. The private vehicle loses any vestiges of individuality, freedom, or adventure as it becomes apparent that, for Lee, it operates as part of a modern technology of oppression. Later in the essay, she equates vehicular travel with tourism, as both are devices "for wasting the kernel of things and filling ourselves with their voluminous husks, and one of the practical ironies which wait on privilege of all kinds" (*Enchanted*, 107). It is class privilege in particular that the author is thinking of here. "Certain it is that what remains clearest in this day's recollections," she argues,

> rather than the landscapes we whirled into and out of, were the faces, enviously gaping or angry, of the people we scattered along the road. It is not good, I am afraid, dear friends, to scatter people along roads and cover them with the dust of our wheels; there is a corresponding scattering of our soul, and a covering of *it* with dust.

The motor here becomes one aspect of a classist system of segregation between the tourist and the locals, the latter being aestheticized as part of the passing scenery, covered literally in the dust of the landscape, perhaps as Stevenson does in *Travels with a Donkey* when he depicts the plodding workers as inferior because of what he imagines are their numb, laborious lives. Simultaneously, modern petrol-fueled transport attains a quasi-spiritual function as the polluter of the countryside and those who live within it. In her extended metaphor, nonvehicular people are the embodied soul of those others (among whom Lee includes herself) who are scattering and polluting the *genius loci* with the engines of their profane modernity. The image operates, in a sense, as an inversion of Antonio Stoppani's modern botanists, discussed in Chapter 1, who vehemently search "the furthest depths, into mountains' fissures, on the highest peaks, for the untamed daughters of virgin nature, that carry unaltered the features of their mother."[80] Stoppani contentedly observes how, with the rise of a Christian Anthropocene, "ancient nature distorts itself, almost flees under the heel of this new nature,"[81] but for Lee the polluting exhaust of contemporary human values brings forward not the rise of a new geologic era, but the indifference to a transhistorical spirituality that in fact overrides the modern fleeting infatuation with speed and efficiency.[82]

"There is, to my mind, a very peculiar pleasure – akin to that of following a river from its source to the sea – in getting to know the different physiognomy, the different mode of being, of various mountainous or hilly regions," Lee writes in *The Enchanted Woods* (186). The

128   The *Genius Loci* as Spirited Vagabond

description brings to mind not only Stevenson's musings in his travelogues, but also Stoppani's celebratory description of "the humble brook, that springs from cliff to cliff, to the river that widens its mouth as it debouches into the sea."[83] Adopting the perspective of an African geologist who is on an excursion with her in Italy, Lee goes on to muse,

> how immensely, and in a way super-humanly, personal, the genealogy, biography, and way of being of localities and districts must become in the light of science, just by a word here and there, accompanied by a nod in the direction of the hills around, or the plain below, or the misty gap where the Alps should be, he was able to make me realize that the geologist and geographer have secrets and have emotions like those of the historical student. (185–86)

Lee comes to believe that, although the geologist approaches the subject with a scientific eye, for him the landscape also holds "an additional and (however unconscious) imaginative interest, not unlike that with which I sometimes caught myself" (186). The author here voices, with a touch of false naiveté, a newfound awareness of the role of the imagination in the burgeoning fields of the earth sciences. With the same gesture, however, she also situates herself as part of the scientific community, legitimizing her record of her own experiences as equivalent in accuracy and import to those of the geologist – her fellow traveler in tourism as well as in intellectual exploration. In this work Lee ultimately suggests the ways in which individuals such as Stoppani, Pater, Müller, Tylor, and Andrew Lang contributed to a growing corpus of scientific works whose imaginative vigor spurred the pagan revival along. As Lee's contemporary, the Scottish social anthropologist James George Frazer, would propose in his highly influential *The Golden Bough* (1890; revised 1900, 1905), imagination was at the core of both scientific and religious knowledge.

Victorian macro-theories of cultural evolution such as Frazer's generally put aside the question of whether the individuals who proposed arguments inflected with spiritualities rooted in the biosphere or cosmos might have identified as pagans or could be understood as pagans. Frazer never actually engaged with the remote peoples who are central to many of his claims, something even he acknowledged as a weakness of his work. By the mid-twentieth century, anthropologists were less invested in Frazer's often ethnocentric views, but nevertheless his emphasis in *The Golden Bough* on folk traditions as a valid source of information, if not scientific proof, appeared during a time when British folklore was itself receiving intense interest, the Folklore Society being founded in London in 1878. He was by no means alone in arguing that a shared set of beliefs formed the basis of much of the scientific, spiritual, and customary knowledge of his time. The influence of Darwinian and Spencerian theory, for example, is apparent in Frazer's view of magic as a precursor for religious and scientific thought. *The Golden Bough*'s analysis builds upon the image of ancient fertility cults patterned on a seasonal cycle of sacrifice and rebirth, and he saw this practice succinctly captured in the landscape of a sacred grove distinguished by the "golden bough" referenced in his study's title. "Who does not know Turner's picture of the Golden Bough?" Frazer asks in his opening sentence, referencing J. M. W. Turner's 1834 painting of the same name (Fig. 4.4), "The scene, suffused with the golden glow of imagination in which the divine mind of Turner steeped and transfigured even the fairest natural landscape, is a dream-like vision of the little woodland lake of Nemi – 'Diana's Mirror,' as it was called by the ancients."[84] The goddess Fraser references is Diana Nemorensis, or Diana of the Wood.

In his painting, Turner depicts a scene from Virgil's *Aeneid*, with the prophetess Sybil holding up the golden bough that Aeneas required in order to gain passage to the Underworld through Lake Avernus. The Fates, depicted dancing next to the lake, capture the element of magic

Figure. 4.4 Joseph Mallord William Turner, *The Golden Bough*. 1834. Tate Museum, London. Engraving of Painting by T.A. Prior. 36.3 by 23.8 cm, 14.3 by 9.4 in., JAK Historical Imates/Alamy Stock Photo.

130 The *Genius Loci* as Spirited Vagabond

and dangerous mystery with which such venerated geological locations were imbued. This is not what Frazer describes, as he uses the image to develop the central theme of his own envisioned mythology. He proposes that in the grove, where "Diana herself might still linger by this lonely shore, still haunt these woodlands wild," "a grim figure might be seen to prowl."[85] This peripatetic character, he tells us, is the head priest, who is always eventually killed by the one who would usurp his title. Like Pater's *Marius*, the story with which Frazer opens *The Golden Bough* creates a peculiar overlay of temporal frames. The chapter's main aim is to establish that this mythic scenario is a generic story reproduced in different forms throughout history. Although the process of repetition may not be recognized as scientific evidence, he argues, it nevertheless offers a strong form of proof of the universality of certain cultural patterns of understanding. Notably, a similar repetition occurs within the story itself, where the vanquishing of the priest recurs, leaving the factuality of the pagan spirit to be affirmed primarily through the reiteration of ritual performance by the next priest and the next and so on. Most curious in this regard, however, is the image of the high priest himself as he constantly walks about the *genius loci*. The hero wanders through the Italian landscape more attentive to his surroundings than to the journey or his destination. In fact, Frazer's chapter is characterized by a parade of travelers – wayfarers and adventurers from Classical history and myth who arrive at the mystical Italian *loci* and depart, their stories interweaving to create an increasingly thicker affirmation of the grove of Nemi as a spiritual place.

Lee brings forward just such a temporal overlay in her various considerations of the relationship of the individual to the spirit of a location. As early as *Genius Loci: Notes on Place* (1899), which appeared not too long after Frazer's *Golden Bough*, Lee addresses the complex relation of time and place in one's sympathetic engagement with the landscape. She refers to participation in this de-individuated process as the "nobler paganism," where existence in deep time is marked by what appear as no more than brief singular moments of death in a life force that is eternal because it is itself built of multiplicity.[86] Lee dedicates *Genius Loci* with gratitude not to people but to trees, the cypresses of Vincigliate, and the oaks of Abbey Leix, and she opens the introduction with a simple acknowledgment that locales, regardless of their history and inhabitants, "can touch us like living creatures; and one can have with them friendship of the deepest and most satisfying sort" (3–4). Her language is neither particularly scientific nor spiritual, as she goes on to declare rather pragmatically that the claim "may seem nonsense" if we have only the common sense of friendship in mind (4). But Lee proceeds to pare away any ideal of such relationships, describing friendship as "a mere practical and in the main accidental relation wherein exchange of ideas and good offices, fetching and carrying for one another, and toiling and moiling in company, plays the principal part." Rather than offering a broader, more philosophic definition of friendship, the author instead maintains a familiar explanation from which she then skims the richest cream of the relationship, a rare ideal element that is also found in one's engagement with places. Through this rhetorical move, she avoids asking her readers to redefine terms with which they feel confidently familiar, and instead encourages them to see their own realities as already engaged in the refined element of the *genius loci* itself. The maneuver thereby encourages individuals to contribute their own experiences to a collective process of knowledge-making akin to the repetition of information that Frazer argues is fundamental to the creation of folklore.

The strategy supports Lee's interests, like Field's and Stevenson's, in a paganism alive within everyday society. "Indeed, when I try to define the greatest good which human creatures can do us, good far transcending any practical help or intellectual guidance," she writes, "it seems to express itself quite naturally in vague metaphors borrowed from those other friends who are not human beings" (4). Stoppani had similarly turned to a rhetoric of natural spirit in his efforts to articulate the soul of a Christian Anthropocene, but while the scientist's efforts to capture the geologic moment led to his rendering of natural locations as mythic characters, Lee here adamantly argues against such humanizing gestures. Benjamin Morgan has observed that, "[w]ithin Lee's theory, to be uplifted by a mountain does not require that the mountain be personified or even imagined as sentient; as a result, her work articulates an unfamiliar kind of empathy whose primary orientation is not toward the social domain."[87] As Lee herself declares, "For mercy's sake, not a personification, not a man or woman with mural crown and attributes, and detestable, definite history[.] ... To think of a place or a country in human shape is, for all the practice of rhetoricians, not to think of it at all" (5). She explicitly challenges the common tendency to envision spirituality as a human phenomenon in form and emotive structure. For her, even the longevity that is often seen to be a defining characteristic of friendship is misleading; while repeated visits to a particular location may result in a sense of the *genius loci*, the experiences are more akin to

132   The *Genius Loci* as Spirited Vagabond

fleeting, erotic engagements – "mere *amours de voyage* (in the most worthy sense) where, though the remembrance may be long, the actual moment of meeting ('now we have met we are safe,' as Whitman says) is necessarily very brief" (7–8). Lee ultimately does rely on her audience's own human relations to evoke the experience of the *genius loci*, but she categorizes this as only one rare component within the realm of friendship, an element more often not encountered there, and one that clearly can be encountered elsewhere.

In emphasizing the brief, passionate quality of these spatial encounters, Lee brings to mind Stevenson's near-drowning in the Oise, but also, more informatively, Pater's conclusion to *Studies in the History of the Renaissance* in which he argues for an intensity of fleeting experience that he situates as much in one's ecological context as he does in the human. In that essay, Pater makes a point of recognizing the individual human as but one element extended and interwoven through a larger landscape. By introducing Whitman, however, Lee gives an original erotic emphasis to the passage, bringing forward a vision of same-sex desire distinctly more worldly than Pater offers when he says of Johann Joachim Winckelmann in *Studies in the History of the Renaissance*, "he fingers those pagan marbles with unsinged hands, with no sense of shame or loss. That is to deal with the sensuous side of art in the pagan manner."[88] Lee's vision, albeit aesthetic in its philosophical argument, does not rely for its intensity on Classical formulations of beauty but on a notion of the natural environment as inherently amoral. Her language conforms to pagan interests while also evoking the pastoral socialism that had gained popularity through the back-to-the-land movement and people such as William Morris and Edward Carpenter. Carpenter, in particular, worked to develop a vision of a universal culture similar to that described in Frazer's *Golden Bough* in its broad strokes and emphasis on myth as a form of confirmation, if not proof. Meanwhile, his fusion of British socialism and Eastern mysticism found a context at his country retreat in Millthorpe, where he moved in 1883 and maintained relationships with other men against an agrarian backdrop characterized by communal living, vegetarianism, and a spirituality that could be described as environmentalist.

One of the men with whom Carpenter was intimate was Whitman,[89] whose 1865 poem "Out of the Rolling Ocean the Crowd" Lee cites for capturing the fleeting quality central to her conception of the *genius loci*. Recalling Stevenson's depiction, in *The Inland Voyage*, of himself as one with the drops of water each in a singular yet collective panic, Whitman's

Vernon Lee's Peripatetic Engagements 133

poem describes a lover as a drop of water that, momentarily individualized, is able to voice its desire:

> I have travel'd a long way, merely to look on you, to touch you,
> (Now we have met, we have look'd, we are safe; Return in peace to the ocean
>   my love;
> I too am part of that ocean, my love – we are not so much separated.[90]

The image can be read as a noncommittal one-night stand, an *amour de voyage*, as Lee puts it. But what Lee wishes to emphasize is that, in Whitman's formulation, the encounter is all the more precious *because of* its brevity, the moment when the two forces acknowledge each other through their encounter being a particular point of queer intensity occurring within the oceanic comingling of all sentient beings, the crowd. "Behold the great rondure," suggests the lover in a non-decadent vision, "the cohesion of all, how perfect!" As with the poem, the *genius loci* elicits in Lee "well-nigh passionate and certainly romantic feelings," her language becoming particularly erotic at this point of singular intensity, just as she is about to end her study (*Genius Loci*, 203). The lovers she describes are the human and the ecological, the latter notably including not just forests and hillsides but also potentially buildings and streets. As she explains elsewhere, "as to enchanted woods, why, they lie in many parks and girdle many cities; only you must know them when you see them, and submit willingly to their beneficent magic" (*Enchanted*, 10).

In these experiences of intimacy, Lee notes, only one of the lovers is human, and so the emotions evoked are "necessarily, from the nature of the case, one-sided." It is this very de-stabilizing of the human in the erotic experiences that makes them strategically decadent, but also, for Lee, "makes them only the more honourable (precluding jealousy, fatuity, and every bitterness), and certainly, to my mind, more really romantic" (207). The inevitable mystery of the nonhuman beloved, the lack of affirmation of the subject's affective reading, enhances for Lee, as for Whitman (and arguably Field, as explored in the previous chapter), the ephemeral intensity of the queer engagement.

In her essay collection *The Enchanted Woods*, which appeared thirteen years after *Genius Loci*, Lee offers a more in-depth analysis of the trans-ecological bonds operating outside the more common emotions of exclusively human relationships. Here, however, she describes the relations as being marked by an emotional reciprocity, declaring that "places like these have moods and emotions on their account, seem to feel something which they transmit to us" (220). It is not just that people themselves have a yearning for relationships with nature, but *genius loci* extend affective invitations to humans as well, albeit ones not open to ready interpretation. In the essay "Nymphs and a River God," for example, she notes a sense of pagan intimacy but also acknowledges her inability to render the emotional exchange: "I know it is the place of the nymphs, I feel their presence, though the nymphs are merely the white singing water, the whispering brake of reeds; not immanent in it all, but *it, itself.* ... I have a very special feeling of the place; and it is all summed up in that misapplied word, the *Nymphæum*" (*Enchanted*, 55–56). It is Lee's emphasis here on avoiding mythological personification – on understanding that it is the brook itself that affects her spirit and is thus the agent, rather than simply a vessel for some otherworldly force – that characterizes her brand of paganism. And it is a respect for the thing *as is* that fits with the de-humanizing elements of the eco-politics found in works such as *The Enchanted Woods*.

This collection repeatedly works a political edge into Lee's eco-pagan vision. She dedicated the work to her close friend Isabella Ford, whose family was deeply engaged in social reform and philanthropy for factory workers. The Fords' home in Leeds often welcomed these laborers, as well as suffragists, labor leaders, Fabians, and socialist and Radical Liberal politicians. It was at the Fords' that she wrote her avant-garde pacifist play *The Ballet of Nations* (1915). By dedicating *The Enchanted Woods* to Isabella, Lee positions herself within this vibrant community, recommending the essays as a balm against "the landscape of chimneys and desecrated rivers and inhuman suburbs" (vii). In *The Enchanted Woods*, Lee creates a highly original model of the *genius loci* that brings together three of her key interests. First, one finds the author's personal investment in a communal eco-sensitive model of industry that respects transspecies partnerships built on mutual reliance. Related to this, she offers a sense of a familiar paganism that envisions the spiritual as moving through and propelling the morality of quotidian human activity. Finally, central to these arguments and found in many of her works is an interest in articulating a range of nonnormative, impassioned attractions worthy of at least the same degree of respect given to heterosexual monogamy.

The essay "A Walk in the Maremma" sees Lee develop her theory of the fleeting, animistic encounter – the most intense of affections – as something performed by the peripatetic, passing traveler. "[I]n the longing for closer acquaintance," she argues, "it is borne in on one that it is only with the feet that complete possession is taken of a country" (165). For Lee, it is "while walking, and walking by one's self, that – to paraphrase

Vernon Lee's Peripatetic Engagements

Swinburne – one touches and tastes it, and breathes it, and lives of its life." The reference to the decadent's poem "The Oblation," from *Songs before Sunrise* (1871), is informative. Dedicated to, and partly inspired by, the Italian patriot Giuseppe Mazzini, Swinburne's collection of poems is built around the formation of the nation of Italy from a series of smaller states in 1861 (Rome joining in 1870). The collection also contains the poem "To Walt Whitman in America," in which the narrator asks Whitman to deliver the "earth-god Freedom" across the ocean.[91] The sentence from Swinburne's "Oblation" that Lee paraphrases in her essay reads:

> All things were nothing to give
> Once to have sense of you more,
> Touch you and taste of you sweet,
> Think you and breathe you and live,
> Swept of your wings as they soar,
> Trodden by chance of your feet.[92]

The word "feet" in fact appears as a stressed metrical foot at the end of three of the poem's eighteen lines, foregrounding the self-subjugating position adopted by the narrator. The steady dactyls, the heavy rhyme, and the three repetitions of each of six words at the ends of the lines work together to create a steady rhythm fostering a sense in the reader of determination or even predestination. However, as with Whitman's "Out of the Rolling Ocean the Crowd," Swinburne's "The Oblation" depicts a fleeting relationship, the narrator laying all of themselves as a sacrifice at the beloved's feet, asking nothing in return other than the pleasure of that moment's intense encounter. The declaration of self-subjugation attains a masochistic tone, with the narrator finding greatest fulfillment in being "Trodden by chance of your feet." In the poem's vibrant imagery, the lover is described as a "heart" laying on the ground to be stepped on, but they can also be read as the very soil on which the foot treads in the erotic moment of passing engagement, an experience that excites in the narrator not only touch, but also taste, thought, and breath. The foot of the beloved becomes, for Swinburne's narrator, a source of poly-sensuality that extends not only to mental engagement but to the very state of being alive.

In her dogged efforts to establish exactly why walking alone through an ecology fosters one's strongest engagement with it, that such a solitary act is indeed required for a full appreciation of the landscape experience, Lee follows Swinburne in venerating the poly-sensual foot. Even more specifically, she describes not just walking but scrambling – an act of engagement that requires full attention and effort – as "the most intimate form of walking, the one bringing the most affectionate knowledge" (*Enchanted* 166). The scrambling foot here becomes the very means of access to an ecological understanding beyond rational comprehension, a pagan knowledge mediated through reciprocal attraction. The model echoes Lee's research in the 1890s with her lover Kit Anstruther-Thomson, a Scottish intellectual and amateur painter whose interests in the sensual relations of humans and objects greatly influenced the couple's articulation of what they called psychological aesthetics, and what might today be read as a form of materialist affect, a knowledge that is intimate to the degree of effecting physical change.[93] On a trip to Florence with Lee, Anstruther-Thomson described the façade of the Santa Maria Novella church as "planted solidly on the ground," encouraging "a faint desire to enclose the form between the pressure of our feet on the ground and the very slight downward pressure of the head."[94] This aesthetic language foreshadows Lee's later emphasis on the scrambling foot, the intensely engaged body as crucial to the experience of intimacy with environment.

Lee had developed her arguments on the sensual physicality of aesthetic experience through her observations of Anstruther-Thomson's body while the latter appreciated an object of beauty. Together, the two wrote essays on such psychological aesthetics, further developed by Lee and eventually published by her as *Beauty and Ugliness* (1912). Diana Maltz describes the two women's observational experiments as ultimately offering "a lively, liberatory forum for an aristocratic lesbian elite," proposing that the cultural sanction of same-sex desire as a nonthreatening element of aesthetic appreciation encouraged the development of a community around such experiences.[95] Maltz's analysis usefully foregrounds the place of same-sex female desire within Victorian aesthetics, a gender correlation that, at the time of Lee's work's publication, was far less recognized than that of same-sex male aesthetic discourse. Maltz also acknowledges Anstruther-Thomson's otherworldly interests, describing her as performing the role of a sort of lesbian spiritualist who "conducted aesthetic empathy as more of a parlor game than a science" and "endow[ed] the project with mystery and herself with second-sight."[96] Maltz is skeptical of Anstruther-Thomson's actual occult potential and argues that her "performance ... emulates a séance" characterized by a "bizarre mysticism," suggesting something of the charlatan in these engagements. Whether this is the case or not, Maltz is nevertheless picking up on the pagan and occult sympathies that were receiving extensive attention at the time and that Lee herself would develop into a philosophical theory of desire beyond the human.

Anstruther-Thomson's own mystical foci make apparent that the sensual element of Lee's aesthetics frequently extends into the object of appreciation itself. As my earlier examples suggest, in works such as *The Enchanted Woods*, Lee's private engagements with the *genius loci* appear so intense that one is encouraged to consider the site of the erotic existing not in the individual but in the affective contact and interchange. The sensuality of Lee's aesthetics is especially apparent in passages such as the one in which she describes the joy of feeling "the soft flood sand under one's feet, to wet one's hands picking the snowdrops in the green moss and sere leaves, to stay listening to the song of the stream, one's ear close to it" (*Enchanted,* 166). In all three of these examples – foot to the sand, hand to the water on snowdrops, ear to the stream – attention is paid to the moment of sensory contact; in fact, each example draws just a bit away from actual contact, enhancing the sense of allusiveness, with the focus becoming even more precisely the moments of engagement. It is this intimacy that has Lee define not just walking, but walking in human solitude, as the ideal mode of spatial engagement, fostering what she refers to as "one of the incidents, the *peripezie*, of the religion of the *genius loci*" (168). As Lee would have well been aware, this term, Italian for incident or adventure, is derived from the same root as "peripatetic," bringing us back to the act of wandering. When Lee declares half-mockingly, "Defend us from the sentimental ups and downs of travel, the caprice and moodiness of the uprooted heart of the wayfarer" (*Enchanted,* 293), she is making a declaration against the more cerebral experience of travel, the sort of distant viewing that she finds the only option with vehicular travel and common tourism.

For both Lee and Stevenson, it is the peripatetic mind, the scrambling mind – precisely because it is an act of physicality demanding affective engagement outside the self – that most effectively renders the *genius loci* as a site of philosophic inquiry. The demand for proof is an attempt to force, in compliance with legitimized sciences, what is precious precisely because it is a queer desiring beyond such calculated capture. As Lee observes in the final essay of *Enchanted Woods*, "Et in Arcadia," "for the humble Genius Loci even like the great divinities of Olympus, is but an intangible idol fashioned out of what we have and of what we want" (321). And yet, this quotation also marks Lee's turn back to human conception, an acknowledgment that the *genius loci* can itself be seen as a

138   The *Genius Loci* as Spirited Vagabond

fabrication of the mind in an effort to make sense of trans-specific experiences of friendship, love, and desire. In this sense, it echoes Stevenson's own declaration, after his and Modestine's weeks of travel, that a return to civilization felt like a form of freedom, a release from a period of sustained eco-pagan immersion.

The Modern *Nymphæum* of the Collective Spirit

In the first chapter of *The Sentimental Traveller*, Lee describes her "passion for localities, the curious emotions connected with lie of the land, shape of buildings, history, and even quality of air and soil"; the "intense and permeating feeling" is "fashioned, before we see them, by our wishes and fancy; we recognize rather than discover them in the world of reality."[97] The primary audience for this explanation, she proposes, is other women who are drawn to her uniquely embodied mode of journeying, a "breed of Sentimental Traveller" that arose among "our mothers and grandmothers."[98] Lee is drawn not simply to the scenario of an all-female collective, but a woman-centered paganism: "Priestesses of the Genius Loci, vestals often, urged by divine frenzy across the picturesque globe," "reputable maenads, bearing instead of thyrsi and haunches of kid, campstools and old-fashioned sunshades," "venerable and exquisite priestesses of the Divinity of Places, sacred and wonderful above all other old ladies." There is no doubt that Lee saw herself as a participant within this time-traveling, global network of independent women whom she affectionately mocks as "sedate with nods and becks and wreathed smiles under caps and bonnets which seem fresh from the bandboxes of 'Cranford'." In contrast to the paganism that Pater's *Greek Studies* renders with decadent style and images of carnivorous frenzy, Lee here offers a more charming vision, with the interfusions among Pater's swarming maenads replaced by a sense of ecological empathy akin to that which Stevenson renders in his depictions of himself as a blithe and joyous youth in *An Inland Voyage* and *Travels with a Donkey*. At the same time, while sidestepping the imperialism inherent to global exploration, Lee alludes to the discrimination that contorts such independent female explorers such as herself into the decadent trope of the dangerously confident and capable female.

This passage is one of Lee's most forceful evocations of not only her life-long emotional and sexual attachment to various women, but also the many strong-willed females within paganism and the ecological tradition of the maternal divine that extends around the globe but also into the recesses of the mind. She is writing at a time when formulations of feminism rooted in essential notions of women's natural powers were gaining greater attention. Although one senses here her imagining the possibility of a same-sex female spiritual collective, Lee never joined any contemporary pagan or pagan-studies groups. Despite her own lesbian relationships and the fact that much of her writing is queerly inflected, the feminist potential of pagan decadence surfaces tenuously, muffled by the language of other intentions. In the following chapter, I turn to other women of the period who were more invested than Lee in actual earth-based spirituality as a means of engaging the transience of space and time. Bringing forward the gender politics that Lee wove through her own formulations of affection and desire, I turn to works by Moina Mathers and Florence Farr, two influential contributors to turn-of-the-century popular occulture. Focusing on ancient Egyptian pagan practices, these women reinforced the admiration for the inconstant, symbolist, and intangible found in Stevenson, Lee, and other contributors to British decadence. For Mathers and Farr, however, engagements through actions – specifically through performance and ritual – were an essential, and essentially eco-feminist, means of spiritual realization.

CHAPTER 5

Occult Ecology and the Decadent Feminism of Moina Mathers and Florence Farr

The thread of Orientalism running through British decadence is apparent in works throughout the Victorian and Modernist periods. Over time, with increased global travel among the British, the predominantly aesthetic character found in decadent works became more realistic, along the lines of first-person travel narration. At the same time, with the rise of symbolism and its developments into the twentieth century, one finds Orientalism manifesting differently in the ritualistic style of decadent dramas such as Oscar Wilde's *Salomé* and William Sharp's *Black Madonna*.[1] This chapter engages with a major source of the decadents' Orientalist interests – the occult conception of eco-spirituality through the lens of Egyptosophy. While interest in Egyptian aesthetics and myth is apparent throughout decadence, it is the spiritual emphasis found in Theosophy, the Hermetic Order of the Golden Dawn, and other occult communities that most richly engages the decadent interest in undermining the modern Western compulsion for a closed, knowable ecology. Focusing on the influence and reimaging of ancient Egyptian culture, this chapter adopts an understanding of decadence not bound by its most strongly promoted contributors and tropes but more open to the visions within works beyond the canons formulated either by Victorian and early-twentieth-century critics and reviewers or by academic scholars of the past century. In the process, I suggest a potential for a decadent feminism that in part challenges some key attributes of the more populist understanding of decadence itself.

Nineteenth-century decadence was dominated by the portrayal of the strong female figure as a sexually aggressive femme fatale often affiliated with the exotically foreign, the occult, and the mystical, as in the case of Frederick Sandys's *Medea*. The authors who then and now first come to mind as decadents are, curiously, those who offered relatively few renderings of such women as life-affirming, dynamic leaders. The pattern of understanding base-decadence, so to speak, through the same

Occult Ecology and the Decadent Feminism

cultural lens for more than a century has resulted in the obfuscation of feminist decadent perspectives, as opposed to the notice of select female authors with some feminist interests. And yet, the popular occulture so tightly interwoven with decadence readily encouraged female authority, incorporated affirmations of womanhood into its structures, and offered the most complex models of pagan feminist empowerment from the period. Occult discussions of the female often complemented key New Woman arguments regarding the vote, prostitution laws, women in positions of authority, and women as particularly attuned to a broad ecological network. Many occult works also tended to appreciate the political potency of women's essential procreative wisdom, an issue that was also politicized by some New Woman advocates. Nevertheless, scholarship on the New Woman, like that on decadence, has not yet fully accounted for the role of the occult in shaping dominant forms of modern feminism. Most notably, more needs to be done to recognize the innovation and influence of an occult politics rooted in an ancient wisdom tradition that foregrounded matriarchy, and the importance of ritual and performance in accessing this tradition. These are, I argue, the principal elements of a feminist occult ecology that was characterized by the acceptance and veneration of an indeterminate, otherworldly reality to the human environment and that gained recognition during an occult revival in many ways conjoined with nineteenth- and early-twentieth-century decadence.

In this chapter, I give the stage to Moina Mathers and Florence Farr, Egyptophile members of the Hermetic Order of the Golden Dawn (1888–1902), one of the largest and most influential occult societies in modern history.[2] It was formed "for the purpose of the study of Occult Science, and the further investigation of the Mysteries of Life and Death, and our Environment."[3] Mathers and Farr were major influences on the shape of popular occulture, bringing their ideas – especially regarding drama and performance – into the urban arts and culture scene dominated by the decadents. Building on my previous chapter's discussion of Robert Louis Stevenson's and Vernon Lee's conceptions of the *genius loci* not as a space but as an act of moving *through* space, I wish to address Mathers's and Farr's efforts to embody feminist practices empowered by another form of movement – that of ritual and theatrical performance. As in previous chapters, I address the decadent movement not as a rigid and distinct singular through line of history but as shifting threads that, starting and ending at different times, collectively wove a cultural network of interests in, among other subjects, powerful women, new modes of spiritual engagement, and the symbolic potential of style and detail. Like many decadents, Mathers and Farr were both drawn into Egyptian paganism, with one of their particular interests being questions of women's innate spiritual force, a subject that explicitly connected to contemporary women's rights and opportunities. Researching ancient Egyptian history, religion, and anthropology, Mathers and Farr used their artistry to turn their knowledge into modern, gender-politicized modes of astral communion. Contributing to the Egyptomania that permeated British decadence, they used performance to engage spiritual forces not only in order to challenge gender-based constrictions, but also, rather thrillingly, *to experience* trans-ecological subject positions in mind, body, and spirit.

In *The Victorians and the Visual Imagination*, Kate Flint notes that, by the end of the century, distinctions among hallucination, illusion, and perception were being heavily debated across the fields of aesthetics, spirituality, the medical profession, and sciences of the brain and mind.[4] If Stevenson and Lee's paganism resides in the engaged movement through space, as I argued in the previous chapter, then – as part of the cultural shift Flint marks – Mathers's and Farr's emphasize one's integration into other dimensions entirely. In this sense, their occult ecology offers a new development to the symbolist strain also running through the decadence of Charles Baudelaire, Walter Pater, Michael Field, Arthur Machen, and Arthur Symons. Their work is particularly unique, however, in its focus on ways in which performance offers both occultists and feminists the strategic maneuverability of the ephemeral. The agency arising from the immateriality of performance appealed to many Golden Dawn members because it situated spiritual experience beyond the conventions of rationality, hard science, and the logic of inclusion and exclusion, mastery and submission. As Mathers and Farr demonstrate, both the impermanence of performance and its ambiguation of a private/public divide draw one into a transtemporal, trans-spatial ecological vision that would, by the middle of the twentieth century, prove pivotal to the Western feminist tradition. In what follows, I first address the gendering of the occult as part of the biological determinism challenged by recent eco-feminism. I then establish the importance of performance for the Golden Dawn's belief system and its access to the otherworldly ecology, before turning specifically to Mathers and Farr's contribution to decadence in their use of Egyptian-inspired ritual to argue for an eco-feminism.

Toward a Feminist Occult Ecology

Made popular by the sage and poet Éliphas Lévis, the French term "occulte" (from the Latin for secret or hidden) arose in the mid-nineteenth century at the same time as modern decadent literature. It referred primarily to practices such as alchemy and natural magic that required training and education in the hermetic knowledge that supposedly gave one the tools to access an alternate, assumedly purer, plane of being. This is the sense in which the word was generally used by Golden Dawn members. However, "occult" also quickly became a catch-all term in the West to address all sorts of new or newly noticed, but not yet institutionalized, spiritual ideas. The decadents themselves saw the dissident potential of the occult, conjoining its exotic interests in Egyptian and other non-European belief systems with contemporary aesthetic, philosophical, and scientific developments. Much as occultists trained in engagement with an otherworldly realm, poets such as Baudelaire and Arthur Rimbaud deployed symbolic correspondences to offer artistic renderings of imagined, alternative realities. With this in mind, Max Nordau melded symbolism and mysticism together, reminding readers of the "old clinical observation that mental decay is accompanied by colour mysticism" and declaring that "Symbolism, like English pre-Raphaelitism," is "nothing else than a form of the mysticism of weak-minded and morbidly emotional degeneration."[5] Just as the arts relied on new spiritualities, the fin-de-siècle occult scene, Alex Owen argues, "owed as much to the *modernité* of Baudelaire or 'the decadents' as it did a particular socialist tradition or the rationalized components of modern Western society."[6] Meanwhile, other Golden Dawn contributors to decadence such as William Sharp and W. B. Yeats turned the occult's transmutability into a means of advocating for their Celtic homelands' spiritual and cultural independence from the English.

Decadents and occultists may have appreciated these new avenues to the otherworldly as a stimulating source of inspiration and power, but many middle-class members of society recognized them as a threat to their cultural and economic authority. Increasing mainstream familiarity with decadence and the occult exacerbated anxieties regarding the exploitative economic agenda of the bourgeoisie. Thus, as Richard King has demonstrated, the term "mystic" was negatively imbued with Orientalist connotations that positioned it in contrast to the rationalist West.[7] In novels such as H. Rider Haggard's *She* (1886) and Joseph Conrad's *Heart of Darkness* (1899), demonized, sexualized Africans and

144   Occult Ecology and the Decadent Feminism

their cultural and spiritual practices – rendered by the tales' heroes as not only exotically pagan but unintelligibly and sensuously mystical – come to signify the abject other of the imperialists' own lack of a moral core. Critics often voiced concern regarding occult claims both of transmutational capabilities and contact with powerful, shrowded authorities – claims that challenged the exceptionalism, privilege, and influence of the white, middle-class, heterosexual, Western male.[8]

As Haggard's and Conrad's novels make evident, this demonization of indeterminate spiritual forces was also strongly nationalist and gendered. The gender politics of such transformability become apparent in the distinctions offered between the occult and mysticism, the former based in education and training, the latter seen as a passive practice of innate receptivity. Mathers and Farr both made claim to mystical engagements. Involving the individual as a docile receptacle open to influences from the spiritual realm, such experiences were often denigrated by association with a sort of anti-empiricist laziness.[9] As Joy Dixon explains, while the occult's rigor and profundity carried masculine connotations, mysticism was portrayed as submissive and feminine: "Over and over again, the same oppositions were rehearsed: occultism had to do with power and wisdom, mysticism with self-surrender and love," formulated on an essential gender binary of male and female.[10] Dixon goes on: "The path of the mystic was a contemplative and solitary one, and as its fruits were almost wholly subjective, its practitioners were exempt from the discipline and hierarchy of occultism." The image of the lone mystic producing obscure works captures to a degree some of Mathers's and Farr's personal spiritual practices. At the same time, it encourages a devaluing of their work as receptive rather than productive, and thus less worthy of engagement by the scientific community, the larger network of amateur scientists, and even the authors and artists who, at the time, were becoming increasingly enamored by a masculine avant-gardism.

Of course, many women such as Mathers, Farr, Annie Besant, and Helena Blavatsky did engage in intensive, methodical studies and practices, but they understood that this did not require their rejection of a belief in a natural correspondence between humans and a more profound reality, one that they themselves often saw as gendered female and more valuable for that. This set of correspondences is reflected in the ways in which Mathers's and Farr's works turn the essentialist conflation of women, nature, and mysticism in which many decadents participated to feminist advantage. In fact, the seeming irrationality of their positions functioned as a source of authority for their claims to having unique access to secret knowledge. The feminization of mysticism, and nonnormative spirituality in general, was part of a broader cultural development around the politics of gender determinism. As Barbara Gates argues, by the end of the century,

> evolutionists, eugenicists, psychologists, anthropologists, educators, poets, and painters alike tended to confer on women attitudes of the "natural." … This kind of biological determinism was so widespread that it can serve as an index to an entire set of discourses that typify Victorian and, later, Edwardian culture in terms of gender definition.[11]

And yet, as various women, decadent and otherwise, who contributed to the pagan revival realized, such essentialism could, in fact, be an effective tool with which to argue for a destabilization of male authority through an enhanced respect not simply for women, but for the planetary community at large.

New Woman writers such as Mona Caird, Kate Chopin, George Egerton, and Sarah Grand engaged and explored a number of perspectives on the subject of biological determinism. Celtic writers such as the Irish Lady Augusta Gregory and Rosa Mulholland, meanwhile, created works either romanticizing the earth mother or, suggestive of Algernon Swinburne's "Hertha" discussed in Chapter 1, depicting the Celtic spirit as an essential female energy. Mulholland's poem "Under a Purple Cloud" is typical of this motif, celebrating "The great brown mother [who] lies and takes her rest, | A dark cheek on her hand, and in her eyes | The shadow of primeval mysteries." The piece takes on a nationalist connotation as "Each flower erect upon its fearless stem" eventually cowers at winter's approach, the cycles of decay, fertilization, and regrowth suggesting the inevitable success of the Celtic revival. As mother earth explains in the closing couplet, "Ye are immortal, children of my pain; | Sleep unafraid, for ye shall live again."[12]

Mulholland's poem sits within a larger anti-colonialist, Celtic agenda exemplified by Patrick Geddes and William Sharp, who coedited *The Evergreen: A Northern Seasonal* as a four-part publication with each volume thematically structured under a different season, each season functioning across the volume as a metaphor for a stage in the Scots Renascence and Celtic revival. In the opening "Proem" of the first volume, William Macdonald and John Arthur Thomson offer a description of social and artistic decadence as part of an organic nationalist resurgence:

> So many clever writers emulously working in a rotten vineyard, so many healthy young men eager for the distinction of decay! And yet, … [a]

> literature of distinguished style and moral vulgarity is indeed a misproduct of the same process that gives us in our meaner streets a degeneration of the restless craving, high and low, for undignified excitement[.] ... Nay, already we seem to see, against the background of Decadence, the vaguely growing lines of a picture of New-Birth.[13]

For Macdonald and Thomson, economic and nationalist change is as inevitable as the seasons. Mulholland, however, extends the metaphor to the planet as an ecology that is, crucially, beyond the comprehension of any one contributor – whether flower or human. The model Mulholland proposes decenters the "healthy young men" of Macdonald and Thomson's narrative, replacing them not with women but with the force of a female, self-nurturing planet.

More recent eco-feminist analyses have also moved toward resolving the conflict inherent within a biologically deterministic feminism that has for centuries sustained the abuse of both women and the environment.[14] Would not a view of feminism as fundamentally rooted in nature (as opposed to science, knowledge, or something else) inevitably cement the very binary logic that the patriarchy has used to leverage its social and cultural dominance? It is because of this conflict that Donna Haraway, in her cyborg manifesto, discredits eco-spiritual feminism for what she sees as its blanket rejection of modern science and technology.[15] However, Chas S. Clifton and Graham Harvey, who note the influence of "second-wave feminism and ... the growing environmental movement" on twentieth-century paganism and occultism, see such feminism as de-essentializing the spiritual or, as they put it, "challenging all hierarchy with the essential plurality of self-constructing individuals and societies."[16] Similarly, a key aim of eco-feminist scholar Val Plumwood's 2002 *Environmental Culture* is to formulate a counter-centric philosophical animism that avoids the dualisms of nature versus human, science, or culture – binaries that tend to position women as neither fully human nor fully natural. To do so, she modifies the vision of deep ecology articulated by Arne Næss and others, advocating for an "ethic of environmental activism" focused on "'standing with' earth others" and "a concept of solidarity ... involving multiple positioning and perspectives," formulations she derives, in large part, from Australian Indigenous spiritual beliefs.[17] Noting that attempts to ignore ethics in establishing environmental models have simply occluded rather than removed them, she proposes adopting a set of "counter-hegemonic virtues, ethical stances which can help minimize the influence of the oppressive ideologies of domination and self-imposition that have formed our conceptions of

Ritual, Politics, and the Occult Theatre Scene

both the other and ourselves." Plumwood defines these as "communicative" virtues, such as listening and paying attention to others, including nonhumans.[18] Key for her is that the model be interactive and that it acknowledge and incorporate the agency of other sentient beings. Plumwood's multi-perspectival paradigm – echoed in some of Haraway's more recent works such as *When Species Meet* (2007) and *Staying with the Trouble: Making Kin in the Chthulucene* (2016) – speaks most accurately to occultists of Mathers's and Farr's time who emphasized the central role of the imagination, performance, and ritual in their own feminism, attentive to the fact that collectivist paradigms need not make claims to holism or override or disregard the everyday systemic subordination and abuse of the female, the nonhuman, and the natural.[19]

Ritual, Politics, and the Occult Theatre Scene

A full sense of Mathers's and Farr's feminist models of occult ecology requires an appreciation of the transformative potency they saw in performance. Approaching the subject from a pagan vantage point, Ronald Hutton defines ritual as "consecrated[,] … formal, dramatic, and unusually stylized action."[20] The Golden Dawn's understanding of ritual is perhaps more accurately suggested in Nina Auerbach's description of theatre in general, which she sees as "the ultimate, deceitful mobility. It connotes not only lies, but a fluidity of character that decomposes the uniform integrity of the self."[21] For Auerbach, the passing temporality of performance and its decompositive character constitute a strategic potential that could be directed toward political ends. Golden Dawn initiates were similarly drawn to performance not despite but because of its tendency to decomposition, its evanescent quality engendering a power they believed to be conjoined to another realm of being. The medium of drama, in this context, allowed the spiritual to serve as the political.

Peggy Phalen observes that "the question of belief always enters critical writing and perhaps never more urgently than when one's subject resists vision and may not be 'really there' at all."[22] While LGBTQ+, Indigenous, Black, and other scholars have noted the disadvantages of having one's identities and values culturally erased and thus delegitimized by a society's homogenizing institutions of power, Phalen points out that there is also "real power in remaining unmarked; and there are serious limitations to visual representation as a political goal."[23] For Phalen, the art of performance is empowered by its marginality, its elusiveness within mainstream systems of control and containment. Understood within this

148   Occult Ecology and the Decadent Feminism

frame, Mathers's and Farr's rituals operate as dissident spirituality – politicized acts of destabilization inspired, paradoxically, by essentialist belief.

Just as occultists were drawn to the art of performance because it engaged the consecrated act of ritual, new developments in decadent and other theatre were notably inflected by the occult. Indeed, "the impact of occultism upon symbolist theatre was so profound," argues Edmund Lingan, "that a deep understanding of symbolism is only possible with some knowledge of the trends of the Occult Revival."[24] At the same time, George Bernard Shaw, despite being Farr's lover and an intimate friend of Theosophist Annie Besant, was notably frightened by the power of the woman's writing and acting, and popular occultism in general. In works such as his play *Caesar and Cleopatra* (1898), he suggests a critique of Farr's feminism, her devotion to the occult, and – as he put it in a letter to her – her "shillings work on exoteric Egyptology."[25] Theatre, in Shaw's view, was a dangerous weapon in the wrong hands. He worried that regular doctors could not compete with the influence on the common public of charlatans, with their "arts of the actor, the orator, the poet, the winning conversationalist."[26] Occult events, such as Farr's performance of works rooted in ancient Egyptian history, were to be understood less as spiritual ventures than as dangerously seductive trickery. Shaw and others were concerned, in particular, with the advocates of spiritualism (with which neither Farr nor Mathers were engaged), who were seen to be using the power of drama to popularize their unfounded beliefs. Echoing Shaw's comparison of medical practitioners and fake occultists, scholar Steven Connor has recently described the public séance room frequently used by spiritualists as functioning both as a "laboratory" and as a "stage."[27] With its "emphasis on staging, spectacle and audience," summarizes Mackenzie Bartlett, "spiritualism can be read as one of the most overtly theatrical cultural trends of the period."[28]

Spiritualists' self-promoting public performances came to characterize much of the new belief systems in general in the popular consciousness. Notably, many members of the Hermetic Order of the Golden Dawn – including writers, designers, actors, producers, and financiers – were also actively involved in public performances, most notably the politicized, cutting edge of theatre, and its engagement with Irish nationalism in particular. Mathers used the skills she had developed while a student at the Slade School of Art (entering at the age of fifteen) to create sets and costumes for a number of Order rituals. Farr and Olivia Shakespear (the latter having first met Golden Dawn member Yeats at the launch party

Ritual, Politics, and the Occult Theatre Scene

for *The Yellow Book*) coauthored and produced two dramas based on ancient Egyptian paganism. Farr also contributed to the production of a play by Yeats, and both were involved in the production of plays by John Todhunter, all of which were influenced by the pagan revival. Meanwhile, Sharp – another Golden Dawn member and a friend of Pater, Dante Gabriel Rossetti, and Yeats – wrote and produced "psychic dramas," as he called them,[29] including *The House of Usna* (1900) and *The Immortal Hour* (1908), both of which draw on Celtic nature-worship for their spirituality. Sharp's works are notable for their ritualist style, with the characters operating less as individuals than as emotive symbols. A previous play by Sharp, *The Black Madonna* (1892), stands as an early attempt at symbolist theatre, with the occult attaining a strong decadent flavor in its Orientalist depiction of a fantastic, tropical culture. Golden Dawn member Annie Horniman's inheritance, meanwhile, allowed her to support many theatrical and occult ventures. She made costumes for Yeats's plays and bankrolled the production of dramas written, directed, and acted by Order members. She also helped financially in establishing the Abbey Theatre in Dublin and the Gaiety Theatre in Manchester, the latter being Britain's first regional repertory theatre.

The Irish interests of Horniman, Yeats, Maude Gonne, and other Order members found inspiration from the Celtic revival, including its eco-pagan mythology, folklore, and political spirit of independence.[30] Oscar Wilde, another Irish connection, was also a friend of Farr. She produced and directed the first English performance of *Salome* (first published in 1893 in French as *Salomé*) at the Bijou Theatre in London in 1905. She herself performed the role of Herodias.[31] Wilde was never a member of the Order, but his wife Constance was. In fact, she was one of the nine women who made up the thirty-two people who joined the Order in 1888, its first year. It is possible she broke the rule of secrecy and shared some knowledge with her husband, as another initiate had declared.[32] Anne de Brémont describes being initiated with Constance in 1888, "a rather theatrical ceremony that would have been amusing had it not been taken so seriously."[33] "Whether the study of the occult accorded well with the aesthetic tendencies of the set that affected the Wilde manner I know not," she writes, "but everyone was possessed with a craze for cheiromancy, star-gazing, planet-reading and the Egyptian cult of the unseen forces of good and evil."[34] She goes on to claim that Constance informed Wilde of her secret teachings and then speculates on the influence of the Golden Dawn on his decadent writings. Wilde himself claimed that the Order's cofounder Samuel Mathers had read his palm.

One can also recognize the influence of an occult aesthetic on *Salome*, which Wilde had written while his wife was actively studying for her exams within the Order. In its arch style of language and movement, its decadent penchant for Eastern exoticism, and its evocation of a nature-based symbolism rooted in mythic belief, the drama evokes both decadence and the ritualist aesthetics of the Golden Dawn, but only generally. Wilde's repeated references in the play to the moon as a female pagan force echo suggestions made by contemporary occultists, most notably Blavatsky in the first major work of the Theosophical movement, *Isis Unveiled* (1877), where Isis is described as a lunar goddess. Isis was also perhaps the most evoked pagan goddess or god within the Golden Dawn. That said, records suggest that, in Ancient Egypt, the moon was more often rendered male, an alternative that Aubrey Beardsley coincidentally captures when – in an illustration for *Salome* – he renders Wilde himself as the moon. A standard trope in dramas by Order members, the eponymous heroine of the play functions as an immortal, spiritual force, like "a woman who is dead," as one of Wilde's characters puts it.[35] At the same time, Salome is both a decadent femme fatale alive in myth and, echoing the Golden Dawn's own history of strong female management, a powerful, leading figure.

Despite this investment in drama, the Golden Dawn was, from its inception, also secretive about much of its origins and lessons. The intense study, memorization, and practice of scripts, rituals, and instructional flying rolls was to enhance the practitioner's self-realization, while the personae, costumes, props, and stage sets were necessary for the power of performance to engage the alternate plane. Needless to say, with such secrecy and introversion, occult performance is not the first thing that comes to mind as an effective resource for enacting feminist change in modern society. But if we remember that, until 1951, it was illegal in Britain to perform or even claim to perform magic,[36] it becomes apparent just what a political lightning rod natural magic already was. The specifically feminist potency of this dramatic force goes back to the Order's beginnings, which can be credited to powerful female leaders such as Blavatsky and Anna Kingsford, the latter an anti-vivisectionist M. D. and Theosophist who founded the Hermetic Society, the precursor of the Golden Dawn. Perhaps the most powerful female influence was a German woman named Anna Sprengel whom Golden Dawn cofounder William Wynn Westcott claimed had first nominated him as head of the Order in Britain. Strong doubts that Sprengel ever actually existed do not take away from the fact that the cofounders wished to root their new

Moina Mathers, Procreativity, and Natural Magic

Order in a female authority. In 1889, the year after the Order was formed, Westcott observed that it saw "no distinction between men and women,"[37] and so the Golden Dawn itself aimed to integrate gender equality within its history and methods, implicitly encouraging an occult feminism that ran parallel to the New Woman movement. Mathers and Farr would have understood the Order's rituals as essential to their aspirations to use the spiritual plane to destabilize the gender codes of modern Western society.

Moina Mathers, Procreativity, and Natural Magic

As with many proponents of twentieth-century eco-feminism, Moina Mathers situated her gender politics not only in pagan myths and values, but also in the idea that women had particularly strong biological and spiritual connections to an ecological reality beyond everyday culture, even if any articulation of this reality was itself enculturated. Her theorization of her performance of the Rites of Isis offers one of the most explicit declarations of a feminist resonance within occult rituals. The influence of ancient Egyptian paganism on both nineteenth-century occultism and decadence is remarkable, even though it is part of a longstanding veneration of ancient Egyptian beliefs. Christopher Partridge has noted that the practice of attributing a high degree of wisdom to the Egyptians (not always with much foundation) goes back to the Classical age.[38] As Hutton observes, "ever since the time of the ancient Greeks, the civilization of Pharaonic Egypt had been regarded as the premier repository of magical lore, being the most stable and enduring of all those that first emerged in Europe and the Near East."[39] Erik Hornung has used the term "Egyptosophy" to refer not to the study of ancient Egypt, but to the construction of conceptions of it as a prime source of esoteric knowledge. "Every period of history has had an Egypt of its own," he writes, "onto which it has projected its fears and its hopes. ... The learned writers of Classical antiquity founded an Egyptosophy that flourishes to this day."[40]

Ancient Egyptian spirituality and culture had struck a particular chord in England following Britain's 1798 defeat of France in the Battle of the Nile, which was followed by a series of archaeological projects that stimulated the British imagination.[41] By 1878, George Ebers could confidently declare that "[n]ot only the learned and cultivated among the inhabitants of the Western world, but every one, high and low, has heard of Egypt and its primeval wonders."[42] Ancient Egyptian beliefs and elements were readily incorporated into many of the new spiritual and artistic

152   Occult Ecology and the Decadent Feminism

movements. Blavatsky, for instance, used *Isis Unveiled* in part to summarize her research in Egypt and elsewhere into Egyptian history and religion. And as late as 1909, the suffragette Theosophist Frances Swiney founded the pseudo-scientific League of Isis, which engaged with women's sexual liberation and eugenics (in highly problematic racial terms) to extol a form of spiritual evolution driven by Isis as the Divine Mother (a trope in Theosophy, as in the Golden Dawn). For Swiney's League, "The Mother, then, is the Supreme Unity, uniting all in Herself. It is not difficult why[,] in the eternal sequence of things in evolution[,] the human race is awakening to the truth of the Divine Feminine in the present stage of the world history."[43]

The Golden Dawn was likewise heavily invested in Egyptology and Egyptosophy, while also holding a strong devotion to the divine feminine, particularly through Isis. Nineteenth-century Egyptian archaeology and Greco-Egyptian papyri had influenced the structure of the Order's initiation grades, and its main pagan deity was a horned figure that fused an Egyptian god-form with Pan and an idol of the Knights Templar.[44] In 1888, the cofounders of the first temple of the Order named it the Isis-Urania Temple, comingling the Egyptian goddess with the Greek muse of astronomy, a link inspired again, in part, by Blavatsky. The Order's next two temples, in Weston-Super-Mare and Bradford, were named the Osiris and Horus temples. Alison Butler notes that elements of Egyptian magic and symbolism permeate the works of William Wynn Westcott, one of the Golden Dawn's three founders.[45] Meanwhile, Samuel Mathers was apparently relatively fluent in Coptic and was deeply interested in Egyptian symbolism. The cofounders had even claimed that the Golden Dawn's secret chiefs – of which the vast majority of members were not allowed to know anything – practiced Egyptian alchemy. Meanwhile, various female members of the Order, such as Mathers, Farr, and Elaine Simpson, claimed to have had ritual-induced visions of Isis.[46]

In 1881, the Egyptian Rooms at the British Museum had become so popular that they were opened daily. Mina Bergson (Henri Bergson's sister) spent time there as an arts student studying Egyptian history and artefacts, and it was here that, in 1887, she met Samuel Mathers.[47] In 1888, Bergson became the Golden Dawn's first initiate, eventually changing her name to "Moina" to emphasize her Irish ancestry. She took for herself the Order motto of *Vestigia Nulla Retrorsum*, Latin for "I do not retrace my steps." The motto's reference is to the erasure through ritual of one's history and material identity in the aspiration to achieve a higher

Moina Mathers, Procreativity, and Natural Magic 153

spiritual state of being, the universal will.[48] But the spiritual motto is also germane to the impermanence of ritual, suggestive of the performative impetus behind all members' self-development within the Golden Dawn. Practitioners did not engage primarily in the worship of a particular deity or deities, but in the scholarly study of magic symbols and rituals believed to affect the sympathetic fusion of one's consciousness with the occluded spiritual realm.[49]

Moina and Samuel married in 1890 and she quickly joined him in becoming one of the Order's most influential members, with the eco-pagan power couple moving to France in 1892 to start the Isis Movement. In Paris, the two often visited the Egyptian collection at the Louvre, with Moina turning her talents to creating artworks and cartoons, as well as designing and constructing costumes and sets for rituals.[50] Meanwhile, Samuel wrote a series of rituals known as the Rites of Isis, combining his studies in Greco-Egyptian articulations of ancient Egyptian religious beliefs with his own creative imaginings. What we know now regarding the actual Rites is through the few articles published on them, with these descriptions making it clear that Moina had a considerable hand in the dramatic realization of the works, with her explanation of them affirming a Goddess tradition. Samuel himself acknowledged a range of influences on this new set of rites, including Tibetan Buddhism, Christianity, magic, and Theosophy (Lees). In light of his creative collage methods, it is not surprising that, as Caroline Tully points out, there are inaccuracies and a "not-quite-right approach to ancient Egyptian religion" in Samuel's description of the rites.[51] These appeared in Frederic Lees's 1900 article on and interview with him and Moina – "Isis Worship in Paris. Conversations With the Hierophant Rameses and the High Priestess Anari." Lees was an American journalist based in Paris who wrote on a range of cultural subjects, including literature, sculpture, and architecture. His works on the occult, mysticism, and hypnotism appeared in *The Humanitarian*, as well as *Light: A Journal of Psychical, Occult, and Mystical Research*. In addition to Moina and Samuel, he published interviews with the physician Georges Gilles de la Tourette (after whom Tourette's syndrome was named) and decadent novelist Joris-Karl Huysmans (whose novel about Satanism and the occult, *Là-Bas*, appeared in 1891).

Lees's article "Isis Worship in Paris" starts, theatrically enough, by setting the scene: "Through the yellow muslin curtains of a window on my right streamed the dim light of a mid-October morning. The winged figure of Isis was facing me, her horned disk circled with an aureola of diffused light, which came through the interstices of the closed shutters of another window behind" (82). The piece then transitions into a conversation with Moina and Samuel about "their studies of a religion dead to the Egyptologist, but so living and so full of vital force to them," interspersed with descriptions of actual rituals, "artistic in the extreme" (83). The conversations are heavily edited and Lees's descriptions are utterly sympathetic, declaring Moina to be a highly accomplished artist who exudes an aura of mysticism and the occult. At one point the interviewer observes that Moina's art would serve as an excellent complement to the writings of Fiona Macleod (unbeknownst to Lees, the pseudonym of William Sharp). As Lees realized, Moina illustrating one of Macleod's highly popular romantic Celtic novels would have done much to popularize the couple's occult paganism back in Britain.

In his article, Lees's attention curiously pivots between, on the one hand, Isis and her centrality to Egyptian worship in contemporary Paris and, on the other, Moina herself – presented respectfully as both the High Priestess Anari and an exemplary artist. Similarly, John Newton (also writing in 1900) proposes that the information in Lees's article be taken as scholarly information that would be of particular interest to those "fascinated by the study of the old religion of Egypt, recognizing as it did the feminine element in its worship" and Isis as "Egypt's chief deity."[52] "Ancient Egypt, at the same time the source of religion and civilization," he writes, "recognized the Divine Mother in the Goddess Isis" and thus, at the feast of Isis, "only the males were sacrificed, the females were spared out of complement to the sex of the Goddess." Following, it would seem, Moina and Samuels's lead, both journalists frame their articles on the Rites of Isis being performed in Paris to focus on a female divinity, and specifically one that extends through the being of Moina herself as a performer of the rites, a medium for Isis, and part of a vital force. Even though the Golden Dawn was a hermetic society, its members and descendant societies wrote out the rituals, illustrated aspects of them, and photographed themselves with ceremonial clothing and other items. In 1910, Aleister Crowley even published extracts of materials on Golden Dawn rituals in his magazine *The Equinox*. Although Crowley's actions apparently angered Samuel, he could not be too critical because he himself, along with Moina, had over a decade earlier begun performing the Rites of Isis in a public theatre. One of the best-known dramas by Golden Dawn members, this ceremony demonstrates the ways in which pagan belief, magic, and theatre engendered occult practice as both eco- and woman-centered. Rather than

Moina Mathers, Procreativity, and Natural Magic

demonstrating a line of influence between the immaterial and the material, or the occult and the public, this formulation of a trans-spatial agency points to a conflation of performance spaces that helps explain why the Matherses were not more uncomfortable with presenting private ritual as public theatre.

The couple began by practicing their Rites of Isis privately in a chapel constructed in the basement of their Parisian residence. As encouraged by the Golden Dawn's hermeticism, they initially rejected an invitation from Samuel's friend, the French writer Jules Bois, to perform at the Bodinière Theatre.[53] But then, as Moina explains in Lees's article, the "goddess Isis herself" intervened, appearing to Moina in a dream to give them permission to proceed (83). It is notable that this affirmation is bestowed by a traceless female deity, echoing the claim made by the cofounders of the Golden Dawn regarding their guidance from the unconfirmable Anna Sprengel. The couple began performing the rituals at the Bodinière in March 1899,[54] with Samuel adopting the priestly identity of the Hierophant Rameses. "Rameses" is an English transliteration of a name given to a number of ancient Egyptian pharaohs, reflecting Samuel's vision of himself as both a seer and a leader of the Golden Dawn. This need not be read as a suggestion of egotism; in his interview with Lees for "Isis Worship in Paris," Samuel foregrounds the way in which he and Moina both, in their worship, subsume themselves in Isis as a force greater than themselves. The claim echoes the Golden Dawn's precept of ritual not as worship of a particular goddess or god, but as a private, consecrated act of extension through another realm.

Moina, meanwhile, took on the role of the High Priestess Anari, an invented persona presented as being in particularly close communication with Isis. In Lees's view, her costume and props made her especially well "adapted for giving a good idea of the symbolism of the Isis worshipper" (84) (Fig. 5.1). The wording of Lees's synopsis suggests that the symbolic relevance of Anari's clothing was actually explained to him by the Matherses, who had taken creative liberties in developing the rites. "Her long, flowing hair expresses the idea of rays of light radiating through the universe," he writes:

> Upon her head is a little cone symbolical of the Divine Spirit, and a lotus flower symbolic of purity and wisdom. "The lotus springs up," said the Hierophant Rameses, "from the muddy waters of the Nile. The cone is the flame of life. The whole idea of the dress of the priestess is that the life of matter is purified and ruled by the divine spirit." (84)

Figure 5.1 Photograph of Moina Mathers, circa 1900, printed in André Gaucher, "Isis à Montmartre," *L'Écho du merveilleux*, 94 and 95 (December 1900), 446–53, 470–73, at 471. The Picture Art Collection/Alamy Stock Photo.

Once "the High Priestess Anari invoked the goddess in penetrating and passionate tones," there followed the "dance of the four elements" by a young Parisian lady who, dressed in long white robes, had previously recited some verses in French in honor of Isis. Evoking perhaps Salomé's dance of the seven veils, the performances are heavily invested in images of Moina as a symbol of Isis and of the universal will, the latter being a broader eco-spiritual force that, while gendered, also disembodies and disturbs the qualities that render the divine as female.

Sensitivity to the feminist potential of Mathers's enactments requires a consideration of the theatre performances as private, despite the invited audience. Discussing Dion Fortune's performance decades later of these same Rites of Isis, Gareth Knight describes them as theatre, observing that enacting rituals in a public forum may not be "the most effective mode of ceremonial magic, for like grand opera and other specialist art forms, it needs a sympathetic and informed audience."[55] There is a significant oscillation in Knight's description between, on the one hand, suggesting the performers have sacrificed their private spirituality to the attention and possible monetary gain of a public spectacle and, on another, understanding the audience as being converted momentarily into part of an occult community. Victor Turner offers an anthropological understanding of such conversion as having been at one time a more common daily experience. Notably, Turner's *From Ritual to Theatre* (1982) is partly inspired by his mother, Violet Witter, a feminist and actor

Moina Mathers, Procreativity, and Natural Magic 157

who contributed to the short-lived Scottish National Theatre. Turner describes it as "the equivalent" of Dublin's Abbey Theatre, even if it "could not emulate the heady nationalist eloquence or stark political metacommentary of an Ireland struggling to be free."[56] Although he notes that, during her career, Witter would perform work by George Bernard Shaw and Fiona Macleod (Sharp "in literary Celtic drag,"[57] as he puts it), Turner's analysis of ritual does not explicitly engage the occult. What he does argue, however, is that all notable experiences in life include a state of performance, "an act of creative retrospection in which 'meaning' is ascribed to the events and parts of experience," "both 'living through' and 'thinking back'."[58] In addressing the connections between symbolic actions within cultures across time, Turner proposes that one can recognize historical gestures within "the symbolic genres of the so-called 'advanced' civilizations, the complex, large-scale industrial societies."[59] He links ancient ritual to modern experimental theatre, for example, offering an anthropological framework useful for understanding Moina and Samuel's claim that their symbolic ritual performances allowed them to commune with ancient Egyptian deities.

Even in a general sense, a theatre event's effectiveness relies in part on the audience's emotional investment in the shared experience. With the performance of the Rites of Isis in a theatre and with the goddess's approval, the audience was to be understood as, like Mathers herself, having been incorporated into the universal will. The majority of her and Samuel's viewers were, indeed, sympathetic to the occult, some even engaging in secondary roles within the ritual. To be present at the performance, therefore, was to be made part of the divine female. Like Auerbach's view of theatre in general as destabilizing one's sense of self, the conflation of private and public that Knight registers is less conflicted in light of the Golden Dawn's understanding of their occult acts as not simply mimicking or rendering the alternate reality to which members gave such importance, but displacing selfhood with an affirmative dispersion of life force through the otherworldly.

In this context, it is also less peculiar that Lees presents the couple, during their interview, in the ritual identities as the High Priestess Anari and the Hierophant Rameses. It is in this role that Moina explicitly articulates their occult performance as a mode of female empowerment. The feminist concerns underlying her vision of ancient Egyptian paganism are most apparent in her critique of the marginalization of the priestess's cosmological role in contemporary, institutional religions, which, she observes, have devalued the "idea of the Priestess [that] is at the root of all ancient beliefs" (86). "What do we find in the modern development of religion to replace the feminine idea, and consequently the Priestess? When a religion symbolizes the universe by a Divine Being," she argues, "is it not illogical to omit woman, who is the principal half of it, since she is the principal creator of the other half – that is, man?" Her language implies a critique of monotheism (and Samuel had, indeed, described their beliefs, in "Isis Worship in Paris," as pantheistic, as well as animist). But her claim is not simply for the inclusion of a goddess within religion, akin to the Pagan Federation's suggestion that all paganism must include a goddess.[60] Rather, she argues for the female spirit as primary because, as biological mothers, females are the principal creators on the planet, the ecological source:

> How can we hope that the world will become purer and less material when one excludes from the Divine, which is the highest ideal, that part of its nature which represents at one and the same time the faculty of receiving and that of giving – that is to say, love itself in its highest form – love the symbol of universal sympathy? (86)

For Mathers, woman "finds her force in her alliance with the sympathetic energies of Nature." She uses the term "nature" twice in this passage, signifying both the essence of the universal will and organic ecology. More precisely, just as performance exists simultaneously both as a mode of otherworldly engagement and as an agent of change in the everyday, nature fulfills the full essence of Golden Dawn paganism: It is the spiritual made manifest not so much as a symbol of the ideal but *as* that actual realm in sentient or animist form, capturing what Mathers calls the "eternal attraction between ideas and matter" (87). Thus, to lack both sympathy for and a sense of integration with the natural (including what is commonly categorized as the human) is to be disconnected from Isis, the eternal maternal. In Mathers's model, it is not the human woman who marks divinity, but the procreative force of nature. She realized that such a seemingly gender-essentialist formulation could be interpreted as reinforcing the technology that privileged the male, scientific, factual, and materialist. But, as she argues, the same essentialist logic is, in fact, a viable position from which to argue for a destabilization of not simply male authority but systemic oppression more broadly.

Mathers's neo-pagan politics accords with Plumwood's argument that a viable eco-feminism will not simply subvert patriarchal logic because such a maneuver – even if it establishes a matriarchy – would still inadvertently sustain the oppressive scaffolding itself. Rather, for Plumwood, eco-feminism must work for a politics focused on multiple perspectives and trans-species solidarity or, as she puts it, "'standing with' earth others."[61] Likewise, for Mathers, the divine feminine that she evokes in her ritual of Isis demands respect not only among women and among humans, but among all of the protean, mutually imbricated pro/creative energies on the planet and beyond. "That is where the magical power of woman is found," explains Mathers, "[s]he finds her force in her alliance with the sympathetic energies of Nature" (86), thereby granting moral standing to fauna, flora, and the planet. This ethical extensionism remains complicated by her vision of the earth as a mother, a view that risks reinscribing procreative heteronormativity into a paganism that her ritual performances encourage one to understand as changeable and disruptive or, in the language of the more recent Pagan Federation, queer and diverse. Mathers's conception of nature and the female, however, is less sutured to a centering of the human within a universalist scheme than the maternal metaphor may initially suggest. Nature is, for her, always also a divine reality – "an *assemblage* of thoughts clothed with matter and ideas which seek to materialize themselves" (86). Woman, meanwhile, "is the magician born of Nature by reason of her great natural sensibility, and of her instructive sympathy with such subtle energies as these intelligent inhabitants of the air, the earth, the fire and water" (87). Structurally similar to the Golden Dawn's conception of the spiritual realm as natural, amorphic, and powerful, Mathers's spirituality also holds that these principal qualities are in greatest sympathy with the constitution of women in particular. But, as I have argued, this is not to say that, in her view, all women are skilled in natural magic; to evoke Simone de Beauvoir's *Second Sex*, in the Golden Dawn one is not born a magician. Mathers strictly adhered to the Order's position that memorization, testing, and complex training are necessary for the practice of natural magic. Her eco-feminism resides not in the sort of essential view of woman as an all-powerful goddess or of the earth as mother that is suggested in some works by male decadents, but in the belief that women's procreative potential (even if it was not fulfilled, as in her own case) reflected their stronger disposition for performing natural magic.

Florence Farr's Feminist Occultism

Moina Mathers articulated an eco-feminism that arises almost exclusively from the context of her ancient Egyptian ritual studies and practices. Her oeuvre, therefore, does not thoroughly address the correlation between

Occult Ecology and the Decadent Feminism

her gynocentric occult practice and British fin-de-siècle gender politics. Florence Farr was as familiar as Mathers with ancient Egyptian renderings of the earth as a goddess and the female as spiritually powerful but, at the same time, she had a more intense engagement than Mathers with the decadent and theatre scenes, as well as with contemporary gender politics. These investments led her to produce feminist works that range from urban New Woman fiction to dramas recreating Egyptian myth and ritual. After leaving Queen's College in 1880 without completing her studies,[62] Farr took up acting, and her investment in the theatre and literary scenes would become enmeshed with her interests in the occult and, later, the Celtic revival. In 1894, with the financial support of Annie Horniman, Farr ran a season of new plays at the Avenue Theatre, including works by W. B. Yeats and John Todhunter (both members of the Golden Dawn), as well as George Bernard Shaw.[63] The poster for the season was Aubrey Beardsley's first. Yeats and Shaw first saw Farr in Todhunter's pagan play *A Sicilian Idyll* (1890), in which she performed the role of Priestess Amaryllis,[64] who prays to the lunar goddess Selene to punish her unfaithful lover. On seeing her perform, Yeats wrote the role of Aleel, in his 1892 *The Countess Kathleen* (later *Cathleen*), specifically for her.[65] Aleel is a mystic male poet and seer devoted to the countess. In 1898, Farr became the stage manager for Yeats's Irish Literary Theatre in Dublin. There was also some talk in 1894 of Farr playing the lead in a production of a play by the decadent authors Michael Field, although the production appears not to have been realized.[66]

As these various connections suggest, Farr spent the 1890s immersed in the London and Dublin theatre and decadent communities. For roughly two decades beginning in the 1890s, she was also highly prolific, writing plays and novels, as well as articles on feminist politics, sociology, and Egyptian antiquity and spirituality that appeared in, among other places, the *British Journal of Art and Politics*, *The Mint*, *The New Age*, *Occult Review*, and *Theosophical Review*. In 1890, Farr was initiated into the Isis-Urania Temple, taking as her magical motto *Sapientia Sapienti Donoa Data* (Wisdom is a gift given to the wise).[67] Her progress through the Order's training was remarkably quick and, within two years, she had become the Outer Order's Praemonstratrix (Latin: prophesier, or lead instructor). By 1897, she was the Chief Adept in Anglia, the Order's most powerful position in Britain.

Throughout this time, Farr was studying ancient Egyptian culture and spirituality, often going to the British Museum to research materials, view exhibits, and make use of the work of chief philologist and Egyptologist

Ernest Wallis Budge, who himself may have contributed to Golden Dawn activities.[68] The feminist element of her studies is apparent from the research she conducted in 1895 for her book *Egyptian Magic*. Farr became interested in a mummy that had been acquired by the museum in 1835, and eventually claimed to have made contact through the mummy with an ancient Egyptian female adept of the Temple of Amun at Thebes.[69] Tully has noted that while X-rays have confirmed that the coffin is indeed that of a "Chantress of Amun, dating from the nineteenth (1295–1186 BCE) or twentieth (1186–1069 BCE) Dynasties, the mummy that lay inside the coffin dates from the Roman period (30 BCE–395 CE) and is actually that of a man."[70] Regardless, Tully notes, "[i]n choosing an ancient Egyptian priestess as a spiritual guide, Farr was asserting herself as a spiritually accomplished woman in a man's world."[71]

As early as 1894, Farr was envisioning occult alchemy as a female-centered practice – the transmutation of the individual mind from everyday perception to a spiritual reality rooted in the "wisdom Goddess" (i.e., Athena), marking the matriarchal paradigm that she would continue to develop for the remainder of her career.[72] It was also in 1894 that Farr published one of her most populist works, the novel *The Dancing Faun*, which, rather than evoking the interests of the Golden Dawn, offers the light, witty banter among middle- and upper-class characters that, thanks in large part to Wilde's plays, had come to give modern decadence both its popularity and its reputation for vapidity and elitism. The title of the novel itself speaks to the paganism that was such a common element of Victorian decadence. The eponymous allusion to the goat god brings to mind that of Machen's own *The Great God Pan*, which appeared the same year and in the same series run by publisher John Lane. Farr's eagerness to gain broad appreciation for her novel is apparent from one of her letters; not satisfied with its tepid reception, she wrote Lane, telling him that people were unsure where to buy the book, and suggested he consider "advertis[ing] *The Dancing Faun* a little." She goes on:

> I saw some good notices of it such as the Athenean and Liverpool Daily Post which seemed as if they would quote well. It might have a chance of selling a little now at Xmas time, if attention were called to it. It was such a misfortune that Smith's catalogue printed it as by Florence Parr so that it lost all the benefit it might have got from my name being known in that direction.[73]

In another letter to Lane, Farr proposed a second book that she wanted first to be serialized in his journal *The Yellow Book*, which was at its peak of decadent infamy.[74]

162 Occult Ecology and the Decadent Feminism

Despite Farr's familiarity with British decadent culture and the related works of French symbolists and people such as Swinburne, Pater, and Wilde, her pagan interests arose primarily from her position of seniority in the Golden Dawn and her skills in natural magic. Thus, at the same time that she labored to position *The Dancing Faun* within fin-de-siècle decadent culture in order to expand her audience, the actual novel undermines the public personae of dandies and upper-class egotists by using the Wildean subgenre to offer a New Woman novel that situates her occult feminist views within the more common context of modern gender politics.

Farr would eventually identify herself as a suffragist,[75] and so it is appropriate that her *Dancing Faun* appeared in Lane's Keynotes series, named after George Egerton's hugely successful *Keynotes* (1893), a collection of New Woman short stories. Reflecting her belief in the power of performance, Farr situates the novel's analysis of women's agency in the (itself rather hermetic) inner circle of the theatre world. The titular hero of *The Dancing Faun* – a manipulative, self-assured young man (believed to be based on Shaw) – is murdered by his beloved, Lady Geraldine, an Ibsenesque character whom the author modeled in part on herself.[76] The strong-willed heroine serves as an easy funnel for Farr's feminist concerns. At one point, Geraldine asks in anger, "Why should there be one law for men and another for women?"[77] Elsewhere, she disparages the inhumane, mechanical system by which young women are brought out for social consumption: "in another season, girls now in the schoolroom will be going through the mill exactly in the same way as I am doing. How one longs for something different!" (13–14). Early in the novel, the heroine's mother, complimenting her daughter's beautiful voice (a talent she shares with Farr), offers some advice that suggests the spiritualized politics of the dramatic arts: "In art all are equal. There is something so beautiful in that thought" (3). Through this axiom, the novel establishes artistic performance as a means to social equality, the fundamental premise behind the novel's gender politics. As Mary K. Greer has pointed out, Farr was well aware of the dramaturgical forces that can be drawn on to actuate the occult.[78] Meanwhile, author Rebecca West, in her 1912 article "English Literature," foregrounds – perhaps inadvertently – the importance of performance's ephemerality for its spiritual impact:

> Miss Farr is the last of those subtle women of the nineties who veiled their loveliness with a becoming melancholy born of tragedies that were, one is sure, very enjoyable while they lasted. Content to be themselves works of art, they did not desire to project their beauty into eternity by becoming

artists. Miss Farr's art of reciting to the psaltery is typical of her period. It is unimportant from every artistic point of view, yet nothing could be more exquisite than the speech of that lovely, level voice, in which the tears glimmer perpetually, like dewdrops in long grass.[79]

It would seem that it is Farr's spiritual investment in her performance on the psaltery, a zither-like instrument played by plucking strings, that West here interprets as an artless earnestness (Fig. 5.2). Instrument-maker Arnold Dolmetsch engaged with Farr and Yeats while designing her psaltery (seemingly with a Celtic knot pattern in the center), and Yeats would go on to write a number of essays on the recitation of poetry to the instrument. In 1902, Farr, Yeats, and Dolmetsch gave a lecture-performance on "Speaking to Musical Notes," where Yeats lectured and Farr played the instrument while reciting poetry by, among others, Yeats, Swinburne, and Lionel Johnson. The room was apparently "*packed* like herrings in a box," according to artist and Golden Dawn member Patricia Colman Smith.[80] They would spend the next four years performing in England, Ireland, and Scotland.[81] In 1907, Farr performed in America. The reviews of these events were mixed, reflecting the growing disinterest after the turn of the century in the image of the female mystic, along with other aspects of decadence that had a peak of popularity in the 1890s.

Having personally familiarized herself with the Enochian language of Elizabethan occultist John Dee, Farr lectured on how the sounds of its

Figure 5.2   Photograph of Florence Farr. Abbey Theatre archives, 1903. The Picture Art Collection/Alamy Stock Photo.

164   Occult Ecology and the Decadent Feminism

vowels have the power to vibrate in sympathy with the ether on the astral plane; there is with this language an essential harmony between art and the otherworldly just as, in *The Dancing Faun*, theatre allows access to a higher realm.[82] In Farr's view, her performances in Britain and North America reciting Yeats's and other's words while playing her psaltery are no less than an invitation for a multi-participatory immersion into the universal will as an ecological network characterized by equanimity and equality.[83] West's depiction of the musician, meanwhile, reflects the common practice of associating male artists within the occult and symbolist traditions with intellectual rigor, and female artists with mysticism, passivity, and a winsome innocence. It also reinforces the common tendency to transpose the ephemeral sensibility perceived to exist in Farr's work onto her personality. As *The Dancing Faun* makes clear, the author's own interests in performance were actually solidly grounded in modern politics.

In Farr's novel, the heroine Geraldine's seeming rival in love is the actor Grace Lovell, another independently minded female who defines her life on the stage as an ephemeral, aesthetic ideal. Grace's husband, George, was at one time himself an actor. Not a sincere artist, though, he mocks Grace: "You appear to think what people say on the stage is real life, and what you see behind the scenes is play acting," to which she counters, suggestive of Sybil Vane in Wilde's *Picture of Dorian Gray* (1890/1891), "[W]e all play our parts there, [in everyday life,] but we put all of reality we have in us into our acting" (46). The conflation of stage performance with the otherworldly follows on the Golden Dawn's view of ritual enactment as a means to the pure divine. At the same time, in contrast to the artifice of social customs such as the marriage market, Grace finds in performance the inspiration for her esoteric feminism: "As she listened to the laments of Beatrice di Cenci, it seemed to her some inspired spirit had entered her body and was making use of her voice to reveal to her what life, and love, and divine sorrow meant" (53). The empowered spirit arises from reciting lines from Percy Shelley's 1819 *The Cenci*, Farr herself having performed the character of Beatrice in select scenes in an 1892 recital of the play.[84] The more vital engagement of Grace's acting, meanwhile, leads her to focus on "making every sound she uttered beautiful" (54), turning art into life, just as it turns spirit into the wellspring of Grace's feminist defiance.

One finds a similar politics in Farr's later novel *The Solemnization of Jacklin* (1911). For West, one of the most entertaining aspects of this novel is its portrayal of an eco-pagan dandy, "a most charming semi-supernatural gentleman, the son of Eros by a wealthy American lady, who picturesquely goes to sleep among the Annunciation lilies or dallies at Fontainebleau talking pantheism and Theosophy and anything else that comes handy to beautiful ladies."[85] Farr takes the now popular persona of the pagan young man, which West here mocks, and juxtaposes it with sociological arguments of women's natural place in modern society. At one point, the narrator offers the heroine's thoughts on encultured gender biases: "Why was it, she asked herself, that it was impossible for women to make money as easily as men did; why was it always slavery or marriage for them? ... She suddenly realised that she belonged to a race of creatures maintained for the pleasure they could give their masters – their paymasters."[86] The heroine, Jacklin, distinguishes herself from the rest of the female race, however, by her self-determination. She leaves her husband for a dissipated artist, goes through various relationships, has a child, and then returns to the husband. Solemnizing – as in the novel's title – refers to performing a ceremony that affirms a particular status or acknowledges a new state of being; in Christianity, for instance, it refers to marriage as a religious rite. But in Farr's novel, the actions that solemnize Jacklin are not her conformity to heteronormative cultural machinery but her self-determined choices, and specifically choices that go against the bourgeois conventions of marriage.

One gets a much stronger sense of Farr's conception of spiritual and cultural solemnization from her study *Modern Woman: Her Intentions* (1910), an anthropological work that she wrote at the same time as *The Solemnization of Jacklin*. Here, the author declares that the twentieth century will be the "Woman's Century," qualifying the conviction by noting that, "in spite of the enthusiasm of the alchemists and the transmuters of base metal into gold, the main body of society is as yet hardly aware of the fire that is to burn it."[87] Her views on the consequences of postponing suffrage are particularly striking:

> Every day of delay in giving women the vote gives them a power far more deadly, a hope more dangerous, an accomplishment far more vital. It gives them the power of standing up for themselves, freed from the belief in the protection of men. It gives them hope in each other. It teaches them to speak for themselves, and discover the force of their eloquence and the ingenuity of their resources.[88]

She even questions the necessity of men for pregnancy. The language here and elsewhere in *Modern Woman* develops rhetorically toward the viability of all-female or female-driven communities. Farr's gender

166   Occult Ecology and the Decadent Feminism

politics do not fit comfortably in the mainstream of New Woman writing, offering, at times, a problematic vision of women's innate nurturing tendencies while simultaneously denying this gender-essentialist compulsion a heteronormative vision of mutual support. As suggested in *The Solemnization of Jacklin*, Farr challenges conventional marriage on anthropological grounds, while also arguing for sanitary conditions for prostitutes and for the serious consideration of eugenics as a way of ensuring the health of the collective.[89] Rachel Blau DuPlessis admires the study's originality and energy, but summarizes it as a "snarl of scapegoating, Semiticized representations, patrician racism, overgeneralized history, and feminism."[90]

Farr's efforts to suture her sociological claims to a spiritual context, meanwhile, raise additional concerns. In *Modern Woman*, she turns to the psychological writings of Henri Bergson (Moina Mathers's brother) to urge pregnant women to maintain the torpid consciousness induced by sleep because it encourages the development of the imagination. This directive seems drawn from the Golden Dawn's attention to the role of the imagination in practices such as alchemy, scrying, spiritual sexuality, and the individual's immersion within the universal will.[91] Mary K. Greer posits that, for Order members, the will was "charged by a desire that was purified of all ego-content and actualized through an imagination that used all the senses," and Hutton similarly notes that members believed "spiritual maturity" could be attained "by inflaming the imagination, providing access to altered states of consciousness."[92] Within the context of the Golden Dawn's artistic occultism, it makes sense for Farr not only to consider the importance of her personal freedom to engage her imagination, but also to develop an understanding of other catalysts for sustained, creative thought. Torpidity, she observes, is "a state cultivated to a high degree by the Eastern mystics, who have given us glimpses of the psychic powers to which it can give birth."[93] "The Eastern sage does not starve his emotional nature," she continues, "but learns to direct it, while he is in a state of apparent torpor. So I believe the wise mother might, if she gave herself the opportunity, direct the future character of her child in the best sense of the word." Just as Mathers emphasizes the potential to give birth as a sign of women's spiritual authority, Farr argues that Eastern mysticism and pregnancy both naturally enhance a woman's openness to a more profound state of being.

The model ultimately relies on problematic assumptions regarding women's essential biological drive; however, Farr also suggests that the condition of imaginative torpor can be extended to others, bringing to

Florence Farr's Feminist Occultism 167

mind the collectivism that Plumwood more recently encourages in her exploration of eco-feminism circumventing a patriarchal structure by developing empathy, collaboration, and mutual respect with other species. The artist and the natural magician, Farr implies, are of the same stock in nurturing the imagination's access to the instinctual consciousness, "an animal faculty cultivated by an outdoor life."[94] Within the anthropological context of *Modern Woman*, Farr celebrates "the old matriarchal village community," which relied heavily on instinct, as an example of "a good way of conducting affairs on a dignified basis without the family unit."[95] In such a society, sexuality would manifest itself not as heteronormative monogamy, but as "temperance with an occasional orgy." Farr bases her argument in the practices of tribes living in tropical locations, as described not much before Farr's text by anthropologists J. F. Hewitt, Herbert Hope Risley, and Cornelis Tiele. According to Farr – as suggested by the village cultures of Egypt, India, and elsewhere depicted in these works – if women once again were to establish greater authority and if people generally adopted a life more attuned to nature, society would replace its emphasis on intellect with an engagement with a collective consciousness rooted in a natural, psychically matriarchal concord.[96]

As these various works suggest, Farr approached the relationship of the occult to a pagan female authority from more than one direction. Her effort to conjoin these issues with contemporary feminist politics proved largely incomplete, however, with her focus rarely settling on pagan ritual – the realm where her spirituality, performance theory, and feminism overlapped most strongly. It is to Farr's coauthored occult dramas that one must turn to find her most fully imagined rendering of such a naturalized eco-feminism. Like *The Dancing Faun*, the plays make use of performance to engage contemporary gender politics. However, they more effectively situate this fusion within an occult context that shifts the debate outside everyday power dynamics to a realm of nonreferential equality beyond issues of human desire, identity, sentience, and, indeed, the material world.

The Beloved of Hathor and *The Shrine of the Golden Hawk* are symbolist plays rooted in ancient Egyptian history, attributed at publication in 1901 to Farr and Olivia Shakespear, although Greer argues that Farr is the principal author of the latter play, if not both.[97] Farr directed and acted in the plays' first productions. For Farr, ancient Egyptian spirituality manifested a connection to other temporal and spatial planes. Through her scrying, for example, she proposed that she had come into contact

168   Occult Ecology and the Decadent Feminism

with the ancient figure of Nenkheftka (Farr referred to him as Nemkheftka), a provincial official from Deshasha, a statue of whom was acquired by the British Museum in 1897.[98] Farr's efforts at such engagement were unique within the Order because her rituals apparently resulted not simply in contact with supernal figures but in her temporary materialization *as* them. Farr saw herself as a manifestation of the ancient Egyptian rendered in the statue, while Nenkheftka was her ka (one aspect of a human's soul, according to ancient Egyptian spirituality). In *Egyptian Magic*, Farr associated the ka with the human ego, but here, five years later, she suggests a more nuanced sense of it as an element of oneself originating within another level of an expanded ecology, the "double" of one's being on "this plane of human earth-life."[99] The logic of this particular formulation of spiritual alchemy builds on the Golden Dawn's view of performance as both conduit and manifestation of the divine, thereby allowing Farr to politicize her engagements in the material world through the trans-dimensional quality of her own being.

With *The Beloved of Hathor* and *The Shrine of the Golden Hawk*, Farr manifests her occult feminism by combining ancient Egyptian history and ritual, imaginative renderings of what they were like, and aspects of the Golden Dawn, including the Matherses' own Rites of Isis. Farr and Shakespear's wish for the plays to function as occult media is apparent from their formulation of the scenes not so much as history or narrative, but as symbolically potent action: "The Authors wish the plays to be represented, not scenically but decoratively, with a simple white background or pale sienna hangings, so arranged that the figures of the actors, moving across the stage, may reproduce the effect of the ancient frescoes or illuminated papyri."[100] They envisioned the actors, within the reality of the performance, to embody the frescoes or illuminations, the spiritually enlivened aesthetic objects themselves, much like the statue of Nenkheftka in which Farr found her ka. Meanwhile, just as this transformation incorporates the performer into the universal will, it also extends the force of the will into the feminist politics being performed in the plays. In the shorter of the two, *The Shrine of the Golden Hawk*, Farr performed the role of Nectoris, the daughter of the King of Egypt, "skilled in the sombre mysteries of Isis." "Having passed through the flames which cleanse [her] from mortality," Nectoris is less a human than a spirit, although "she has yet some part in what is mortal." Farr was thus perfectly cast, having already demonstrated her dual positioning through her ability to use her skill at scrying to become quite literally (it was felt) a supernal force, while nevertheless still struggling with fin-de-siècle femi-

Florence Farr's Feminist Occultism

nist politics. Because Nectoris is part mortal, when she goes to retrieve a magic amulet of the god Heru from Gebuel, an evil magician intent on "overwhelming the power" of the king, her victory is not guaranteed. As the heroine's ka explains, Egypt is not simply a nation, but "is great and skilled in august mysteries; and to reign over her and to follow her wisdom is to become equal with the gods; and when the last mysteries are won, even greater." The heroine's struggle is not simply a battle of nations or empires, but a divine struggle from which the material conflict cannot be separated. Occult ecology in this framework must be recognized as not distending only temporal and spatial scales, but also those of other dimensions – modern feminism, in this scenario, playing a role in the power dynamics that shape the universal will itself.

With a rhetorical seductiveness suggestive of the heroine of Wilde's *Salome*, Nectoris manages to trick Gebuel into giving her access to the amulet. When she puts it on, rather than being destroyed by Heru (as is expected of any mortal), she becomes the god: "His eyes are my eyes, and his power is my power, his spirit is my spirit." As the heroine then explains, "Whoso is made one with the gods makes their holy place desolate, and himself becomes their sanctuary. … For [Heru] has devoured their mystical rites and symbols, he has swallowed their shining forms." Thus, Nectoris (and Farr as the actor performing the role) becomes not a symbol or messenger of Heru but "the will of Heru made manifest"; the result is a matriarchal system being destined to rule Egypt. The success is marked by Nectoris's dancing, although, because the performance is driven by "a splendour which is beyond the eye of man," it must occur offstage, while the character Ka, the heroine's "sister soul," imitates the performance on stage. The audience members see only a simulacrum of what is to be understood as the now utterly divine heroine. This is a crucial distinction because the audience members are made to question whether they have simply witnessed a play, or whether, in a sense, they have been drawn – from the occult actor's perspective – into becoming participants in the ritual. In *The Shrine of the Golden Hawk*, the audience is encouraged to consider the actor, Farr, as a potential manifestation of the divine. In the logic of the ritual, just as Nectoris's faith was tested, each audience member's degree of belief will determine the result of their own trial by conviction.

Nectoris's survival after putting on the divine amulet echoes Farr's own experience while scrying of living through Nenkheftka, becoming an embodiment of the spiritual force of the entity to which she has exposed herself through ritual. *The Shrine of the Golden Hawk* both explains Farr's

Occult Ecology and the Decadent Feminism

scrying methods from a spiritual standpoint and itself functions as a ritual that engages the audience in its alchemy. In other words, the mediation from the god Heru to the semi-mortal Nectoris to the sister-soul Ka is doubled in the mediation from the universal will to Farr to the audience. In this process, the occult feminism is likewise enacted, with a shift in social models where kings and male magicians are replaced by females. As Nectoris's father informs her, "If you, a woman wise with the serpent wisdom, should gain that sanctuary and bring back the amulet, I will give the throne of Egypt to you and to your daughters for ever; that honor may be paid to the woman of splendid courage. And no man shall reign over Egypt, in his own right, from that day." And so, after attaining the amulet, Nectorus affirms, "Yes, you are in the presence of the Flame of Life. I, a woman of Egypt, have been chosen to pierce this mystery." As Farr and Shakespear explain in a closing note to *The Shrine of Hathor*,

> the final ecstasy of Nectoris is quoted thought for thought from the earliest Egyptian texts which have yet been discovered. Just as the Modern World has come to think of Heaven as a state rather than as a place, so we learn from these texts that the wise men of the Ancient World had gone a step farther, and knew the gods to be states and not persons.

The displacement of male authority by a matriarchal lineage is, then, not a change of those in power but a reconfiguration of power itself as not constituted in the individual or the human, but in an occult ecology beyond the organicist holism we so often imagine.

A similar conceptual shift in social structures occurs in *The Beloved of Hathor*, the premier performance of which occurred at Victoria Hall in London in 1901 as part of the first meeting of the London Egyptian Society.[101] The society's inaugural president was Marcus Worsley Blackden, a member of the Golden Dawn. With Farr in the main role of the thirty-five-year-old Ranouter, the High Priestess of Hathor, the play depicts the hero Ashmes as the chosen one of Ranouter, "great diviner of beauty, who rulest in those places where desire fails, and the substance of human life fades and passes into eternal truth." Farr's character is not simply a matriarch but the very force of the divine plane beyond humans' shifting passions and emotions. Under her protection, Ashmes is expected to be victorious in battle against "the Asians" and to restore Egypt, understood as a spirituality rather than a nation. With that restoration, Ashmes and Ranouter will become king and queen. Ashmes, however, is also tempted by Nouferou, a rebellious young sorceress with "the wild instincts of her mother." Crucially, for Farr's politics, this femme fatale is also a feminist. "I burn for knowledge, for the freedom of a bird upon the wing," she declares, "I am weary of the speech of the wise, who have not wisdom; who would tell me that Egyptian women must always be discreet and secret." Nouferou had been abandoned by her mother, who had heard her own call to freedom, suggesting a lineage of independent females. However, as the daughter attempts to seduce Ashmes to love her above all else, her selfishness contradicts the submission to an indeterminate universal will on which Farr's feminism is founded.

Meanwhile, throughout the last section of *The Beloved*, a war chant, delivered by a chorus of soldiers offstage in mid-battle, thrums in the background of the key characters' dialogue. As the authors acknowledge in a footnote, the chant is actually taken from decadent poet Lionel Johnson's "The Coming of War" (1889). Shakespear's cousin, Johnson was a cofounder of the Rhymers Club and the person who introduced Wilde to Lord Alfred Douglas. His friend Katharine Tynan, a feminist and contributor to the Irish literary revival, singled out "The Coming of War" in a 1915 article on Johnson in *The Bookman* as an inspiration for resilience in the face of the First World War. Noting Johnson's attachment to Ireland (despite his being English) and that "many Celtic strains met within him,"[102] Tynan hints at the poem as an inspiration for a Celtic Revival and Irish rebellion. For her, the piece is one of Johnson's poems that should "live by reason of their loftiness, their pure passion, their uplifted ecstasy." "The Coming of War" fulfills a similar function in *The Beloved of Hathor*, symbolizing a constancy of devotion to a set of values universal in their ethical import, and larger than any one individual can wholly comprehend. While the male Ashme's ultimate choice is, from the seductive Nouferou's perspective, between her love and Ranouter's wisdom, the work's opening preface defines the overarching choice as being between "the mere splendour of material victory" (embodied in Nouferou) and restoring "the great spiritual kingdom of Egypt" (embodied in Ranouter), where "Egypt" refers not to a nation or its sanctioned religion but to a divine ecology.[103]

In *The Beloved of Hathor*, Egyptology and Egyptosophy are used to evoke a feminism that initially appears to support the aspirations of the individual spirit. The model holds a dangerous appeal for the male hero, Ashmes, who, easily seduced by Nouferou, risks the kingdom and the wrath of the High Priestess Ranouter. However, when Nouferou declares, "I am weary of the speech of the wise, who have not wisdom," the authors are evoking Farr's own Golden Dawn motto *Sapientia Sapienti*

Donoa Data. The teenager's rebelliousness and her seduction of the hero seem to situate the dynamics within the heteronormative conventions that gave rise to the decadent persona of the femme fatale. However, Farr and Shakespear use this rebelliousness to aggravate the conflict central to Farr's own spiritual politics – the struggle between the independence and self-agency encouraged by New Woman feminism, on the one hand, and the Order of the Golden Dawn's ideal of a de-individuated universal will, on the other. As per Farr's arguments in *Modern Woman*, based on anthropological claims regarding communal living, *The Beloved of Hathor* ultimately does not celebrate rebellious individuality, but nor does it essentialize a model akin to that outlined by Paul Bourget in his articulation of decadence, in which supplication assures the coherence and constancy of an oppressive social order. To secure the kingdom of the divine, Ranouter does not debase her female competitor Nouferou, but takes the time to convince the younger feminist to engage with a more altruistic, sympathetic understanding of the divine. The result is a society envisioned within the everyday as an organic, matriarchal harmony, and within the ecology of the spiritual as the forever indeterminate, dissipative state of the universal will.

Occult Ecology and Decadent Feminism

The occultism of Mathers and Farr's time was marked by innovative, forceful women who were crucial to imagining, articulating, and leading a range of belief systems, including that of the Golden Dawn. While both popular and avant-garde culture often demonized such new spiritualities as a rebellious female nature threatening the established order of modern Western society, both Mathers and Farr found in Isis occulture and magic ritual an eco-feminism that overrode the dualist logic that, even today, reinscribes patriarchal privilege into certain arguments for women's rights and equality. There are, however, principal discrepancies within their own works – such as the apparent sites of tension, if not conflict, between supporting both feminist agency and the universal will, and between the view of women as primarily responsive to nature and the view of them as self-determined leaders. For Mathers and Farr, the resolution lay in appreciating the spirituality that is part of the planet's ecology as not simply influencing everyday politics but defining and driving humans' experiences in general. Thus, in Mathers's understanding of the Rites of Isis and in Farr's *Modern Woman* and coauthored *The Shrine of the Golden Hawk*, the two women develop models of gynocen-

Occult Ecology and Decadent Feminism

tric communities that function within the framework articulated by the Golden Dawn as an organization, but that also understand both occluded and apparent realities as conjoined within one universal will. Although their visions are distinct from each other, Mathers's and Farr's arguments both support the indeterminacy and flux of the open ecologies formulated by other decadent authors such as Swinburne and Pater. At the same time, they forcefully maintain a conviction to a woman-identified formulation of that network. Woman, in their works, is presented as a uniquely adept medium for a deeper experience of nature-based spirituality. Meanwhile, the allusiveness and lack of a distinct referent within occult ritual performance proffered a power of unaccountability that carried the possibility of political change in their time. Their interests thus offer a unique contest to the male privilege within not only their heteronormative society but also that of decadence itself.

CHAPTER 6

Sinking Feeling
Intimate Decomposition in William Sharp, Arthur Machen, and George Egerton

The blood-red sunset turns the dark fringes of the forest into a wave of flame. A hot river of light streams through the aisles of the ancient trees, and, falling over the shoulder of a vast, smooth slab of stone that rises solitary in this wilderness of dark growth and sombre green, pours in a flood across an open glade and upon the broken columns and inchoate ruins of what in immemorial time had been a mighty temple, the fane of a perished god, or of many gods. As the sun rapidly descends, the stream of red light narrows, till, quivering and palpitating, it rests like a bloody sword upon a colossal statue of black marble, facing due westward.

– William Sharp, "The Black Madonna"[1]

In William Sharp's one-act play "The Black Madonna" (1891), the lush excess of what are impossible stage instructions places the piece squarely within the murky terrain of decadence. As with many works of decadence, it also relies on an especially exaggerated rendering of the trope of the sphinx-like femme fatale, conflating the Christian Madonna with a pagan goddess who rules by fear. The mise-en-scène instructions continue:

The statue is that of a woman, and is as of the Titans of old-time.

A great majesty is upon the mighty face, with its moveless yet seeing eyes, its faint inscrutable smile. Upon the triple-ledged pedestal, worn at the edges like swords ground again and again, lie masses of large white flowers, whose heavy fragrances rise in a faint blue vapour drawn forth with the sudden suspiration of the earth by the first twilight-chill.

A member of the Hermetic Order of the Golden Dawn with Moina Mathers and Florence Farr, Sharp reinforces in this work, albeit from a far less supportive perspective, the female authors' eco-feminist fusion of women with nature that I explored in the previous chapter. As such, the play also fits conceptually and stylistically within the subgenre of occult drama that Mathers and Farr conceived of as ritual.

Sinking Feeling 175

"The Black Madonna" is brief, its action swift. In short order, a group of priests bind and sacrifice five female virgins in the name of the titular heroine, who is either an actual woman or a demi-goddess. For the remainder of the play, center stage is taken up by the rotting corpses of the sacrificed virgins, covered by decaying petals of exotic flowers drenched in their blood. The femme fatale, meanwhile, chooses a young chief, Bihr, to be her high priest but he, having fallen in love with her, forces himself on her physically. The two then retire into the forest depths where, we are encouraged to assume, the Madonna kills Bihr and herself seemingly in sacrifice. The implication ultimately is that individuals such as the Madonna and Bihr have less authority than their positions connote. Even the hero-worshipping imaginary pagan religion, with its seemingly impotent cluster of priests and homogenized chorus of trepidatious, wailing tribespeople, holds out little promise of resolution from the crisis. It is the ecological network at large that offers any prospect of a universal will. Throughout the play, the humans repeatedly step out of and recede into the depths of the wilderness from which the sounds of wild animals are heard. The fertile landscape is all-consuming and the play's final moments, in which all agents of the pagan religion have apparently either been killed or made ineffective, leave the reader with nothing but the seductive palpitations of the rising and setting sun, now signaling the end of an era of human fear and submission and the dawn of a spirituality sustained by the environment itself.

"The Black Madonna" is highly problematic in its gender and racial politics and its reliance on stereotypes and clichés. Nor can one argue that these issues are resolved when Sharp evokes the "suspiration of the earth,"[2] putting forward a vision of interconnected, mutually moderating components of the biosphere – with deaths, decompositions, and re-compositions evoked as the planet's collective breathing. The fall and demise of the society in fact emphasizes humans' inability to comprehend, or even imagine, the pulsations and seductions through which the greater ecological network communicates. The comparison of the planet's methods with that of humans' mimics Sharp's own notion of an over-arching, empathetic vision, on the one hand, and the problematic object-ification in this story of non-European identities, on the other.

The ideal of an ecological system of mutual sustenance is not unique to Sharp, nor is his skepticism of its viability. Various decadent writers turned to disruptive geopoetics and models of decomposition *as* re-composition to envision biosystems not reliant on human existence (let alone understanding) and, as such, not accommodating the comfort of closure. Recent scholars have become equally uncertain of humans' capacity to develop an environmental agenda that could, in fact, address what is increasingly envisioned as an eco-apocalypse or, as presented by Elizabeth Kolbert, a sixth extinction.[3] In his introduction to *The Earth and I* (2016), James Lovelock declares today's eco-politics as too idealistic, proposing too little too late with regard to "saving" the planet.[4] His critique is aimed at those humans who continue to put faith in themselves as the beings most capable of managing a crisis of our own making, rather than engaging with other members of the biosphere, let alone considering the possibility that others are already modifying their systems to address damaging changes. For Lovelock, the state of crisis has now left little feasible resolution unless technology can step in and take over. Similarly, Bruno Latour in *Facing Gaia* (2015) defines a naïve and unrealistic hope for salvation behind much of past and current eco-politics, what he calls "secular paganism."[5] For Latour, the environmentalist movement is most accurately understood as a populist eco-faith. Meanwhile, Christopher Hamlin has effectively argued that "[w]hile many first generation ecocritics distanced themselves from postmodernism in embracing scientific realism, there was ambivalence: in reifying the distinction between humans and the nature they studied and appreciated, ecocritics had reintroduced the alienation the artists hoped to combat."[6] As scholars of eco-science, both Lovelock and Latour turn to pagan paradigms to argue *against* our need for them; while they suggest their gesture is rhetorical or figurative, I believe there is something richer and, indeed, necessary being gained from the pagan engagement. Fin-de-siècle authors such as Sharp, Arthur Machen, and George Egerton, I propose, found in the intricacies of ecological excess and scalar distortion effective means of dismantling the conceptual division between belief and the secular or scientific, thereby moving toward a sense of human limits that have always existed, even if Lovelock suggests that they have only recently become a serious concern. These decadent works address the restricted agency and cross-lines of affection and intimacy through which humans and their lives are formulated, a tangle that they recognized as being incomprehensibly vast – reflecting what Arthur Symons described as, among the decadents, a "finer sense of things unseen."[7]

Deep into Ecological Decay

Decadent ecology has always been affiliated with rot – ecological, mental, moral rot: decomposition, putrefaction, the rot of bodies, the decay of societies, mental degeneracy, the dissolution of civilizations and eras. The

Deep into Ecological Decay 177

writers I address in this chapter deployed the possibilities of decay to engage philosophically with the inseparability of humans and the larger ecological network from which they anxiously attempt to distinguish themselves. George Egerton's story "An Ebb Tide," for example, raises existential worries regarding the inevitable decomposition of the body: "It's hard to look at a day like this [sob], and know that tomorrow I rot" (brackets in original).[8] One of the characters in William Sharp's play *House of Usna* (1900) extends the paradigm to the rise and fall of civilizations: "The sons of Usna are dead. May the dust of Naysha rot among the worries of the earth."[9] And in Arthur Machen's *Hill of Dreams* (1907; written 1897), the entire ecosystem is defined by "that odour of decay, of the rank soil steaming, of rotting wood, a vapour that choked the breath and made the heart full of fear and heaviness."[10]

The concept of decay has for centuries been incorporated into our understanding of the aesthetic and philosophical phenomena of decadence, often steering its principal definitions. As "The Black Madonna" suggests, decadence has commonly been conceived as the process of a society's birth, development, and then ruin – often as a punishment for arrogance or immorality. This perception of cultural artefacts moving through a spiritualized organic cycle has been the result of humans patterning complex, often unfathomable ecological processes on their understanding of their own individual life narratives, even in some cases personifying cultures and societies as sentient mortal entities. Visions of species enhancement, industrial progress, and imperial expansion are mutually reinforcing, brought together through a rhetoric that discredits anything that either does not contribute to or stymies developments seen to improve the lives of middle-class, white, Western humans. Particularly concerning to these cultural institutions were any forms of growth that nobody yet knew how to harness, and which would, as a result, be characterized as threatening and potentially contagious, while also being denigrated as useless waste and excess.

In my articulation of decadent ecology in the introduction to this book, I discussed Théophile Gautier's explanation of Charles Baudelaire's poetry as the decadent waste product of modernity, as meat "savouring of" the rot of a civilization.[11] Paul Bourget followed soon after with his *Essays on Contemporary Psychology* (1883) and the claim that what Baudelaire calls "the phosphorescence of decay"[12] is perhaps the repulsive but nevertheless inevitable abject element of any civilization or era. At the same time that Bourget encourages the cooperation of individuals working toward the long-term, collective health of their society, he also suggests the inevitable dissipation of any such order.[13] Meanwhile, for Max Nordau, writing a few years later, the authors and artists who contributed to the rise of decadence were not commenters on the rot of modernity itself, but its first signs. However, for the actual contributors themselves, as Bourget suggests, cultural decay is a necessary element of processes of growth and replenishment. But it is, moreover, also an oblique reflection of other perspectives, compulsions, and modes of engagement beyond the human – therefore often perceived by humans as incoherent noise, as dissidence within the harmonious masterwork toward which they believe themselves to be evolving.

This conception of trans-species dis-communication has found new traction in more recent eco-related scholarship. The anxious response of Nordau can be found echoed in what Simon Estok has described as "ecophobia"[14] and Dawn Keetley as "plant horror" regarding vegetal nature's "untameability, its pointless excess, its uncontrollable growth."[15] Cary Wolfe's recommendation that humans adopt a "mutational logic" echoes the decadents' conception of the oblique and even incomprehensible as communication in itself, with Wolfe suggesting this may result, on occasion, in the convergence in "a consensual domain ... by autopoetic entities that have their own temporalities, chronicities, perceptual modalities, and so on." As Wolfe argues, "systems, including bodies, are both open *and* closed as the very condition of possibility for their existence (open on the level of structure to energy flows, environmental perturbations, and the like, but closed on the level of self-referential organization)."[16] That is, a system's being and our knowing exist as different phenomenological orders; thus "language is fundamental to our embodied enaction, our bringing forth the world, as humans. And yet it is dead" in that it is outside the system's own being (albeit not ineffective because of this). Karen Houle, meanwhile, has proposed "partnerings" as a means of short-circuiting the phenomenological divide, of disrupting the common tendency to presume individuals or even something like individual species are the fundamental starting point for understanding ecologies.[17] Her aim is, in part, echoing Henry Salt's work in his 1892 *Animals' Rights*,[18] to remove the extensionism by which we measure and value nonhumans based on their similarity to humans. As she observes, "[v]ery little attention has been devoted to imagining what these unique expressions of plant-livings might actually be," what may result from "our extension and ideas entering into composition with something else."[19] Even Heinrich Kaan's early sexological work in *Psycopathia Sexualis* (1844) encouraged a sense of the "chaos," as he called it,[20] which naturally

Deep into Ecological Decay 179

occurred in the cross-species integrations on the level of organisms among plants and animals, including humans. Houle points out that Charles Darwin also saw plant behavior as a form of agency and communication, an invitation to partnering.[21]

The works by Sharp, Machen, and Egerton on which this chapter focuses stand out for the complexity with which they challenge not only the tendency to approach the human as the starting point of inquiry or creative exploration, but also the approach to ecology as something separate from the human, as something for humans to judge as if distinct and distinguishable from ourselves. Decadence demonstrates the considerable imaginative investment given to exploring the indeterminate attractions across species or in utter disregard for humans' stock in species classification and extensionism. As Latour suggests, some pagan spiritualities are scientifically naïve (and, on occasion, willfully so), but this does not easily apply to the decadents who were engaged and interested in developments in the natural and human sciences, and yet also recognized paganism as offering an imaginative sensual excess that crucially respects seemingly nonproductivist longings and pleasures. Pagan decadents often disrupted the species distinctions on which Houle notes that she and other scholars tend to rely, in the process dissolving the philosophical skin of the human individual through scenarios of re/decomposition and interminglings that shift emphasis from subjects to the infinite means of sensual engagement.

In Chapter 3, I looked at works by Simeon Solomon and Michael Field to argue that the sinew of decadent ecology is enforced by species co-reliance, systems – often cultural and political – of beckoning, attraction, and intimacy across animals, plants, and other ecological components in a not-always-harmonious community. Such a queer ecological approach turns a skeptical eye toward human exceptionalism, while understanding acts of mutual support as forms of communicative intimacy. The recent turn in eco-studies to paradigms of decay and degeneration as constitutive and resourceful supports this affective model, a combination that had already been considered in the work of scientists such as Ernst Haeckel, Darwin, and Kaan, who considered the roles of decay and excess in ecological systems. As I argue in this chapter, Sharp, Machen, and Egerton also engaged this set of subjects, each through their own politics of pagan decomposition. Contrary to the common tendency to incorporate decay within a model of development or an idealistic holism, the decadent ecology of these writers refuses an implicit teleology toward a collective harmony. As we have seen, works early in British decadence, such as Swinburne's "The Leper," appreciated decay but, in a sort of atheistic echo of a natural theology, still offered a sense of grander coherence, this time demarcated by the author and his works. A similar formulation can be found in later works of British decadence such as Oscar Wilde's *The Picture of Dorian Gray* (1890/1891).[22] The decadents whom I turn to in this chapter, however, each in their distinctive way, derail the catharsis of textual closure. Rather, each sustains doubt, skepticism, or incomprehensibility that quashes humans' sense of control and management not only in moments of crisis such as global pandemics or climate disasters but, more profoundly, also in day-to-day life.

William Sharp's Eco-Poetics of the Breath

Among the contributors to British decadence, William Sharp stands as one of those who sustained a career-long interest in desire as an ephemeral and transient mode of ecological communication. He represented these views through the lens of a general image of earth veneration, but usually through pagan but especially Celtic models, with the latter often promoting a Scottish nationalist position. As Michael Shaw argues, Sharp's works – especially those written under the pseudonym of Fiona Macleod – have been read as adopting an Arnoldian Celticism engaging an essentialism that sees all Celtic culture as innately "feminine, intuitive, emotional and relatively illogical."[23] The characterization led many to critique Sharp (or Macleod) as defeatist in his view of Scottish nationalism under British imperialism, although Sharp himself more than once represents the feminine as resilient, generative, and adaptable. Meanwhile, Sharp's portrayals of earth veneration prove gender dualism far too limited a schema for grasping his vision. Although the Scottish revival was definitely a key concern for the author, the majority of his writings can be read as attempts either to represent or to enter into the sensual correspondences among the vegetal, animal, and elemental.

Sharp spent much of his life hiking, traveling, and writing about his experiences; he envisioned himself woven deep into the fabric of nature. As a youth, he would on occasion leave his home in Paisley and then Glasgow for the Highlands to live in the open air, spending time with various wanderers. One summer, he spent roughly two months living outdoors with what he referred to as a group of gipsies. "I suppose I was a gipsy once," he conjectured later in life, "a 'wild man' before: a wilder beast of prey before that."[24] But his difficult health persistently reminded him of the limits of his own body and the potentiality of death, resulting in not only his spiritual but also his physical intimacy with the landscape becoming a part of his aesthetics. In his writing, he portrays himself as reveling in an intimate, constantly changing co-reliance with energies that ultimately remain elusive not simply because they are changeable, but – as was poignantly apparent to Sharp, whom doctors were sending off to the Highlands, Italy, and Australia for his health – because humans, too, are but mutating variables of these forces. As his poetry collection *Sospiri di Roma* (1891) demonstrates, the impact of his illness did result in writing that took up the sort of decadent investments in debilitation, sickness, or putrefaction that can be found in Simeon Solomon, Algernon Swinburne, and Walter Pater. As with Stevenson, Sharp's sensitivity to the ecology that sustained his constitution resulted in a pagan spiritualization of the body as part of a biosphere of emotional interchange, fostering, most notably, an eco-poetics of the breath.

Of the British decadents, Pater was the person to whom Sharp was especially drawn – an "intimate and valued friend" whom he first met in 1880, when Sharp was twenty-five and Pater forty-two.[25] He dedicated his poetry collection *Earth's Voices, Transcripts from Nature* (1884) to Pater and, in 1889, Pater wrote in support of his friend's candidacy for the Chair of English Literature at University College London; the application was ultimately withdrawn for health reasons.[26] In his biography of Dante Gabriel Rossetti (1882), Sharp describes Pater as "one of the most masterly and cultivated art-writers of our time."[27] Sharp also became close to Rossetti, who, by the late 1870s, entertained only a small group of friends. Rossetti's main circle at this time also included Swinburne, whom Sharp also admired. He speaks of Rossetti's "deep and strong" influence, the way his sonnets "almost took my breath away" (*Memoir*, 1:75). "I can find no language," Sharp declares, "to express my admiration of his supreme genius and it is with an almost painful ecstasy that I receive from time to time fresh revelations of his intellectual, and artistic splendour." His devotional biography of Rossetti appeared the year of the Pre-Raphaelite's death and was well received overall, although Wilde (perhaps a touch jealous of the friendship) critiqued it as a rush job.[28] Sharp later dedicated to Rossetti his anthology *The Sonnets of This Century* (1886), in which he included Wilde's "Libertatis Sacra Fames" (1880).

Even as Sharp changed styles and genres over the years, his work retained a decadent sensuality verging at times on the erotic, as well as an attention to the details of the organic environment. Regarding Sharp's story "The Rape of the Sabines" (1892), a writer for the *Saturday Review* opines over "the overloaded style which distinguishes new pagan from

182   Sinking Feeling

ancient pagan literature. The tendency to cloud over the matter with layer upon layer of heavy cloying adjectives marks the work of most modern pagans who write about Italy."[29] Pater, Rossetti, and Swinburne all emphasized Greco-Roman paganism in their writings but, while the Classical also arises in Sharp's work, it is notable that this later decadent represented diverse forms of paganism in his periodical *The Pagan Review* (1892), in which "The Rape of the Sabines" and "The Black Madonna" appeared. Lasting only one issue, Sharp wrote all the contributions himself under various male pseudonyms. He attempts to propose a global range of paganism both in theme and, to a lesser degree, in style – an impossible task, but one that now usefully offers a measure of his breadth of pagan interests and actual knowledge, the latter appearing to have been rather limited. Under the pseudonym of W. H. Brooks, Sharp uses his manifesto-like Foreword to *The Pagan Review* to declare the journal's aim of "thorough-going unpopularity" among the general public by being "frankly pagan: pagan in sentiment, pagan in convictions, pagan in outlook."[30] As the "mouthpiece" of a "younger generation,"[31] it also offers a feminism characterized by "a frank recognition of copartnery":

> This new comradeship will be not less romantic, less inspiring, less worthy of the chivalrous extremes of life and death, than the old system of overlord and bondager, while it will open perspectives of a new-rejoicing humanity. ... [T]he "new paganism" would fain see that sexual union become the flower of human life. But, first, the rubbish must be cleared away; the anomalies must be replaced by just inter-relations; the sacredness of the individual must be recognized; and women no longer have to look upon men as usurpers, men no longer to regard women as spiritual foreigners.[32]

In his Foreword, references to art for art's sake and Gautier make clear that Sharp saw the periodical's paganism as engaged with decadence,[33] and the representations of women in "The Black Madonna" and other works in *The Pagan Review* do reflect the misogynistic objectification and, on occasion, demonization also found in works by Gautier, Baudelaire, Swinburne, and others. Meanwhile, the combination of organic metaphors and a notion of women as not "spiritual foreigners" speaks to the possibility of an eco-feminism with the earnestness of those of Mathers and Farr. However, Sharp is quick to clarify that one should not expect the feminism espoused in his Foreword to be parroted in all of the new paganism, or even all of the contributions to the periodical.

Reviewers of *The Pagan Review*, often writing for Christian vehicles, were unable or unwilling to consider his paganism as rooted in recent political and aesthetic developments, such as the suffrage and decadent movements, rather than in the distant past. *The Christian Union*'s critic assures readers that Sharp's journal "indicated the blowing of no very violent wind." They note that, while the Foreword claims to break from "the religion of our forefathers," it then states that their work "is still fruitful of vast good," and claims to mark a "new epoch," but illogically one that Sharp declares has already started.[34] Writing for *Lippincott's Monthly*, the American Episcopal minister Frederic Bird deflates any pretentions at spiritual revision, while also glibly pointing out that it is too soon after having just opened colleges to women to imagine gender equality. He sums up the publication's mantra as a paean to youthful passions: "Since the dominant note of Nature is the sexual, let girls and boys be free to rush into each other's arms, and let us who are older give the most of our time and minds to noting how they do it."[35] Meanwhile, the writer for *The Saturday Review* is hung up on the lack of knowledge that these new pagans apparently have of the old: "Real paganism to the modern Neo-Pagan would have seemed Tory in politics, bald in art, and unadventurous in morals. The Neo-Pagan is a revival of the young man whom ARISTOPHANES particularly detested. If the New Pagan had any knowledge of the old paganism he would choose for himself some other nickname."[36] Thus, while Sharp defined his vision not by Classical predecessors, but by an engagement with current eco-spiritualities, aesthetics, and sex and gender politics, reviewers chose to ignore much of this, choosing to reject his claims on Classical terms, despite his explicit declarations of currency.

Sharp even more richly engages the shift from a human to an ecological perspective that he depicts at the end of "The Black Madonna" when he turns in his writing to his own Celtic identity. The Celtic revival was one of the most sustained influences on paganism at this time, even though the problems with promoting a Celtic literature or innate Celticism were explicitly noted as early as Matthew Arnold's lecture series (1867), one of the first and most influential works contributing to the Celtic revival that brought Sharp his fame. Against Arnold's intentions, the notion of an innate Celtic identity captured in its art and writing fortified an intensely nationalist investment in Irish and Scottish independence, directly linking it to what Grant Allen described, in 1891, as "the Celtic upheaval of radicalism and socialism."[37] This element continues to reverberate today in recent pagan efforts to influence the 2014 Scottish vote for independence and in anti-Brexit agitation. The revival itself arose as a re-affirmation of Celtic literature, art, spirituality,

184 Sinking Feeling

and ethnicity, including the Insular Christianity of the fifth to tenth centuries.[38] Romanticism's conception of Celticism as imbued with an innate, primitive spirituality and poeticism also influenced the most popular Celtic identity models of the fin de siècle. Allen declared aestheticism itself to be the product of men who were "either confessedly a Welshman, a Highlander, an Irish Celt, or else had a demonstrable share of Celtic blood, and a marked preponderance of Celtic temperament."[39] "[F]rom the very beginning," he conjectures, "the Celtic race in Britain has been marked by a strong taste for the decorative side of art"; "it is something profound, poetic, mysterious, vague, dim, magical, beautiful," "in a manner instinct with soul and with some indefinite spiritual yearning."[40] Also in 1891, Wilde would pronounce, in the revised version of "The Critic as Artist – Part II," that "the creative instinct is strong in the Celt, and it is the Celt who leads in art."[41] As Isobel Murray notes,[42] he was likely responding to Allen's inclusion of Wilde among influential Celts, describing him as "Irish to the core."[43]

By the turn of the century, however, the craze for the Celtic was seen by many as wilting on the vine. In his 1905 *Beautiful Wales*, the English author Edward Thomas associated the penchant for the Celtic with "a class of 'decadents,' not unrelated to Mallarmé, and of æsthetes, not unrelated to Postlethwaite. They are sophisticated, neurotic – the fine flowering of sounding cities – often producing exquisite verse and prose; preferring *crème de menthe* and *opal hush* to metheglin or stout."[44] Postlethwaite was a caricature of the dandy-aesthete created by George du Maurier in a series of cartoons for *Punch*. At one point Thomas refers to the Welshman Morgan Rhys as "something of a Celt in the bad, fashionable sense of that strange word" but, at the same time, he notes rather admiringly that Rhys, during his childhood, would become "intoxicated by the mere trees and the green lawn" or "the voluptuousness of sheer silence," and as an adult loved poetry because it "revealed to him the possibility of a state of mind and spirit in which alone all things could be fully known at their highest power."[45] Thus, when Sharp was most devoted to a Celtic identity (one more invested in spirituality than nationalism), the overlap between the Celt and the decadent had become so strong that it didn't really matter which was sinking or swimming in popular opinion; the two were knotted together. Daniel G. Williams has observed that the fin-de-siècle culture of Celticism operated as "an internally inflected variant of imperial Orientalism," emerging at a time when "the metropolitan or imperial mind, far from dominating and categorizing a pliable native environment to the scientific and epistemological

William Sharp's Eco-Poetics of the Breath

categories of the centre, finds itself being relativized, at a loss, disoriented, and being forced to turn back on itself."[46] One result of such disorientation was the production of a variety of Celticisms, with some being constructed not from the center but from a paganism rooted, in Sharp's case, in the body and the breath.

A coeditor of the nationalist Celtic periodical *The Evergreen: A Northern Seasonal* (1895–1897), launched by Patrick Geddes as the voice of the Scots Renaissance, Sharp was keenly invested in the ways in which nationalist identity is the product of history, myth, and aesthetics. It is this combination of interests as they sustain a particular spirituality that drew fellow occultist W. B. Yeats to Sharp's work, especially his later explicitly Celtic writings. As Flavia Alaya proposes, regarding Sharp's style of prose-poetry, he referred to his work as "chants" in order to conjure an otherworldly correspondence with "overtones of poetic vision and prophesy." Alaya explains, "The use of 'chant' is itself intimately connected with the pervasive tendency of the Celts, as Sharp often described them, to see 'the thing beyond the thing,' to view surface phenomena as signs and symbols, a tendency which was quite legitimately extended to language."[47] Meanwhile, Frank Rinder, in a piece published in *The Art Journal* in February 1906, only months after Sharp's death, emphasizes the mystic element of his occultism in noting that "in his dream-scheme of the cosmos – nearer to the heart of truth than most of our 'realities' – many of the limitations of time and of space were swept away."[48] He goes on:

> Intermittently at first, but of late day by day, hour by hour, he prayed: "Oh, beloved Pan, and all ye gods that haunt this place, give me beauty in the inner man, and may the outer man and all that I have be at peace with the inner." Man thus attains his just stature, becomes a spiritual alchemist, transmuting into pure gold the dross of life.[49]

Albeit somewhat potted, Rinder's observation effectively reflects the mosaic of paganism, decadence, and occultism embodied in Sharp's identity.

Nowhere was this unique embodiment more succinctly sustained than in Sharp's pseudonymous persona of Fiona Macleod. Sharp offered ample suggestions that Macleod was more than a ploy to offer a more romantic, populist idealization of paganism. As early as 1879, he had begun articulating his sense of self as transgendered, apologizing to his friend John Elder for the depth of his love and friendship: "Don't despise me when I say that in some things I am more a woman than a man" (*Memoir*, 1:51).

As Sharp's wife explained in *A Memoir* of her husband that she edited and published in 1910, Macleod was very much a part of her husband's identity and of their relationship. Sharp and the invented persona Macleod wrote letters to each other. She even autographed and then gifted her novels to him. He kept his two identities secret from almost everybody throughout his life, and it was Macleod whom Yeats championed most strongly of the two. When Lord Salisbury offered Macleod a Civil List pension, Sharp turned it down in order to keep up what had proven a highly effective deception. As Macleod, Sharp's reconstructionist vision was focused on recording the dignity of the Celts and their culture – at times, clearly Scottish, but not always. Macleod was hugely popular for her romantic and richly sonorous pagan works, such as the collection of nature essays *Where the Forest Murmurs* (1905), the poetry collection *From the Hills of Dream: Threnodies, Songs and Later Poems* (1901), and the novels *Green Fire: A Romance* (1896) and *The Mountain Lovers* (1895). Like Farr's and Machen's first novels, *The Mountain Lovers* is yet another work of the pagan revival published in John Lane's decadent Keynotes series. It offers an idyllic portrayal of the pastoral Highland life of a golden-haired woman named Oona who could not be more enmeshed in the landscape: "She was like the spirit of woodland loneliness[,] … as absolutely one with nature as though she were a dancing sunbeam, or the brief embodiment of the joy of the wind."[50] Another romance, *Green Fire* offers a similar declaration of impassioned transmutation: "What the seedlings feel in the brown mould, what the sap feels in the trees, what the blood feels in every creature from the newt in the pool to the nesting bird – so feels the strange, remembering ichor [blood] that runs its red tides through human hearts and brains."[51] Scottish readers are repeatedly reminded to understand this idealized heroine, and themselves, as a sort of eco-spirit, "at once a child of nature, a beautiful pagan, a daughter of the sun; … at once this and a soul alive with the spiritual life[.] Indeed, the mysticism which was part of the spiritual inheritance come with her northern strain."[52] Virtually all of Macleod's many works turn to an eco-spirituality embodied by the Celtic female, evoking a sense of the folklore as a living, organic contribution to the biosphere, while at the same time being rendered an inspiration for Scottish liberation.

Scholars to date have recognized Sharp's use of the pseudonym of Fiona Macleod for most of his publication during the second half of his career as a means for him to engage the importance of women in Celtic culture and myth and the fluidity of his gender.[53] However, recalling Sharp's lifelong sensitivity to his health (which continued to decline

William Sharp's Eco-Poetics of the Breath

187

during the 1890s when Macleod came into being), one is drawn to consider his identification with a vital, spirited Celtic woman-of-the-woods as also a venture into an ecological state of being, a form of eco-submersion that extends across his oeuvre. One finds a string of health issues in Sharp's memoir – made up of diary entries, letters, and personal recollections – that his wife Elizabeth published upon his death in 1905. The poet suffered from chronic heart and nervous conditions. In 1872, when only sixteen, he developed typhoid, symptoms of which generally include fever, weakness, and exhaustion. Four years later, upon his father's death, his health broke down again. In 1880, he is "out of health, ill-nourished, owing to his slender means, and overworked" (*Memoir*, 1:65). In 1886, Sharp ends a birthday note to a friend with the distinctly unfestive lines "sometimes I am very tired – very tired" (1:196), a phrase he repeats more than once elsewhere in his letters. Throughout the letters in his *Memoir*, Sharp and others record him as "ill," "so ill," "seriously ill," "ill – and seriously," in "ill-health," and in "dubious and ever varying health"; he is recorded as having suffered from fever, scarlet fever, a heart attack, a "severe nervous collapse" and "acute depression," "nervous prostration," rheumatism, relapses, and being "at the gates of death." In one of Sharp's more creative renderings, in a letter dated April 1905, nine months before he dies, he observes, "The cold is very great, and it is a damp cold, you couldn't stand it. When I got up my breath swarmed about the room like a clutch of phantom peewits. No wonder I had a dream I was a seal with my feet clemmed on to an iceberg" (2:290). Meanwhile, in a 1907 article, Ernest Rhys recalled Sharp's illness from scarlet fever in the 1880s as being followed by a strong "spirit of fun, boyish mischief even" and an "extravagance of energy."[54] Sharp, his wife, and their friend Mona Caird all reference his boyish qualities as well. Sharp wrote to Rhys, regarding a bout of illness, that "the rigorous treatment, … the not less potent and marvellously pure and regenerative Llandrindod air – and my own exceptional vitality and recuperative powers – have combined to work a wonderful change for the better" (*Memoir*, 2:244). As in his earlier articulations, the landscape itself here becomes an embodiment of regenerative vigor.

Both Sharp and his wife also began to see Fiona Macleod as invested in his health and well-being. In a letter to a friend, Sharp smoothly shifts from describing his own sickness to describing that of his alter-ego. Elizabeth at one point observes that the "wet winter and long hours of work told heavily on my husband, whose ill-health was increased by the enforced silence of his 'second self'," one of her ways of alluding to

Macleod (*Memoir*, 1:195–96). She observes the other woman's influence again later on, while Macleod herself, in a letter to Sharp, chastises him for not looking after his health, and even threatens to stop working with him: "as to *our* collaboration I see no way for its continuance unless you will abrogate much of what is superfluous, ... and generally serve me loyally as I in my turn allow for and serve *you*" (*Memoir*, 2:313). Such exchanges and medical analyses shared among Macleod, Sharp, and his wife address the affective transience of identity but, more importantly for my argument, also enact Sharp's conception of nature as a system of mutating, interactive forces. More precisely, Macleod became an alternative embodiment for Sharp that allowed him – through her vigor and that of her Celtic heroines – to feel a part of the vitality of the wild landscape. As Macleod writes in a letter to Grant Allen,

> What you say about the survival of folklore as a living heritage is absolutely true – how true perhaps few know, except those who have lived among the Gaels, of their blood, and speaking the ancient language. The Celtic paganism lies profound and potent still beneath the fugitive drift of Christianity and Civilisation, as the deep sea beneath the coming and going of the tides. No one can understand the islander and remove Alban Gael who ignores or is oblivious of the potent pagan and indeed elementally barbaric forces behind all exterior appearances. (*Memoirs*, 2:20)

More than just the pseudonymous name under which he wrote his Celtic novels, Macleod existed for Sharp as a palpitating, pagan force. While his other engagements with nature were directed and limited by his health, Macleod's experiences mark Sharp's notion of living mythology as a potent element of the eco-network. "I am writing to you from Florence," he has Macleod inform a correspondent in 1901:

> You know it perhaps? The pale green Arno, the cream-white, irregular, green-blinded, time-stained houses opposite, the tall cypresses of the Palatine garden beyond, the dove-grey sky, all seem to breathe one sigh ... *La Pace! L'Oblio!*
> But then – life has made these words "Peace," "Forgetfulness," very sweet for me. Perhaps for you this vague breath of another Florence than that which Baedeker described might have some more joyous interpretation. (*Memoir*, 2:184)

The fluid sentences dragging out beyond the expected breath of common conversation draw the reader into a physical awareness of the sensual elements of nature, as Sharp puts it, breathing a single sigh together. And then, in the next sentence, he refers to his own description as itself a breath of Florence, subtly incorporating his own writing into the intimate respiration of the landscape it would, otherwise, be seen simply as representing.

Through this investment in the breath of nature, Sharp positioned himself in a tradition that M. H. Abrams outlines in *Correspondent Breeze: Essays on English Romanticism*. As Abrams notes, "the symbolic equations between breeze, breath, and soul, respiration and inspiration, the reanimation of nature and of the spirit … are inherent in the constitution of ancient languages, are widely current in myth and folklore, and make up some of the great commonplaces of our religious tradition."[55] The "pagan" Percy Shelley[56] had, Abrams observes,

> ample precedent, pagan and Christian, for his West Wind, both breath and spirit, destroyer as well as preserver, which is equally the revitalizing Zephyrus of the Romans and the trumpet blast of the book of Revelation, announcing the simultaneous destruction of the present world and a new life in a world re-created.[57]

The description is paralleled by my own reading of Sharp's "Black Madonna" at the start of this chapter, and Sharp himself notes his place within this tradition when, in his *Life of Percy Bysshe Shelley* (1887), he suggests a marked affinity between himself and the earlier poet, who had fallen ill while wandering through a Florentine autumn "watching the tumult of the driving rain-clouds, and hearkening to the triumphant voice of the wind."[58] It is in this state of illness and turbulence, Sharp tells us, that Shelley wrote "Ode to the West Wind," the most "epically grand" lyrical poem in English. Weak health, Sharp observes, fosters a heightened sensitivity to one's ecological inter-reliance.

In a letter written in Germany in 1891 during "the vintage season" (*Memoir*, 1:299), he alludes to Shelley's poem as he no less than merges himself with the palpitations of the landscape:

> I revel in this summer gorgeousness, and drink in the hot breath of the earth as though it were the breath of life. … The bloom on the fruit was as though the west wind had been unable to go further and had let its velvety breath and wings fade away in a soft visible death or sleep. … There was the fragrance of a myriad odours from fruit and flower and blossoms and plant and tree and fructifying soil – with below all that strange smell as of the very body of the living breathing world. (*Memoir*, 1:300–1)

George Meredith had noted of *Sospiri di Roma* (Sharp had sent him a copy) some contrivance: "But you have at times (I read it so) insisted on your impressions. That is, you have put on your cap, sharpened your pencil, and gone afield as the impressionistic poet" (*Memoir*, 1:295). One can sense this in the letter by Sharp just cited, as it shifts from the pastoral to a Whitmanesque philosophical rapture: "I seemed to inhale it – to drink it in – to absorb it at every pore – to become *it* – to become the heart and soul within it" (*Memoir*, 1:301). Meanwhile, his conjecture in the letter that "I suppose I was a gipsy once – and 'a wild man o' the woods'" refines the same idea that he had written out a month earlier in his diary: "I suppose I was a gipsy once: a 'wild man' before: a wilder beast of prey before that" (*Memoir*, 1:302–3). What Meredith marked as contrivance was, in short, an author working out through his poetry, fiction, and correspondences an eco-poetics of illness mapped onto a sense of inevitable re/degeneration.

"In work," Sharp proposes, "creative work above all, is the sovereign remedy for all that ill which no physician can cure: and there is a joy in it which is unique and invaluable" (*Memoir*, 1:298). In his poetry, we find him celebrating not the self but his "becom[ing] the heart and soul" of the breathing earth, as the *plein-air* poetry of *Sospiri di Roma* effectively attests. The Italian "sospiri" is commonly translated as "sighs," as in the Ponte dei Sospiri (Bridge of Sighs) in Venice. Sharp, however, in *Sospiri di Roma* and in a later letter to Alfred Austin, translates the term as "breaths," bringing attention to his conception of the act of breathing out in nature as a form of eco-spirituality. An American reviewer, writing for the magazine *Current Literature* in 1891, informs us that Sharp has "like the artists of the day, taken to doing his work – yes, even getting his inspiration – out of doors. He has virtually thrown up his lucrative literary connections in London in order to live under less strain."[59] The choice of the word "inspiration," echoing the poetry collection's title (inspire, from Latin: breath into), was perhaps intentional. Describing *Sospiri di Roma* as "Italian color studies" and "impressionist studies in verse," the reviewer captures the sense of both realistic immediacy and fleeting impermanence of many of the poems, as well as Sharp's move away from narrative that led his pieces to be recognized as some of the earliest English works of prose poetry.

In a letter to John Elder written in 1880, Sharp explicitly describes "sospiri" as a "spiritual breath," a force that passes through all things "like a vague wind blowing through intricate forests" (*Memoir*, 1:48). He used rolling lines of scarcely punctuated free verse and other techniques to help his readers engage with his own experience, the poems' spirit, and so that of the landscape, breathing through them. Images of such eco-aspiration are also apparent in poems such as "Sussurro" ("Whisper"), with its "Breath o' the grass, | Ripple of wandering wind," and "High Noon at Midsummer on the Campagna," which evokes "Scarce any breath of wind | Upon this vast and solitary waste."[60] William Halloran points out that, in "High Noon," as the narrator "contemplates evening and darkness, the past comes to life as a 'low deep whisper from the ground'."[61] The narrator voices a wish "To be as the Night that dies not," which Halloran interprets as a melancholy plea for immortality or, in Halloran's words, "a possible means of preserving the individual soul from annihilation." Within a de-individuated, pagan context, the poem evokes not a personification of immortality but a universal will beyond human conceptions of time. When Sharp declares that time's "vast holocausts lie here, deep buried from the ken of men," it is a submersion of human histories (past, present, future) within a notion of universal mutability, "where no breath of wind | Ruffles the brooding heat, | The breathless blazing heat of Noon." The image of deep time as a brooding maternal hen evokes the metaphor of the earth goddess found in "The Black Madonna" and the later Celtic work he wrote as Fiona Macleod. That said, Sharp does little here to realize the image, the inability to personify or mythologize this system perhaps speaking to its very expansiveness.

"The Fountain of the Acqua Paola" explores the motif more deeply as a practice of difficult and expansive breathing, opening first with an image of the landscape's expulsion of noxious air: The Tiber's "turbid wave | Flowing Maremma-ward, moves heavily" (23). The Maremma (between Florence and Rome) was known for centuries for its malarial marshlands and swamps. The ancient Romans first popularized the belief that the illness came from the fumes released by swamps, with the term – from *mal aria*, or "bad air" – being coined in Italy during the Middle Ages. During Sharp's time, the Maremma remained recognized symbolically and medically as a source of such foul air. There had been repeated attempts to drain the Maremma – none wholly successful until the twentieth century. In "The Fountain," however, Sharp quickly leaves the toxic air of the lowlands to offer a painterly rendering of higher altitudes. Here he turns to long sentences with distinctly short lines, creating in the reader both a sense of disjuncture and actual difficulty breathing:

> Bright too and joyous,
> [The waves], in the moonshine,
> When the falling waters
> Are as wreaths of snow
> Falling for ever

192 Sinking Feeling

> Down mountain-flanks,
> Like melting snows
> In the high hill-hollows
> Seen from the valleys
> And seeming to fall,
> To fall forever
> A flower of water,
> Silent, and stirred not
> By any wind. (25–26)

The positive energy in this passage, as water tumbles downward, becomes almost straining as one searches for the end of the thought, from "falling" to "falling" to "fall" to "fall" to "flower," such that one feels ironically a sense of relief, at the end of the piece, to return to the "turbid wave" "flowing heavily" to the swamps. From this state of sunken breathlessness, the poem moves fluidly upward into the "cloudy vapours," then to the night sky, and then back to the waves.

The poem's cycle of sickly and revivifying forces patterns Sharp's sense of his eco-embodiment, extending his breathing in the landscape to his readers, but also envisioning it as part of a Celtic ecology. His portrayal in this poem of the joy-inducing "norland forest," "where the echoing pines | Whisper to high wandering winds," reflects his growing sense of the Scottish Highlands as the wellspring of spiritual rejuvenation. In another poem "The Norland Wind," published in 1895 in *The Evergreen*, Sharp presents "the north wind on the sea" as "fearless and elate," the "Spirit of dauntless life."[62] In a complex editorial maneuver, his description of the north wind is equated with breath through a headpiece in which illustrator John Duncan personifies it as a spiritual force visibly expelling air while being led by a bird, probably a raven or crow, both of which are popular symbols in Celtic myth (Fig. 6.1). Celtic goddesses often take the form of ravens, while both types of birds were seen as portents of future events.[63] In this issue of *The Evergreen*, the bird draws the wind toward the previous two pages, which contain an image and anonymous description of the "Anima Celtica" (Latin: Celtic soul), which Duncan illustrates with a woman imagining various Celtic artefacts and mythico-historical figures. The over-riding sensual energy in Sharp's poem is ecological, with the female figure – as in Macleod's novels – embodying his sense of organic intra-permeability. The representation of the female as the changeable relations dissipating through the components of the environment became a mainstay of Sharp's writing. Although romanticized, his efforts render a queer ecology of trans-species attractions and engagements.

William Sharp's Eco-Poetics of the Breath 193

Figure 6.1 William Sharp, "The Norland Wind," Headpiece by John Duncan, *The Evergreen*, 1 (1895), 109. Dennis Denisoff.

194 Sinking Feeling

In his earlier *Sospiri di Roma*, it is the piece "Fior di Memoria" ("memory's flower" or "the best of memories"), the longest poem in the collection, that most effectively demonstrates Sharp's early investment in this decadent ecology. Written in trochaic tetrameter,[64] it opens with a vivid rendering of the Maremma landscape as degenerate illness:

> From the swamp the white mist stealeth,
> Wendeth slowly through the grasses,
> Like a long lithe snake it circleth
> Breathing from its mouth its poison,
> Breathing fumes of the malaria. (16)

This serpentine sentence relies for whatever propulsion it musters on sibilants and the repetition of the word "breathing." The decadent description continues in long, inert phrasing, as the mist becomes a thin, white snake that just as quickly turns into a "veil of smoke-drift" that eventually enters a hollow of timeless ruins:

> Nought is seen around but grasses,
> Flower-filled grasses, ...
> Nought above, but the blue hollow
> With its infinite depths of azure.
> Nought to meet the wandering vision
> But the ruins mid the grasses. (17)

The sense of stymied imagination, the lack of propulsion reinforced by the panting rhythm all work to evoke the sense of an individual outdoors looking to the landscape for inspiration. The vagueness and inertia reflect an evanescence that is key to the de-individuated spirituality of Sharp's poetics. With the spirit residing throughout the elements of the environment, the poet seems to avoid pursuing any imaginative thread, instead returning repeatedly, as if in the act of meditation, to the breath and the moment as it is. His description of sky, for example – "the wide deep dome of purple, | Cloudless, speckless, save when darkling | for a moment drifts a shadow | Far in the aerial distance" (17) – evokes both a purposelessness and a detailed presence. It takes four pages of such vague renderings before the narrator, having progressed to "the uplands" (16), finally encounters something seemingly more tangible, a naked "wild mountain-girl" (20). Any hope of human-to-human action, however, is soon squelched, as she spends the entire poem asleep in a rosebush. Of course, the figure is not simply human. The narrator first wonders whether it is a statue, "some stone goddess, nymph, or naiad" "glowing | With the multitudinous breaths of sunlight" (19–20). But this prospect is undermined by the rise and fall of the figure's flesh, a breathing that then extends to the landscape and the movement of the winds – a force "whose arms have claspt the hill-wind," "whose swelling breast has quivered | 'Neath the soft south-wind's caresses," and whose "white limbs have felt the kisses | Of the wander wind, thy lover" (20). In the poem, the figure is initially seen as a goddess that "the soul can know and see" (21), and then re-envisioned again as a mortal – "no goddess here, | Only a wild mountain-girl" – and then folded outward to an image of her as a timeless spirit where "the winds alone shall call thee" (22). The mortal/immortal fluctuations duplicate the narrator's own breathing, which has moved in its rhythm and fluidity from the heavy swamps to "the kisses of the wandering wind" to the eco-pulsations of the idealized female figure.

The poem enacts a respiratory gesture, shifting from a vision of the planetary winds to an erotic attention to the naked female's gentle breaths and then out again and then back. The chant-like rhythms and repetitions are, for Sharp, recuperative, allowing him to submerge into the biosphere or, more effectively, recognize himself as having always been but a part of this stronger system of respiration. As the poem demonstrates, Sharp's sensitivity to his health and breathing impacted his writing and his spirituality – resulting in an innovative eco-poetics and, in his later work, an embodiment of the spirit of the "wild mountain-girl" as Fiona Macleod. "On the 14th, in an hour of lovely sunshine," Elizabeth writes of Sharp's burial in December 1905, "the body was laid to rest in a little woodland burial-ground on the hillside within sound of the Simeto," a river in Sicily (*Memoir*, 2:325–26). Later, an Ionic cross, carved in lava, was placed there, with an inscription written by Sharp himself that captures the pagan mystery he sensed through his life-long efforts to breath as landscape:

> Farewell to the known and exhausted,
> Welcome the unknown and illimitable. W. S.

Arthur Machen's Eco-Piquarism

Throughout much of his career, Arthur Machen tried to extricate himself and his work from the vortex of the decadent and occult movements, which he felt had become inauthentic through their appropriation into mainstream culture. The former affiliated him, against his own views, with an urbane dandy-aesthete persona that mainstream society was often satirizing as shallow and effete. Popular occulture, meanwhile, often rendered an image of the otherworldly as accessible, understandable, and eager to communicate with the living, and on the living's terms. "Our age, which has vulgarized everything," he laments, "has not spared the unseen world, and superstition, which was once both terrible and picturesque, is now thoroughly 'democratised'."[65] In "The Literature of Occultism" (published in 1899, the year he joined the Hermetic Order of the Golden Dawn), Machen explicitly mentions automatic writing and the "modern disciples of Isis" as part of "the squalid back-parlour magic, ... the inanities, the follies, the impostures of modern theosophy and modern spiritualism."[66] Machen himself, however, was strongly drawn to the elements of mystery and self-dissolution that both decadence and occultism suggested; for him, they were important not in a cultural sense but as personal, albeit ephemeral, engagements with the reality beyond the façade of daily life. In this sense, decadence and occultism bring to mind what Arthur Symons refers to, in his essay on the decadent movement, as "not general truth merely, but *la vérité vraie*, the very essence of truth – the truth of appearances to the sense, of the visible world to the eyes that see it; and the truth of spiritual things to the spiritual vision."[67] The senses were, for Machen, the site of exchange among various realities (that is, truths).

Similar to Sharp, a major impetus behind Machen's investment in and devotion to pagan spirituality was the location where he grew up. He was born in 1863 in the small Welsh town of Caerleon in Monmouthshire – although Machen referred to the county by its medieval Welsh name of Gwent to bring forward its Celtic roots. Throughout his oeuvre, he refers or alludes to it as a source of inspiration and spiritual centeredness found as much in the environment as in his heritage. Caerleon is buried deep in pagan history and myth. Its Celtic origins were followed historically by the classical influences from its time as a Roman fortress. "Caerleon" is Welsh for "fortress of the legion," and it was built on a hillfort named Isca (from the Brythonic – an ancient Celtic language – for water), and was used for various spiritual and civic purposes from the fifth century BCE to the fourth century CED.[68] Its rounded amphitheatre and other remains were an inspiration to Machen, most notably for his *Hill of Dreams*, in which Roman elements are mingled with Celtic pagan allusions to create a system of correspondences that leave the hero Lucian Taylor, and the reader, in a state of symbolic limbo. According to Geoffrey of Monmouth's *Historia Regum Britanniae* (*The History of the Kings of Britain*, c. 1136), King Arthur was crowned at the hillfort and, prior to the site's excavations, locals referred to the amphitheatre as King

Arthur Machen's Eco-Piquarism

Arthur's Round Table. This history led Alfred Tennyson to visit Caerleon while writing *Idylls of the King* (1859–1885).

In his autobiography *Far Off Things* (1922), Machen evokes his love and devotion for the ecology of his youth in an extended paean to Gwent. Musing on his own "sense of a constant wonder latent in all things," Machen – noting that Robert Louis Stevenson "had some sense of this doctrine as applied to landscape" – explains that, for him as a child, such encounters

> made the soul thrill with an emotion intense but vague in the sense in which music is vague … : everything to me was wonderful, everything visible was the veil of an invisible secret. Before an oddly shaped stone I was ready to fall into a sort of reverie or meditation, as if it had been a fragment of paradise or fairyland. There was a certain herb of the fields that grew plentifully in Gwent, that even now I cannot regard without a kind of reverence; it bears a spire of small yellow blossoms, and its leaves when crushed give out a very pungent, aromatic odour. This odour was to me a separate revelation or mystery, as if no one in the world had smelt it but myself, and I ceased not to admire even when a countryman told me that it was good for stone, if you gathered it "under the planet Juniper."[69]

This personal recollection brings to mind the scene from Machen's *The Great God Pan*, in which the character Clarke, smelling a concoction made by his friend Dr. Raymond, drifts into a recollection of his childhood, "the scent of summer, the smell of flowers mingled, and the odour of the woods, of cool shaded places, deep in the green depths, drawn forth by the sun's heat; and the scent of the good earth, lying as it were with arms stretched forth, and smiling lips, overpowered all."[70] The landscape has become for Clarke an active agent, inviting his acceptance of his submergence into the ecology, the character finding himself facing

> a presence, that was neither man nor beast, neither the living nor the dead, but all things mingled, the form of all things but devoid of all form. And in that moment, the sacrament of body and soul was dissolved, and a voice seemed to cry "let us go hence," and then the darkness of darkness beyond the stars, the darkness of everlasting.[71]

Machen's recollection of his early days in Caerleon are transformed, through his art, into a rendering of occult reverie, a momentary dissolution into the immeasurable. In fact, in his memoir, Machen goes so far as to declare that

> anything which I may have accomplished in literature is due to the fact that when my eyes were first opened in earliest childhood they had before

them the vision of an enchanted land. As soon as I saw anything I saw Twyn Barlwm, that mystic tumulus, the memorial of peoples that dwelt in that region before the Celts left the Land of Summer.[72]

Through the image of Twyn Barlwm, a hill in South Wales distinctive for the ancient burial mound at its top, Machen defines his Celticism as the very environment, the topography as the landscape of his being, just as in *Great God Pan* it is the earth itself beckoning Clarke to feel himself, sensually and emotionally, dispersed through the natural surroundings.

Of equal relevance to my argument, Machen defines his own writing as valuable only as it exists as a contribution to the transhistorical life of his Celtic identity. To be clear, Machen did not support Grant Allen, Patrick Geddes, and others who found in the Celtic tradition some essential or spiritual core that resulted in exceptional art and literature. In *Landscapes of Decadence*, Alex Murray has summarized the eager efforts in the 1890s to venerate an innate Celticism within British literature of the period. Although noting admiration for Fiona Macleod and W. B. Yeats, Machen had no patience for this "craze" propounded by the "pseudo-scientific," "fanatical race-theorist" "of tracing literary genius to racial origin."[73] "The very idea of Celtic literature," Murray argues, "was inimical to Machen who refused any racial, national or regional definition of art."[74] Rather than measuring his own writing as a nationalist cultural product, Machen more often suggested its value existed in its integration through the "miracle" (as he refers to it) of what I characterize as his decadent ecology. Susan J. Navarette captures the poetics of this vision in Machen's indirect style and meandering narratives when she notes that the "omissions and ellipses of Machen's [*Great God Pan*] disclose an essentially decompositive strategy" intended to create "emotional and intellectual short-circuits in which reason gives way to elemental human emotions."[75] Navarette emphasizes readers' required emotional involvement in using their own imaginations to stimulate feelings of "fear, anxiety, and shame"; however, as my excerpt from Machen's memoir makes clear, his prose also reflects an eco-pagan poetics that he envisioned as a votive marking his devotion to a larger mystery of being. It is not so much fear, in this sense, as self-erasure through a state of spiritual awe.

Machen's formulation speaks to the conflation of biological, social, and literary conceptions of decadence articulated by Gautier, Bourget, and others. Just as Bourget put forward the idea that authors and artists who were more extreme in their claims or style had a stronger influence on the perceptions of their society in general, Machen suggests that it is only

Arthur Machen's Eco-Piquarism 199

writers of truly "fine" literature – literature of "ecstasy" – who create works of long-term impact. Machen, however, explains ecstasy as "rapture, beauty, adoration, wonder, awe, mystery, a sense of the unknown, desire for the unknown,"[76] his definitions shifting gradually from pleasure to awe and then to an occultist veneration of the absolute real beyond human comprehension. His decadent vision emphasizes a diminishment of human perspective within an immersive engagement that his descriptions of his Caerleon childhood suggest are more akin to Karen Houle's desire to challenge human extensionism by enabling "acts of understanding performed with the maximum perspective possible" or, more specifically, "to truly think ecosophically."[77] Edward Thomas recalls the Welshman Morgan Rhys "pointing to a fair, straight hawthorn that stood, with few branches and without leaves on the mountain side" and declaring, "If only we could think like that!"[78] In this conception of thought and reality, Machen's disruptive aesthetic is a source of fear and trepidation only for those like Nordau already anxious for the comforts of materialist closure. For many others, it operates as an invitation, an enticement to recognize one's existence in and complicity within copresent realities on a universal level.

It is crucial to remember that the British paganism of the nineteenth and early twentieth centuries was not strongly connected to the simultaneous developments in environmentalism, the latter driven by different, often politicized, groups that took on practical agendas aimed at establishing legislation and practices of protection and stewardship, ones more often directed at maintaining byways and historically important architecture as addressing the health of nonhuman sentient beings. Also, unlike most contemporary scholars of animality and vegetality, Machen's ecosophical thinking was not formed through an effort to examine interconnected perspectives and ways of being, what has recently been referred to as the pluriverse. His vision arose first from a combination of the Anglicanism in which he was raised, forms of occultism, folklore, and Welsh and English history that caught his interest, and his love of and veneration for the Welsh countryside of his boyhood – not a "pure" wilderness either, but one richly inlaid with myth, mystery, and ancient histories. The end result is not a claim for how nature, the earth, or the universe is in reality, but to multiple ways in which they are understood. Through his Celtic pagan imagination, ecologies are seductive and humbling in their transhistorical and trans-spatial capacities, and all-inflecting in their disruption of conceptual divisions between the organic, the built, and the imagined.

200 Sinking Feeling

Machen engages with the excess and agency of nature in most of his works, but it becomes a particularly erotic fulcrum in his novel *The Hill of Dreams* (1907, written 1897), the text on which I wish to focus. The novel opens with its hero, Lucian Taylor, on a walk, as he "penetrated" the Welsh countryside (111). Eventually, he "found himself, as he had hoped, afar and forlorn; he had strayed into outland and occult territory"; viewing the mysterious landscape, he felt like he was "reading a wonderful story, the meaning of which was a little greater than his understanding" (111). In the conflation of pagan mystery, Welsh terrain, and occult reading, Lucian was drawn to a mound, a site of worship like the one in Caerleon, that had been added to by Romans. Encircled by ancient oak trees that suggest it may have been, even earlier, a Druidic place of spiritual practice, the hill layered various spiritual perspectives upon each other, collectively stirring up the very atmosphere itself:

> The wind blew wildly, and it came up through the woods with a noise like a scream, and a great oak by the roadside ground its boughs together with a dismal grating jar. As the red gained in the sky, the earth and all upon it glowed, even the grey winter fields and the bare hillsides crimsoned, the water pools were cisterns of molten brass, and the very road glittered. He was wonder-struck, almost aghast, before the scarlet magic of the afterglow. The old Roman fort was invested with fire; flames from heaven were smitten about its walls, and above there was a dark floating cloud, like a fume of smoke, and every haggard writhing tree showed as black as midnight against the blast of the furnace. (113)

Machen's imagery spreads its decadent excess over pages; almost alchemical, "the air was all glimmering and indistinct, transmuting trees and hedges into ghostly shapes" (112). A local woman, Annie Morgan, passed by in the distance, she, too, seemingly a spirit of the landscape. The anthropomorphism of the screaming wind and the oak dismally grinding its limbs against each other hints at an ecological agency beyond the hero's comprehension. Meanwhile, the author's layering of Lucian's mystical experience over the Roman fort and Druidic oak circle signals a sense of the spiritual energy extending the experience of the hero beyond conventional notions of history. There was nothing special about Lucian to have provoked this violent environmental activity; it is not even clear that this was a reaction to his presence. What the passage does affirm is a collocation of mutations and intercommunications across vast spatial and temporal fields – forces of living, interpenetrative experiences that Lucian (and Machen) found seductive in their very incomprehensibility.

Arthur Machen's Eco-Piquarism

Not surprisingly, Lucian was soon drawn to return to the "dark green vault" covered in peculiar nettles with a "sting that burns like fire" (119). The teenager made his way through the "ugly," "deformed" trees and "rank, unknown herbs, that smelt poisonous," eventually coming upon an ancient foundation made of "stones white with the leprosy of age." Machen writes, "The earth was black and unctuous, and bubbling under the feet, left no track behind. From it, in the darkest places where the shadow was thickest, swelled the growth of an abominable fungus, making the still air sick with its corrupt odour, and he shuddered as he felt the horrible thing pulped beneath his feet." Meanwhile, Lucian saw in the landscape "forms that imitated the human shape, and faces and twining limbs," mosses like hair, branches like limbs, and bark like the "masks of men" (120). This is not the sort of positively inspiring *genius loci* that Sharp addresses, or that Robert Louis Stevenson and Vernon Lee had chosen to engage in their works discussed in Chapter 4. Rather, the topography is configured as an animate, threatening, autopoetic force that, eventually, drew a willing Lucian into itself, just as his psyche sank into an ecological mesh of memories: "Quick flames now quivered in the substance of his nerves, hints of mysteries, secrets of life passed trembling through his brain, unknown desires stung him … ; the wood was alive. The turf beneath him heaved and sank as with the deep swell of the sea" (121).

The scene culminates with Lucian dropping into the pulpy moss, while also submerging into a disturbed sleep and an erotic encounter with a faun. Crucially, this pagan creature that arose from the natural context also looked exactly like Lucian; more precisely, Machen implies that the two were one. Semi-conscious, Lucian stripped himself naked and laid down among the stinging nettles; his "eyes were fixed and fascinated by the simulacra of the wood, and could not see his hands, and so at last, and suddenly it seemed, he lay in the sunlight, beautiful with his olive skin, dark haired, dark eyed, the gleaming bodily vision of a strayed faun" (120). Upon waking, he "stretched out his hands, and cried to his visitant to return; he entreated the dark eyes that had shone over him, and the scarlet lips that had kissed him. And then panic fear rushed into his heart" (121), the word "panic" being an allusion to Pan (its etymological root) or, in Roman mythology, Faunus. The narcissistic sexual encounter is not an uncommon decadent trope – found, for example, in Wilde's *Picture of Dorian Gray*, Laurence Housman's illustration "The Reflected Faun" (1894), and John William Waterhouse's painting *Echo and Narcissus* (1903). In *Hill of Dreams*, however, it is a self-directed act not because Lucian found some sort of spiritual "simulacra," but because his selfhood momentarily merged, sunk into a psycho-geographical sense of being. Machen enacts what Houle later formulates as ecosophical thinking, albeit with an emphasis on a decadent paganism that also acknowledges his wish to recognize the limits of human comprehension.

In these early passages of the novel, Machen's use of luscious style and imagery makes his readers feel, perhaps, some sense of the loss of self within the transmutations communicated across species, ecologies, and time. Lucian moves from forcefully penetrating nature to being willingly penetrated by it, a dehumanizing perspectival shift that Machen explores further in a particularly erotic representation of self-piquerism. In his various ventures in the Welsh countryside, Lucian was repeatedly pierced by thorns. At one point, he became lost and agitated: "The hour in the matted thicket rushed over the great bridge of years to his thought; he had sinned against the earth, and the earth trembled and shook for vengeance" (143). His imagination having gotten the better of him, he concluded that his earlier sexual relations with the landscape were somehow being judged and so, as he fled the wilderness, the very effort became a form of self-flagellation: "As he plunged through the hedges, the bristling thorns tore his face and hands; he fell amongst stinging-nettles and was pricked as he beat out his way amidst the gorse" (144). Having already been absorbed into the terrain, however, this very pain defined the spiritual awakening of his "virgin mind" (120). Just as the judgment was the product of his own cultural knowledge, the interpenetration was the experience of ecological and philosophical decomposition: "Quick flames now quivered in the substance of his nerves, hints of mysteries, secrets of life passed trembling through his brain, unknown desires stung him" (120). It is the sense of burning flames and the stinging of the penetrating thorns and nettles, we are told, that remained with him the longest. The enigmatic sensorium engaged on the hill remained with Lucian as an incoherent force that shifted across genders, species, and energies. The novel's hero shares this sense of indeterminacy with central characters in *The Great God Pan*, capturing for Machen the enticing occultism or unknowability of the macro-networks of the universe. For the same reason, Lucian found himself re-enacting his prickling, penetrative interaction with a faun that became himself or, more accurately, that he came to understand as an intimacy decaying from encounter to memory.

Lucian's experience on the hill fostered not only a new decadent "ritual" of occult writing, but also a ritual of self-penetration. Hiding some "spiked and prickly gorse" in his bedroom,

> he would draw out the gorse-boughs, and place them on the floor, and taking off his nightgown, gently lay himself down on the bed of thorns and spines. Lying on his face, with the candle and the book before him, he would softly and tenderly repeat the praises of his dear, dear Annie, and as he turned over page after page, and saw the raised gold of the majuscules glow and flame in the candle-light, he pressed the thorns into his flesh. At such moments he tasted in all its acute savour the joy of physical pain; and after two or three experiences of such delights he altered his book, making a curious sign in vermilion on the margin of the passages where he was to inflict on himself this sweet torture. (164)

Upon rising, "here and there a spine would be left deep in the flesh, and he would pull those out roughly, tearing through the skin." "[H]is thighs would stream with blood, red beads standing out on the flesh, and trickling down to his feet."

Machen never denied his Christian faith, and the allusions to Christ in this extended metaphor are thick; the narrator even describes Lucian as a martyr. As the scene affirms, he did not see Christianity as anathema to an eco-spirituality that seduces the human into self-subjugation. In the earlier episode in the novel, Lucian is shown being violently pierced by the thorns and thistles but, by the end of his hilltop ecstasy, there is a shift in perspective, with the character having become unable to differentiate himself from the rest of the biosphere. Layered upon this model is also the author's sense of fine literature as that which produces ecstasy, the type of wonder he also found in the spiritual potency of the countryside of his childhood. Key here is recognizing Machen's concerted effort not to leap conceptually from an ecological empathy to a pagan occultism, but instead to offer a detailed, intimate rendering in which the spirituality remains evoked but never confidently declared or demarcated. Machen thereby encourages us, as readers, to avoid seeing his hero as a singular agent choosing self-piquerism, and instead considering his ritual as an erotic transmutation. The bedroom activities are hidden from other humans, but they are not private; instead, they are an element of the historical communication through nature that Lucian had experienced earlier. In many of his works, Machen explores what he describes elsewhere as the alchemical ability of, as he puts it in his preface to Richard Middleton's *The Ghost-Ship and Other Stories*, "something formless transmuted into form," to reveal that "the universe is a great mystery."[79] "The consciousness of this mystery," he explains, "resolved into the form of art, expresses itself usually (or always) by symbols, by the part put for the whole."[80] Transmutability is central to Machen's spiritual synecdochic

204 Sinking Feeling

symbolism and, through his rendering in *The Hill of Dreams* of Lucian's growing appreciation for transmutation, he formulates a queer ecology where the sense of ecstasy is as close to spiritual affirmation as one can hope to comprehend.

George Egerton and the Plots of Women

By the mid-1890s, Michael Field (Edith Cooper and Katharine Bradley) sensed themselves increasingly slipping away from the core of the avant-garde literary scene. Writing in January 1893 in their joint diary *Works and Days*, Cooper blames the publisher of *Sight and Song*, Elkin Mathews, which by then had become John Lane and Elkin Mathews of The Bodley Head: "We have not got on friendly terms with any of the Bodley Head set, & younger authors than we are have been pushed before us."[81] Fearing that their drama *Stephania: A Trialogue* (1892) is a "deader," Cooper adds with black humor, "we want a grave publisher"; soon after, she writes, "all friends avoid discussing our art as if it were a dead husband" (258, 261).

Born in Australia to Welsh and Irish parents, George Egerton (Mary Chavelita Dunne) was soon to be seen as the brash voice of this new literary vanguard that Field felt was pushing them aside. Recent scholarship on Egerton has situated her as a major voice within fin-de-siècle British decadence. The same year of Cooper's diary observations, The Bodley Head published Egerton's game-changing collection of eco-feminist short stories, *Keynotes* (1893). And the next huge event in the London literary scene after that was the start of Lane's decadent quarterly *The Yellow Book* (1894–1897), its inaugural issue including Egerton's short story "The Lost Masterpiece." Highly descriptive and saturated in issues of female desire, Egerton's stories have commonality with Field's own lush, decadent works, but they are unique in their impressionistic casualness, contemporary contexts, and bold, informal language and style, much of which developed through her familiarity with contemporary Scandinavian writers such as Knut Hamsun and Ola Hansson, as Tina O'Toole notes. They also differ from Field's writing in focusing not on a Classical paganism but on an intensely earthy entanglement arising from, but not locked down by, Egerton's regionalist interests. O'Toole, building on Iain Chambers's notion of migrancy as "a movement in which neither the points of departure nor those of arrival are immutable or certain," describes Egerton's Irish identity as fluid, as "a way of being in the world rather than a journey between two fixed points."[82] Thus, while Egerton's

George Egerton and the Plots of Women 205

work is often semi-autobiographical and reflects her regional knowledge, it is a regionalism, much like Sharp's or Machen's, that flows through and shapes contexts outside of any circumscribed geographic domain. It is an embodied, organic regionalism that resurfaces in her very writing.

In February of 1894, Field submitted work to *The Yellow Book*'s literary editor, Henry Harland, but nothing by the two women was published in the first issue, which appeared that April. Cooper's response in their diary was pointed. After seeing the Bodley Head's window display glowing with rows of the first volume of the bright yellow journal, she wrote, "We have been almost blinded by the glare of hell. ... The window seemed to be gibbering our eyes to be filled with incurable jaundice" (261). Inspired, perhaps, by seeing multiple copies of the face of a masked woman coyly grinning on the cover of the inaugural issue, Cooper envisions the publication as an unashamedly immoral female: "One felt as one does when now & then a wholly lost woman stands flaming on the pavement with the ghastly laugh of the ribald crowd in the air round her. One hates one's eyes for seeing! But the infamous window mocked & mowed, & fizgiged, saffron & pitchy." According to Field's diary, Harland had already accepted a piece by the poets for the second issue but, for some reason, he held off including it; the couple then, having read the first two issues, withdrew their submission and asked for the typed copy to be returned. Harland – "the Cad" – asked for a stamped self-addressed envelope; they complied, but spitefully noted their inclusion also of a half-penny stamp to cover the cost of his own note to them – "a break forever from the hated Bodley Head" (262–63).

All the contributions to the first issue, Cooper concludes, range in quality from being no more than clever to downright damnable but Egerton, based on her work, "does not even deserve damnation, but something weightier – crushing-out silence" (262). In a letter written within days of the diary entry, Bradshaw extends the criticism of the periodical, again singling out Egerton, "that shameless creature," for her horrible writing: "[D]o glance through <u>A Lost Masterpiece</u> – & note the expression 'a chunk of genius.' ... They should never be admitted into the society of good books – who sin such sins. I am sick & ashamed of belonging to the corruptors of my own language" (331). The letter goes on in its attack on both the periodical and Egerton, declaring "We must not let these women go rampant," conflating the image of Egerton as uncontrollable with that of the periodical itself as a mass-displayed "lost woman" "flaming" in the street. In addition to the displeasure of seeing Egerton's glowing success in contrast to their own muted recognition,

Field perceived in the new author a more explicit and grounded investment in the gender debates of their time.

Notably, Egerton herself did not identity as a New Woman or suffragette, writing in 1900 that she had "no propaganda in view – no emancipation theory to propound, no equality idea to illumine."[83] Instead, in a witty conflation of literature and the earth, she encouraged women to write their own stories: "There was only one small plot left for her to tell: the terra incognita of herself, as she knew herself to be."[84] The conception of woman as unknown land recalls the essentialist eco-feminism of Moina Mathers, and Egerton's writing has more than once in recent decades been analyzed for its depiction of women's innate affiliation with nature, and its considerations of the fundamental urges and desires that result in women's ongoing confinement within positions of cultural subordination. For Egerton, these issues exist outside contemporary politics and even time; they are neither "new," as in the phrase "New Woman," nor propogandist, but submerged within the mysterious gendered make-up of the earth itself, represented in Roman mythology as the goddess Terra Mater, in Greek as Gaia.

Like Rachilde, the leading French female decadent of the time, Egerton often draws attention to the discontinuities among women – the ways in which individuals inadvertently support the very prejudices that oppress them as a gender, for example, or act out of self-interest rather than on behalf of an imagined female collective. Egerton evokes just as much sympathy for the characters who act independently, even when momentarily supporting institutions of oppression by engaging in micro-level tactics that may appear to ignore long-term feminist strategies. Egerton turns to formulations often rooted in paganism in order to encourage consideration of these gestures as occurring within an ecological system whose agency is not limited to the human. Her particularly decadent ecology resides in her displacement of the anthropocentric assumptions not only found in late-Victorian feminist politics, but also often adopted in more recent scholarly analyses of her representation of nature as a reflection of gender. But what new relations and contingencies become apparent when gender is disturbed by a pagan-sensitive model of ecological sustainability? More common Victorian understandings of environmentalism have hinged heavily on a model of stewardship, resulting in an overemphasis on human agency in the management of a pseudo-pastoral ideal that, in fact, has never existed. Egerton offers an alternative construction, turning, in her stories, to a paradigm foregrounding

George Egerton and the Plots of Women 207

an ecological diversity characterized by trans-species attractions and an acceptance of and self-submersion within the terra incognita.

Like Sharp and Machen, Egerton returns repeatedly in her writing to a notion of eco-collective history. For her, however, the decomposition of selfhood within such a model fosters a frustration with the misogynistic opportunities that it suggests cannot be countered. In short, the eco-decadence she demarcates could encourage fatalism. The first sentence of "A Cross Line," the first story published in *Keynotes*, opens with a clause that connotes the issues that have come to characterize her entire oeuvre: "The rather flat notes of a man's voice float out into the clear air."[85] There is an incongruity, the narrator observes, between the man's prosaic tone and his surroundings, the latter comingling brambles, fallen trees, burbling waters, and a woman whom he initially does not notice. The scene situates Egerton squarely in the New Woman debate regarding the innate strengths and weakness of males and females, but the story, like many of her others, suggests nature is not simply a set of metaphors affirming particular gender relations, but a community of agents who all contribute to the instability of their collective body. Often rooted in paganism, Egerton's formulation offers an ecological system whose agency and possibilities are not limited to the machinations of the human.

The eco-feminism of Carolyn Merchant, Karen Warren, and others has been keenly attentive to the fact that various systems of devaluation are mutually imbricated, where intra-human abuse – including racism, classism, and misogyny – is buttressed through other systems of oppression such as speciesism and naturism. As elaborated in the previous chapter, Val Plumwood's principal argument is that feminism and environmentalism do not only usefully reinforce each other's aims, but together more effectively destabilize the structural logic by which the dominant order (including the patriarchy) is able to maintain its oppression even as the individuals involved shift position and even switch roles. Plumwood finds in this solidarity the ethics by which she argues for an unstructured ecology that first and foremost celebrates its multiplicity of kinships and differing channels of communication in order to retain a sense of difference even when envisioning points of coherence. Writing to John Lane, Egerton declares, "I hate books with a purpose" (White 36), signaling her unwillingness to write pieces that focused on the politics of the time, particularly the suffrage movement.[86] As Plumwood encourages, however, Egerton does not offer a critique of modern feminism in her works but, rather, puts forward an ecological vision of oppressed heroines who do not attempt to attain equal gender rights within an order that retains other modes of oppression such as speciesism, but who come to appreciate and try to engage with a larger organic network of solidarity. That these efforts are often unfulfilled or indeterminate reflects Egerton's unwillingness to succumb to a holistic vision or a summarial offering of hope. That they are themselves, in her renderings, often entangled if not complicit with human industry and exploitation suggests a particularly decadent form of self-destabilization and a skepticism that is not allowed to assume that its own position of judgment is secure.

Despite her affiliations with decadence, nature worship, and Celtic culture, Egerton's representations of the natural environment have, to date, usually been read as reflecting her concern regarding women's rights, a perspective that has encouraged the erasure of the nonhuman agents depicted in her work. With no extensive articulation of Egerton's writing through an ecological paradigm, some scholars have interpreted her as essentializing both women and the natural. Kate McCullough, for instance, argues that the author's proclamation of a "shared inherent wildness" among women creates a sense of solidarity at the same time as it erases real-world differences of race, religion, class, and nation.[87] For McCullough, it is always interhuman relations that drive Egerton's notion of wildness or her conception of ecological engagement. Elaine Showalter in *Daughters of Decadence* likewise criticizes the author's reliance on biological essentialism, assuming that gender-based concerns take full precedence for Egerton over her representation of environmental oppression and abuse.[88] The few readings of her work that give some consideration to ecological issues often risk reducing nature to metaphor. Maureen O'Connor argues that Egerton deploys representations of the brutalization of animals not to challenge such abuse, but to argue against gender and colonial oppression.[89] Laura Chrisman, meanwhile, takes the opposite approach, claiming that Egerton's idealization of the English countryside is an imperialist fantasy that works to legitimize the established hierarchy.[90]

What Connie Bullis calls the "womanizing of nature and naturizing of woman"[91] was, in Egerton's time, depicted and debated by various female and male writers. Barbara Gates has demonstrated that popular culture, spirituality, and science made models of the maternal earth goddess familiar to many Victorians. Stories by Egerton such as "The Third in the House," "Virgin Soil," "A Cross Line," and "Pan" drew on the image of the modern woman not only as confident, independent, and intelligent, but also as instinctually attuned to nature. As Martha Vicinus observes, however, Egerton did not simply equate the natural environment with women's essential character, but "rather saw the outdoors as a freeing agent, providing the space and climate for personal growth."[92] In addition to offering a context for permitting and representing women's self-development, Egerton configures the environment as itself a living organism, with humans not operating with the superiority of semi-autonomous stewards, but acting individually, collectively, and unconsciously through the flows and stresses of the networks in which they remain entangled.

The story "The Third in the House," for example, focuses on a village on the Yorkshire coast enmeshed with the "flotsam and jetsam" of commerce cast upon the shore. Here, it mingles with marine plants, anemones, and rocks that look like "strange sea monsters or basking ocean lizards, with shell- and seaweed-encrusted backs."[93] The species that inhabit tidal ecosystems, Chelsea Miya observes in her analysis of the story, "have uniquely evolved to survive both underwater and on land. Human scavengers likewise are part of the intertidal lives of the beaches, loading up their carts with shells, driftwood, and other items that have been left behind. Houses cling to the base of the rocky cliffs like sea barnacles, extra additions tacked one on top of the other."[94] "Inter-marriage was common" in the village, the narrator tells us, going on to note how "the natural conditions of this crabbed little place" have protected it from tourism.[95] The description of the homes as "crabbed" among the craggy shoreline re-enforces a conceptual fusion of the humans and other life already together clinging to the encrusted rocks. Egerton then imbues this ecological inter-marriage of species with Celtic myths and beliefs that encourage a nonrational understanding of the environment. Meanwhile, allusions to the inevitable aestheticization and commodification of this very ecology – through references to things such as casinos, funiculars, and pier entertainments – discourage a false ideali-zation of the impoverished villagers' realities. The story of relationships across generations and species occurs not against a natural backdrop intended to reflect the struggles of the human, but as part of an ecosystem that incorporates and mutates whatever detritus is brought to the village by the pull and push of ocean tides and industry.

Egerton's story "Her Share" in the collection *Discords* (1894) similarly formulates biospheric entanglements in which the human is portrayed as one interacting component among many, but it offers a more thorough sense of the fundamental influence of desire within them. It begins with the narrator describing the sensation one feels

> sitting on a stile on a summer's day, when the whole world about you basks in sunshine, and the gladness of the time whispers round you in the fields, and the trees hold long talks together in the woods, and the mystery of it speaks to you and works in you in some subtle way so that you too feel summer in you.[96]

Despite the comforting intimacy of the imagery, the perspective is, in fact, global, capturing the sense of solar warmth longed for by all the planet's sentient elements. Only then does the writing begin to focus gradually on individual human characters. The personification of the trees and the "leaves fluttering into a surprised murmur" first insinuate the human into the landscape (72). They are followed by the tolling of a dead-bell which – generally rung to safeguard a corpse from evil spirits – alludes as much to the absence, as the presence, of the human. Similarly, in describing the sound as "a mocking whisper of relentless Fate," the narrator reminds the reader of the inevitability of death, bringing attention to the lack of individual agency within this larger system. Egerton only then introduces her heroine: a recently engaged woman who, wishing to escape her unhappily married sister and the other people intruding on her bliss, chooses to take a vacation, "to run down to the country on my bicycle, to get out into the fields and listen to the birds singing, to match the melody in my own heart" (73). At the inn, she meets another cyclist – a woman further along in her lifecycle. The older female recounts her experience of love and loss, now symbolized by the melody of a song her beloved sang in a language she could not understand. The two cyclists both feel their youthful love to be original and unique, but the cyclicality of their life stories, Egerton suggests, affirms their roles as comparable participants in an ecology characterized by fluid engagements of longing. The women are similar not only to each other, but also to the leaves, trees, and others that are part of a cosmos whose "mystery … speaks to you and works in you in some subtle way so that you too feel summer in you" (72).

Like "Her Share," the story "Virgin Soil," also first published in *Discords*, muses over fate's cyclicality but uses the ecological model more forcefully to critique customs of desire. As with many decadent works, the piece also turns to an image of decay as part of a process of renewal and as an opportunity for change. The story is principally about the "legal prostitution, a nightly degradation" (154) that marriage places on wives. The work's eco-decadence, however, suggests that marital oppression is in fact part of the same fluid network with which the heroine, a naïve newlywed named Flo, associates after she has liberated herself from a marriage for which she was not prepared. The man whom she had wed is described early on as a sort of pagan figure – "florid, bright-eyed, loose-lipped" with "ears peculiar, pointed at their tops like a faun's" (145). He is confident – "an animal of strong passions" (155) – and yet bumbling in this new role he is expected to perform in the cultural narrative. Egerton obviously criticizes the assumption of men's authority over women, but she complicates the situation by making Flo's mother complicit in the oppression, chastised by the heroine for having encouraged the marriage and having sent Flo into the relationship with no practical knowledge of what to expect. The mother, like the husband, is described as animalistic: a frog watching a snake, a "kitten with a claw in her paw," and a creature with "dove-like eyes" or "startled, fawn-like eyes," the latter being a trait that she tellingly shares with her daughter (156, 157, 145, 146). The mother's "piping voice" (145) meanwhile suggests the pipe-playing demi-god Pan who has just been evoked in the young husband's faun-like visage. It is thus not only marital rape that Egerton is challenging, but also a set of cultural practices that leave young women unfamiliar with the potential of their own desires. "You reared me a fool, an idiot, ignorant of everything I ought to have known," Flo accuses her mother, "my physical needs, my coming passion, the very meaning of my sex" (156). By situating the crisis within a context of pagan-inflected animalism, however, Egerton deflates such individuated accusations by suggesting that there exists, beyond the control of any individual and outside any particular episode, a cosmology with its own set of competing desires.

At the end of the story, Flo leaves her husband and is submerged into a world of autumnal decay which the narrator presents through a piece of prose-poetry reminiscent of Swinburne in its exploration of desire as pain:

> The first whisper of the fall, the fall that turns the world of nature into a patient suffering from phthisis – delicate season of decadence, when the loveliest scenes have a note of decay in their beauty; when a poisoned arrow pierces the marrow of insect and plant, and the leaves have a hectic flush and fall, fall and shrivel and curl in the night's cool; and the chrysanthemums, the "good-bye summers" of the Irish peasants, have a sickly tinge in their white. (160–61)

Neither the departure from her marriage nor the argument with her mother fosters a complete sense of freedom within the heroine. As this passage suggests, acts that she and others in the story may have recognized as monumental are subsumed by a cycle of "flush and fall" captured in the collage of autumn images and the baroque language itself. Alliterative phrases such as "first whisper of the fall, the fall" and "delicate season of Decadence" attain a pulsating cadence lulled by the mid-length clauses themselves as each layers a new image of decay upon the previous one. Almost reassuring in its plodding repetitiveness, the composition results in a poetics of circularity. "Wither and die, wither and die," says Flo, "make compost for the loves of the spring, as the old drop out and make place for the new, who forget them, to be in their turn forgotten" (161). While the heroine suggests that the decay be read as a metaphor for her wasted youth, the repetition of words and concepts in her phrasing converts her self-reflection on desire into but another layer in the composting, ecological cycle.

The same vision of submergence and decay does not hold for the story "A Cross Line," from *Keynotes*, with which I began my analysis of her work. While the male character in the story's opening scene does perceive the heroine to be immersed in the landscape, this is not exactly the case. She herself is occupied elsewhere as she reads a description of "a fountain scene in Tanagra" that "her vivid imagination has made ... real to her" (1–2). Just as her physical environment has been enlivened by ancient Greek culture, the statues described in the text she is reading themselves have been animated by her own imagination: "The slim, graceful maids grouped around [the fountain] filling their exquisitely-formed earthen jars, the dainty poise of their classic heads, and the flowing folds of their draperies have been actually present with her" (2). Emphasizing the sense of the historical as present, Egerton suggests that the heroine, with a shawl and cream-colored gown covering her "duskily foreign" skin (7), is herself one of these sculptures come to life. The author, like others at the time, was inspired by the recent discovery in the ancient Greek town of Tanagra of a bounty of figurines from the fourth and third centuries BCE. Wilde compares a woman to a Tanagra statue in both *The Picture of Dorian Gray* and *An Ideal Husband* (1895). The items were seen as particularly unique because they were so expertly manufactured for what was viewed as such a minor location far from any major urban center.[97] As Sheila Dillon notes, "many of the Tanagra figurines represent women in the world of religious rituals and public festivals"[98] but, despite being part of a tradition of pagan idealization, the statuettes are notably realistic in their rendering of the individuals.

Like the Tanagra statuettes, the opening scene of "A Cross Line" marks a fusion of the rustic with the civilized, as well as of Classical paganism

George Egerton and the Plots of Women

with the everyday culture of its time. While the heroine sustains this ecological point of view, it remains impenetrable to the "flat notes" of the male that she encounters. In the opening scene, she is described as

> sitting on an incline in the midst of a wilderness of trees; some have blown down, some have been cut down, and the lopped branches lie about; moss and bracken and trailing bramble, fir-cones, wild rose bushes, and speckled red "fairy hats" fight for life in wild confusion. A disused quarry to the left is an ideal haunt of pike. (2)

Any wish on the reader's part to imbue the landscape with a sense of the bucolic is undermined by an ecology characterized by signs of confusion and violence in which the human is present but minimized. The forest is damaged – trees lay helter-skelter – and the damage is neither wholly environmental nor wholly the result of human intervention. The eco-decadence of Egerton's formulation is most succinctly captured in the image of an industrial quarry falling into ruin while simultaneously rewilding into a new state. Moss, roses, mushrooms, and other plants struggle both with and against each other in an orgiastic compulsion for growth, a longing that extends into even the heroine, who finds herself perplexed by a desire to give birth despite her disinterest in the conventional role of the mother. We are given here not an idealized vision of the maternal earth goddess, but an ecological collage in which human desire operates neither rationally nor harmoniously.

One of Egerton's most nuanced turns to paganism to render a sexually charged ecological vision occurs in the story "Pan" in the collection *Symphonies* (1897). In the Victorian period, Pan's image shifted from that of a pastoral trickster to an increasingly philosophical rebuttal to industrialization and consumerism.[99] In addition to his resultant role as a symbol for a bucolic ideal of nature in works such as Kenneth Grahame's *Wind in the Willows* (1908), the figure also developed as a threatening persona increasingly affiliated with sexual violence, as in works such as Machen's *The Great God Pan* and Aleister Crowley's "Hymn to Pan" (1919). Egerton's depiction incorporates elements of both the economic critique found in Grahame and the sexual violence of Machen and Crowley. Her contribution to Pan's lineage is unique in engaging the perspective of an abused woman. In addition, Egerton disturbs the urge for resolution by refusing to situate the figure purely on the side of a human-designed pastoral ideal, his sexual energy being used not only to demarcate him as a liberating rebel but to acknowledge the ecological damage that often comes with renderings of such liberty.

214   Sinking Feeling

The story opens with a scene saturated in "a honey golden noontide": "gold of saffron, gold of topaz, gold of jonquil ... turning the world into an orange dream with changeful shafts of ochre and gamboge."[100] "The maize fields stood proudly," we are told, "like a phalanx of golden spears guarding the hill sides." What begins as an image of natural splendor gradually reveals the aggressive mining industry at the core of the Basque region of France in which the story takes place, as the echo of gold, gold, gold eventually turns to images of ochre shafts and a phalanx of spears. During the nineteenth century, industrialization had led to the Basque landscape being mined for its iron ore. The workers – many new to the region – met with wretched living and working conditions, resulting in general strikes and outbreaks of violence.[101] Egerton chooses to depict this inhumane experience through a conflation of animal types that extends economic oppression to speciesism, even first introducing, among the members of the village, "troops of shaggy mules," "pannier-laden asses," and maize-colored oxen (220). When people do enter the scene, they seem somewhat other than human – workers with feet "shod in hempen solid *espartinac*, ankle-bound," a group of women with their "shrill laughter and guttural Basque" (220), and then – the first individual – an old witch, Maria Andrerea, familiar with the "mystic goat pastures, where the warlocks and witches hold an evil sabbat" (221). Egerton's march continues with "a troop of reformatory children," a contrabandist, a miserable donkey, an unkempt beggar with a "gangrened stump," and manacled prisoners banished across the border as anarchists (222–23). The glorious "honey golden" "world of quivering yellows" (219) is revealed on closer inspection to be a confusion of beings participating in acts of oppression that are the grim reality of modern economic plunder.

The heroine – a girl with red-gold hair that "seemed to catch and imprison the sun itself" (224) – is named Tienette, from the Greek for "crowned in victory," suggesting her affiliation with the Trois Coronnes of the mountain landscape. Her hair of gold, the language of capture and imprisonment, and Egerton's comparison of the woman's features to that of "the image on an Iberian coin" (225), confirm her being fully enmeshed within the industrial machinery sustaining her village. But Tienette senses a possibility of escape in a lame, feminine lutist with "dove-like eyes" who appears to operate outside the economic order. His "witchery," she declares, "vibrated in between the regenerative cry of the earth in her, and around her, until she seemed to listen for it with her very blood" (225–26).[102] Tienette can soon hear his music everywhere – in

George Egerton and the Plots of Women

the sea, the trees, the wind, even at vespers (227). With her resistance worn down by this newfound passion, the heroine puts up little struggle when she is taken into the forest and raped by a fiery man known as the Toro Negro, or Black Bull. "The witch melody that was keyed by the wan musician's hand," the narrator tells us, "seemed to be struck into rougher chords by the man at her side," much as she hears the rapist's own callous laughter echoed by "the wood-spirit – the goat-man" (227–28, 231). Just as the gentle lutist with his witchery is linked to the witch who encouraged the Toro Negro to rape the heroine, the musician and the Toro Negro are both presented as elements of Pan, a force that Egerton ultimately presents as no less than ecological interpenetrations beyond full comprehension. In this story, then, Pan signifies an ongoing resistance to turning the heroine into a pure victim and turning Pan into a rebel victory that would serve, at best, as no more than a temporary release from an economic system built on abuse and oppression. Unlike the figure found in, for example, Stevenson's early works, Egerton has Pan's seemingly amoral complicity serve as a reminder of our own.

Notably, the narrator observes that the rapist's very presence frightened the heroine so much that she "almost desired to be hurt in some way as a relief" (230). Evoking the opening description of Tienette's golden ecology as both natural and economic, organic and inorganic, Egerton suggests the reader consider the heroine as part of the desire and conflict embodied in the alluring yet violent Pan. Spring passes into autumn, and a wealthy uncle gives the now-pregnant Tienette a dowry and a gold chain, before sending her to demand marriage from the Toro Negro, who happens to be taking part in a hunting expedition at the Palombier, "the pass of the pigeons" (240). The patriarch's gift of a chain is, of course, another thread in the economic network, but Egerton brings the sustained metaphor to a new level of horror when she extends it to the vast nets the men use to capture the flocks of birds migrating through a narrow cleft between two remote mountain cliffs. The hunters have over the years spanned the cleft with a line of trees from which they now suspend nets that catch the pigeons:

> She held her breath, and waited with throbbing pulses. Nearer, nearer, surely on the wings of a great wind; – beat, beat – the noise has become deafening, like the charge of hundreds of invisible aerial warriors treading the air above her. Now they have entered the pass; thousands of birds, a grey-white throbbing mass of wing-beating units, driving as one compact body straight to their doom. ... The smell of powder and the blood-stained feathers fluttering on every side made her feel faint. The men

216 Sinking Feeling

> plunged their hands into the net, clutching the struggling birds, many
> maimed, all half-paralysed with terror. (245–46)

With Tienette elsewhere being compared to a hummingbird, a magpie,
and a wild hawk, there is a clear parallel to the birds' capture and the
heroine's – and women's in general. The pigeons' inability to fathom
action that does not conform to their past migratory practices raises the
sense of inevitability also found in stories such as "The Third in the
House" and "Her Share." Foreshadowing Plumwood's feminism,
however, Egerton is not simply inverting a binary here, with Tienette also
maintaining a pagan sense of herself as part of the ecology, along with all
sentient and animist beings including the lutist and even the Toro Negro,
both of whom – like the woodlands themselves – Egerton explicitly affili-
ates with Pan. One is reminded of the opening scene of a dismal pageant
of humans and other animals marching through the village, a futility
echoed later, in a depiction of Tienette's wedding, where everybody
dances "with mechanical steps and a kind of forced gravity," the
"rhythmic tramp of feet … [striking] like hammer-blows on her senses"
(249–51). Recognizing her marriage as another cog in the system of
oppression, the heroine flees to a cliff top, the sea below "bubbl[ing] as in
a cauldron" (253). The lame musician who has followed her professes his
love and she has him play "the goat-man's call" for her again, returning
"all the old witchery to her eyes and lips" (255). When he ends his tune
and looks to the heroine, he finds her gone, but, as the narrator says,
"Pan still lives" (256).

In her well-known 1844 poem "The Dead Pan," Elizabeth Barrett
Browning repeats the phrase "Pan is Dead" a numbing twenty-nine
times; Egerton ends her story with a rebuttal to that sentiment, one that
suggests he lives on but as part of an ecology that maintains, in part,
systemic abuse. At the turn of the century, the notion of environmental
sustainability carried a sense that humans have a responsibility to manage
the welfare of other sentient beings and nature in general. As the violent
climax of "Pan" suggests, Egerton encourages less humans' investment in
how to sustain what they envision to be a healthy or holistic ecology,
than their consideration of the possibility that the vitality of their own
species is largely the result of a decadent ecology incomprehensible in its
magnitude and ethics (if it has any). Sustainability is not a form of
human planning and agency, but a politically inflected state-of-mind or
worldview. Whether Tienette has jumped, has been drawn over the cliff
by the winds, or has dispelled into the environment of which she has
always been and remains a part, she is both the victim of an oppressive

economic order and a constituent of a decadent ecology. Like the other stories by Egerton discussed here, "Pan" offers an important complement to broader ecological models of the period, turning to earth-venerating spirituality to consider, and not wholly celebrate, what Plumwood calls an "interspecies communicative ethic."[103] The story presents the gendered, classist, and speciesist violence of a modern industrial economy. In it, the earth is not recognized by humans as a living force manifested through species inter-reliance, but is seen as a planet on which they have a privileged status that sanctions their efforts at domination. Attentive to the realities of her own cultural context, Egerton remains skeptical, constructing Pan as an ecology that appreciates longing and codependence, but also acknowledges the networks of abuse on which it continues to rely.

The Loam of Desire

In this chapter, I have turned to three writers who made use of pagan tropes and mythology, but not simply as symbols of nonpagan issues concerning humans at the turn of century. Rather, each of them found in pagan decadence an articulation of the indeterminate continuities across modes of sentience and consciousness. Each developed a distinct decompositive model and style addressing their understanding of the purpose of the category human within a vast ecology – a network warranting respect and, in the views of Sharp and Machen, spiritual veneration. Latour explores this indeterminacy in *Pandora's Hope* (1999), describing humans and nonhuman entities negotiating and allying with each other, all with their own "history, flexibility, culture, blood."[104] Just as Latour warns against the benign idealism and innate racism of modern venerations of "primitive" cultures and their paganism,[105] the decadents' perspectives here do not see paganism as a weak fallback position characterized by the mystical worship of the unknown. These authors' writings do much more than settle into a comfortable sense of the beauty of faith or the idealistic promise of the hereafter; in fact, both Machen's and Egerton's oeuvres tend toward states of disturbing uncertainty and distress, while Sharp often formulates a Celtic landscape that appears indifferent to distinguishing human presence, its sentient participants content to continue their rich lives with or without them. Sharp, Machen, and Egerton were not friends or even acquaintances. These distinctions make it all the more interesting that all three were part of the paganism of their moment – influenced by and contributing to the popular culture of decadence, heavily invested in and characterizing The Bodley Head's publishing ventures, and, in the case of Sharp and Machen, contributing to the cultural fusion of paganism with popular occulture. In this sense, rather than simply voicing the value of an ecological understanding that demands sensitivity to multiple perspectives and paradigms of cognition, they enacted something like it in their influence on the decadent scene in Britain. Vegetal excess, scalar distortions, decomposition – their works contributed to the rich loam of desires that characterize the status of humans, like that of the Black Madonna, as confluences of trans-specific attractions and demands forming and unraveling, realized only in those moments of intimacy, and only for those moments' sake.

Epilogue

> The only explanation that suggested itself to his unimaginative mind was that the forces of nature hereabouts were – overpowering; that, after the slum streets and factory chimneys of the last twelve months, these towering cliffs and smothering pine-forests communicated to his soul a word of grandeur that amounted to awe. Inadequate and far-fetched as the explanation seems, it was the only one that occurred to him; and its value in this remarkable adventure lies in the fact that he connected his sense of danger partly with the bed and partly with the mountains.
>
> – Algernon Blackwood, "Special Delivery"[1]

The short story "Special Delivery" (1912) by Algernon Blackwood – member of the Hermetic Order of the Golden Dawn and, like Vernon Lee and Arthur Machen, one of the early masters of weird fiction – is dominated by the consternations of a curate who, stopping for the night at an alpine inn, is saved from a landslide by a shape-shifting force that he ultimately concludes must have been the protective *genius loci*, which notably had no qualms about wiping out the entire sawmill on which the mountain community relied. That this energy first visits him in the form of a man at his bedside instills the piece with an erotic potential that manifests as a beckoning to which the curate fortunately succumbs. In one sense, the short piece reads as a rewriting of Mary Shelley's *Frankenstein*, an analysis of the monstrous night-time visitant as the sublime discourse of nature itself – the "word of grandeur" (as opposed to "world," as a reader might expect) to which the curate, unlike Shelley's doctor, readily responds. In the last chapter of this book, I addressed the way in which the often erotically painful attractions and intimacies are presented as communications that serve as the locus of identification itself. In a discussion of how to understand Blackwood's fiction, David Punter points to some of the conceptual difficulties arising from such a shift of attention away from the human perspective:

220 *Epilogue*

> We are confronted always and inevitably with a dilemma: either we impose human agendas and strategies on to the world of the other, or we treat that world as its own thing, in which case we may feel that we are awarding it due dignity while in fact our admission that we know nothing of it may rob us of all "fellow-feeling" in our dealings with it.[2]

While the curate's mind may be "unimaginative," as Blackwood's narrator proposes, the works of British decadence demonstrate the considerable creative investment and "fellow-feeling" given to exploring the indeterminate attractions operating across animist entities and often in utter disregard for humans' investments in extensionist classification or seemingly reductive materialism. Throughout my book, I have been interested in unmooring British decadence somewhat from its familiar contributors and works in order to emphasize its revolutionary interpenetrations across categories, reconceiving of participants and communities as vital tendrils of ecological engagement. Ideas about decadence changed throughout the time period on which I focus, with authors and artists personalizing certain tropes, politics, or characteristics in some works, but not in their entire oeuvres. Many of these developments were inflected and at times driven by values and investments arising from the pagan revival. We see an exciting shift in perspective, for example, from the pained passion of the lover of Swinburne's leper early in British decadence to the leprous landscape in which the hero of Machen's *Hill of Dreams* loses himself. This is not a concise clear trajectory, but rather shifts in emphases brought on by the humility, uncertainty, and imaginings inspired by a variety of paganisms, including the Egyptian, Greco-Roman, Germanic, Celtic, and occult.

In 1892, Henry Salt would call for the "imaginative sympathy" and "sense of affinity" necessary to move beyond models of relationships that retain the privilege of the human over other species;[3] it makes no sense, Salt argues regarding nonhuman animals, to see humans as "beings of a wholly different order, and to ignore the significance of their numberless points of kinship with mankind."[4] Some decadents of the latter half of the nineteenth century contributed by turning to paganism as a vital force that conceives of the human as something blurring beyond the lines of the skin and the self. Meanwhile, some conceived of the environment as the living embodiment and source of beliefs, or as an essential element of one's identity (gender, desire, or ethnicity, for example). Contributors to the multi-threaded decadent movement and the pagan revival were more often than not city-dwellers, often cosmopolitan, with privileged educations and financial security. Like many of today's pagans (the majority of whom also live and/or work in urban environments), their eco-spiritualism engaged with politics that were both specific to their time and transhistorical. In his poetry collection *Nature Poem* (2017), Tommy Pico, a queer member of the Kumeyaay nation, writes: "I can't write a nature poem | bc it's fodder for the noble savage | narrative. I wd slap a tree across the face." And later:

> Nature asks aren't I curious abt the landscapes of exoplanets – which,
> I thought we all understood planets are metaphors
> like the Vikings, or Delaware [...]
> It's hard for me to imagine curiosity as anything more than a pretext for colonialism
> so nah, Nature I don't want to know the colonial legacy of the future.[5]

Such recent poetry is Indigenous in politics and spirit. Pico's work is not readily part of Western decadence and its philosophies and perspectives, although the dramatics of slapping a tree across its face does take part in the sort of camp excess first made popular by decadent authors such as Oscar Wilde and Ronald Firbank. Like eco-decadence, Pico's poetry does engage in politicizing expansive notions of time and space when it renders extraplanetary landscapes and scientific curiosity as the kernel of colonial exploitation – sticking flags into planets like pins into insects. This evokes the skepticism of the eco-pagan decadents regarding the rise of scientific materialism, suggesting Pico and the decadents might share an inspiration for their ecological visions.

In this book, I have explored the works of a range of individuals who contributed to the cultural imagining of decadent ecology. Those individuals who are most commonly recognized as part of the British movement themselves encourage models of decadence that are often more expansive and volatile than scholars to date have tended to recognize. While often portraying urbane, hyper-encultured characters or personae, these authors and artists repeatedly formulate decadence itself as an ecological force of entangled processes and communications operating beyond humanly conceivable scales of space, time, dimension, and perspective. Not determinist or fatalist, they downplayed the role of the human by emphasizing communications of attraction, desire, or integration mediated through rot, decay, dissipation, and regeneration. This diffusion of the human and the individual fosters scenarios of humility or even surrender – scenarios often read as tragic but that, within the pagan visions introduced into the works, can also be understood as affectionate or even generative.

222   *Epilogue*

Recognizing that decadence of this period rendered visions of ecologies beyond human articulation, frequently presented through forms of eco-veneration, establishes a broader cultural canon of decadence. It also gives us a stronger sense of authors such as Robert Louis Stevenson, Florence Farr, and Machen as central to the ecological fulcrum on which decadence pivots. While often focusing on particular individuals, I have made a concerted effort in this book to note communities and linkages among contributors, working toward a group portrait of British decadents that positions eco-pagan investments in the foreground, while demonstrating their consort with other people holding related eco-interests in the fields of science, spirituality, activism, and aesthetics. I have emphasized the often overlooked correlations among those decadents who used myths as metaphors for developing new perspectives on species, gender, sexuality, race, and nationalism; those who wished to engage spiritually and culturally with paganisms (such as those found in Celtic, Egyptian, Greco-Roman, and modern occult cultures); those who used their art to communicate into otherworldly realities; and those whose admiration or veneration of the organic elements of their ecology vibrated with panpsychic or animist potency. In addition to being a cultural movement encouraging radical engagements with the politics and aesthetics of its time and place, British decadence also challenged the idea of decadence itself as temporally and spatially situated; it put forward perspectives that were transient, transhistorical, trans-spatial, and (often problematically) multinational and multicultural. Recent theoretical developments in the field of eco-studies suggest that, rather than envisioning new foundations and canons of decadence studies, it is more accurate to acknowledge not only that ecology is decadently open but that the cultural phenomenon of decadence is itself an open ecology beyond our complete comprehension.

Contributors to eco-pagan decadence were similar to each other in having earth-venerating spiritual interests and in often engaging the political relevance of these interests, but also in their sense of trans-species affective communications. The vital emotional bonds that characterize decadent paganism are evoked, for example, in what Walter Pater describes, in reference to the maenads' frenzy, as "the swarming of bees together, ... the sympathies of mere numbers."[6] In their poetry, Michael Field foreground desire as an eco-pagan discourse, using their work as part of this "intimate" engagement "by suppressing the habitual centralisation of the visible within ourselves."[7] Pater and Field both celebrate in their writing forms of ecological communication that foster exchanges that humans often understand as empathy, kinship, or the compulsion to care. Decadent ecology is not principally about how canonical authors represent their versions of nature but, rather, about the politics and communications of empathy and affect among forces making up the organic and inorganic environment. The diversity of attractions as modes of emotional transaction not exclusive to humans usefully undermines humans' tendency to exceptionalism, demanding the reconsideration of standard methods of establishing identities (such as species categorization) and, likewise, of whether it is the singular beings who communicate or the exchanges themselves that form and dissolve our nodules of being, that lick us into shape.

An issue to which my analyses have returned is how scholars might understand the communication of affection and desire across species without colonizing Others through the very discourses of our engagement. Among the decadents, these acts of empathy are rendered ephemeral, transient, beyond human control. Rarely do we find a representation in decadent writings in which the individual has the agency to invite such encounters; they may be portrayed as moving through the environments in which they believe they are likely to experience the engagements (scrambling over the Italian mountainside, for Lee, or exploring the Highlands, for William Sharp and Stevenson), but ultimately these authors suggest that, while they or their characters may recognize themselves being drawn to certain intimacies, the actual moment is not of their making. These ecological formulations are queer in David Halperin's sense of evoking desires that are "at odds with the normal, the legitimate, the dominant."[8] The human attempt to manage these queer tendrils or even prove their presence is dismissive of the value of the oblique and, ultimately, futile. As the decadent works that I have explored often suggest, there is an irresponsible but rich pleasure in the experience of this seeming hermeneutic chaos, and there is a value in expectantly waiting for and appreciating the desiring outreach of the indeterminate.

About ten years ago, I noticed in rereading Pater's *Studies in the History of the Renaissance* that it evoked for me a less urbane, less processed, and less contentious vision of sensualism than my study of decadence had led me to expect. In retrospect, I believe it was this occasion that began to shift my sense of my decadent field of inquiry, expanding it to accommodate more diverse interests and a broader set of cultures, including the cultures of the petri dish. This book is, in one sense, my effort to consider what decadence means and who it includes if we accommodate what contributors to the British movement themselves offered as pagan-invested models of ecology.

224 *Epilogue*

I have worked to conceptualize decadence as a trans-species discussion among entangled disciplines regarding attractions, affiliations, and reconfigurations. By encouraging a consideration of less familiar decadent voices, my process has also drawn me both to an acceptance of one's self as a subject of engagement and to a willingness to be written upon – a passive mode of scholarship that operates against the grain of conventional academic demands. I have hesitated many times and will no doubt continue to hesitate to open myself up to being engaged in this way. There are many questions that *Decadent Ecology* has not asked about its subjects, and just as many that I have not yet allowed to be asked of myself. This is, I believe, the threshold of intimacy and submission that Blackwood evokes in "Special Delivery," writing of his protagonist:

> With this realization there came over him, he declares, a singular mood in which, as in a revelation, he knew that Nature held forces that might somehow communicate directly and positively with – human beings. This thought rushed upon him out of the night, as it were. It arrested his movements. He stood there upon the bare pine boards, hesitating to open the door.[9]

Notes

Introduction

1 Jeremy Harte, *English Holy Wells: A Source Book* (London: Heart of Albion, 2008).

2 David Horan, *Oxford: A Cultural and Literary Companion* (New York: Interbook Books, 2000), 121.

3 F. Max Müller, *Theosophy or Psychological Religion* (London: Longmans, Green, 1895), 89–90.

4 Billie Andrew Inman, *Walter Pater and His Reading, 1874–1877, With a Bibliography of His Library Borrowings, 1878–1894* (New York: Garland, 1990), xii, 126. Lene Østermark-Johansen, *Walter Pater and the Language of Sculpture* (Farnham, UK: Ashgate, 2011), 231.

5 Luce Irigaray and Michael Marder, *Through Vegetal Being: Two Philosophical Perspectives* (New York: Columbia University Press, 2016), 6.

1 Decadent Ecology and the Pagan Revival

1 Ernst Haeckel, cited in Robert C. Stauffer, "Haeckel, Darwin, and Ecology," *The Quarterly Review of Biology*, 32.2 (June 1957), 138–44 at 140.

2 Devin Griffiths and Deanna K. Kreisel, "Introduction: Open Ecologies," *Victorian Literature and Culture*, 48.1 (Spring 2020), 1–28 at 3.

3 Edward Gibbon, *The Decline and Fall of the Roman Empire*, 6 vols. (London: A. Strahan, 1788), 1: 10.

4 Gibbon, *Decline and Fall*, 5:515, 516.

5 Charles Baudelaire, *Ouevre complète* (Paris: Gallimard, Bibliothèque de le Pléiade, 1961) 322–23. My translation.

6 Théophile Gautier, "Charles Baudelaire," in Charles Baudelaire, ed., *Les Fleurs du mal* (Paris: Calmann-Lévy, 1868), 1–75 at 17. My translation.

7 Paul Bourget, *Essais de psychologie contemporaine*, 1878 (Paris: Plon-Nourrit, 1908), 19. My translation.

8 Bourget, *Essais de psychologie contemporaine*, 25.

9 Bourget, *Essais de psychologie contemporaine*, 25.

10 Bourget, *Essais de psychologie contemporaine*, 20.

Note of pages 11–14

11 Alfred Egmont Hake, *Regeneration: A Reply to Max Nordau*, 1895 (New York: G. P. Putnam's Sons, 1896), 208.

12 Hake, *Regeneration*, vi.

13 Hake, *Regeneration*, 27, 28.

14 Regenia Gagnier, *Individualism, Decadence and Globalization: On the Relationship of Part to Whole, 1859–1920* (Basingstoke: Palgrave Macmillan, 2010); Kristin Mahoney, *Literature and the Politics of Post-Victorian Decadence* (Cambridge: Cambridge University Press, 2015); Robert Stilling, *Beginning at the End: Decadence, Modernism, and Postcolonial Poetry* (Cambridge: Harvard University Press, 2018); Liz Constable, Dennis Denisoff, and Matthew Potolsky, eds., *Perennial Decay: On the Aesthetics and Politics of Decadence* (Philadelphia: University of Pennsylvania Press, 1999); and Kate Hext and Alex Murray, eds., *Decadence in the Age of Modernism* (Baltimore: Johns Hopkins University Press, 2019).

15 Mary Ellis Gibson, "Regionalism and Provincialism: Where Is the Local?" in Dennis Denisoff and Talia Schaffer, eds., *The Routledge Companion to Victorian Literature* (New York: Routledge, 2020), 449–61 at 449.

16 William Barry, *Heralds of Revolt: Studies in Modern Literature and Dogma* (London: Hodder and Stoughton, 1904), 310.

17 Robert Buchanan, "The Fleshly School of Poetry: Mr. D. G. Rossetti," *The Contemporary Review* 18 (October 1871), 334–50 at 349, 336.

18 Gowan Dawson, *Darwin, Literature and Victorian Respectability* (Cambridge: Cambridge University Press, 2007), 20.

19 Buchanan, "The Fleshly School of Poetry," 349, 343. It is likely that Buchanan or the editors made an error, and meant "pangenesis," Darwin's theory of hereditary transmission, including in asexual reproduction. See chapter 27 of Darwin's *The Variation of Animals and Plants under Domestication* (1868). I thank Gowan Dawson for his help in clarifying this.

20 John Morley, "Review of Swinburne, Poems and Ballads," *Saturday Review* (4 August 1866), 147.

21 Algernon Swinburne, "The Poems of Dante Gabriel Rossetti," 1870, *Essays and Studies* (London: Chatto and Windus, 1876), 60–109 at 80.

22 Algernon Swinburne, *Uncollected Letters of Algernon Charles Swinburne*, vol. 2, edited by Cecil Lang and Terry Meyers (London: Pickering and Chatto, 2004), 45.

23 Swinburne, *Uncollected Letters*, 98.

24 Margot K. Louis, *Swinburne and His Gods* (Montreal: McGill University Press, 1990), 111–2.

25 Jerome McGann "Swinburne, 'Hertha,' and the Voice of Language," *Victorian Literature and Culture*, 36.2 (2008) 283–97 at 285.

26 Algernon Swinburne, "Garden of Proserpine," *Poems and Ballads* (London: John Camden Hotton, 1866), 196–99 at 197.

27 Sara Lyons, *Algernon Swinburne and Walter Pater: Victorian Aestheticism, Doubt and Secularisation* (Oxford: Legenda, 2015), 100.

Note of pages 14–20

28   Swinburne, "Garden of Proserpine," 196.

29   Swinburne, "Garden of Proserpine," 196.

30   David Thomas Ansted, "Our Natural Enemies," *The Cornhill Magazine* 2 (December 1860), 709–17 at 710.

31   Ansted, "Our Natural Enemies," 710.

32   Ansted, "Our Natural Enemies," 711.

33   Clyde K. Hyder, "The Medieval Background of Swinburne's *The Leper*," *PMLA*, 46.4 (December 1931), 1280–88.

34   "Mr. Buchanan on Immorality in Authorship," *The Spectator*, 39.1995 (22 September 1866), 1049–50 at 1049.

35   John Skelton, "Mr. Swinburne and His Critics," *Fraser's Magazine* 74 (3 November 1866), 637–48 at 641.

36   Untitled, Review of Algernon Swinburne's "Notes on Poems and Reviews," *The Athenæum* 2036 (3 November 1866), 564–65 at 564.

37   The narrator of "The Leper" defines himself as a scribe and refers to wearing a "clerk's hood." Sara Lyons notes that the term "clerk," within the medieval context of the poem, was used at that time both to refer to a "cleric in holy orders" and "more loosely as a synonym for a scholar, secretary, or man of letters." Lyons, *Algernon Swinburne and Walter Pater*, 66.

38   Algernon Swinburne, *The Swinburne Letters*, vol. 1, edited by Cecil Y. Lang (New Haven: Yale University Press, 1959), 273.

39   Austin Dobson, "Notes," *London Lyrics*, edited by Frederick Locker Lampson (London: Macmillan, 1904), 165–96 at 171.

40   Christopher Hamlin, "Providence and Putrefaction: Victorian Sanitarians and the Natural Theology of Health and Disease," *Victorian Studies*, 28.3 (Spring 1985), 381–411 at 381.

41   "The Leper," John S. Mayfield papers: Algernon Charles Swinburne series. MS#214: Manuscript "The Leper," 01/01/1860–12/31/1866. n.d.

42   Algernon Swinburne, "Notes on Some Paintings of 1868," *Essays and Studies* (London: Chatto and Windus, 1901), 358–80 at 371.

43   Algernon Swinburne, "The Leper," *Poems and Ballads* (London: John Camden Hotton, 1866), 137–43 at 141.

44   Swinburne, "The Leper," 137.

45   Swinburne, "The Leper," 143.

46   Henry Schuster, "Domestic Terror: Who's Most Dangerous?" CNN (24 August 2005), www.cnn.com/2005/US/08/24/schuster.column/.

47   While there are fundamental differences between Wicca and modern paganism, the members of the American Council of Witches also incorporated skepticism of authority into their social position, officially declaring that they "do not recognize any authoritarian hierarchy," quoted in Margot Adler, *Drawing Down the Moon: Witches, Druids, Goddess-Worshippers, and Other Pagans in America Today* (Boston, MA: Beacon, 1986), 102.

48   Emma Restall Orr, "The Ethics of Paganism," in Ly De Angeles, Emma Restall Orr, and Thom van Dooren, eds., *Pagan Visions for a Sustainable Future*, (Woodbury, MN: Llewellyn, 2005), 1–37 at 7.

228   *Note of pages 20–4*

49   On neofascists' appropriations, see Nicholas Goodrick-Clarke, *Black Sun: Aryan Cults, Esoteric Nazism and the Politics of Identity* (New York: New York University Press, 2002).

50   L. Crow, "Official Statement on the Events Today at the US Capital," *The Troth*. www.thetroth.org/news/20210106-192450.

51   "Mission Statement," *The Troth*, www.thetroth.org/faqpolicies/mission .html.

52   Starhawk, "Towards an Activist Spirituality," in Ly De Angeles, Emma Restall Orr, and Thom van Dooren, eds., *Pagan Visions for a Sustainable Future*, (Woodbury, MN: Llewellyn, 2005), 215–20 at 215–16.

53   Thom van Dooren, "Dwelling in Sacred Community," in Ly De Angeles, Emma Restall Orr, and Thom van Dooren, eds., *Pagan Visions for a Sustainable Future*, (Woodbury, MN: Llewellyn, 2005), 255–82 at 259.

54   Ronald Hutton, *The Stations of the Sun: A History of the Ritual Year in Britain* (Oxford: Oxford University Press, 1996).

55   Anonymous, "Greek Superstitions Concluded – Household Gods – Æsculapian Mysteries – The Sortes," *Chambers's Edinburgh Journal*, 9.417 (November 1839), 356–57 at 356.

56   The term "folklore" was coined by William Thoms in 1846. Jason Marc Harris notes that the words "folk" and "lore" both reinforced Thoms's condescending view of such superstitions and scientifically unfounded narratives; see Marc Harris, *Folklore and the Fantastic in Nineteenth-Century British Fiction* (London: Routledge, 2006), 16. Thoms's embedded critique echoes what is believed to be the original use of the word "pagan" to devalue rural beliefs as less sophisticated.

57   Michael Shaw offers a nuanced analysis of pagan decadence in Scotland in Michael Shaw, *The Fin-de-siècle Scottish Revival: Romance, Decadence and the Celtic Identity* (Edinburgh: Edinburgh University Press, 2020). As Shaw demonstrates, neo-pagan and occult aesthetics and fashions created new artefacts and constructed memories that reinforced claims to an indigenous Celtic spirituality crucial to the modern Scottish struggle for national independence. For a contemporary consideration of the pagan element of the Celtic Renaissance, see the chapter "Celtic Revivals of Paganism" in John Kelman, *Among Famous Books* (London: Hodder and Stoughton, 1912), 89–124.

58   David Hempton, *Religion of the People: Methodism and Popular Religion c. 1750–1900* (London: Routledge, 1996).

59   James Obelkevich, *Religion and Rural Society: South Lindsey 1825–1875* (London: Clarendon, 1976), 14.

60   Obelkevich, *Religion and Rural Society*, 305–6.

61   W.B. Yeats, cited in "Yeats Replies to His Critics," *Boston Post*, 5 October 1911, 8. Rpt. in William Butler Yeats, *W.B. Yeats: Interviews and Recollections*, vol. 1, E. H. Mikhail, ed. (London: Macmillan, 1977), 70–72 at 71.

62   See Richard Dellamora, *Masculine Desire: The Sexual Politics of Victorian Aestheticism* (Chapel Hill: University of North Carolina Press, 1990); Linda

Dowling, *Hellenism and Homosexuality in Victorian Oxford* (Ithaca: Cornell University Press, 1994); Stefano Evangelista, *British Aestheticism and Ancient Greece: Hellenism, Reception, Gods in Exile* (Basingstoke: Palgrave Macmillan, 2009); Margot K. Louis, *Persephone Rises, 1860–1927: Mythography, Gender, and the Creation of a New Spirituality* (Farnham, UK: Ashgate, 2009); and Yopie Prins, *Victorian Sappho* (Princeton: Princeton University Press, 1999).

63 Joyce Kilmer, "Absinthe at the Cheshire Cheese," *The Circus and Other Essays and Fugitive Pieces, 1916* (New York: George H. Doran, 1921), 153–8.

64 Edmund Gosse, *The Life of Algernon Charles Swinburne* (London: Macmillan, 1917), 135–56.

65 T. Earle Welby, *A Study of Swinburne* (London: Faber & Gwyer, 1926), 14.

66 Dowling, *Hellenism and Homosexuality*, 116.

67 Mrs Humphry Ward, "A Writer's Recollections: Part III," *Harper's Magazine*, 136.1895 (April 1918), 680–91 at 689.

68 Goldsworthy Lowes Dickinson, "How Long Halt Ye," *The Independent Review*, 5.17 (February 1905), 27–36 at 29.

69 Dickinson, "How Long Halt Ye," 31–32.

70 Dickinson, "How Long Halt Ye," 35.

71 Dickinson, "How Long Halt Ye," 36.

72 Ronald Hutton, *The Triumph of the Moon* (Oxford: Oxford University Press, 1999), 20.

73 G. K. Chesterton, *Heretics* (London: John Lane, 1908), 50.

74 Bénédicte Coste, "Late-Victorian Paganism: The Case of the Pagan Review," *Cahiers victoriens et édouardiens*, 80 (Autumn 2014), https://journals .openedition.org/cve/1533.

75 Barry, *Heralds of Revolt*, 272.

76 Barry, *Heralds of Revolt*, 292–93.

77 Barry, *Heralds of Revolt*, 295.

78 Barry, *Heralds of Revolt*, 300.

79 Barry, *Heralds of Revolt*, 310.

80 Barry, *Heralds of Revolt*, 310, 309.

81 Barry, *Heralds of Revolt*, 295.

82 Barry, *Heralds of Revolt*, 342.

83 William Michael Rossetti and Algernon Swinburne, *Notes on the Royal Academy Exhibition, 1868* (London: John Cambden Hotten, 1868), 31–51 at 42–43.

84 Elizabeth Prettejohn, "Medea, Frederick Sandys, and the Aesthetic Moment," in Heike Bartel and Anne Simon, eds., *Unbinding Medea: Interdisciplinary Approaches to a Classical Myth from Antiquity to the 21st Century* (Abingdon, Oxon: MHRA, 2010), 94–111 at 101.

85 Rossetti and Swinburne, *Notes on the Royal Academy Exhibition*, 25 (Rossetti), 43–44 (Swinburne).

86 Algernon Swinburne, "Morris's Life and Death of Jason," 1867, *Essays and Studies* (London: Chatto & Windus, 1875), 110–22 at 119.

230 *Note of pages 32–8*

87 Alfred Bate Richards, "Preface," *Medea: A Poem* (London: Chapman & Hall, 1869), iii–x at vi.
88 Alfred Bate Richards, *Medea: A Poem* (London: Chapman & Hall, 1869), 19.
89 A similar sense can be found in George Henry and Edward Atkinson Hornel's *The Druids: Bringing in the Mistletoe* (1890). The intensity of detail, flattened perspective, and use of gold leaf combine in an image of pagan worshippers and white cattle bedecked with mistletoe cut from the sacred oak with a golden sickle. They proceed down a steep, snow-covered slope into the foreground in a disorienting crush upon the viewer akin to the proximity of Medea to the front of the perspective in Sandys's painting.

2   "Up & down & horribly *natural*"

1   Walter Pater, *Greek Studies* (New York: Macmillan, 1895), 58. All further citations of this work appear in the main body of the text.
2   Walter Pater, *Marius the Epicurean*, 1885 (Oxford: Oxford University Press, 1986), 92. All further citations of this work appear in the main body of the text.
3   In his "Introduction" to the novel, Ian Small observes that this sort of play "with quotation, authority, and intertextuality" sets Pater apart from other authors of his time for his avant-garde formal experimentation (Pater, *Marius the Epicurean*, xiii).
4   Edmund Gosse recalls Pater's very process of composition as a sort of meandering, burdensome challenge. "I recollect the writing of the opening chapters of 'Marius,' and the stress that attended it – the intolerable languor and fatigue, the fevers and the cold fits, the grey hours of lassitude and insomnia, the toil as at a deep petroleum well when the oil refuses to flow." Writing as ecological industry. Edmund Gosse, "Walter Pater: A Portrait," *The Contemporary Review*, 66 (December 1894), 795–810 at 806.
5   Timothy Morton, *Ecology without Nature: Rethinking Environmental Aesthetics* (Cambridge, MA: Harvard University Press, 2009), 12.
6   Morton, *Ecology without Nature*, 5.
7   Cited in Robert C. Stauffer, "Haeckel, Darwin, and Ecology," *The Quarterly Review of Biology*, 32.2 (1957), 138–44 at 140.
8   Stauffer, "Haeckel, Darwin, and Ecology," 141.
9   Ernst Haeckel, *The History of Creation*, 1868 (New York: Appleton, 1880), 94–95.
10 Haeckel, *The History of Creation*, 285–86.
11 For a concise introduction to eighteenth- and early nineteenth-century Western conceptions of race, see Irene Tucker, "Race: Tracing the Contours of a Long Nineteenth Century," in Dennis Denisoff and Talia Schaffer, eds., *The Routledge Companion to Victorian Literature* (New York: Routledge, 2020), 330–41.

Note of pages 38–44 231

12 Timothy Morton, "Art in the Age of Asymmetry: Hegel, Objects, Aesthetics," *Eventual Aesthetics*, 1.1 (2012), 121–42.

13 Paul J. Crutzen, "Geology of Mankind," *Nature*, 415.23 (2002), DOI: 10.1038/415023a. On Stoppani, see Gian Luici Daccò, ed., *Antonio Stoppani tra scienza e letteratura* (Lecco: Musei Civici, 1991).

14 Antonio Stoppani, quoted in Etienne Turpin and Valeria Federighi, "A New Element, a New Force, a New Input: Antonio Stoppani's Anthropozoic," in E. Ellsworth and J. Kruse, eds., *Making the Geologic Now* (Brooklyn: Punctum Books, 2012), 34–41 at 38.

15 Paul J. Crutzen and E. F. Stoermer, "The 'Anthropocene'," *Global Change Newsletter*, 41 (2000), 17–18 at 17.

16 Crutzen and Stoermer, "The 'Anthropocene'," 17–18.

17 Tylor was a major contributor to discussions of the "International Congress of Prehistoric Archæology" of which Stoppani was an Honorary President. Billie Andrew Inman has declared it "obvious that Pater got his anthropological orientation from Edward B. Tylor": Billie Andrew Inman, *Walter Pater and His Reading, 1874–1877* (New York: Garland, 1990), ix. Sebastian Lecourt offers an insightful discussion of Pater's interest in Tylor: Sebastian Lecourt, "'To surrender himself, in perfectly liberal inquiry': Walter Pater, Many-Sidedness, and the Conversion Novel," *Victorian Studies*, 53.2 (2011), 231–53.

18 Walter Pater, *Studies in the History of the Renaissance*, 1873 (Oxford: Oxford University Press, 2010), 99. Further references to this text appear in the main body of the chapter.

19 Michael Levey, *The Case of Walter Pater* (London: Thames & Hudson, 1978), 71.

20 Gowan Dawson, "Walter Pater's *Marius the Epicurean* and the Discourse of Science in *Macmillan's Magazine*: 'A Creature of the Nineteenth Century'," *English Literature in Transition, 1880—1920*, 48.1 (2005), 38–54.

21 Kate Hext, *Walter Pater: Individualism and Aesthetic Philosophy* (Edinburgh: Edinburgh University Press, 2013), 133.

22 Curtzen similarly describes the Anthropocenic perspective as a paradigm shift, his sense of wonderment being captured in the closing sentence of his essay "Geology of Mankind," where he describes the epoch as "terra incognita."

23 Stoppani, "A New Element," 37.

24 Stoppani, "A New Element," 37.

25 Stoppani, "A New Element," 36.

26 See William Cronon, "Foreword: Look Back to Look Forward" in David Lowenthal's *George Perkins Marsh: Prophet of Conservation* (Seattle: University of Washington Press, 2000), x–xiii.

27 David Lowenthal, *George Perkins Marsh: Prophet of Conservation* (Seattle: University of Washington Press, 2000), 58.

28 Lowenthal, *George Perkins Marsh*, 609.

29 Mario Cermenati, *Antonio Stoppani: commemorazione pronunziata nel Teatro sociale di Lecco* (L. Rioux: Torino-Rome, 1891), 46.

232 *Note of pages 44–53*

30 Stoppani, "A New Element," 37–38.

31 Stoppani, "A New Element," 39.

32 In contrast to this nineteenth-century articulation, the contemporary concept of the Anthropocene is principally secular. Writing in 2011, Paul Crutzen and Christian Schwägerl declare an utterly human authority as fundamentally characterizing the era: "it's we who decide what nature is and what it will be. To master this huge shift, we must change the way we perceive ourselves and our role in the world. Rather than representing yet another sign of human hubris, this name change would stress the enormity of humanity's responsibility as stewards of the Earth." This emphasis on human environmentalist responsibility accords with Morton's earlier argument. Paul J. Crutzen and Christian Schwägerl, "Living in the Anthropocene: Toward a New Global Ethos," *Environment*, 360. (2011), e360.yale.edu/feature/living_in_the_anthropocene_toward_a_new_global_ethos_/2363.

33 Maureen Moran explores this multiplicity of spiritualities through the trope of the conversion narrative. Maureen Moran, "Pater's 'Great Change': *Marius the Epicurean* as Historical Conversion Romance," in Laurel Brake, Lesley Higgins, and Carolyn Williams, eds., *Walter Pater: Transparencies of Desire* (Greensboro, NC: ELT, 2002), 170–88.

34 Stefano Evangelista, "Outward Nature and the Moods of Men: Pater's Romantic Mythology," in Laurel Brake, Lesley Higgins, and Carolyn Williams, eds., *Walter Pater: Transparencies of Desire* (Greensboro, NC: ELT, 2002), 107–18 at 109.

35 Lene Østermark-Johansen, "Introduction," Lene Østermark-Johansen, ed., *Walter Pater's Imaginary Portraits* (London: Modern Humanities Research Association, 2014), 38.

36 Both Kate Hext and Thomas Lütkemeier have argued that it is likely Pater was familiar with Schopenhauer's work. See Kate Hext, *Walter Pater*, 21.n; Thomas Lütkemeier, *chez soi – The Aesthetic Self in Arthur Schopenhauer, Walter Pater and T.S. Eliot* (Berlin: Verlag Königshausen and Neumann, 2001), 9–11.

37 David Harris Sacks, "Rebuilding Solomon's Temple: Richard Haklyut's Great Instauration," in Chloë Houston, ed., *Travel and Utopia in the Earlier Modern Period* (Burlington, VT: Ashgate), 17–55 at 36.

38 R. M. Seiler, ed., *Walter Pater: The Critical Heritage* (London: Routledge and Kegan Paul, 1985), 124.

39 John Addington Symonds, *The Renaissance: An Essay* (Oxford: Henry Hammans, 1863), 10.

40 Michael Levey, *The Case of Walter Pater*, 104–5.

41 Seiler, *Walter Pater*, 124.

42 Richard Crinkley, *Walter Pater, Humanist* (Lexington: University of Kentucky Press, 1970), 136.

43 Gosse, "Walter Pater: A Portrait," 807.

44 Seiler, *Walter Pater*, 228.

Note of pages 55–66 233

45 For those Victorians engaged in modern art, architecture, and aesthetics, Lucca would bring to mind the work of John Ruskin, who visited the city a number of times to study its art and architecture, and who incorporated this research into his aesthetic theories, which would go on to influence many other artists and scholars, including the Pre-Raphaelites. Caroline Levine has argued that, with *Studies in the History of the Renaissance*, Pater is not so much challenging Ruskin's advocation of "the irregular, self-effacing aesthetics of the Gothic" in *The Stones of Venice* (1851), as formulating his own ideas regarding realism through Ruskin. Caroline Levine, *The Serious Pleasures of Suspense: Victorian Realism & Narrative Doubt* (Charlottesville: University of Virginia Press, 2003), 183.

46 Walter Pater, *The Renaissance: Studies in Art and Poetry* (London: Macmillan, 1888), 246.

47 Gosse, "Walter Pater: A Portrait," 801.

48 On the sustainability of paganism in Christianity, see Lecourt's "To surrender himself, in perfect liberal inquiry." See also Lesley Higgins's "A 'Thousand Solaces' for the Modern Spirit: Walter Pater's Religious Discourse," in Jude V. Nixon, ed., *Victorian Religious Discourse: New Directions in Criticism* (New York: Palgrave, 2004), 189–204.

3 The Lick of Love

1   Review of *Moths*, *Examiner* (10 July 1880), 835.

2   "Ouida's Decadence," *Munsey's Magazine*, 11.5 (August 1894), 550.

3   Review of *Ariadne: A Dream*, *The Saturday Review*, 43.1128 (9 June 1877), 709–10 at 710.

4   Review of *Ariadne*, 709.

5   Pierre Loti, quoted in Ouida, "Death and Pity," *The Fortnightly Review*, 57 (April 1892), 548–65 at 550.

6   Elizabeth Pennell, "The Two Salons," *The Fortnightly Review*, 57 (April 1892), 840–45 at 843.

7   Arthur Symons, "J.K. Huysmans," *The Fortnightly Review*, 57 (April 1892), 402–14 at 409 and 403.

8   Benjamin Morgan, *The Outward Mind: Materialist Aesthetics in Victorian Science and Literature* (Chicago: Chicago University Press, 2017), 261.

9   Pierre Loti, quoted in Ouida, "Death and Pity," 548–65 at 550.

10 David M. Halperin, *Saint Foucault: Towards a Gay Hagiography* (Oxford: Oxford University Press, 1995), 62.

11 Jeremy Bentham, *Introduction to the Principles of Morals and Legislation*, 1802 (Oxford: Clarendon, 1879), 310.

12 Jeremy Bentham, *Theory of Legislation*, 1802 (London: Trübner, 1871), 10.

13 Ivan Kreilkamp, "The Ass Got a Verdict: Martin's Act and the Founding of the Society for the Prevention of Cruelty to Animals, 1822," in Dino Franco Felluga, ed., *BRANCH: Britain, Representation and Nineteenth-Century History*. www.branchcollective.org/?ps_articles=ivan-kreilkamp-the-ass-got-

234   *Note of pages 66–70*

a-verdict-martins-act-and-the-founding-of-the-society-for-the-prevention-of-cruelty-to-animals-1822.

14 Mario Ortiz-Robles, "Animal Acts: *1822, 1835, 1849, 1850, 1854, 1876, 1900*," in Dino Franco Felluga, ed., *BRANCH: Britain, Representation and Nineteenth-Century History*. www.branchcollective.org/?ps_articles=mario-ortiz-robles-animal-acts-1822-1835-1849-1850-1854-1876-1900.

15 John Stuart Mill, *Utilitarianism* (New York: Liberal Arts, 1949), 8.

16 Mill, *Utilitarianism*, 8.

17 John Stuart Mill, *Principles of Political Economy with Some of Thier Applications to Social Philosophy*, vol. 5 (London: Longman, Green, 1885), 578.

18 Monica Flegel, *Conceptualizing Cruelty to Children in Nineteenth-Century England* (Aldershot, UK: Ashgate 2009).

19 Henry Salt, *Animals' Rights Considered in Relation to Social Progress*, 1892 (Clarks Summit, PA: Society for Animal Rights, 1980), 28. Further references to this text are cited in the main body of this study.

20 Bentham, *Theory of Legislation*, 425.

21 Alfred Russell Wallace, "The Origin of Human Races and the Antiquity of Man Deduced from the Theory of Natural Selection," *Journal of the Anthropological Society*, 2 (1864), clviii–clxxxvii at clxix.

22 Vernon Lee, "Vivisection: An Evolutionist to Evolutionists," *Contemporary Review*, 41 (May 1882), 788–811 at 803.

23 Keith Tester, *Animals and Society: The Humanity of Animal Rights* (New York: Routledge, 1991).

24 Peter Singer, *Animal Liberation, 1975* (New York: Harper Collins Publishers, 2002), 20, 19.

25 Brian Massumi, *What Animals Teach Us about Politics* (Durham, NC: Duke University Press, 2014), 3.

26 Cary Wolfe similarly shifts the conceptual field when he argues that, rather than challenging speciesism whenever it arises within our humanist worldviews, it is necessary to erase the sense of species distinctions entirely, fostering a "fundamental change or mutation" in our shared assumptions about how species engage. Cary Wolfe, *What Is Posthumanism* (Minneapolis: University of Minnesota Press, 2010), xvii.

27 Catriona Sandilands, "Queer Ecology," in Joni Adamson, William A. Gleason, and David N. Pellow, eds., *Keywords for Environmental Studies* (New York: New York University Press, 2016), 169–71 at 171.

28 See Myra Hird, "Animal Trans," in Noreen Giffney and Myra Hird, eds., *Queering the Non/Human* (Hampshire, UK: Ashgate, 2008), 227–47; and Elizabeth Wilson, "Biologically Inspired Feminism: Response to Helen Keane and Marsha Rosengarten, 'On the Biology of Sexed Subjects'," *Australian Feminist Studies*, 17.39 (2002), 283–85.

29 Sandilands, "Queer Ecology," 169.

30 Catriona Mortimer-Sandilands and Bruce Erickson, "Introduction: A Genealogy of Queer Ecologies," in Catriona Mortimer-Sandilands and

Bruce Erickson, eds., *Queer Ecologies: Sex, Nature, Politics, Desire* (Bloomington: Indiana University Press, 2010), 1–47.

31 Anna Maria Wilhelmina Stirling, ed., *The Richmond Papers, from the Correspondence and Manuscripts of George Richmond R. A., and his son Sir William Richmond R. A., K. C. B.* (London, n.p., 1926), 160.

32 Gerard Manley Hopkins, *The Journals and Papers of Gerard Manley Hopkins* (London: Oxford University Press 1959), 167.

33 Catherine Maxwell, "Pater and the Pre-Raphaelites," *The Pater Newsletter*, 63 (Spring 2013), 77–90 at 78.

34 Elizabeth Prettejohn, "Solomon's Classicism," in Colin Cruise, ed., *Love Revealed: Simeon Solomon and the Pre-Raphaelites* (London, Merrell, 2005), 39–45 at 45.

35 Walter Pater, *Studies in the History of the Renaissance*, 1873 (Oxford: Oxford University Press, 2010), 119.

36 Pater, *Studies in the History of the Renaissance*, 118.

37 Walter Pater, *Greek Studies* (New York: Macmillan, 1895), 3.

38 Pater, *Studies in the History of the Renaissance*, 112, 99.

39 Roberto C. Ferrari, "Solomon's Life Before 1873," *Simeon Solomon Research Archive*. Simeonsolomon.com/simeon-solomon-biography.html. Richard Kaye has noted the steady criticism that over much of the past 150 years has been doled out to nineteenth-century decadent visual art – which in Britain (other than Aubrey Beardsley's work) was often seen as synonymous with Pre-Raphaelitism. The criticism has principally arisen not for its eroticism but for its costuming, preciousness, sentimentality, idealized bodies, and limited innovation. Latent within this criticism is a conceptual misogyny – a critique of the small, the detailed, the pretty against the context of the seeming realism, bold honesty, and modernity of the impressionists and those who came later. Of course, there is also misogyny within decadent art. Richard Kaye, "Decadence in Painting," in Alex Murray, ed., *Decadence: A Literary History* (Cambridge: Cambridge University Press, 2020) 234–53 at 236.

40 Algernon Swinburne, "Simeon Solomon: Notes on his 'Vision of Love' and Other Studies," *The Dark Blue*, 1 (July 1871), 568–77 at 572.

41 Catherine Maxwell, *Swinburne* (Tavistock: Northcote House, 2006), 100.

42 "Studio-Talk," *The Studio*, 37 (1906), 67–68 at 67.

43 "Biography of Simeon Solomon," Birmingham Museums and Art Gallery. www.bmagic.org.uk/people/Simeon+Solomon.

44 Susan Moore, "Simeon Solomon gets his time in the spotlight," *Apollo: The International Art Magazine*, 9 July 2018, www.apollo-magazine.com/simeon-solomon-gets-his-time-in-the-spotlight/. For a counter-reading of the history of scholar's queer rendering of Solomon's career, see Richard Kaye, "The New Other Victorians: The Success (and Failure) of Queer Theory in Nineteenth-Century British Studies," *Victorian Literature and Culture*, 42 (2014), 755–71.

45 Dustin Friedman, *Before Queer Theory: Victorian Aestheticism and the Self* (Baltimore: Johns Hopkins University Press, 2019), 4.

236   *Note of pages 74–84*

46   Colin Cruise, "Introduction," in Colin Cruise, ed., *Love Revealed: Simeon Solomon and the Pre-Raphaelites* (London: Merrell, 2005), 9–11 at 9.

47   Gayle Seymour, "The Old Testament Paintings and Drawings: The Search for Identity in the Post-Emancipation Era," in Colin Cruise, ed., *Love Revealed: Simeon Solomon and the Pre-Raphaelites* (London: Merrell, 2005), 13–21 at 13.

48   "The Royal Academy. The One Hundred and First Exhibition. Second Notice." *The Art-Journal* (July 1869), 201; "The London Art Season." *Blackwood's Edinburgh Magazine* (August 1869), 220–39 at 224.

49   "Dudley Gallery. Fourth Winter Exhibition," *The Art-Journal* (1 December 1870), 373.

50   "The Fourth General Exhibition of Water-colour Drawings. Dudley Gallery," *The Art-Journal* (1 March 1868), 45.

51   "The Fourth General Exhibition," 57.

52   Pater, *Greek Studies*, 37.

53   Pater, *Greek Studies*, 42.

54   Algernon Swinburne, "Simeon Solomon: Notes on his 'Vision of Love' and Other Studies," *The Dark Blue*, 1 (July 1871), 568–77 at 574.

55   Gayle Seymour, "The Old Testament Paintings and Drawings," 21.

56   Winter Exhibition catalogue, cited in Colin Cruise, ed., *Love Revealed*, 77.

57   E. H. Plumptre, "Jeremiah," in Charles John Ellicott, ed., *An Old Testament Commentary for English Readers*, vol. 5 (London: Cassell, 1884), 3–177 at 168.

58   Seymour, *The Life and Work of Simeon Solomon*, 17.

59   Seymour, *The Life and Work of Simeon Solomon*, 49.

60   Merrill Fabry, "Where Does the 'Thumbs-Up' Gesture Really Come From?" *Time* (25 October 2017), https://time.com/4984728/thumbs-up-thumbs-down-history/.

61   Christopher Epplett, "Roman Beast Hunts," in Paul Christesen and Donald G. Kyle, ed., *A Companion to Sport and Spectacle in Greek and Roman Antiquity* (Hoboken, NJ: A. Wiley-Blackwell, 2013), https://onlinelibrary.wiley.com/doi/abs/10.1002/9781118609965.ch34.

62   Walter Pater, *Marius the Epicurean*, 1885 (Oxford: Oxford University Press, 1986), 135, 136. All further citations of this work appear in the main body of the text.

63   Algernon Swinburne, "Faustine," 1862, *Poems and Ballads* (London: Saville and Edwards, 1866), 122–29 at 127.

64   Pater, *Studies in the History of the Renaissance*, 60.

65   Stefano Evangelista, "Greek Textual Archaeology and Erotic Epigraphy in Simeon Solomon and Michael Field," *Cahiers victoriens et édouardiens*, 78 (Automne 2013), http://journals.openedition.org/cve/909.

66   Mary Sturgeon, *Michael Field* (London: George G. Harrap & Co, 1922), 20.

67   Emma Donoghue, *We Are Michael Field* (London: Absolute, 1998), 33.

68   Sturgeon, *Michael Field*, 21.

Note of pages 84–97   237

69 Jill Ehnenn, "Looking Strategically: Feminist and Queer Aesthetics in Michael Field's *Sight and Song*," *Victorian Poetry*, 42.3 (Fall 2004), 213–59; Yopie Prins, *Victorian Sappho* (Princeton: Princeton University Press, 1999).

70 Michael Field, *Whym Chow: Flame of Love* (London: Eragny Press, 1914), 14.

71 David Banash, "To the Other: The Animal and Desire in Michael Field's Whym Chow: Flame of Love," in Mary Sanders Pollock and Catherine Rainwater, eds., *Figuring Animal: Essays on Animal Images in Art, Literature, Philosophy, and Popular Culture* (New York: Palgrave, 2005), 195–205 at 196.

72 Halperin, *Saint Foucault*, 62.

73 Marion Thain, *Michael Field: Poetry, Aestheticism and the Fin de Siècle* (Cambridge: Cambridge University Press, 2007), 71.

74 Michael Field, *Sight and Song* (London: Elkin Mathews and John Lane, 1892), 4. All further references to this poetry collection appear in the main body of the chapter.

75 Richard Kaye, "'Determined Raptures': St. Sebastian and the Victorian Discourse of Decadence," *Victorian Literature and Culture*, 27.1 (March 1999), 269–303 at 271.

76 Kaye, "Determined Raptures," 269–303.

77 Vasari, *Lives of the Most Eminent Painters, Sculptors, and Architects*, 1550, vol. 4, translated by Gaston du C. de Vere (London: Philip Lee Warner, 1912–14), 126–27.

78 Vasari, *Lives of the Most Eminent Painters, Sculptors, and Architects*, 134 and 133.

79 Joseph Bristow, "How Decadent Poems Die," in Jason Hall and Alex Murray, eds., *Decadent Poetics: Literature and Form at the British* Fin de Siècle (Basingstoke: Palgrave Macmillan, 2013), 26–45 at 38.

80 Michael Field, *Whym Chow: Flame of Love*, 15.

81 Ouida, *Ariadnê: The Story of a Dream*, 3 vols. (London: Chapman & Hall, 1877), 1:1–2.

82 Ouida, *Ariadnê*, 1:3.

83 Ouida, *Ariadnê*, 1:5.

84 Review of *Ariadne: A Dream*, *The Saturday Review of Politics, Literature, Science and Art*, 43.1128 (9 June 1877), 709–10 at 710.

85 Edward Carpenter, *Civilization, Its Cause and Cure, and Other Essays*, 1889 (London: George Allen, 1921), 132–33.

4 The *Genius Loci* as Spirited Vagabond in Robert Louis Stevenson and Vernon Lee

1 Robert Louis Stevenson, "Walking Tours," *Cornhill Magazine*, 33 (1876), 685–90 at 685–86.

2 Walter Pater, *Studies in the History of the Renaissance*, 1873 (Oxford: Oxford University Press, 2010), 120.

238   *Note of pages 97–9*

3   Although not a common term for Pater, Stevenson, or Lee, "life force" gained increased use during the Victorian period with the rise of spiritualism to define the energy of the soul, which spiritualists believe continues to exist and evolve after death. The movement is defined by the belief that the dead wish and try to communicate with the living and that nature is an expression of a greater, collective force. This usage of the term "life force" gradually became a part of the pagan movement, albeit not due to the views of spiritualists.

4   Andrea Kaston Tange, "Travel Writing," in Dennis Denisoff and Talia Schaffer, eds., *The Routledge Companion to Victorian Literature* (New York: Routledge, 2020), 473–84 at 473.

5   Tange, "Travel Writing," 474.

6   In the past thirty years, extensive scholarship has been done on Victorian travel writing, with particular emphasis on its relations to postcolonialism, imperialism, amateur science, and gender politics. Key early works of scholarship on the subgenre with regard to the period on which *Decadent Ecology* focuses include Mary-Louise Pratt, *Imperial Eyes: Travel Writing and Transculturation* (New York: Routledge, 1992); James Buzard, *The Beaten Track: European Tourism, Literature and the Ways to "Culture," 1800–1918* (Oxford: Oxford University Press, 1993); Lila Marz Harper, *Solitary Travelers: Nineteenth-Century Women's Travel Narratives and the Scientific Vocation* (Madison: Farleigh Dickinson University Press, 2001); Peter Hulme and Tim Youngs, eds., *The Cambridge Companion to Travel Writing* (Cambridge: Cambridge University Press, 2002); and Wolfgang Schivelbusch, *The Railway Journey: The Industrialization of Time and Space in the 19th Century* (Berkeley: University of California Press, 2014).

7   Vernon Lee, "Dionysus in the Euganean Hills, Walter Pater in Memorium," *The Contemporary Review*, 120 (September 1921), 346–53 at 347.

8   Edmund Gosse, "Walter Pater: A Portrait," *The Contemporary Review*, 66 (December 1894), 795–810, 807.

9   In recent years, a particularly insightful approach to exploring this subject has arisen in the study of affect and landscapes – the ways in which humans relate to and interact with their environments emotionally and sensually. Although the scholarship does not explore notions of the *genius loci* or pagan panpsychism, the works offer nuanced paradigms for considering the relationship between geography and emotion. Key works contributing to the subject include Christine Berberich, Neil Campbell, and Robert Hudson, eds., *Affective Landscapes in Literature, Art and Everyday Life* (Farnham: Ashgate, 2015); and Melissa Gregg and Gregory J. Seigworth, eds., *The Affect Theory Reader* (Durham, NC: Duke University Press, 2010).

10 Aurelius Prudentius Clemens, quoted in John J. I. Döllinger, *The Gentile and the Jew in the Courts of the Temple of Christ: An Introduction to the History of Christianity*, Vol. II, trans. N. Darnell (London: Longman, Green, Longman, Roberts, and Green, 1862), 62.

Note of pages 100–5

11 J. P. Alcock, *A Brief History of Roman Britain* (London: Robinson, 2011), 246.

12 Since its formulation by the psychologist Richard Ryder in 1970, the accusation of speciesism has been directed primarily against humans; see Richard D. Ryder, *Animal Revolution: Changing Attitudes Towards Speciesism* (London: McFarland, 1989). Peter Singer popularized the term through his foundational discussion of speciesism in his 1975 *Animal Liberation* (New York: Harper Collins Publishers, 2002).

13 For recent influential yet differing analyses of panpsychism within the humanities, see Jane Bennett, *Vibrant Matter: A Political Ecology of Things* (Durham: Duke University Press, 2010); Bruno Latour, *Reassembling the Social* (Oxford: Oxford University Press, 2007); and the essay collection by David Skrbina, ed., *Mind that Abides: Panpsychism in the New Millenium* (Amsterdam: John Benjamins, 2009). As the latter attests, the recent debate around panpsychism has far from completed its run, with particular attention having been given to clarifying distinctions between the concept and animism, and whether panpsychism is to be understood as addressing consciousness at all; on this issue, see Galin Strawson, ed., *Consciousness and Its Place in Nature: Does Physicalism Entail Panpsychism?* (Exeter: Imprint Academic, 2006).

14 Adela Pinch, "The Appeal of Panpsychism in Victorian Britain," *RAVON: Romanticism and Victorianism on the Net*, 65 (2014–15), 6.

15 George Henry Lewes, *Problems of Live and Mind*, Series 3 continued (London: Trübner, 1979), 23–24.

16 Lewes, *Problems of Live and Mind*, 26, 20.

17 Lewes, *Problems of Live and Mind*, 27.

18 Lewes, *Problems of Live and Mind*, 34–35.

19 Gregory Nixon, Review of *Mind that Abides. Journal of Consciousness Studies* (Amsterdam: John Benjamins, 2009), 116–21, 116.

20 *James Lovelock, Gaia: A New Look at Life on Earth* (Oxford: Oxford University Press, 2000), 25.

21 James Lovelock, "Gaia: The World as a Living Organism," *New Scientist* (18 December 1986), 25–28 at 25.

22 Lovelock, "Gaia," 28.

23 Paul Maixner, "Introduction," *Robert Louis Stevenson: The Critical Heritage* (New York: Routledge, 1971), 1–46 at 8.

24 Anonymous, cited in Paul Maixner, ed., *Robert Louis Stevenson: The Critical Heritage* (New York: Routledge, 1971), 48.

25 William Archer, cited in Maixner, *Robert Louis Stevenson*, 160.

26 William Archer, cited in Maixner, *Robert Louis Stevenson*, 169.

27 Robert Louis Stevenson, *The Letters of Robert Louis Stevenson*, Vol. 1, edited by Sidney Colvin (New York: Charles Scribner's Sons, 1902), 436.

28 Henry James, *Partial Portraits* (London: Macmillan, 1919), 143.

29 Richard Le Gallienne, *Robert Louis Stevenson: An Elegy, and Other Poems Mainly Personal* (London: John Lane, 1895), 7, 9.

240 *Note of pages 105–11*

30 Le Gallienne, *Robert Louis Stevenson*, 8.

31 Jason Boyd, "Richard Le Gallienne," in Dennis Denisoff and Lorraine Janzen Kooistra, eds., *The Yellow Nineties Online*, http://1890s.ca/HTML. aspx?s=legallienne_bio.html.

32 Philip Gilbert Hamerton, "The Yellow Book: A Criticism of Volume I," *The Yellow Book*, 2 (July 1894), 179–90.

33 Le Gallienne, *Robert Louis Stevenson*, 9.

34 Le Gallienne, *Robert Louis Stevenson*, 9.

35 Le Gallienne, *Robert Louis Stevenson*, 8–9.

36 G. K. Chesterton, *Heretics* (London: John Lane, 1905), 153.

37 G. K. Chesterton, "Robert Louis Stevenson," 1927, *Collected Works of G. K. Chesterton*, Vol. 18 (San Francisco: Ignatius, 1991), 39–148 at 69.

38 Chesterton, "Robert Louis Stevenson," 119.

39 Robert Louis Stevenson, *Men and Books* (London: Chatto & Windus, 1882), 100.

40 Robert Louis Stevenson, *The New Arabian Nights* (New York: Charles Scribner's Sons, 1905), 424.

41 Robert, Louis Stevenson, *An Inland Voyage* (London: C. Kegan Paul, 1878), 222. Further citations of this work are made directly in the text.

42 Stevenson, *The Letters of Robert Louis Stevenson*, 30–31. Stevenson acknowledged his lack of Greek, but he had studied Latin for two years and, according to Eli Edward Burriss, "his Latin reading, so far as it affected his intellectual life, was a pursuit, not of his school days, but of his maturity," Eli Edward Burriss, "The Classical Culture of Robert Louis Stevenson," *The Classical Journal*, 20.5 (February 1925), 217–79 at 271–72.

43 Stevenson, *The Letters of Robert Louis Stevenson*, 436.

44 Stevenson, *The Letters of Robert Louis Stevenson*, 144.

45 Walter Pater, *Greek Studies* (London: Macmillan, 1910), 15. Pater foregrounds the confusion of species when he describes Pan and his followers as "speculating wistfully on their being, because not wholly understanding themselves and their place in nature." Wolfgang Iser has noted Stevenson's indebtedness to Pater's pagan philosophy: Wolfgang Iser, *Walter Pater: The Aesthetic Moment*, trans. David Henry Wilson (Cambridge: Cambridge University Press, 1987).

46 Burriss, "The Classical Culture of Robert Louis Stevenson," 277.

47 Robert Louis Stevenson, "Pan's Pipes," 1878, *Virginibus Purisque and Other Papers* (London: C. Kean Paul, 1881), 279–87 at 281.

48 Stevenson, "Pan's Pipes," 279–80.

49 Robert Louis Stevenson, "An Autumn Effect," *Essays of Travel*, 1905 (London: Chatto & Windus, 1918), 98–121 at 112.

50 Jean Perrot, "Pan and Puer Aeternus: Aestheticism and the Spirit of the Age," *Poetics Today*, 13.1 (Spring 1992), 155–67 at 156. On Stevenson's early discussions of Pan, see also the last chapter of William Gray, *Fantasy, Art, and Life: Essays on George MacDonald, Robert Louis Stevenson and Other Fantasy Writers* (Newcastle Upon Tyne: Cambridge Scholars, 2011).

Note of pages 112–23 241

51   Stevenson, "Pan's Pipes," 285.

52   Stevenson, "Pan's Pipes," 281.

53   Stevenson, "Pan's Pipes," 279.

54   Stevenson, "Pan's Pipes," 281.

55   William Gray, "On the Road: Robert Louis Stevenson's Views on Nature," *New Formations*, 64 (Spring 2008) 90–98 at 93, 90.

56   Robert Louis Stevenson, *Familiar Studies of Men and Books*, 1882 (London: Chatto & Windus, 1896). For an analysis of Thoreau's and Whitman's influences on Stevenson's ecological vision, see Louisa Gairn, *Ecology and Modern Scottish Literature* (Edinburgh: Edinburgh University Press, 2008).

57   Walter Pater, "Poems by William Morris," 1868, in Peter Faulkner, ed., *William Morris: The Critical Heritage* (London: Routledge & Kegan Paul, 1973), 79–92 at 89.

58   Pater, "Poems by William Morris," 82.

59   Robert Louis Stevenson, "Books that Have Influenced Me," 1887, *The Art of Writing*, 1905 (Los Angeles: Indo-European, 2011), 40.

60   Robert Louis Stevenson, *Travels with a Donkey in the Cévennes* (Boston: Roberts Brothers, 1879), 45. All further references to this work are made in the main body of the text.

61   Stevenson celebrates and engages with Hazlitt's essay in his own responding essay "Walking Tours."

62   William Hazlitt, "On Going a Journey," *The New Monthly Magazine*, 4 (January 1822), 73–79 at 73.

63   Morgan Holmes, "Donkeys, Englishmen, and Other Animals: The Precarious Distinctions of Victorian Interspecies Morality," Richard Ambrosini and Richard Dury, eds., *European Stevenson* (Newcastle upon Tyne: Cambridge Scholars, 2009), 109–26.

64   William Wordsworth, "She dwelt among the untrodden ways," *The Poetical Works of William Wordsworth* (London: E. Moxon, Son, 1871), 64.

65   Stevenson's second published book is *Edinburgh: Picturesque Notes* (London: Seeley, Jackson & Halliday, 1878).

66   In the frontispiece to the second book, the characters performing the scenes in the background are all Stevenson and Modestine at stages of travel yet to occur. Both of Crane's images for Stevenson portray the author disappearing more or less into the sunset. Both also position human and equine together in a circle at the top – one with a centaur, the other with the traveling companions encompassed by the setting sun. At the risk of over-reading, Stevenson and Pan are also conflated through the image of each of them enjoying their pipes.

67   Michael Field, *Sight and Song* (London: Elkin Mathews and John Lane, 1892), vi.

68   Pater, *Greek Studies*, 15.

69   Hazlitt, "On Going a Journey," 73.

70   Vernon Lee, *The Enchanted Woods, and Other Essays on the Genius of Places* (London: John Lane, 1905), 259–60. All further references to this work appear in the main body of my text.

Note of pages 124–35

71 Vernon Lee, "The Craft of Words," *New Review*, 11 (1894), 571–80 at 579.
72 Vernon Lee, *Renaissance Fancies and Studies* (London: Smith, Elder, & Co, 1896), 258.
73 Lee, *Renaissance Fancies and Studies*, 259–60.
74 Nicholas Dames, *The Physiology of the Novel* (Oxford: Oxford University Press, 2007), 176.
75 Lee, "The Craft of Words," 575–76.
76 Pinch, "The Appeal of Panpsychism in Victorian Britain," 18.
77 Paul Bourget, *Essais de psychologie contemporaine*, 1878 (London: Brace, 1926), 25.
78 Gordon W. Smith, ed., "Letters from Paul Bourget to Vernon Lee." *Colby Library Quarterly*, 3.15 (August 1954), 2–9.
79 Smith, "Letters from Paul Bourget to Vernon Lee," 7.
80 Antonio Stoppani, quoted in Etienne Turpin and Valeria Federighi, "A New Element, a New Force, a New Input: Antonio Stoppani's Anthropozoic," in E. Ellsworth and J. Kruse, eds., *Making the Geologic Now* (Brooklyn: Punctum Books, 2012), 34–41.
81 Stoppani, "A New Element," 37.
82 Lee's position begs consideration in relation to Filippo Tommaso Marinetti's *Manifesto of Futurism*, which first appeared in 1909, a few years after Lee's *Enchanted Woods*. One is encouraged by Marinetti's work to understand the distinction as the shift from a Victorian to a Modernist zeitgeist or, more specifically, from the Romanticist aspect of some of the decadents to the aggressive compulsion for experimentation and novelty that defines the historical avant-garde. As I am suggesting, however, Lee's writings are particularly sensitive to the potential of modern industry, with her discussion explicitly engaging with and incorporating human influence into her eco-aesthetics.
83 Stoppani, "A New Element," 37–38.
84 James George Frazer, *The Golden Bough: A Study of Magic and Religion*, 1890 (New York: Macmillan, 1922), 1.
85 Frazer, *The Golden Bough*, 1–2.
86 Vernon Lee, *Genius Loci: Notes on Place*, 1899 (London: John Lane, the Bodley Head, 1907), 198. All further references to this work appear in the main body of the text.
87 Benjamin Morgan, *The Outward Mind: Materialist Aesthetics in Victorian Science and Literature* (Chicago: University of Chicago Press, 2017), 222.
88 Pater, *Studies in the History of the Renaissance*, 112.
89 Gavin Arthur, *The Circle of Sex*, 1962 (New Hyde Park, NY: University Books, 1966). See also Martin G. Murray, "Walt Whitman, Edward Carpenter, Gavin Arthur, and the Circle of Sex," *Walt Whitman Quarterly Review*, 22.4 (2005), 194–98.
90 Walt Whitman, *Leaves of Grass* (Philadelphia: David McKay, 1881), 92.
91 Algernon Swinburne, *Songs before Sunrise* (London: F. S. Ellis, 1871), 148.
92 Swinburne, *Songs before Sunrise*, 265.

Note of pages 136–43 243

93 Kathy Psomiades offers an insightful consideration of Lee's same-sex desires as they relate to her aesthetics: Kathy Psomiades, "'Still Burning from This Strangling Embrace': Vernon Lee on Desire and Aesthetics," Richard Dellamora, ed., *Victorian Sexual Dissidence* (Chicago: Chicago University Press, 1999). For a summary of scholarship on the place of Lee's lesbianism in her writing, see the thoughtful third chapter of Christa Zorn's *Vernon Lee: Aesthetics, History, and the Victorian Female Intellectual* (Athens: Ohio University Press, 2003).

94 Vernon Lee, *Beauty and Ugliness and Other Studies in Psychological Aesthetics* (London: John Lane, the Bodley Head, 1912), 188.

95 Diana Maltz, "'Delicate Brains': From Working Class Enculturation to Upper-Class Lesbian Liberation in Vernon Lee and Kit Anstruther-Thomson's Psychological Aesthetics," in Talia Schaffer and Kathy Alexis Psomiades, eds., *Women and British Aestheticism* (Charlottesville: University of Virginia Press, 1999), 211–29 at 213.

96 Maltz, "Delicate Brains," 222.

97 Vernon Lee, *The Sentimental Traveller: Notes on Places* (London: John Lane, the Bodley Head, 1908), 4.

98 Lee, *The Sentimental Traveller*, 5.

5 Occult Ecology and the Decadent Feminism of Moina Mathers and Florence Farr

1 In this chapter, I do not capitalize the term "symbolism" because I use it not only to refer to the well-known movement in French literature and Charles Baudelaire's theory of correspondences, but also and principally to address the use of symbols in writing, art, and ritual by members of the occult.

2 The actual end of the Order cannot be dated precisely. Rifts arose in the later 1890s, with the Ahathoor temple in Paris and Isis-Urania temple in London battling for authority and resources. While Farr and other members of the London temple challenged the wishes of Samuel Mathers (Moina's husband) to promote Aleister Crowley too quickly, Crowley attempted to take over the Isis-Urania Temple physically, but W. B. Yeats stopped him with magic. This was soon followed by two imposters infiltrating the Order, stealing some of its hermetic records, and then being found guilty of sexual misconduct. By 1902, the Golden Dawn separated into factions, some of which continue in some form to the present day.

3 Order of the G.D., quoted in R. A. Gilbert, *Revelations of the Golden Dawn: The Rise and Fall of a Magical Order* (London: Quantum, 1997), 21.

4 Kate Flint, *The Victorians and the Visual Imagination* (Cambridge: Cambridge University Press, 2003), 261–64.

5 Max Nordau, *Degeneration*, 1892 (Lincoln: University of Nebraska Press, 1993), 142, 144.

Note of pages 143–7

6   Alex Owen, *The Place of Enchantment: British Occultism and the Culture of the Modern* (Chicago: Chicago University Press, 2004), 9.

7   Richard King, *Orientalism and Religion: Postcolonial Theory, India and "the Mystic East"* (New York: Routledge, 1999). See also Christopher Partridge, "Orientalism and the Occult," in Christopher Partidge, ed., *The Occult World* (New York: Routledge, 2015), 611–25.

8   The scientific fields that authors portrayed as being infiltrated by the paranormal were diverse; innovations in astronomy developed in hand with telepathy; electricity was integral to an interstellar Christianity; hypnotism to automatic writing; brain surgery to Classical paganism.

9   In *Mysticism and the Way Out* (1920), physiologist and ophthalmologist Ivor Tuckett, who made his name by exposing proofs of psychic phenomena to be fake, disparages mysticism as "the mental attitude of persons who believe in hypotheses which elude empirical inquiry and are satisfied by merely verbal explanations of phenomena. This attitude is the reverse of that of Huxley." See Ivor L. L. Tuckett, *Mysticism and the Way Out* (London: Watts, 1920), 8. See also Pamela Thurschwell, *Literature, Technology, and Magical Thinking: 1880–1920* (Cambridge: Cambridge University Press, 2005); and Robert Crossley, *Imagining Mars: A Literary History* (Middleton, Conn: Wesleyan University Press, 2011).

10 Joy Dixon, *Divine Feminine: Theosophy and Feminism in England* (Baltimore: Johns Hopkins University Press, 2001), 86.

11 Barbara Gates, *Kindred Nature: Victorian and Edwardian Women Embrace the Living World* (Chicago: University of Chicago Press, 1998), 12.

12 Rosa Mulholland, "Under a Purple Cloud," *The Evergreen: A Northern Seasonal*, 2 (Autumn 1895), 25–26 at 25, 26.

13 William Macdonald and John Arthur Thomson, "Proem," *The Evergreen: A Northern Seasonal*, 1 (Spring 1895) 9–15 at 10–11.

14 The Pagan Federation in the United Kingdom (founded in 1971) – the largest, multi-faith pagan organization of our time – declares that "a religion without goddesses can hardly be classified as Pagan," while also articulating its complete commitment to the equality of all sexual orientations, thereby characterizing both gender equity and queer diversity as fundamental to paganism. There seems, however, to be a potential contradiction between the association's sexual constructionism and its declaration that all paganisms must recognize goddesses. See "Welcome," *The Pagan Federation*, www.paganfed.org/cms/.

15 Donna Haraway, *Simians, Cyborgs and Women: The Reinvention of Nature* (New York: Routledge, 1991).

16 Chas S. Clifton and Graham Harvey, "Introduction," in Chas S. Clifton and Graham Harvey, eds., *The Paganism Reader* (New York: Routledge, 2004), 1–5 at 1.

17 Val Plumwood, *Environmental Culture: The Ecological Crisis of Reason* (London: Routledge, 2002), 196, 206.

18 Plumwood, *Environmental Culture*, 195, 206.

Note of pages 147–9

19   Further insightful discussions of fin-de-siècle feminisms, sexuality, and procreation can be found in, among other works: Ann Heilmann, *New Woman Strategies: Sarah Grand, Olive Schreiner, Mona Caird* (Manchester: Manchester University Press, 2004) and Angelique Richardson's *Love and Eugenics in the Late Nineteenth-Century: Rational Reproduction and the New Woman* (Oxford: Oxford University Press, 2008).

20   Ronald Hutton, *The Triumph of the Moon: A History of Modern Pagan Witchcraft* (Oxford: Oxford University Press, 1999), x.

21   Nina Auerbach, *Private Theatricals: The Lives of the Victorians* (Cambridge, MA: Harvard University Press, 1990), 4.

22   Peggy Phalen, *Unmarked: The Politics of Performance* (New York: Routledge, 1993), 10.

23   Phalen, *Unmarked*, 6.

24   Edmund B. Lingan, *The Theatre of the Occult Revival: Alternative Spiritual Performance from 1975 to the Present* (New York: Palgrave Macmillan, 2014), 10.

25   Clifford Bax, *Florence Farr, Bernard Shaw, and W. B. Yeats* (Dublin: The Cualla Press, 1941), 13.

26   Bax, *Florence Farr, Bernard Shaw, and W. B. Yeats*, xv.

27   Steven Connor, "The Machine in the Ghost: Spiritualism, Technology and the 'Direct Voice'," in Peter Buse and Andrew Stoff, eds., *Ghosts: Deconstruction, Psychoanalysis, History* (Basingstoke: Macmillan, 1999), 203–25 at 204.

28   Mackenzie Bartlett, "Mirth as Medium: Spectacles of Laughter in the Victorian Séance Room," in Tatiana Kontou and Sarah Willburn, eds., *The Ashgate Research Companion to Nineteenth-Century Spiritualism and the Occult* (Burlington, VT: Ashgate, 2012), 267–84 at 273. See also Tatiana Kontou, "The Case of Florence Marryat: Custodian of the Spirit World/ Popular Novelist," in Tatiana Kontou and Sarah Willburn, eds., *Nineteenth-Century Spiritualism and the Occult* (Burlington, VT: Ashgate, 2012), 221–30. Advocates even distributed manuals on how to hold your own séances, creating a culture of amateur performers and parlor-practicing enthusiasts; see, for example, Florence Marryat, *The Spirit World* (New York: Charles B. Reed, 1894), 286.

29   Herbert V. Fackler, "William Sharp's 'House of Usna' (1900): A One-Act Psychic Drama." *The South Central Bulletin*, 30.4 (Winter, 1970), 187–89 at 187.

30   Golden Dawn cofounder Samuel Mathers was himself a Celtophile – dressing in a kilt and being captivated by all people Celtic – including Sharp, Yeats, and Wilde. Samuel fashioned himself "Count MacGregor," "a Scotch gentleman of fortune," as the journalist Frederic Lees wrote, although the man was in fact neither wealthy nor Scottish nor a count (Scotland does not have counts); see Frederic Lees, "Isis Worship in Paris. Conversations with the Hierophant Rameses and the High Priestess Anari," *The Humanitarian*, 16.2 (February 1900), 82–87 at 83. All further references to this piece appear in the main body of the text.

Note of pages 149–54

31 Mary K. Greer, *Women of the Golden Dawn: Rebels and Priestesses* (Rochester, VT: Park Street, 1995), 310.

32 Franny Moyle, *Constance: The Tragic and Scandalous Life of Mrs. Oscar Wilde* (London: John Murray, 2011), 173–75.

33 Anna de Brémont. *Oscar Wilde and His Mother: A Memoir* (London: Everette, 1911), 39.

34 de Brémont, *Oscar Wilde*, 95.

35 Oscar Wilde, *Salome: A Tragedy in One Act*, 1891 (London: John Lane, 1907), 2.

36 Owen Davies, *Witchcraft, Magic and Culture 1736–1951* (Manchester: Manchester University Press, 1999), 76.

37 William Wynn Westcott, "A Society of Kabalists," *Notes and Queries*, 7 (9 February 1889), 116–17 at 116.

38 Christopher Partridge, "Orientalism and the Occult," in Christopher Partridge, ed., *The Occult World* (New York: Routledge, 2015), 611–25.

39 Hutton, *Triumph of the Moon*, 77.

40 Erik Hornung, *The Secret Lore of Egypt: Its Impact on the West*, 1999, trans. David Lorton (Ithaca: Cornell University Press, 2001), 191.

41 James Stevens Curl, *Egyptomania: The Egyptian Revival: a Recurring Theme in the History of Taste* (Manchester: Manchester University Press, 1994).

42 George Ebers, *Descriptive, Historical, and Picturesque*, vol. 1, trans. Clara Bell (New York: Cassell, 1885), iii.

43 Frances Swiney, *The Ancient Road* (London: Bell and Sons, 1918), 485.

44 Hutton, *Triumph of the Moon*, 83.

45 Alison Butler, *Victorian Occultism and the Making of Modern Magic: Invoking Tradition* (Basingstoke: Palgrave Macmillan, 2011), 55.

46 Greer, *Women of the Golden Dawn*, 118, 208.

47 R. A. Gilbert, *The Golden Dawn Companion: A Guide to the History, Structure and Workings of the Hermetic Order of the Golden Dawn* (Wellingborough: Aquarian, 1986), 45.

48 Donald Michael Kraig, *Modern Magick* (St. Paul, UK: Llewellyn, 1988), 9.

49 This is why the Order strongly discouraged practices popular among spiritualists, such as mesmerism, séances, and hypnotism, where an intermediary so often was necessary, thus standing between the individual and the celestial forces. R. A. Gilbert, *The Golden Dawn Companion*, 45.

50 André Gaucher, "Isis à Montmartre," *L'Écho du merveilleux: Revue bimensuelle*, 94 and 95 (December 1900), 446–53, 470–73, at 448.

51 Catherine Tully, "Samuel Liddell MacGregor Mathers and Isis," in Dave Evans and Dave Green, eds., *Ten Years of Triumph? Academic Approaches to Studying Magic and the Occult* (Harpenden: Hidden, 2009), 62–74 at 68. In this article, Tully offers a succinct assessment of the man's creative envisioning of ancient Egyptian spirituality and its deities, noting that much of his Rites of Isis were built around misinformation from ancient Greek works or simply fabricated by Mathers himself.

52 John Newton, "Isis Worship in Paris," *The Humanitarian*, 16.4 (April 1900), 296–98 at 296.

Note of pages 155–61

53   Directed by Charles Bodinière from 1890 to 1902, the theatre offered lectures and performances of interest to a combination of intellectuals, artists, and the well-to-do. Bois was best known at this time for works such as *Satanism and Magic* (1895), which claimed Satanism was being practiced across France, and *The Minor Religions of Paris* (1894), in which he describes secret societies intermingling various belief systems including Satanism, paganism, and Buddhism.

54   David Huckvale, *Ancient Egypt in the Popular Imagination: Building a Fantasy in Film, Literature, Music, and Art* (Jefferson, NC: McFarland, 2012), 104.

55   Gareth Knight, "Dion Fortune: Her Rites and Her Novels," in Gareth Knight, ed., *Dion Fortune's Rites of Isis and of Pan* (Cheltenham, UK: Skylight, 2013), 7–17 at 8.

56   Victor Turner, *From Ritual to Theatre: The Human Seriousness of Play* (New York: PAJ, 1982), 7.

57   Turner, *From Ritual to Theatre*, 7.

58   Turner, *From Ritual to Theatre*, 18.

59   Turner, *From Ritual to Theatre*, 23.

60   "Welcome," *The Pagan Federation*, www.paganfed.org/cms/.

61   Plumwood, *Environmental Culture*, 196.

62   Greer, *Women of the Golden Dawn*, 23.

63   Nicholas Grene, "W. B. Yeats," in Brad Kent, ed., *George Bernard Shaw in Context* (Cambridge: Cambridge University Press, 2015), 44–50 at 45.

64   Josephine Johnson. *Florence Farr: Bernard Shaw's "New Woman"* (Gerrard Cross, UK: Colin Smythe, 1975), 39

65   Greer, *Women of the Golden Dawn*, 224.

66   Johnson, *Florence Farr*, 59.

67   In *Egyptian Magic* (1896), she suggests her own interpretation of the motto, when she writes "The Kings and Priests of Egypt were the elect of those who had studied with success in the 'School of Wisdom,' a Philosophical Aristocracy; they were chosen because they were not only wise, but could use their wisdom"; Florence Farr, *Egyptian Magic* (London: Theosophical Publishing Society, 1896), 1.

68   Greer, *Women of the Golden Dawn*, 152, 430 n.4; see also Butler, *Victorian Occultism and the Making of Modern Magic*, 88–89.

69   Greer, *Women of the Golden Dawn*, 195.

70   Caroline Tully, "Egyptosophy in the British Museum," in Christine Ferguson and Andrew Radford, eds., *The Occult Imagination in Britain, 1875–1947* (New York: Routledge, 2018), 131–45 at 135.

71   Tully, "Egyptosophy in the British Museum," 139.

72   Florence Farr, "An Introduction to Alchemy," *A Short Enquiry Concerning the Hermetic Art, and Euphrates or the Waters of the East, by a Lover of Philalethes*, 1714 (London: Theosophical Publishing Society, 1894), 9–13, 10.

73   Collections of Sir Hugh Walpole, MS. Walpole d. 19, fols. 28–36, folio 32.

74   Collections of Sir Hugh Walpole, MS. Walpole d. 19, fols. 28–36, folio 32.

248   *Note of pages 162–7*

75   Florence Farr, *Modern Woman: Her Intentions* (London: Frank Palmer, 1910), 17.
76   Farr was the first English actor to perform Ibsen – specifically, the character Rebecca West in the English premier of the 1891 Vaudeville Theatre production of *Rosmersholm*. Kumari Jayawardena, *The White Woman's Other Burden: Western Women and South Asia During British Colonial Rule* (New York: Routledge, 1995), 137.
77   Florence Farr, *The Dancing Faun* (London: Elkin Matthews and John Lane, 1894), 99. Further references from this novel appear directly in the main text.
78   Greer, *Women of the Golden Dawn.*
79   Rebecca West, "English Literature," *The Freewoman* (25 July 1912), reprinted in Jane Marcus, ed., *The Young Rebecca: Writings of Rebecca West 1911–17* (New York: Virago, 1982), 49–52, 52.
80   Patricia Colman Smith, Letter of 12 June 1902 to Lady Gregory, Berg Collection, New York Public Library, Astor, Lenox and Tilden Foundations. Quoted in Ronald Schuchard, "The Countess Cathleen and the Revival of the Bardic Arts," *The South Carolina Review*, 32.1 (Fall 1999), 24–37 at 33.
81   Ronald Schuchard, "The Countess Cathleen and the Revival of the Bardic Arts," 33.
82   In her study *The Music of Speech* (1909), Farr declares that "sound is the elemental correspondence of etheric spaces," adding that "the mystery of sound is made manifest in words and in music." Florence Farr, *The Music of Speech* (London: Elkin Mathews, 1909), 21.
83   For a useful discussion of Farr's psaltery recitals as engagements with pagan ritual and contemporary music theory, see Muriel Pécastaing-Boissière, "'Wisdom is a gift given to the Wise': Florence Farr (1860–1917): New Woman, Actress and Pagan Priestess," *Cahiers victoriens et édouardiens*, 80 (Autumn 2014) http://journals.openedition.org/cve/1542/.
84   "Dramatic Gossip," *The Athenæum*, 3376 (July 9, 1892), 76.
85   Rebecca West, "Men, Minds, and Morals," *The Freewoman* (25 April 1912), rpt. *The Young Rebecca*, 37–38, 37.
86   Florence Farr, *The Solemnization of Jacklin: Some Adventures on the Search for Reality* (London: A. D. Fifield, 1912), 73.
87   Farr, *Modern Woman*, 7.
88   Farr, *Modern Woman*, 17.
89   Farr, *Modern Woman*, 38.
90   Rachel Blau DuPlessis, *Blue Studios: Poetry and Its Cultural Work* (Tuscaloosa: University of Alabama Press, 2006), 132.
91   Donald Michael Kraig, *Modern Magick* (St. Paul, UK: Llewellyn, 1988), 9.
92   Greer, *Women of the Golden Dawn*, 57; Hutton, *Triumph of the Moon*, 82.
93   Farr, *Modern Woman*, 72.
94   Farr, *Modern Woman*, 74.
95   Farr, *Modern Woman*, 73.

Note of pages 167–77

96 Earlier anthropological works such as Johann Jakob Bachofen's *Mother Right: An Investigation of the Religious and Juridical Character of Matriarchy in the Ancient World* (1861) and John McLennan's *Primitive Marriage* (1865) had contributed to a growing interest among Victorians in a matriarchal source for modern social structures.

97 Greer, *Women of the Golden Dawn*, 266.

98 Tully, "Egyptosophy," 140.

99 Farr, *Egyptian Magic*, 5, 3 (London: Theosophical Publishing Society, 1896).

100 Florence Farr and Olivia Shakespear, *The Beloved of Hathor* and *The Shrine of the Golden Hawk*. Because the first publication of these two plays appears in a single, unpaginated work, I do not cite pages, but make it clear in the main body of my text which play is being quoted.

101 Pécastaing-Boissière, "'Wisdom is a gift given to the Wise,'" http://journals.openedition.org/cve/1542/.

102 Katherine Tynan, "Lionel Johnson," *The Bookman*, 49.290 (November 1915), 50–52 at 51.

103 The sexual framing of the conflict, through Nouferu's seduction of Ashme, also suggests that Farr was recalling Crowley's recent efforts to incorporate sexual rituals into the Golden Dawn. She had overseen his initiation in 1897, but word of his apparent bisexuality and his affair with a married member of the order had soon troubled members, and it is believed these are the reasons why Farr and others chose to deny Crowley admission to the second order, despite his renowned talents in magic; the reason given was "sex intemperance" (Sharon E. Cogdill, "For Isis and England: The Golden Dawn as a Social Network," in Alisa Clapp-Intyre and Julie Melnyk, eds., *"Perplext in Faith": Essays on Victorian Beliefs and Doubts*, (Newcastle upon Tyne: Cambridge Scholars, 2015), 209–34 at 223). Samuel Mathers would initiate him instead.

6   Sinking Feeling

1 William Sharp, "The Black Madonna," *The Pagan Review*, 1 (1891), 5–18 at 5.

2 Sharp, "The Black Madonna," 5.

3 Elizabeth Kolbert, *The Sixth Extinction: An Unnatural History* (New York: Henry Holt, 2014).

4 James Lovelock, *The Earth and I* (London: Taschen, 2016).

5 Bruno Latour, *Facing Gaia: Eight Lectures on the New Climatic Regime, 2015*, translated by Catherine Porter (Cambridge, UK: Polity, 2017).

6 Charles Hamlin, "Charles Kingsley: From Being Green to Green Being," *Victorian Studies*, 54.2 (Winter 2012), 255–81 at 257.

7 Arthur, Symons, "The Decadence Movement in Literature," *Harper's New Monthly Magazine* (November 1893), 858–67 at 859.

8 George Egerton, *Keynotes* (London: Elkin Mathews and John Lane, 1893), 170.

250   *Note of pages 177–81*

9   William Sharp, "The House of Usna," in Mrs William Sharp, ed., Vol. 7, *The Works of "Fiona Macleod"* (London: William Heinemann, 1919), 391–443 at 406.

10   Arthur Machen, *The Hill of Dreams*, in Dennis Denisoff, ed., *Arthur Machen: Decadent and Occult Works* (Cambridge: MHRA, 2018), 110–250 at 243. Further references to this work are noted parenthetically in the text.

11   Théophile Gautier, "Charles Baudelaire," in Charles Baudelaire, ed., *Les Fleurs du mal* (Paris: Calmann-Lévy, 1868), 1–75 at 17. Translations are my own.

12   Gautier, "Charles Baudelaire," 31.

13   Gautier, "Charles Baudelaire," 25.

14   Simon C. Estok, "Theorizing in a Space of Ambivalent Openness: Ecocriticism and Ecophobia," *ISLE: Interdisciplinary Studies in Literature and Environment*, 6.2 (2009), 203–24 at 203.

15   Dawn Keetley, "Introduction: Six Theses on Plant Horror; or, Why are Plants Horrifying?" in Dawn Keeley and Angela Tenga, eds., *Plant Horror: Approaches to the Monstrous Vegetal in Fiction and Film* (London: Palgrave Macmillan, 2016), 1.

16   Cary Wolfe, *What Is Posthumanism?* (Minneapolis: University of Minnesota Press, 2010), xxiv–xxv.

17   Karen L. F. Houle, "Animal, Vegetable, Mineral: Ethics as Extension of Becoming? The Case of Becoming-Plant," *Journal for Critical Animal Studies*, 9.1–2 (2011), 89–116 at 102.

18   Henry Salt, *Animals' Rights Considered in Relation to Social Progress*, 1892 (Clarks Summit, PA: Society for Animal Rights, 1980).

19   Houle, "Animal, Vegetable, Mineral," 97.

20   Heinrich Kaan, *Psychopathia Sexualis*, 1844, translated by Melissa Haynes (Ithaca, NY: Cornell University Press, 2016), 44.

21   Houle, "Animal, Vegetable, Mineral," 94.

22   Dennis Denisoff, "Ecology: the Vital Forces of Decay," in Jane Desmarais and David Weir, eds., *The Oxford Handbook of Decadence* (Oxford: Oxford University Press, 2021): www.oxfordhandbooks.com/view/10.1093/oxfordhb/9780190066956.001.0001/oxfordhb-9780190066956-e-3.

23   Michael Shaw, *The Fin-de-siècle Scottish Revival: Romance, Decadence and Celtic Identity* (Edinburgh: Edinburgh University Press, 2020), 161.

24   William Sharp, *A Memoir*, edited by Elizabeth A. Sharp, vol. 1 (New York: Duffield, 1910), 188. All subsequent references to this work are noted parenthetically in the text.

25   William Sharp, *A Memoir*, edited by Elizabeth A. Sharp, vol. 2 (New York: Duffield, 1910), 25. All subsequent references to this work are noted parenthetically in the text.

26   Walter Pater, *Letters of Walter Pater*, edited by Lawrence Evans (London: Clarendon, 1970), 92.

27   William Sharp, *Dante Gabriel Rossetti: A Record and a Study* (London: Macmillan, 1882), 115.

Note of pages 181–5

28 Joseph Bristow and Rebecca N. Mitchell, *Oscar Wilde's Chatterton: Literary History, Romanticism, and the Art of Forgery* (New Haven: Yale University Press, 2015), 145.

29 "The Pagan Review," *The Saturday Review*, 74 (3 September 1892), 268–69 at 269.

30 William Sharp, "Foreword," *The Pagan Review*, 1 (15 August 1892), 1–4 at 1.

31 Sharp, "Foreword," 3, 2.

32 Sharp, "Foreword," 2.

33 Sharp, "Foreword," 3, 4.

34 "The Pagan Review," *The Christian Union: A Family Paper*, 46.16 (15 October 1892), 694.

35 Frederic M. Bird, "An Organ and a Reform," *Lippincott's Monthly Magazine*, 51 (February 1893), 249–53 at 249.

36 "The Pagan Review," *The Saturday Review of Literature, Politics, Science and Art*, 74 (3 September 1892), 268–69 at 269.

37 Grant Allen, "The Celt in English Art," *Fortnightly Review*, 55 (1 February 1891), 267–77 at 273.

38 The term "insular," from the Latin for "island," refers to the Celtic-inflected Christianity found in Ireland and Britain during the Middle Ages. Although committed to the Christian authorities of Rome, it incorporated elements of Celtic culture and spirituality and thus serves as a major source of information on the Celts themselves. For extended histories of Celtic-inflected Christianity, see Ian Bradley, *Celtic Christianity: Making Myths and Chasings Dreams* (Edinburgh: Edinburgh University Press, 1999) and Caitlin Corning, *The Celtic and Roman Traditions: Conflict and Consensus in the Early Medieval Church* (Basingstoke, UK: Palgrave Macmillan, 2006).

39 Allen, "The Celt in English Art," 273.

40 Allen, "The Celt in English Art," 271, 270.

41 Oscar Wilde, "The Critic as Artist – Part II," in Oscar Wilde, ed., *The Major Works* (Oxford: Oxford University Press, 1989), 267–97 at 287.

42 Josephine M. Guy, *The Complete Works of Oscar Wilde*, Vol. 4: Criticism (Oxford: Oxford University Press, 2007), 513.

43 Allen, "The Celt in English Art," 273.

44 Edward Thomas, *Beautiful Wales* (London: A. & C. Black, 1905), 11. Opal hush was a drink made of claret and lemonade possibly invented by Yeats and seen as a preferred drink of the British 1890s decadent and occult community.

45 Thomas, *Beautiful Wales*, 88, 90, 91.

46 Daniel G. Williams, "Celticism," in Laura Marcus, Michèle Mendelssohn, and Kirsten E. Shepherd-Barr, eds., *Late Victorian into Modern* (Oxford: Oxford University Press, 2016), 69–82 at 70, 70–1.

47 Flavia Alaya, *William Sharp – "Fiona Macleod"* (Cambridge: Harvard University Press, 1970), 180, 181.

48 Frank Rinder, "William Sharp – 'Fiona Macleod': A Tribute," *Art Journal*, 68.1 (1906), 44–45 at 44.

252   *Note of pages 185–94*

49   Rinder, "William Sharp," 45.

50   William Sharp (aka Fiona Macleod), *The Mountain Lovers* (London: John Lane, 1895), 7–8.

51   William Sharp (aka Fiona Macleod), *Green Fire: A Romance* (Westminster: Archibald Constable, 1896), 7.

52   Sharp, *Green Fire*, 57–58.

53   See C. E. Andrews and M. O. Percival, "Introduction," in Clarence Edward Andrews, ed., *Poetry of the Nineties* (New York: Harcourt, Brace, Jovanovich, 1926), 1–51; Edward Engleberg, *The Symbolist Poem* (New York: Dutton, 1967); and William F. Halloran, "William Sharp as Bard and Craftsman," *Victorian Poetry*, 10.1 (Spring 1972), 57–78.

54   Ernest Rhys, "William Sharp and Fiona Macleod," *The Century Magazine*, 74 (May 1907), 111–16 at 114.

55   W. H. Abrams, *The Correspondent Breeze: Essays on English Romanticism* (New York: Norton, 1984), 33–34.

56   Abrams, *The Correspondent Breeze*, 29.

57   Abrams, *The Correspondent Breeze*, 35.

58   William Sharp, *Life of Percy Bysshe Shelley* (London: Walter Scott, 1887), 150. See also Helen Rossetti Angeli, *Shelley and His Friends in Italy* (New York: Brentano's, 1911).

59   "Gossip of Authors and Writers," *Current Literature: A Magazine of Record and Review*, 7 (May–August 1891), 344–45 at 344.

60   William Sharp, *Sospiri di Roma* (Rome: La Societá Laziale, 1891), 13, 14. All subsequent references to this work are noted parenthetically in the text. In the table of contents, the title of the latter poem reads "High Noon on the Campagna at Midsummer." As Sharp arranged and paid for the publication himself, it is most likely he made the change in the main body and forgot to revise the table of contents.

61   Halloran, "William Sharp," 69.

62   William Sharp, "The Norland Wind," *The Evergreen: A Northern Seasonal*, 1 (Spring 1895), 109. I wish to thank Lorraine Janzen Kooistra, with whom I had conducted an initial analysis of this poem.

63   See Marion Davies, *Sacred Celtic Animals* (Milverton, UK: Capall Bann, 2001).

64   Notably, the most popular English poem in trochaic tetrameter is Henry Wadsworth Longfellow's "Song of Hiawatha" (1855), which itself offers a narrative built around Indigenous pagan beliefs formulated as myths. It is likely Sharp had read the poem, as he was familiar with Longfellow's work and relished his visit to "Evangeline's country," alluding to Longfellow's famous poem, when on a tour of Canada and the United States in 1889. See William Sharp, *A Memoir*, edited by Elizabeth A. Sharp, vol. 1 (New York: Duffield, 1910), 242. In a letter written in Italy in 1881, he includes Longfellow with Rossetti, Swinburne, William Morris, and his friend Philip Marston among the contemporary English authors he most admires. I thank Herbert Tucker for noting the connection between the poems' meters.

65	Arthur Machen, "Science and the Ghost Story," *Literature*, 48 (17 September 1898), 250–52 at 251.
66	Arthur Machen, "The Literature of Occultism," *Literature: An International Gazette of Criticism*, New Series: 2 (17 January 1899), 34–36. Reprinted in Arthur Machen, *Arthur Machen: Decadent and Occult Works*, edited by Dennis Denisoff (Oxford: MHRA Press, 2018), 277.
67	Symons, "Decadent Movement," 859.
68	See Peter Guest and Mike Luke, "Isca: The Roman legionary fortress at Caerleon," cardiff.ac.uk/share/research/projectreports/caerleon/; and J. Wiles, "Lodge Wood Camp," *Royal Commission on the Ancient and Historical Monuments of Wales.* www.coflein.gov.uk/en/site/93396/details/LODGE+WOOD+CAMP/.
69	Arthur Machen, *Far Off Things* (London: Martin Secker, 1922), 24–25.
70	Arthur Machen, *The Great God Pan* (1894), Reprinted in Arthur Machen, *Arthur Machen: Decadent and Occult Works*, edited by Dennis Denisoff (Oxford: MHRA Press, 2019), 48.
71	Machen, *The Great God Pan*, 48–49.
72	Machen, *Far Off Things*, 8–9.
73	Arthur Machen, "The All-Pervading Celt," *Literature*, 12.8 (8 January 1898), 1–3 at 1.
74	Alex Murray, *Landscapes of Decadence: Literature and Place at the Fin de Siècle* (Cambridge: Cambridge University Press, 2016), 137.
75	Susan J. Navarette, *The Shape of Fear: Horror and the Fin de Siècle Culture of Decadence* (Lexington, KY: University Press of Kentucky, 1998), 202.
76	Arthur Machen, *Excerpt from Hieroglyphics: A Note upon Ecstasy in Literature*, 1902. Reprinted in Arthur Machen, *Arthur Machen: Decadent and Occult Works*, edited by Dennis Denisoff (Oxford: MHRA Press, 2019), 283–91 at 283.
77	Houle, "Animal, Vegetable, Mineral," 93.
78	Thomas, *Beautiful Wales*, 90–91.
79	Arthur Machen, *Preface, The Ghost-Ship and Other Stories*, by Richard Middleton (London: T. Fisher Unwin, 1912), vii-xiv at ix, xi.
80	Machen, *Preface*, xii.
81	Michael Field, *Michael Field, The Poet: Published and Manuscript Materials*, edited by Marion Thain and Ana Parejo Vadillo (Peterborough: Broadview, 2009), 258. All subsequent references to this work are noted parenthetically in the text.
82	Tina O'Toole, *The Irish New Woman* (Houndmills, Basingstoke: Palgrave, 2013), 130.
83	George Egerton, quoted in Ann Heilmann, ed., *The Late-Victorian Marriage Question: A Collection of Key New Woman Texts, Volume 5* (New York: Routledge, 1998), 221.
84	George Egerton, "A Keynote to *Keynotes*," in John Galsworthy, ed., *Ten Contemporaries: Notes Toward Their Definitive Bibliography* (London: Ernest Benn, 1932), 58.

254 *Note of pages 207–14*

85 George Egerton, *Keynotes* (London: Elkin Mathews and John Lane, 1893), 1. All subsequent references to this collection are noted parenthetically in the text.

86 George Egerton, *A Leaf from* The Yellow Book: *The Correspondence of George Egerton*, edited by Terence de Vere White (London: The Richards Press, 1958).

87 Kate McCullough, "Mapping the 'Terra Incognita' of Woman: George Egerton's *Keynotes* (1893) and New Woman Fiction," in Barbara Leah Harman and Susan Meyers, eds., *The New Nineteenth Century: Feminist Readings of Underread Victorian Novels* (London: Garland, 1996), 205–23 at 207.

88 Elaine Showalter, *Daughters of Decadence: Women Writers of the Fin-de-Siècle* (New Brunswick, NJ: Rutgers University Press, 1993).

89 Maureen O'Connor, *The Female and the Species: The Animal in Irish Women's Writing* (Oxford: Peter Lang, 2010).

90 Laura Chrisman, "Empire, 'Race' and Feminism at the *fin de siècle*: the Work of George Egerton and Olive Schreiner," in Sally Ledger and Scott McCracken, eds., *Cultural Politics at the Fin De Siècle* (Cambridge: Cambridge University Press, 1995), 45–65.

91 Connie Bullis, "Retalking Environmental Discourses from a Feminist Perspective: The Radical Potential of Ecofeminism," in James G. Cantrill and Christine L. Otavec, *The Symbolic Earth: Discourse and Our Creation of the Environment* (Lexington, KY: University Press of Kentucky, 1996), 125.

92 Martha Vicinus, "Rediscovering the 'New Woman' of the 1890s: The Stories of 'George Egerton'," in Vivian Patraka and Louise A. Tilly, eds., *Feminist Re-Visions: What Has Been and Might Be* (Ann Arbor, MI: University of Michigan Press, 1983), 12–25 at 17.

93 George Egerton, *Flies in Amber* (London: Hutchinson, 1905), 66.

94 Chelsea Miya, "The Ecological Ebb-Tide of George Egerton's Short Fiction," MA thesis (Department of English, Ryerson University, 2013), 5.

95 Egerton, *Flies in Amber*, 67.

96 George Egerton, *Discords* (Boston: Roberts, 1894), 72. All subsequent references to this collection are noted parenthetically in the text.

97 Department of Greek and Roman Art, "Tanagra Figurines," *Heilbrunn Timeline of Art History* (New York: Metropolitan Museum of Art), metmuseum .org/toah/hd/tafg/hd_tafg.htm.

98 Sheila Dillon, "Hellenistic Tanagra Figurines," in Sharon L. James and Sheila Dillon, eds., *Women in a Cosmopolitan World: The Hellenistic and Late Republican Periods* (London: Blackwell, 2012), 231–34 at 233.

99 For a thorough record of references to Pan in Victorian literature, see Patricia Merivale, *Pan, the Goat God: His Myth in Modern Times* (Cambridge, MA: Harvard University Press, 1969).

100 George Egerton, *Symphonies* (London: John Lane at The Bodley Head, 1897), 109. All subsequent references to this collection are noted parenthetically in the text.

Note of pages 214–24 255

101 Ludger Mees, "Politics, Economy, or Culture? The Rise and Development of Basque Nationalism in the Light of Social Movement Theory," *Theory and Society*, 33.3 (2004), 311–31 at 319–20.

102 On the lute as a symbol for unarticulated sexual feelings, see Julia Craig-McFeely, "The Signifying Serpent: Seduction by Cultural Stereotype in Seventeenth-Century England," in Linda Phyllis Austern, ed., *Music, Sensation, and Sensuality* (New York: Routledge, 2002), 299–317.

103 Val Plumwood, *Feminism and the Mastery of Nature* (London: Routledge, 1993), 192.

104 Bruno Latour, *Pandora's Hope: Essays on the Reality of Scientific Studies* (Cambridge: Harvard University Press, 1999), 3.

105 Latour, *Pandora's Hope*, 289.

Epilogue

1 Algernon Blackwood, "Special Delivery," in *Pan's Garden: A Volume of Nature Stories* (London: Macmillan, 1912), 387–400 at 391.

2 David Punter, "Algernon Blackwood: Nature and Spirit," in Andre Smith and William Hughes, eds., *EcoGothic* (Manchester: Manchester University Press, 2013), 44–57 at 49.

3 Henry Salt, *Animals' Rights Considered in Relation to Social Progress*, 1892 (Clarks Summit, PA: Society for Animal Rights, 1980), 21.

4 Henry Salt, *Animals' Rights*, 9.

5 Tommy Pico, *Nature Poem* (Portland, OR: Tin House, 2017), 2, 40.

6 Walter Pater, *Greek Studies* (New York: Macmillan, 1895), 53.

7 Michael Field, *Sight and Song* (London: Elkin Mathews and John Lane, 1892), iv.

8 David M. Halperin, *Saint Foucault: Towards a Gay Hagiography* (Oxford: Oxford University Press, 1995), 62.

9 Algernon Blackwood, "Special Delivery," 392.

Index

Abrams, M.H., 189
Africa/African, 11, 82, 128, 143 (see also: Egypt/Egyptian)
alchemy, 31, 143, 152, 161, 165, 166, 168, 170, 185, 203–4
Allen, Grant, 183, 184, 188, 198
animal rights, 62, 64–69, 80–81, 84, 94, 100, 118
animism, 40, 48–50, 72, 100–2, 110, 115, 134, 146, 158, 216, 220, 222
Ansted, David Thomas, 15, 17
Anstruther-Thomson, Kit, 85, 136–37
Anthropocene, 5, 38–45, 46, 59, 63, 96, 127, 131, 232
anthropology, 11, 14, 22, 40, 68, 128, 142, 145, 156, 157, 165, 166, 167, 172, 231, 249
archaeology, 21, 22, 45, 100, 151, 152
Archer, William, 104–5
Arnold, Matthew, 180, 183
Auerbach, Nina, 147, 157

Bacchus, 24, 71, 73, 75–76, 78, 84, 93–94 (see also: maenads)
Banash, David, 84
Barry, William Francis, 13, 26–28
Bartlett, Mackenzie, 148
Baudelaire, Charles, 5, 8–10, 13, 18, 19, 142, 143, 177, 182, 243
Beardsley, Aubrey, 4, 6, 150, 160, 235
Bennett, Jane, 239
Benson, E.F., 23
Bentham, Jeremy, 65, 67
Bergson, Henri, 152, 166
Besant, Annie, 67, 144, 148
biology, 8, 10, 11, 15, 19, 125, 145–47, 151, 158, 166, 198
Blackwood, Algernon, 219–20, 224
Blake, William, 73
Blau DuPlessis, Rachel, 166
Blavatsky, Helena, 2, 144, 150, 152
botany, 2, 44, 97, 127

Botticelli, 88, 89, 91
Bourget, Paul, 5, 9–10, 37, 62, 114, 124, 125, 172, 177, 178, 198
Boyd, Jason, 105
Brémont, Anne de, 149
Bristow, Joseph, 90
Brown, Horatio, 28, 53
Browning, Elizabeth Barrett, 216
Browning, Robert, 13, 18
Buchanan, Robert, 13, 15
Budge, Ernest Wallis, 161
Bullis, Connie, 208
Burriss, Eli Edward, 111, 240
Butler, Alison, 152, 247
Buzard, James, 238

Caird, Mona, 145, 187
Carpenter, Edward, 23, 25, 67, 94, 132
Celtic culture, 2, 3, 22, 100, 143, 145, 149, 154, 157, 160, 163, 171, 180, 183–88, 191, 192, 196, 198, 199, 208, 209, 217, 220, 222, 228, 245 (see also: Ireland/Irish, Scotland/Scottish, and Wales/Welsh)
Chesterton, G.K., 25, 26, 28, 107, 112, 114
Chopin, Kate, 145
Chrisman, Laura, 208
Clifton, Chas S, 146
Coleridge, Samuel Taylor, 51
Connor, Steven, 148
Conrad, Joseph, 143
Constable, Liz, 12
Correggio, 86–88, 91
Cosimo, Piero di, 89–93
Coste, Bénédicte, 26
Crane, Walter, 110, 118–22
Crinkley, Richmond, 53
Cronon, William, 36, 231
Crossley, Robert, 244
Crowley, Aleister, 106, 154, 213, 243, 249
Cruise, Colin, 74, 76, 236
Crutzen, Paul J., 38, 40, 232

Index

257

Dames, Nicholas, 124

Darwin, Charles, 5, 7, 13, 26, 37, 39, 40, 41, 43, 45, 68, 100, 102, 129, 179, 226

Dawson, Gowan, 13, 41, 226

deep ecology, 146

deep time, 41, 43, 54, 56, 59, 96, 97, 130, 191, 221

Dellamora, Richard, 228

Dickinson, Goldsworthy Lowes, 24–26, 28

Dixon, Joy, 144

Dowling, Linda, 24, 229

Druce, George Claridge, 2

Druids, 20, 200, 230

Duncan, John, 192

earth as mother, 39, 44, 102, 122, 127, 145, 146, 159, 160, 191, 206, 208, 213 (see also; Gaia)

Egerton, George, 6, 145, 162, 176, 177, 179, 204–18

Egypt/Egyptian, 2, 22, 23, 31, 139, 140–43, 148, 149, 150, 151–58, 159–61, 167–73, 220, 222

Ehnenn, Jill, 84

Ellis, Havelock, 67

Emerson, Ralph Waldo, 114

environmentalism, 6, 20, 36, 43, 44, 45, 58, 67, 97, 132, 146, 176, 199, 206, 207, 208, 216, 232

Erickson, Bruce, 70

Estok, Simon, 178

eugenics, 145, 152, 166

Evangelista, Stefano, 47, 83, 229

Evergreen: A Northern Seasonal, The, 145, 185, 192

Far East/Far Eastern, 8, 11, 28, 31

Farr, Florence, 1, 6, 139, 141–42, 144, 147–49, 151, 152, 159–73, 174, 182, 186, 222

feminism, 3, 6, 21, 84, 95, 103, 134, 139, 140–73, 182–83, 206–7, 216 (see also: suffrage)

femme fatale, 18, 140, 150, 171, 172, 174, 175

Ferrari, Roberto C., 73

Field, Michael, 5, 60, 61, 63, 64, 67, 68, 69, 70, 84–93, 94–95, 97, 106, 121, 131, 133, 142, 160, 179, 204–6, 222

Sight and Song, 61, 63, 85–93, 95, 204

Whym Chow: Flame of Love, 84, 92

Flint, Kate, 142

folk culture, 22, 24, 100, 128, 149, 186, 188, 189, 199, 228

Fortune, Dion, 156

Frazer, James George, 128–31, 132

Friedman, Dustin, 74

Gagnier, Regenia, 12

Gaia, 102–3, 176, 206 (see also: earth as mother)

Gates, Barbara, 145, 208

Gautier, Théophile, 9–10, 177, 182, 198

Geddes, Patrick, 22, 145, 185, 198

genius loci, 5, 6, 75, 97–100, 101, 103, 108–10, 114, 115, 123, 127–34, 137–38, 141, 201, 219

geography, 5, 39, 43, 56, 96, 97, 128, 202, 205, 238

geology, 15, 17, 38–40, 41–45, 46, 57, 58, 59, 96, 127, 128, 131

Gibbon, Edward, 8, 10, 12

Gibson, Mary Ellis, 12

Gilbert, R.A., 246

Goethe, Johann Wolfgang von, 26, 37

Gonne, Maude, 22, 149

Gosse, Edmund, 24, 53, 230

Grahame, Kenneth, 1, 2, 25, 126, 213

Grand, Sarah, 145

Gray, Keomi, 30

Gray, William, 112, 240

Greer, Mary K., 162, 166, 167, 246, 247

Gregory, Augusta, 22, 23, 145

Griffith, Francis Llewellyn, 2

Griffiths, Devin, 7

Haeckel, Ernst, 5, 7, 36–38, 42, 43, 45, 48, 179

Haggard, H. Rider, 143

Hake, Alfred Egmont, 11

Halperin, David, 64, 85, 223

Hamlin, Christopher, 17, 19, 176

Haraway, Donna, 146, 147

Harland, Henry, 205

Harvey, Graham, 146

Hazlitt, William, 115, 122, 241

health, 10–12, 13, 15, 16, 18, 19, 22, 25, 28, 52, 58, 77, 82, 83, 109–10, 145, 146, 166, 177, 180, 181, 186–90, 191, 194, 195, 201, 205, 211, 216

Hegel, Georg Wilhelm Friedrich, 37, 46

Heilmann, Ann, 245

Henry, George, 230

Hermetic Order of the Golden Dawn, 6, 23, 100, 140–73, 174, 196, 219, 247, 249

Hext, Kate, 12, 41, 232

Higgins, Lesley, 233

Hird, Myra, 234

Holmes, Morgan, 117

Holywell Cemetary, 1–3, 6

Hopkins, Gerard Manley, 71

Hornel, Edward Atkinson, 230

Horniman, Annie, 149, 160

Hornung, Erik, 151

Houle, Karen L.F., 178–79, 199, 202

Huggan, Graham, 36

Hulme, Peter, 238

hunting, 62, 80, 86, 90, 91, 215

Hutton, Ronald, 22, 25, 147, 151, 166

258 *Index*

Huxley, Thomas Henry, 2, 244
Huysmans, Joris-Karl, 61, 62, 153

Ibsen, Henrik, 248
illness: see: health
imperialism, 11–12, 27, 97, 98, 144, 145, 177, 180,
   184, 208, 221, 238
industrialism, 45, 97, 127, 134, 177, 208, 209,
   213–14, 217, 219
Inman, Billie Andrew, 225, 231
Ireland/Irish, 12, 22, 23, 100, 145, 148, 149, 152,
   160, 163, 171, 183, 184, 204, 211 (see also:
   Celtic culture)
Irigaray, Luce, 4
Isis, 150, 151, 152–59, 168, 172, 196

James, Henry, 105, 108
Johnson, Lionel, 163, 171

Kaan, Heinrich, 178, 179
Kaye, Richard, 235, 237
Keetley, Dawn, 178
King, Richard, 143
Kingsford, Anna, 150
Knight, Gareth, 156, 157
Kooistra, Lorraine Janzen, 252
Kreilkamp, Ivan, 66
Kreisel, Deanna K., 7

Lane, John, 161, 162, 186, 204, 207, 218
Lang, Andrew, 128
Latour, Bruno, 176, 179, 217, 239
Le Gallienne, Richard, 105–6, 107, 108,
   112, 115
Lecourt, Sebastian, 231, 233
Lee, Vernon, 5, 6, 61, 68, 85, 97–99, 123–39, 141,
   142, 201, 223, 237, 238
   Genius Loci: Notes on Place, 130–32
   The Enchanted Woods, 123, 126–27, 133–36,
   137–38
Lees, Frederic, 153–55, 157, 245
Leighton, Angela, 54
Lessing, Gotthold, 26
Levey, Michael, 41, 52
Levine, Caroline, 233
Lévis, Éliphas, 143
Levy, Amy, 125
Lewes, George Henry, 101, 103
Lingan, Edmund, 148
Locker, Frederick, 16–17, 19
Longfellow, Henry Wadsworth, 252
Loti, Pierre, 62–63
Louis, Margot K., 14, 229
Lovelock, James, 102–3, 122, 176
Lütkemeier, Thomas, 232

Lyell, Charles, 40
Lyons, Sara, 14, 227

Machen, Arthur, 6, 23, 142, 176, 179, 186,
   195–204, 205, 207, 217, 218, 222
   The Great God Pan, 106, 161, 197, 198, 202, 213
   The Hill of Dreams, 61, 106, 177, 196, 200–4,
   220
Macleod, Fiona (aka William Sharp), 154, 157,
   180, 185–88, 191, 192, 195, 198
maenads, 24, 46, 50–51, 78, 83, 138, 222
magic, 22, 100, 129, 143, 150, 151, 152, 153, 154,
   156, 159, 160, 161, 162, 167, 169, 170, 172,
   196, 243, 247, 249
Mahoney, Kristin, 12
Mallarmé, Stéphane, 184
Maltz, Diana, 136
Marinetti, Filippo Tommaso, 242
Marryat, Florence, 245
Marsh, George Perkins, 43
Marz Harper, Lila, 238
Massumi, Brian, 69–70
Mathers, Moina, 6, 139, 141–42, 144, 147–48,
   151, 152–60, 166, 168, 172–73, 174, 182,
   206
Mathers, Samuel, 149, 152–58, 243, 245, 249
Maxwell, Catherine, 73
McCullough, Kate, 208
McGann, Jerome, 14
Medusa, 81–83
Meredith, George, 189
Mill, John Stuart, 66–67, 103
Millais, John Everett, 18
Miya, Chelsea, 209
Moore, Susan, 73
Morgan, Benjamin, 63, 131
Morris, William, 23, 31, 67, 113, 132, 252
Mortimer-Sandilands, Catriona, 70
Morton, Timothy, 36, 37, 38, 44
Mulholland, Rosa, 145, 146
Müller, Max, 2–3, 128
Murray, Alex, 12, 198
Murray, Isobel, 184
mysticism, 13, 34, 62, 71, 73, 78, 101, 107, 132,
   143, 144–45, 153, 154, 160, 163, 164, 166,
   217

Næss, Arne, 146
natural theology, 7, 17, 19, 180
Navarette, Susan J., 198
Near East/Near Eastern, 8, 9, 10, 22, 23, 76, 78,
   151 (see also: Egypt/Egyptian)
Nesbit, Edith, 23, 67
New Woman, 6, 24, 141, 145, 151, 160, 162, 166,
   172, 206, 207, 248

Index

259

Nordau, Max, 5, 10–11, 143, 178, 199
Northern Europe/Northern European, 14, 20–21, 22, 100, 220, 221
nymphs, 90, 93, 119, 124, 134, 194

O'Connor, Maureen, 208
O'Toole, Tina, 204
Obelkevich, James, 23
occultism, 2, 3, 6, 22, 23, 29, 30, 67, 100, 136, 139, 140–73, 174, 185, 195, 196, 197, 199, 202, 203, 218, 220, 222, 228, 251
Orientalism, 28, 31, 140, 143, 149, 150, 184
Orr, Emma Restall, 20, 41
Ortiz-Robles, Mario, 234
Østermark-Johansen, Lene, 48, 225
Ouida, 4, 61–63, 67, 68, 93–94
Ovid, 30, 48, 90
Owen, Alex, 143

Pagan Federation, 20, 158, 159, 244, 247
Pagan Review, The, 174, 182
Pan, 26, 78, 90, 93, 101, 106, 110–13, 120–22, 124, 152, 185, 197, 201, 211, 213, 215, 216, 217
panpsychism, 47, 48, 49, 56, 60, 100–3, 105, 106, 114, 124, 222
pantheism, 107, 158, 165
Partridge, Christopher, 151, 244
pastoral, 110, 112, 132, 186, 190, 206, 213
Pater, Walter, 1, 3, 4, 5, 24, 26, 27, 28, 34–60, 61, 63, 68, 70, 71, 78, 80–83, 85, 98, 104, 107, 122, 123, 124, 125, 128, 142, 149, 162, 173, 181, 182, 222, 231
 Greek Studies, 34, 47, 48, 50–52, 72, 76, 110, 138
 Marius the Epicurean, 5, 27, 28, 34–35, 38, 41, 42, 45, 52–60, 63, 69, 80, 83, 96, 114, 130
 *Studies in the History of the Renais*sance, 5, 24, 40, 41, 46, 47, 49–50, 51, 52, 55, 56, 57, 60, 71, 76, 97, 111, 113, 132, 223
Pécastaing-Boissière, Muriel, 248
Pennell, Elizabeth, 62
Perrot, Jean, 111
Phalen, Peggy, 147
Pico, Tommy, 221
Pinch, Adela, 101, 124
Plumwood, Val, 146, 147, 158, 167, 207, 216, 217
Poe, Edgar Allan, 18
polytheism, 20, 22, 86, 103
Potolsky, Matthew, 12
Pratt, Mary-Louise, 238
Pre-Raphaelites, 4, 5, 17, 18, 28, 29, 71, 72, 143, 181, 233, 235
Prettejohn, Elizabeth, 30, 31, 71
Prins, Yopie, 84, 229

Psomiades, Kathy, 243
Punter, David, 219

queer ecology, 4, 70, 85, 87, 92, 179, 192–95, 201–4, 207
queerness, 5, 21, 27, 55, 62, 63–64, 65, 70–95, 102, 103, 122, 125, 133, 135, 137, 139, 147, 159, 185, 201–4, 221, 222, 223, 244

race, 12, 27, 38, 43, 48, 65, 66, 68, 70, 80, 103, 128, 145, 147, 166, 175, 184, 198, 207, 208, 217, 221, 222, 230
Rachilde, 61, 206
Rhys, Morgan, 184, 199
Rhys, John, 2
Richards, Alfred Bate, 32
Richardson, Angelique, 245
Rimbaud, Arthur, 143
ritual, 3, 6, 20, 50, 75, 76, 100, 130, 139, 140, 141, 142, 147–51, 152–60, 164, 167, 168, 169, 172–73, 174, 202, 203, 212
Robinson, Mary, 52, 53, 54, 125
Rolleston, George, 2
Romanticism, 9, 24, 36, 37, 44, 59, 98, 99, 108, 184, 189, 219, 242
Rops, Félicien, 61
Rossetti Angeli, Helen, 252
Rossetti, Dante Gabriel, 4, 13, 14, 15, 17, 72, 73, 82, 149, 181, 182, 252
Rossetti, William Michael, 30
Royal Academy, 18, 30, 56, 71, 72
Ruskin, John, 22, 28, 233
Ryder, Richard, 239

Saint Sebastian, 88
Saki, 23, 61
Salt, Henry, 5, 67–68, 69, 81, 94, 178, 220
same-sex desire, 5, 63, 73–74, 83, 132
 female, 73, 84, 85, 88, 125, 136, 138, 243
 male, 25, 27, 88, 136, 219
Sandys, Frederick, 5, 6, 17, 18
 Medea, 28–33, 56, 71, 140
Schaffer, Talia, 226, 238
Schivelbusch, Wolfgang, 238
Schwägerl, Christian, 232
Scotland/Scottish, 12, 22, 100, 109, 128, 136, 145, 157, 163, 180–95, 228, 245 (see also: Celtic culture)
Scott, Sir Walter, 17, 18
Seymour, Gayle, 74, 77, 78
Shakespear, Olivia, 148, 167–72
Shakespeare, William, 49, 73
Sharp, William, 6, 22, 140, 143, 145, 149, 154, 174–76, 177, 179–96, 205, 207, 217, 218, 223, 245 (see also: Macleod, Fiona)
Shaw, George Bernard, 67, 148, 157, 160, 162

Index

Shaw, Michael, 180, 228
Shelley, Mary, 219
Shelley, Percy Bysshe, 164, 189
Showalter, Elaine, 208
Singer, Peter, 69, 239
Small, Ian, 230
Smith, Patricia Colman, 163
socialism, 25, 125, 132, 134, 143, 183
Solomon, Simeon, 5, 60, 61, 63, 64, 67, 69,
    70–84, 92, 94–95, 97, 104, 179, 181
    Babylon Hath Been a Golden Cup, 76–79, 86
    Bacchus, 71, 73, 75, 76, 78
    Habet!, 79, 81, 82–84
speciesism, 32, 65, 96, 100, 103, 108, 207, 208,
    214, 217
Spencer, Herbert, 129
spiritualism, 148, 196, 238, 246
Sprengel, Anna, 150, 155
St. Sebastian, 90
Starhawk, 21, 41
Stevenson, Robert Louis, 5, 53, 96–99, 103–23,
    125, 126, 128, 131, 132, 137, 138, 139, 141, 142,
    181, 197, 201, 215, 222, 223
    An Inland Voyage, 104, 108, 109, 110, 112–15,
    118, 120, 132, 138
    Strange Case of Dr. Jekyll and Mr. Hyde, 104,
    108, 109
    Travels with a Donkey in the Cévennes, 108,
    109, 115–23, 127, 138
Stilling, Robert, 12
Stoermer, Eugene F., 39
Stoppani, Antonio, 5, 38–46, 49, 57, 59, 127,
    128, 131
suffrage, 84, 94, 134, 152, 162, 165, 183, 206, 207
Swinburne, Algernon Charles, 3, 4–5, 7, 12, 13, 24,
    26, 27, 29, 30, 31, 36, 61, 67, 73, 76, 104, 107,
    110, 124, 135, 162, 163, 173, 181, 182, 211, 252
    "Faustine", 82
    "Hertha", 13–14, 145
    "The Garden of Prosperine", 13–14
    "The Leper", 5, 13, 14, 16–19, 180, 220
    "The Oblation", 135
symbolism, 23, 28, 63, 74, 85, 139, 140, 142, 143,
    148, 149, 150, 152, 155, 167, 185
Symonds, John Addington, 24, 27, 28, 52–54, 59
Symons, Arthur, 62, 142, 176, 196

Tange, Andrea Kaston, 97
Tennyson, Alfred, 18, 197
Thackeray, William Makepeace, 15, 16, 17
Thain, Marion, 85
Theosophy, 2, 23, 140, 148, 150, 152, 153, 165, 196
Thomas, Edward, 184, 199

Thoms, William, 228
Thoreau, Henry David, 113
Thurschwell, Pamela, 244
Tiffin, Helen, 36
Todhunter, John, 149, 160
trans-species relations, 5, 48, 49, 60, 61–95, 112,
    115, 118, 133, 134, 138, 159, 178, 192, 207, 209,
    217, 218, 222, 224
tree empathy/worship, 20, 72, 86, 89, 100, 105,
    106, 115, 130, 186, 200, 221, 230
Tucker, Herbert, 252
Tucker, Irene, 230
Tully, Caroline, 153, 161, 249
Turner, J.M.W., 129
Turner, Victor, 156, 157
Tylor, E.B., 40, 41, 100, 128

van Dooren, Thom, 21, 41, 103
Vasari, Giorgio, 89, 90, 91
vegetality, 4, 5, 50, 61, 101, 115, 178–79, 199, 218
vegetarianism, 64, 67, 132
Vicinus, Martha, 208
Virgil, 109, 110, 129
vivisection, 62, 64, 66, 68, 80, 84, 150
Voltaire, 8

Wales/Welsh, 100, 184, 196, 199, 204 (see also:
    Celtic culture)
Wallace, Alfred Russel, 68
Ward, Mrs. Humphry, 24
West, Rebecca, 162, 164
Westcott, William Wynn, 150, 152
Whistler, James McNeill, 4
Whitman, Walt, 108, 113, 116, 132–33, 135, 190
Wicca, see: witchcraft
Wilde, Constance, 149
Wilde, Oscar, 1, 4, 6, 24, 25, 104, 125, 140, 149,
    161, 162, 164, 169, 171, 180, 181, 184, 201,
    212, 221, 245
Williams, Daniel G., 184
Williams, Raymond, 36
Wilson, Elizabeth, 234
Winckelmann, Johann, 26, 132
witchcraft, 22, 100, 105, 214, 215, 216, 227
Wolfe, Cary, 178, 234
Wordsworth, William, 112, 118

Yeats, W.B., 22, 23, 143, 148, 149, 160, 163, 164,
    185, 186, 198, 243, 245, 251
Yellow Book, The, 105, 149, 161, 204, 205
Youngs, Tim, 238

Zorn, Christa, 243

CAMBRIDGE STUDIES IN NINETEENTH-CENTURY
LITERATURE AND CULTURE

General Editors
Kate Flint, *University of Southern California*
Clare Pettitt, *King's College London*

Titles published

1. *The Sickroom in Victorian Fiction: The Art of Being Ill*
   MIRIAM BAILIN, *Washington University*
2. *Muscular Christianity: Embodying the Victorian Age*
   edited by DONALD E. HALL, *California State University, Northridge*
3. *Victorian Masculinities: Manhood and Masculine Poetics in Early Victorian Literature and Art*
   HERBERT SUSSMAN, *Northeastern University, Boston*
4. *Byron and the Victorians*
   ANDREW ELFENBEIN, *University of Minnesota*
5. *Literature in the Marketplace: Nineteenth-Century British Publishing and the Circulation of Books*
   edited by JOHN O. JORDAN, *University of California, Santa Cruz and Robert L. Patten, Rice University, Houston*
6. *Victorian Photography, Painting and Poetry*
   LINDSAY SMITH, *University of Sussex*
7. *Charlotte Brontë and Victorian Psychology*
   SALLY SHUTTLEWORTH, *University of Sheffield*
8. *The Gothic Body: Sexuality, Materialism and Degeneration at the Fin de Siècle*
   KELLY HURLEY, *University of Colorado at Boulder*
9. *Rereading Walter Pater*
   WILLIAM F. SHUTER, *Eastern Michigan University*
10. *Remaking Queen Victoria*
    edited by MARGARET HOMANS, *Yale University*
    and ADRIENNE MUNICH, *State University of New York, Stony Brook*
11. *Disease, Desire, and the Body in Victorian Women's Popular Novels*
    PAMELA K. GILBERT, *University of Florida*
12. *Realism, Representation, and the Arts in Nineteenth-Century Literature*
    ALISON BYERLY, *Middlebury College, Vermont*
13. *Literary Culture and the Pacific*
    VANESSA SMITH, *University of Sydney*
14. *Professional Domesticity in the Victorian Novel Women, Work and Home*
    MONICA F. COHEN
15. *Victorian Renovations of the Novel: Narrative Annexes and the Boundaries of Representation*
    SUZANNE KEEN, *Washington and Lee University, Virginia*

16. *Actresses on the Victorian Stage: Feminine Performance and the Galatea Myth*
GAIL MARSHALL, *University of Leeds*

17. *Death and the Mother from Dickens to Freud: Victorian Fiction and the Anxiety of Origin*
CAROLYN DEVER, *Vanderbilt University, Tennessee*

18. *Ancestry and Narrative in Nineteenth-Century British Literature: Blood Relations from Edgeworth to Hardy*
SOPHIE GILMARTIN, Royal Holloway, *University of London*

19. *Dickens, Novel Reading, and the Victorian Popular Theatre*
DEBORAH VLOCK

20. *After Dickens: Reading, Adaptation and Performance*
JOHN GLAVIN, *Georgetown University, Washington DC*

21. *Victorian Women Writers and the Woman Question*
edited by NICOLA DIANE THOMPSON, *Kingston University, London*

22. *Rhythm and Will in Victorian Poetry*
MATTHEW CAMPBELL, *University of Sheffield*

23. *Gender, Race, and the Writing of Empire: Public Discourse and the Boer War*
PAULA M. KREBS, *Wheaton College, Massachusetts*

24. *Ruskin's God*
MICHAEL WHEELER, *University of Southampton*

25. *Dickens and the Daughter of the House*
HILARY M. SCHOR, *University of Southern California*

26. *Detective Fiction and the Rise of Forensic Science*
RONALD R. THOMAS, *Trinity College, Hartford, Connecticut*

27. *Testimony and Advocacy in Victorian Law, Literature, and Theology*
JAN-MELISSA SCHRAMM, Trinity Hall, Cambridge

28. *Victorian Writing about Risk: Imagining a Safe England in a Dangerous World*
ELAINE FREEDGOOD, *University of Pennsylvania*

29. *Physiognomy and the Meaning of Expression in Nineteenth-Century Culture*
LUCY HARTLEY, *University of Southampton*

30. *The Victorian Parlour: A Cultural Study*
THAD LOGAN, *Rice University, Houston*

31. *Aestheticism and Sexual Parody 1840–1940*
DENNIS DENISOFF, *Ryerson University, Toronto*

32. *Literature, Technology and Magical Thinking, 1880–1920*
PAMELA THURSCHWELL, *University College London*

33. *Fairies in Nineteenth-Century Art and Literature*
NICOLA BOWN, *Birkbeck, University of London*

34. *George Eliot and the British Empire*
NANCY HENRY *The State University of New York, Binghamton*

35. *Women's Poetry and Religion in Victorian England: Jewish Identity and Christian Culture*
CYNTHIA SCHEINBERG, *Mills College, California*

36. *Victorian Literature and the Anorexic Body*
ANNA KRUGOVOY SILVER, *Mercer University, Georgia*

37. *Eavesdropping in the Novel from Austen to Proust*
    ANN GAYLIN, *Yale University*
38. *Missionary Writing and Empire, 1800–1860*
    ANNA JOHNSTON, *University of Tasmania*
39. *London and the Culture of Homosexuality, 1885–1914*
    MATT COOK, *Keele University*
40. *Fiction, Famine, and the Rise of Economics in Victorian Britain and Ireland*
    GORDON BIGELOW, *Rhodes College, Tennessee*
41. *Gender and the Victorian Periodical*
    HILARY FRASER, Birkbeck, *University of London*
    JUDITH JOHNSTON and STEPHANIE GREEN, *University of Western Australia*
42. *The Victorian Supernatural*
    edited by NICOLA BOWN, *Birkbeck College, London*
    CAROLYN BURDETT, *London Metropolitan University*
    and PAMELA THURSCHWELL, *University College London*
43. *The Indian Mutiny and the British Imagination*
    GAUTAM CHAKRAVARTY, *University of Delhi*
44. *The Revolution in Popular Literature: Print, Politics and the People*
    IAN HAYWOOD, *Roehampton University of Surrey*
45. *Science in the Nineteenth-Century Periodical: Reading the Magazine of Nature*
    GEOFFREY CANTOR, *University of Leeds*
    GOWAN DAWSON, *University of Leicester*
    GRAEME GOODAY, *University of Leeds*
    RICHARD NOAKES, *University of Cambridge*
    SALLY SHUTTLEWORTH, *University of Sheffield*
    and JONATHAN R. TOPHAM, *University of Leeds*
46. *Literature and Medicine in Nineteenth-Century Britain from Mary Shelley to George Eliot*
    JANIS MCLARREN CALDWELL, *Wake Forest University*
47. *The Child Writer from Austen to Woolf*
    edited by CHRISTINE ALEXANDER, *University of New South Wales*
    and JULIET MCMASTER, *University of Alberta*
48. *From Dickens to Dracula: Gothic, Economics, and Victorian Fiction*
    GAIL TURLEY HOUSTON, *University of New Mexico*
49. *Voice and the Victorian Storyteller*
    IVAN KREILKAMP, *University of Indiana*
50. *Charles Darwin and Victorian Visual Culture*
    JONATHAN SMITH, *University of Michigan-Dearborn*
51. *Catholicism, Sexual Deviance, and Victorian Gothic Culture*
    PATRICK R. O'MALLEY, *Georgetown University*
52. *Epic and Empire in Nineteenth-Century Britain*
    SIMON DENTITH, *University of Gloucestershire*
53. *Victorian Honeymoons: Journeys to the Conjugal*
    HELENA MICHIE, *Rice University*

54. *The Jewess in Nineteenth-Century British Literary Culture*
    NADIA VALMAN, *University of Southampton*
55. *Ireland, India and Nationalism in Nineteenth-Century Literature*
    JULIA WRIGHT, *Dalhousie University*
56. *Dickens and the Popular Radical Imagination*
    SALLY LEDGER, *Birkbeck, University of London*
57. *Darwin, Literature and Victorian Respectability*
    GOWAN DAWSON, *University of Leicester*
58. *'Michael Field': Poetry, Aestheticism and the Fin de Siècle*
    MARION THAIN, *University of Birmingham*
59. *Colonies, Cults and Evolution: Literature, Science and Culture in Nineteenth-Century Writing*
    DAVID AMIGONI, *Keele University*
60. *Realism, Photography and Nineteenth-Century Fiction*
    DANIEL A. NOVAK, *Louisiana State University*
61. *Caribbean Culture and British Fiction in the Atlantic World, 1780–1870*
    TIM WATSON, *University of Miami*
62. *The Poetry of Chartism: Aesthetics, Politics, History*
    MICHAEL SANDERS, *University of Manchester*
63. *Literature and Dance in Nineteenth-Century Britain: Jane Austen to the New Woman*
    CHERYL WILSON, *Indiana University*
64. *Shakespeare and Victorian Women*
    GAIL MARSHALL, *Oxford Brookes University*
65. *The Tragi-Comedy of Victorian Fatherhood*
    VALERIE SANDERS, *University of Hull*
66. *Darwin and the Memory of the Human: Evolution, Savages, and South America*
    CANNON SCHMITT, *University of Toronto*
67. *From Sketch to Novel: The Development of Victorian Fiction*
    AMANPAL GARCHA, *Ohio State University*
68. *The Crimean War and the British Imagination*
    STEFANIE MARKOVITS, *Yale University*
69. *Shock, Memory and the Unconscious in Victorian Fiction*
    JILL L. MATUS, *University of Toronto*
70. *Sensation and Modernity in the 1860s*
    NICHOLAS DALY, *University College Dublin*
71. *Ghost-Seers, Detectives, and Spiritualists: Theories of Vision in Victorian Literature and Science*
    SRDJAN SMAJIĆ, *Furman University*
72. *Satire in an Age of Realism*
    AARON MATZ, *Scripps College, California*
73. *Thinking about Other People in Nineteenth-Century British Writing*
    ADELA PINCH, *University of Michigan*
74. *Tuberculosis and the Victorian Literary Imagination*
    KATHERINE BYRNE, *University of Ulster, Coleraine*

75. *Urban Realism and the Cosmopolitan Imagination in the Nineteenth Century: Visible City, Invisible World*
    TANYA AGATHOCLEOUS, *Hunter College, City University of New York*
76. *Women, Literature, and the Domesticated Landscape: England's Disciples of Flora, 1780–1870*
    JUDITH W. PAGE, *University of Florida*
    ELISE L. SMITH, *Millsaps College, Mississippi*
77. *Time and the Moment in Victorian Literature and Society*
    SUE ZEMKA, *University of Colorado*
78. *Popular Fiction and Brain Science in the Late Nineteenth Century*
    ANNE STILES, *Washington State University*
79. *Picturing Reform in Victorian Britain*
    JANICE CARLISLE, *Yale University*
80. *Atonement and Self-Sacrifice in Nineteenth-Century Narrative*
    JAN-MELISSA SCHRAMM, *University of Cambridge*
81. *The Silver Fork Novel: Fashionable Fiction in the Age of Reform*
    EDWARD COPELAND, *Pomona College, California*
82. *Oscar Wilde and Ancient Greece*
    IAIN ROSS, *Colchester Royal Grammar School*
83. *The Poetry of Victorian Scientists: Style, Science and Nonsense*
    DANIEL BROWN, *University of Southampton*
84. *Moral Authority, Men of Science, and the Victorian Novel*
    ANNE DEWITT, *Princeton Writing Program*
85. *China and the Victorian Imagination: Empires Entwined*
    ROSS G. FORMAN, *University of Warwick*
86. *Dickens's Style*
    edited by DANIEL TYLER, *University of Oxford*
87. *The Formation of the Victorian Literary Profession*
    RICHARD SALMON, *University of Leeds*
88. *Before George Eliot: Marian Evans and the Periodical Press*
    FIONNUALA DILLANE, *University College Dublin*
89. *The Victorian Novel and the Space of Art: Fictional Form on Display*
    DEHN GILMORE, *California Institute of Technology*
90. *George Eliot and Money: Economics, Ethics and Literature*
    DERMOT COLEMAN, *Independent Scholar*
91. *Masculinity and the New Imperialism: Rewriting Manhood in British Popular Literature, 1870–1914*
    BRADLEY DEANE, *University of Minnesota*
92. *Evolution and Victorian Culture*
    edited by BERNARD LIGHTMAN, *York University, Toronto*
    and BENNETT ZON, *University of Durham*
93. *Victorian Literature, Energy, and the Ecological Imagination*
    ALLEN MACDUFFIE, *University of Texas, Austin*
94. *Popular Literature, Authorship and the Occult in Late Victorian Britain*
    ANDREW MCCANN, *Dartmouth College, New Hampshire*

95. *Women Writing Art History in the Nineteenth Century: Looking Like a Woman*
HILARY FRASER BIRKBECK, *University of London*

96. *Relics of Death in Victorian Literature and Culture*
DEBORAH LUTZ, *Long Island University, C. W. Post Campus*

97. *The Demographic Imagination and the Nineteenth-Century City: Paris, London, New York*
NICHOLAS DALY, *University College Dublin*

98. *Dickens and the Business of Death*
CLAIRE WOOD, *University of York*

99. *Translation as Transformation in Victorian Poetry*
ANNMARIE DRURY, *Queens College, City University of New York*

100. *The Bigamy Plot: Sensation and Convention in the Victorian Novel*
MAIA MCALEAVEY, *Boston College, Massachusetts*

101. *English Fiction and the Evolution of Language, 1850–1914*
WILL ABBERLEY, *University of Oxford*

102. *The Racial Hand in the Victorian Imagination*
AVIVA BRIEFEL, *Bowdoin College, Maine*

103. *Evolution and Imagination in Victorian Children's Literature*
JESSICA STRALEY, *University of Utah*

104. *Writing Arctic Disaster: Authorship and Exploration*
ADRIANA CRACIUN, *University of California, Riverside*

105. *Science, Fiction, and the Fin-de-Siècle Periodical Press*
WILL TATTERSDILL, *University of Birmingham*

106. *Democratising Beauty in Nineteenth-Century Britain: Art and the Politics of Public Life*
LUCY HARTLEY, *University of Michigan*

107. *Everyday Words and the Character of Prose in Nineteenth-Century Britain*
JONATHAN FARINA, *Seton Hall University, New Jersey*

108. *Gerard Manley Hopkins and the Poetry of Religious Experience*
MARTIN DUBOIS, *Newcastle University*

109. *Blindness and Writing: From Wordsworth to Gissing*
HEATHER TILLEY, *Birkbeck College, University of London*

110. *An Underground History of Early Victorian Fiction: Chartism, Radical Print Culture, and the Social Problem Novel*
GREGORY VARGO, *New York University*

111. *Automatism and Creative Acts in the Age of New Psychology*
LINDA M. AUSTIN, *Oklahoma State University*

112. *Idleness and Aesthetic Consciousness, 1815–1900*
RICHARD ADELMAN, *University of Sussex*

113. *Poetry, Media, and the Material Body: Autopoetics in Nineteenth-Century Britain*
ASHLEY MILLER, *Albion College, Michigan*

114. *Malaria and Victorian Fictions of Empire*
JESSICA HOWELL, *Texas A&M University*

115. *The Brontës and the Idea of the Human: Science, Ethics, and the Victorian Imagination*
    edited by ALEXANDRA LEWIS, *University of Aberdeen*
116. *The Political Lives of Victorian Animals: Liberal Creatures in Literature and Culture*
    ANNA FEUERSTEIN, *University of Hawai'i-Manoa*
117. *The Divine in the Commonplace: Recent Natural Histories and the Novel in Britain*
    AMY KING, *St John's University, New York*
118. *Plagiarizing the Victorian Novel: Imitation, Parody, Aftertext*
    ADAM ABRAHAM, *Virginia Commonwealth University*
119. *Literature, Print Culture, and Media Technologies, 1880–1900: Many Inventions*
    RICHARD MENKE, *University of Georgia*
120. *Aging, Duration, and the English Novel: Growing Old from Dickens to Woolf*
    JACOB JEWUSIAK, *Newcastle University*
121. *Autobiography, Sensation, and the Commodification of Identity in Victorian Narrative: Life upon the Exchange*
    SEAN GRASS, *Rochester Institute of Technology*
122. *Settler Colonialism in Victorian Literature: Economics and Political Identity in the Networks of Empire*
    PHILLIP STEER, *Massey University, Auckland*
123. *Mimicry and Display in Victorian Literary Culture: Nature, Science and the Nineteenth-Century Imagination*
    WILL ABBERLEY, *University of Sussex*
124. *Victorian Women and Wayward Reading: Crises of Identification*
    MARISA PALACIOS KNOX, *University of Texas Rio Grande Valley*
125. *The Victorian Cult of Shakespeare: Bardology in the Nineteenth Century*
    CHARLES LAPORTE, *University of Washington*
126. *Children's Literature and the Rise of 'Mind Cure': Positive Thinking and Pseudo-Science at the Fin de Siècle*
    ANNE STILES, *Saint Louis University, Missouri*
127. *Virtual Play and the Victorian Novel: The Ethics and Aesthetics of Fictional Experience*
    TIMOTHY GAO, *Nanyang Technological University*
128. *Colonial Law in India and the Victorian Imagination*
    LEILA NETI, *Occidental College, Los Angeles*
129. *Convalescence in the Nineteenth-Century Novel: The Afterlife of Victorian Illness*
    HOSANNA KRIENKE, *University of Wyoming*
130. *Stylistic Virtue and Victorian Fiction: Form, Ethics and the Novel*
    MATTHEW SUSSMAN, *The University of Sydney*
131. *Scottish Women's Writing in the Long Nineteenth Century: The Romance of Everyday Life*
    JULIET SHIELDS, *University of Washington*

132. *Reimagining Dinosaurs in Late Victorian and Edwardian Literature: How the 'Terrible Lizard' Became a Transatlantic Cultural Icon*
RICHARD FALLON, *The University of Birmingham*

133. *Decadent Ecology in British Literature and Art, 1860–1910: Decay, Desire, and the Pagan Revival*
DENNIS DENISOFF, *University of Tulsa*

Printed in the United States
by Baker & Taylor Publisher Services